Right Foot in the Pacific/ Left Foot in the Atlantic

David Stoess

Right Foot In the Pacific — Left Foot In the Atlantic

Published by Hellgate Press, an imprint of PSI Research, Inc.
Copyright 2000 by David Stoess

For information or to direct comments, questions, or suggestions regarding this book and other Hellgate Press books, contact:

Editorial Department
Hellgate Press
P.O. Box 3727
Central Point, Oregon 97502

Email at *info@psi-research.com*

Editor: Kathy Marshbank
Cover designer: Steven Burns & J. C. Young

Stoess, David
   Right foot in the Pacific, left foot in the Atlantic / David Stoess. 1st ed.
     p. cm.
   ISBN 1-55571-521-4 (paper)
   1. United States—Description and travel. 2. United States—Social life and customs—1971 – 3. Stoess, David—Journeys—United States.
   4. Walking—United States. I. Title

E169.04 .S828 2000
917.304'92—dc21

Printed and bound in the United States of America

First edition   10 9 8 7 6 5 4 3 2 1

Contents

To Nancy Baker Stoess — the grandest person I ever knew.

Chapter 1
Right Foot in the Pacific

All of us see pennies on the ground occasionally. And I suppose it's a sign of the times that most people don't think them worth the effort of bending over. But sometimes you'll see a nickel, dime or quarter which most people still consider worth the stretch.

Maybe you've never given it much thought, but has it ever made you wonder what the value of all the coins would be if you walked from Los Angeles to New York City? Probably not. But then, my mind marches to some pretty strange drummers. I indeed know how many of those coins you'd find between Los Angeles and New York City. I've walked every inch and I picked up every coin I saw. I've included the total of those coins on the last page of this book but I don't want you to look just yet.

There are many stories I want to tell you. Stories such as one about a frustrating, soap-dried, ten-second bath in the desert; one about a nudist at a windmill; one about a man who felt sorry for me and literally gave me the shirt off his back; one about kissing the plaque on the Empire State Building, and even one about the time I drank water at a border patrol station that was only intended for flushing toilets.

Wait until the last page to learn the coin total. Hopefully you'll enjoy the rest of the stories that will lead to that final climactic revelation.

One summer in the '90s I walked from Huntington Beach in Los Angeles to the Empire State Building in Manhattan. I left Huntington Beach on the 8th of April and arrived at the Empire State Building on the 24th of September.

On occasion I've been asked how many rides I got. When I say I was often offered rides but refused because I wanted to say I walked every inch, people look at me slightly askew. The look says, Should you be out without a guardian? "You *wanted* to walk! Why? What "cause" were you walking for?" I tell them the only "cause" was 'cause I wanted to. I wanted to see if I had it in me.

My walk started in California, and when most people think of that state they see lots of sun, seas of cars, beautifully-bodied young people on beaches, with every store being on Rodeo Drive.

And California is nice, in many places even beautiful, but California is partly desert. Though in its own right the desert is pretty too. It's just hard to picture a desert and the beautiful parts of California existing side by side.

They do. And very early in my walk I learned about those two starkly contrasting worlds. The pretty and the ugly parts of California come together at almost the same location as two other opposing forces. They are divided along the two plates of the San Andreas Fault, and like the fault below they grind against each other like two chained and snarling dogs straining to get at one another. As you leave the pretty part and enter the desert, something much more than a simple change in aesthetics or cosmetics greets you. Something stark and foreboding awaits through the door marked "Desert." I wouldn't say the door should read: "Abandon ye hope all who enter" but it could serve well the hapless traveler if the Boy Scouts had hand-lettered on the door their unimpeachable motto "Be prepared."

I was about a hundred miles southeast of L.A. and still in the pretty part of California when I came to a small resort town called Julian. Julian is a neat, high-elevation town. Vail or Aspen could be sister cities. A hundred miles must have been enough distance for Julian to escape L.A.'s infamous smog because the town had the bluest sky and the softest, cleanest air. It's strange that a town as neat as Julian should be sitting astride that ugly/pretty fault line. As you head east on the main road out of Julian, at the bottom of a long descent, there's the desert door smack in your face.

If you are brave (or foolish) and decide to pass through that door the next "town" is a spot by the side of the road 35 miles to the east called Ocotillo Wells.

Julian sounded so European, green and Anglo-Saxon and Ocotillo Wells so southwestern-American-Indian-ish. The contrast in names should have told me something.

I learned that in the southwestern desert if a place is named anything Wells, it means that for miles and miles around the wells are the only thing of note. The wells seem to be the only reason everything else exists. Wells are water and if you've got water in this place you are king of all you survey. Take away the wells and you got squat. Thirty-five miles of desert, though, separated me from the dessert of these wells called Ocotillo.

Even though it was early in my walk and I was naive and green, I'd been around the block enough and seen enough maps to suspect I'd better make some enquiries. At the last possible jump-off in Julian, I approached the lady behind the counter at a small mom and pop grocery.

As I paid for all the treats and sweets and drinks I thought I could possibly carry (I had strong suspicions) I addressed the lady behind the counter, "Ma'am, are there any places to get food or drink between here and Ocotillo Wells?"

I guess she thought she was finished with me because she'd already turned her back and was adding cigarettes to an overhead rack. She turned her head and her sly smile said it all. After thinking about it she decided someone so simple needed more than a smile to get her message. In a moment the smile was replaced with, "No, no, there aren't any restaurants, filling stations or convenient stores between here and Ocotillo Wells."

I was so surprised all I could say was, "Not anything?" Again the sly smile. But I detected something additional in the eyes. I felt foolish. The eyes said, "Which is it? Are you simply dumb or are you crazy?"

Thirty-five grueling, scorching, waterless, foodless miles of Anzo-Barrero Desert. I squeezed every ounce of energy and every drop of liquid from the candy, chips and drinks I had purchased. It was my first desert experience.

I kept thinking if I could hang on I'd be rescued by Ocotillo Wells. It had earned a dot on the map so that meant it had to be a town, right? Towns need, indeed require, Snickers and Coke, don't they?

I never saw any wells in Ocotillo Wells. Maybe it was an old Indian trick played on Rand McNally so they'd get themselves a dot on the map. "If we tell 'em we gottum wells we gettum dot!"

Ocotillo Wells is a campground. That's the long and short of it.

It did have a relatively nice store at the campground so it was all the oasis this weary, bone-dry hiker could hope for.

Its campstore held things cold and wet, sugary and artery clogging.

Unless you've been there, done that, got the T-shirt, you can't appreciate how glad I was to see Ocotillo Wells after 35 grueling miles straight out of Dante's Inferno.

I never did grasp Ocotillo Wells raison d'etre but I think it was a starting point for people with all-terrain vehicles who wanted to race through the desert.

After filling my innards dangerously close to bursting I continued eastward.

I began seeing signs by the road indicating I would eventually come to a place called Blu-In Park (I'm not kidding.) The billboards indicated it was an R.V. Park with 24-hour coin-operated showers. It sounded so delicious. At this point there was no doubt in my mind I could have taken a 24-hour shower.

I didn't allow my hopes to soar too high. Already I'd found that words can be cheap, and dots on the map can just be dots on the map.

The Blu-In Park looked like a migrant worker's mobile home park but everyone seemed to be gone. A lone, none-too-spirited, nor healthy-looking dog greeted me.

"Hey Buddy," I said as I gave him an understanding Yeah-I-guess-we're-in-the-same-boat pat on the head.

I checked out the showers. Pretty shabby, but out here you find your standards aren't very high.

The coin-operated showers took quarters. A hurried but thorough search of my pack turned up one lone quarter. The signs I read as I came down the road created excitement but no concern about change. Wouldn't there be a nice camp store with gobs of change?

I didn't back down an inch. The thought of having my body splashed with a cool stream of water gave me all the backbone I needed. I wasn't going to give up on my shower — last quarter or no.

Insert quarter, heavenly water flows, I lather quickly (I wasn't that naive). Ten seconds, water stops! I stand there incredulously soapy-crotched. I knew this was the desert but *ten seconds*! No one to complain to. No one gives a damn if I have to walk 50 miles in the desert with a soap-dried crotch.

They say God looks after drunks, little children, and fools. As I stood there with the drying soap starting to sting I knew I'd gladly accept any of the three classifications if He could see his way clear to rescue me. I had foolishly (I think we just stumbled upon the precise classification for me) drunk all my water way back down the road after the Blu-In Park signs lulled me into throwing caution to the wind.

In desperation I began checking all my water bottles. Glory be! One still contained about three-fourths of a quart of precious (not a strong enough word) drinking water.

I looked at my crotch, thought of my throat. Only about a half-second of hesitation was required. The choice seemed clear to me. Maybe you'd say the throat was the logical choice. The prudent thing would be to walk straddle-legged and save the water for your insides. And my reply would be, "It isn't your crotch on fire!"

I used the water at the spot needing the most attention. Not a drop was wasted, but that would have been true in this place, be it throat or crotch. Luckily, it was barely adequate. The fire was extinguished. But down the road I longed for a drink for my insides.

Without meaning to I've jumped ahead in my storytelling. As you know this walk began at a beach in Los Angeles. Let's go back there and start again.

When you saw this book weren't you a little puzzled as to what the title meant? I planned, no before planning, I thought for years about how much fun it would be to walk from Los Angeles to New York City. And I would tell myself that when I started I'd put my right foot in the Pacific, and if I was successful in completely crossing the U.S., I'd put my left foot in the Atlantic. I knew where I wanted to start at L.A., so where I'd put my right foot was obvious, but since I wanted to walk through the deep south and up the East coast to New York, I wasn't sure where the left-foot-in-the-Atlantic part would actually take place. Without giving it much thought I just assumed Savannah.

I had left my home in Gatlinburg, Tennessee on the first of April and it had taken me exactly a week to reach my starting point in L.A., traveling by thumb.

I was approaching L.A. and beginning to get apprehensive about the scary bigness of it all. Then to compound matters, just as the freeway craziness began to really become apparent, my ride dumped me on the San Bernardino Freeway. There's not a worse place in the Western Hemisphere to get put out of a car. Standing on the side of the road you feel like you're in a jug of bees. And, in California you definitely don't let the police catch you hitchin' on the freeway. Entrance ramps they don't say much, that is, if you look halfway decent. I quickly began looking for the nearest entrance ramp.

If Mark Twain really did say, "The coldest winter I ever spent was a summer in San Francisco", he was right. It even applies to canyon-country in southern California. If it's the least bit cold, the wind whistling down those canyons at gale force digs right for your bones.

So there I was, cold, alone and vulnerable with cars careening by at what seemed like one-and-a-half-times the speed limit. You want desperately to convey to the people in those cars that your sole desire is to have a ride, cutting their throats never entered your mind. You wish you could put a big sign on your chest saying that there's no reason to be afraid — you're a gentle, kind person, a good conversationalist, clean and sweet smelling, (well, at least not sour smelling). And that you'd be eternally grateful if they'd stop.

It's been my experience with hitchhiking that there's always a ride out there somewhere with your name on it. The guy who's going to pick you up will be there. You must just resolve that right now he may be sleeping, working, eating, or making love to his old lady. But he'll be there.

When it's warm and sunny and there's an ample supply of cars passing you it's easy to philosophize and reassure yourself about the driver who is going to pick you up. But substitute cold, rain, and great passages of time and severe doubts begin to cloud your reason. The doubts had begun to rear their ugly heads when I noticed a pickup truck slowing down for me.

I was so glad that someone, anyone, had stopped that where he was taking me seemed secondary. He had stopped and I was getting out of this awful place.

Imagine then, if you will, the utter thrill when I learned that this kind man was not only going to remove me from this bad place, but take me clear across L.A. to my ultimate destination, Huntington Beach.

Getting through Los Angeles had always been one of my prime concerns. I knew I'd hitchhike to L.A. but getting through the city would be a problem. My first choice for getting to the beach was city buses. But I could just picture the driver saying, "Hey buddy, you can't get on here with that pack." If that happened I could fall back on Plan B, a taxi. I dreaded the thought of spending that much money, though.

I was heaven-blessed when this kind man, after hearing my story was so taken by it that he decided to take me all the way. He was a young man whom I judged had the desire for a walk across the U.S. but a job-related accident had crippled him and forced him into early retirement.

"All I was going to do today was wash my truck, so I'd just as soon help you and take you to Huntington Beach", he said.

Music to my ears! I didn't realize at the time that his act of kindness was to be the first in a long string of kindnesses shown me over the next five-and-a-half months. I was so grateful that I treated him to lunch. He wheeled his pickup into the parking lot of a small open-air restaurant complete with palms, brightly colored umbrellas, and tables with checkered tablecloths. The restaurant was conveniently located next to the Huntington Beach Pier.

As he squeezed into a spot between two very expensive looking cars he smiled and said, "You couldn't tell it by this old pickup but in high school my taste in clothes and cars earned me the nickname Rolls. My old, beat up pickup might make these Jags and Mercedes a little nervous but I guess that nickname has always made me feel like I belonged. Let's eat here." I had to quickly get over any qualms I had about being out of place. He rolled out of the truck and was waving me on. I noticed his industrial limp as we crossed the parking lot.

"See why I can't go with you?" He smiled and gave an offhand swipe at his knee.

"How'd it happen?"

"I'll explain over a beer".

I told him to get whatever he wanted. He gave no more than a cursory look at the menu and ordered a Bud and turkey club. "Hey, I owe you. I'm more than a beer and sandwich grateful to you."

"No problem, man," he said.

He either felt he shouldn't put too much of a financial strain on me or the Bud was what he really wanted anyway.

While we waited he stuck his hand across the table. "Darrell's my name."

Something in the way he said it made me think he really preferred Rolls.

"David's mine."

"Where you from?" he asked.

"Well, I was born and grew up in Kentucky but I've lived about twelve years in Tennessee.

"Kentucky, huh? My wife is originally from Kentucky, down around Paducah. You know where that is? She'd like to go back, misses the green."

"Yeah, Kentucky can hold its own in the pretty department." I said, "How's the smog affect you?"

"You get used to it, sorta. Well, not really, but it's not as constant or as bad as people other places believe. L.A.'s in a bowl of sorts. It creates air inversion. Problem is some days neither bad nor good air can escape."

"You said you'd explain about your leg."

"Oh, you ever hear of metal fatigue?"

"I kinda know what you're saying," I said.

"About five years ago I was running a big machine making parts for car crankshafts. Lot's of big steel and torque. One day, in just one more of what must have been a million turnings, a long arm gave way and headed toward me. Before I could even blink, much less move, a three foot piece of steel blew through my knee. Cartilage and all that stuff is gone. Now it's bone-against-bone in my knee socket. I damn sure wish I had my knee back. But the good news is the company has to take care of me the rest of my life."

Darrell was a nice guy. I'd have liked him even if he hadn't picked me up.

"So, when you going to start on your walk?"

"I thought I'd get a motel room and get a fresh start in the morning."

"All the way to New York? Jees, I wish it were me."

"Well, right now it's all the way to Laguna Beach," I smiled. I try not to focus on New York just yet."

It was about two o'clock in the afternoon when we finished our lunch and he pulled away in his old pickup. I swear a collective sigh of relief came from those fancy-smancy cars.

I had meant it when I said I was going to find a motel and get a fresh start the next morning. But after we'd said our good-byes, I realized that my mental make-up wouldn't allow me to waste time in a motel when there was so much daylight left.

The fact that I could see my starting point from the restaurant parking lot did little to dissuade me from starting that very moment what I'd been thinking about for so long. I crossed the street and walked across the beach to the waters edge.

Henry David Thoreau once wrote, "If you are ready to leave father and mother, and brother and sister, and wife and child and friends, and never see them again...if you have paid your debts, and made your will, and settled all your affairs, and are a free man...then you are ready for a walk." I met most of Thoreau's criteria but was I ready? "Ready as I'll ever be, I thought."

I sat down and took off my right boot and sock. I made my symbolic touch of the water. After drying my foot and replacing my sock and boot, I walked over and touched the pier that jutted out into the Pacific. I can't say why. I guess it was just another solid thing to tell me that this point represented so much to me. As I turned to take the first few steps back across the beach, the first steps that I thought — hoped — would eventually take me across all the vastness that is these United States, there were no bells, no whistles, no marching bands. My strange looking safari hat and backpack and walking stick turned no heads. I had the feeling that the young people playing volleyball on the beach and the rollerbladers on the boardwalk had seen more than the likes of me, and I deserved little attention.

Chapter 2
Out of the Grasp of L.A.

As I walked away from Huntington Beach that afternoon what I felt is a little hard to put into words. Sorta awed, I guess, by the enormity of what I had bitten off.

As a safeguard to my ego, I had never declared to myself nor anyone else that I was going to walk across the U.S. If I ever reached the Empire State Building, *then* I could say I had walked all the way across. There's a daylight and dark difference between saying, "I walked across the U.S." and saying, "I'm *going to* walk across the U.S." At 25 you might be able to make such statements and feel confident that your body would cooperate. A wise man doesn't do that at 50.

I was in Louisiana before I actually thought New York might be within my grasp.

And after actually walking all the way I know that there's no magic formula. It's simple: Day one: Get up in the morning, walk 'til dark. Day two: Repeat day one. Then one day you're in the next state.

I heard there is a story in an old McGuffey's Reader that seems apropos here.

It seems there was an old clock that was tired and toward the end of the year it began thinking about how many ticks it would have to make during the next year. When the clock figured the seconds and it came to 31,536,000 it got so depressed it said, "I can't do it." But then someone reminded the clock that it did not have to tick the 31,536,000 seconds all at one time, but rather one by one. Then the clock was relieved and happy again and knew that it could do it.

As I left Huntington Beach that fine April afternoon, goals really didn't play much of a part in my thinking. Where I would spend the night was more of a concern. I'd never been in this part of Los Angeles, and I pictured big city stretching for miles and days.

As warm-ups for this walk I'd taken a few hundred mile walks in Florida, North Carolina and Tennessee. So I wasn't completely unaware of what to expect. I knew from past experience that the most traumatic daily experience was finding a place to spend the night. For most Americans, where they'll spend the night is a given. And if you have a home it's something that never crosses your mind. Not having a secure place to spend the night is a big, big thing. So, I knew that the pre-walk euphoria consisting of thoughts of warm sunshine and exciting new places and people should include a hard look at where to put down for the night.

In addition to my warm-up walks, my wife, Nancy, and I had ridden bicycles from Louisville, Kentucky to Daytona Beach, Florida on our honeymoon. That, too, was good training.

Traveling alone, as I was on this walk was easier on the find-a-place-to-spend-the-night score, though. When it's only you the available places to stay are greatly increased. Well, the actual places are always the same, but there's infinitely less whining about not liking your choice of places.

I remember on the second night of our honeymoon bike trip, a gracious owner of a small country store had offered us the use of his barn as a place to spend the night. After dark, and we'd settled down in our sleeping bags among the hay bales, several dogs who must have called the barn home too, cautiously ventured close to check out the interlopers. As dogs are want to do, they did their chief investigating with their noses. The sniffing was very clear and audible in the dark confines of the barn. I tried to dismiss it simply as dogs being dogs, doing what dogs do. But Nancy saw it in an entirely different light. Finally, the combination of a completely weird honeymoon, a long, dusty day of bike riding with no hope of a regular bed and bath broke Nancy's usual stalwart dam. In tears, she blurted out, "I wish I'd never agreed to come on this trip!" Youth and only one day of marriage under my belt were poor training for the proper response to her lament. Foolishly, I laughed at her. Definitely not a good move for a young or old husband.

I suppose she forgave me, though, as we continued on to complete our trip to Florida and make it through 25 years of marriage. And I like to think I could have talked her into joining me on this Los Angeles to New York walk if cancer hadn't ended her life at age 44. To have her on this walk I'd let her choose our place to stay every night, even if my poor wallet screamed every time as she said, "Motel!" It would be a small price to pay to have her with me.

This first day, finding a place to put down for the night was looking rather bleak as I passed yacht clubs and Mercedes dealerships in Laguna Beach. Californians have a reputation for being forward thinking. And, to their credit, they tolerate the weird and different better than most people throughout the U.S. But I felt these Laguna Beach Californians would be much more tolerant of me if I looked as if I owned a yacht and a Mercedes.

I learned an object lesson along those lines when I asked a policeman where I could find the nearest laundromat. His look told me that Laguna Beach was above laundromats. I got the impression that if you asked for a laundromat there, you'd get a better reception if you didn't look as if you needed a laundromat. I'm afraid that wasn't the case with me. I had hitchhiked from Tennessee and hadn't washed clothes since leaving there.

When I'd left Huntington Beach that first day I'd just assumed that I'd stay in a motel that night. In my Tennessee mind, Los Angeles would take days to escape from and there wouldn't be any fields or woods for me to sleep in. And, in fact, it did take about four days for me to escape. By "escape" I mean before I was completely out of the influence of Los Angeles — cars racing before dawn with people going there to work and dodging those same cars as they raced back down the homestretch in the evening. I guess as any city grows it pushes the limits that people are willing to drive to keep from living in that city. Maybe that's why they are called City Limits.

It was a good feeling when I finally made it far enough away from Los Angeles that it didn't affect people's lives one way or the other.

It was my first afternoon of this epic walk, sunset was approaching and I was beginning to become a little worried because it didn't look likely that I was going to find a field or a woods, a junkyard, a schoolyard, a haystack or even a motel that I could afford. But all of a sudden on the left there was a giant, open expanse of lush grass and trees overlooking an even bigger expanse of beautiful Pacific Ocean.

Naturally, if you're an interloper you want to put down where there's the least likelihood of being seen, and even though there was a house from which it was theoretically possible to see me I knew this was where I would spend the night. I crossed my fingers as I snuck over a fence to get to the best possible spot.

Confronted with the accusation of trespassing you can say, "Oh, I was exhausted and saw this beautiful open field" (your tone insinuating that the owner must be a wise and fortunate person to have such a veritable Eden.) Of course, when confronted by the owner on whose land you have squatted you assume the my-you're-so-lucky tone even if you've been caught in his prize flowerbed or his junkyard. It's his garden and his Eden and you'd best acknowledge and glorify that.

All of this fawning may or may not get you off the hook. And your chances of success are in direct proportion to whether you climbed the guy's fence or not. No fence and you can imply that since there were no impediments to control your exhaustion induced stupor you somehow found yourself on his land. All this is out the window when it is evident that you climbed the dudes' fence to be at the point where your behind now resides. In effect, you're *nolo contendere*.

Anyway, I thought if God wants me to have this field, He isn't going to spoil it by letting the owner see me.

The grass was so tall I had to use my feet to mash down an area the size of my tent. That doesn't sound like much of a problem, but if you get in the tent when it's on top of so much grass, your body weight on the floor causes the walls and roof to sag inward. If they touch your body, the vapor that your body gives off during the night condenses on the inside and make you wet, cold, and miserable. Not something you want to wake up to. Although I stayed dry that night, the next morning when I poked my head out I realized that one of the heaviest dews I'd ever seen had fallen. The tent was soaked. Before I could sleep again I'd have to go through the bothersome drying-out process. Every single article of clothing and sleep gear had to be spread out in the sun to dry thoroughly. If you tried to cheat and leave something in the pack that was a little damp, that article would invade all the newly dried clothes and make them wetter than you thought possible. That one merely damp-of-no-consequence piece becomes like Typhoid Mary in the darkness of the pack. Well, maybe Mildew Mary. Such a stink she could raise.

My home field by the bay was a lucky find for my first night's stay with such a beautiful location and view. Before going to sleep I had lain in the open doorway of my tent and looked out over the bay with its dark water contrasting the bright lights of the boats and yachts moored there. The motion of the waves made the lights dance across the water.

A thousand years ago a buddy of mine named Gus and I drove from Kentucky to California in my 1954 Corvette. That's when I first fell in love with California. I said then, and continue to say, that if I'd been born a hundred years earlier that's where I'd have gone to live.

I'm sure Ol' Mother Nature was up to her earthquake-wildfire-droughts trick-bag even then, but subtract from the equation pollution, traffic gridlock, gang warfare, riots and high taxes and add the sun, the climate, and the beauty. The sum of these parts make for a wonderful place to be. Remember I said a hundred years ago. Too many crazies today — 'nuff said.

The next day, the Pacific Coast Highway was typical Southern California. Just picture in your mind the most glorious weather you can imagine and you have their average day.

Earthquakes, mudslides, droughts, pollution and no-respecter-of-wealth wildfires may be what comes to mind when you think of Southern California, but if you've experienced just one day like this day, then the earthquakes, wildfires, and mud-slides are pushed aside by the beautiful, blond-haired, blue-eyed baby day you are now holding.

Later in the afternoon, I was to realize that this blond, blue-eyed baby also has an evil twin with red hair and a temper. And this twin was the afternoon sun. During the next five-and-a-half months that fiery ball and I were to have quite a love-hate relationship. Love was mornings when it lifted the cold stiffness from my bones, and hate was afternoons when it beat down relentlessly on the backs of my hands threatening, no promising to turn them into a char-broiled hamburger.

My number 15 sunscreen was a weak match for this afternoon sun, 93 million miles or no.

Since I was using my walking stick, one or the other hand was continually jutting out in front of me with the back of the exposed hand taking a terrible beating from the sun. What defensive weapon could I come up with to give my poor hands relief?

A mental search of my backpack brought to mind something I was to learn you can't have too many of — bandannas. Not only, are they backs-of-the-hand savers but can also be washcloths, towels, Kleenex, adornments, sweatbands, a granny scarf on cold nights, in dire straits toilet paper, and even an ever-so-flimsy addition to soften what you lie on at night. An unfolded bandanna might seem like thin, useless mattress material, but I soon found that in the Walking Across America Game, the same rules apply as the ones at hog-killing time — nothing is wasted.

When everything you own, and every defense you have, is contained in a pack on your back you quickly learn to find as many uses as you can for everything you're carrying.

But that heavy backpack was one of the things I could never find more than one use for. It eluded all my efforts. It seemed to know that without its services it would be paper or plastic for me. With seeming immunity from prosecution it smugly and lazily stuck to its one designated assignment. Not that being the container for all my worldly goods wasn't meritorious, I just didn't like the smirk I'd see on its face. As that pack continued to pull at my neck and shoulder muscles for hour upon endless hour I wondered what other use I could put it to.

Of the three basic needs — food, clothing, and shelter — two were contained in an area approximately 24 inches long by 15 inches wide and 10 inches deep on my back.

Not only was my towel a towel, it also became a chair when there was nothing else to sit on but hot asphalt. At night its softness kept my head from the cold, slick nylon bag I had to use for a pillow.

And when menacing dogs came too close my walking stick did double-duty as a lion tamer's chair. It became a lever to pry me back up steep roadside banks after I'd scrambled down for an emergency nature call.

And my clothes didn't just lounge around at night. They worked the third shift as my pillow.

The nylon bag that stood daytime duty as sleeping bag container served as a pillowcase.

And at night when my hands woke me because they were dry and burning my sunscreen became hand lotion.

I found one more use for that bandanna at night one became my tent doormat.

On my second afternoon I was to start a practice that made me the focus of many stares in the following months — I wrapped bandannas around my hands. Imagine if you can, walking through Alabama with a pack on your back, a walking stick, a funny-looking safari hat on your head, and dangling bandannas tied around your hands. I was fair game in an open season. No matter. The baddest dude in the whole state couldn't do to you to what the sun could do.

About the same time I cured my roasted hands problem, I approached a turning point in my walk. It was to be both mental and physical. I was to leave the Pacific Coast Highway and turn east toward San Juan Capistrano.

Euphoria descended upon me when I realized that no longer would I be wasting steps going south along the Pacific coast, but from now on all my steps would be gainful, productive, eastward, Empire-State-Building-direction steps.

It's a feeling that's hard to understand unless you've walked many miles in the heat. Oh sure, I knew that this ground had to be covered but there was no pleasure in that type of walking. The realization that each step is one less step in the big picture, those were the rewarding steps.

Chapter 3
The Returned Swallow

My first eastward direction town was San Juan Capistrano. A clean, pretty little town. (Would those cute little swallows want to return every year to a dirty, ugly little town?) Funny how a small boy growing up in a tiny, rural Kentucky town would have heard about the swallows returning to Capistrano, but for as long as I can remember I've known that. My mother told me about it when I was very young. But why would she tell me about birds in California, a world away from Kentucky? Maybe she reasoned that a young boy would be fascinated by the story, too.

Since the swallows had been a part of my life for so long I couldn't be in their home without finding out what I could about them.

I'm a forge ahead kind of guy and am happiest when moving toward my goal. That doesn't mean, however, that I can't stop and appreciate things and the Capistrano swallows thing was worthy of appreciation. I can appreciate fairly quickly, though. Besides I knew that finding out why the swallows really come back to Capistrano was too big a fact-finding mission for a guy whose real mission was walking Los Angeles to New York. I wondered if anyone really knew why, or how, they came back on the same day. And I'm skeptical enough that if someone gave me a definitive, factual-sounding, reason I'd still doubt they really knew. How does anyone really know why birds do what they do? How do you talk to a bird? Still I couldn't go through the town without seeing the mission.

This was my second night out and the sun was inching toward the horizon. The mission to see the mission would have to wait until tomorrow. I knew from experience that out of sight wooded areas were the best places to spend the night if Holiday Inn wasn't in the equation. The object is simply to be as invisible as possible. You must try your best to not get caught in the middle of town with darkness coming on. Of course, the fly in this walking ointment is that you don't know what lies ahead. You get some idea by looking at the map but, unlike being in an automobile, you can't be out of town in a matter of minutes. On foot it might take hours to get out of town and darkness will not wait. And, maps show cities and towns, but not out-lying communities. If you can be seen from even one house, it's no different from being caught in the largest city.

On the second night of my walk, San Juan Capistrano presented itself at just the wrong time. Towns, darkness, and cross-country walkers do not good bedfellows make. Sadly for it, but gladly for me, an Interstate nearly dissects the town. I knew from past experience that

Interstates offered better places to bed down than a town does. I know it's hard to picture Interstates offering places to hide, but it takes the practiced eye of someone whose been there to see them.

As you might imagine noise is a major drawback. If because of rain you are forced to sleep under an overpass and not in the landscaping along the Interstate the roar from those 18-wheelers will, as Jerry Lee Lewis says, "Shake your nerves and rattle your brain." Still you'll gladly put up with that to have a relatively safe place to put down. Darkness was approaching and I knew it was going to catch me. Why does it always come more quickly when you don't want to be caught?

Just about that time I noticed the sign for the Interstate. I had to walk out of my way to reach it, though that mattered little.

I noticed a fairly high hill next to the Interstate and decided that would be my home for the night. It wasn't an easy climb and after reaching the top I discovered by the flotsam that it must be a hangout for lovers and druggies; neither of whom I wanted around this night. As I unrolled my sleeping bag I rationalized that this was a weeknight and hopefully, loving and drugging were more likely on the weekend. Sometimes self-delusion makes it easier to cope with situations you can't change.

The next morning I walked back into San Juan with a mission on my mind. As luck would have it the mission lay right on my original walking route. It was early morning, though, and the mission wasn't open yet. It was visible over the wall and through the gate surrounding it so I could, at least, say I'd seen it.

Did you ever notice that if a town has an outstanding feature or something of historical significance or a natural wonder everything is named after it? The Peachtrees alone in Atlanta must drive the postal service buggy. There's Peachtree Street, Peachtree Boulevard, Peachtree Way, probably even a Peachtree Alley. The list goes on ad nauseam. The Peachtree Laundromat, the Peachtree Robo-Wash…Gimme a break! The Atlanta Peachtrees alone would curl your toenails but after these come the Taras, Rhetts and Scarletts. It wouldn't surprise me to learn that Atlanta has a "Prissy Git It and Go."

I've heard that San Antonio has the same problem with the Alamo. Are the Alamo Pawn Shop, Alamo Auto Parts, Alamo Video Rental and Tanning Bed really relevant to the Alamo? I think not.

I suppose San Francisco has its "Bays" and New York its "Big Apples."

Although I just passed through San Juan Capistrano fairly quickly I couldn't help wondering if there weren't a Swallow's Dominos and a Mission Wrecker Service. You know, (make me stop!) I'll bet in Hinckley, Ohio there's a "Buzzard Cut & Curl."

But I still hadn't answered the have-they/have-they-not returned swallow question. I began to look around for someone to ask. I couldn't just pass through without asking the most important question that San Juan had to offer.

I spied a man working on a car in a garage. Oh boy, a native. Who better to resolve my lifelong wonderings? As I got a closer look, I saw what may have been the most rustic native San Juan had to offer. When he heard me approach, he withdrew from under the car hood and turned toward me. I was stopped dead.

When I was little I'd sometimes come in the house after playing and my mother would look at my face, arms, shirt and pants and ask me if there was any dirt left in the yard.

That's kinda the feeling I got when this guy turned around. If cars need oil and grease to operate, I hoped he'd left some inside.

It wasn't the first greasy car mechanic I'd seen with a cigarette dangling from his lower lip. It was the first I'd seen with a top tooth and bottom tooth missing at the same location, thereby creating a very unique cigarette holder.

I thought, "Well, you've blundered into this let's see you if you can dig yourself out of it. See if San Juan's Birdman from Alcatraz can answer your swallows-to-Capistrano-question."

He'd seen me and it was too late to turn back. If I'd been quicker on my feet I could have simply asked for a drink of water. I found that the pack on my back always made that appear to be a logical request. It was early in the morning, cool, and I wasn't thirsty so it didn't occur to me fast enough. All I could do was blurt out my question about whether the swallows had returned or not.

"Excuse me. I hate to bother you but I'm just passing through and was wondering if you could answer a question for me?"

Blank stare, up and down movement from the cigarette preceded by some sucking sounds from the blow hole.

Lord, if it takes this long just to get the okay to ask a question, how long would it take to get the actual answer?

After a long pregnant pause and no sign of life other than the sucking sounds, I decided to just ask without his permission.

"I'm not from around here but I've heard most of my life about the swallows returning to the mission. Do you know if they've come back yet?"

In an instant I summed up the look on his face. The look that told me that swallows returning might be the town's business, but he had little time nor sympathy for people who asked dumb questions about birds.

With a hint of disdain he turned back and just before he disappeared under the car hood he said, "I think they came back about two weeks ago."

It was time to move on. More than time to move on. This man had made me lose interest, at least for the moment, in the swallows. He had made *me* feel dirty.

As I walked toward the edge of town questions still played in my head.

Exactly when did the people living in Capistrano realize the swallows were coming back at the same time every year? For scores of years had people not even associated bunches of birds with dates on a calendar? Did they just remark, "Those danged birds are always around here about March!" The day I'd like to have witnessed is the one when that first Sharpy said, "About March, nothing! Those suckers come back here every March 19th.

Chapter 4
Hopefully, Not the Signs of Our Times

I'm going to get letters for saying this, but, to a boy from Kentucky and Tennessee, San Juan Capistrano is pretty much an extension of Los Angeles. Just as you reach the far eastern edge of San Juan you enter "country" for the first time. And soon to follow is a national forest with lots of trees, canyons, and mountains.

My map and a few well-placed questions, told me there was nothing out there. I grew accustomed to hearing that. Some people seemed to delight in saying, "Grocery store? Filling station? Hell, there's nothing for forty miles!" I think those people enjoy the I-know-something-you-don't-know feeling. It gives them a sense of importance. And they like to use it to make you aware that you're in their territory and you'd better be brave.

I prepared all I could for "nothing out there" by filling my internal water tank and my external water bottles, and by buying what was to become my staff of life — Doritos tortilla chips.

Being in a national forest I did escape houses and it felt good to be out in the country at last. But the highway I was on was still busy with commuters. And Lord help the poor soul who isn't cut from the commuter cloth and has to share the road with them. A car made of steel is puny enough protection from commuters. Walking down the road you'd better hope your guardian angel has his hand on your shoulder.

I hadn't gone far out of town before I felt the need for a break coming on. Mainly it was my feet. When you carry a pack on your back it seems the only part of you that escapes the strain is the top of your head. The pack pulls at your shoulders, which ache, which pull on your neck muscles, which ache. It's the old thigh-bone-connected-to-the-hip-bone thing. That heavy pack creates a chain reaction and the buck stops at your feet.

I took off my pack and got out my stool. I know, "stool" sounds incongruous with "pack" so let me explain.

Down through my life I'd hitchhiked over most of the United States but never felt really comfortable standing there facing traffic with the required beseeching look on my face. I didn't mind asking for a ride, I just didn't like the appearance of begging. Though there were many times I would have done it gladly.

So, when I decided I'd hitchhike from Tennessee to California to start my walk, I thought I'd use another slant. I'd just sit by the side of the road, put out a sign indicating my next destination, and catch up on my reading.

It was no fault hitchhiking. Since my eyes never met the drivers, I hadn't the embarrassment of beseeching, and since the driver didn't have to look into my eyes he could zip on by me without the guilt feeling.

If I was going to sit and read what would I sit on? The ground? Naw. Too hard. The pack? Naw. Too soft, might damage something. I put my thoughts to inventing a stool. Just right, Goldilocks! Looks weren't important, compactness and weight were.

I sat on a narrow three-inch wide board and put a pencil mark on either side where my hips came — 13½ inches (no snickering, please). I cut the board 13½ inches by 3 inches and had the seat portion solved. I placed the board against my bottom and "sat" on my imaginary stool to check for height.

Twelve and a half inches seemed about right. Now for the legs. I then found a piece of one-inch diameter plastic PVC pipe, which is used in plumbing and is light and strong. I cut a piece 12½ inches long. I then bored a hole halfway through the seat in which to insert the pipe. Apart it was simply a piece of pipe and a length of board. Together it became a "T" shaped stool — one like farmers used to use when they milked cows by hand. Something probably better suited to a Chinese Acrobats School, but it was a functional stool if you didn't wiggle around too much.

It was while I was sitting there on my stool resting my feet that I realized I'd stopped across the road from a business. The frontage to the place was grown up in trees and bushes and the working part of the business was sitting back off the highway. Through small peepholes I could see movement and hear lots of quick Spanish talk.

I hurried to put my shoes and socks back on. It seems silly now, sitting in the safety of my home, that I should have become apprehensive over movement and Spanish talk. It just created a strange feel in me and I wanted to move on. Why should I have been apprehensive because the workers were speaking Spanish? They may have been discussing the Dow-Jones Index for all I knew. I guess when you are in a strange place and feeling a little vulnerable, you just don't need to feed that vulnerability.

The road started to climb and wind up through a national forest and I began to walk through canyons and high cliffs.

I looked down from those high cliffs into the gorges far below and on more than one occasion I spotted the remains of a Volkswagen carcass. The reason for their contorted deaths was obvious. Boys had pushed them off the cliffs to watch them crash down the mountainside, Hollywood movie style. And they just stayed there 'cause even if it were possible to raise them such a long distance you wouldn't have anything but twisted junk for your efforts.

It was when I had gotten out in the country of California that I began noticing something that surprised me. I'd always thought of California as being one of the most environmentally conscious states so it surprised me that its roadsides were so trash-laden. And it wasn't just new trash. After looking at trash for awhile you can distinguish between recent trash and trash that's been lying there for a long time.

The Volkswagens I could understand. It wasn't feasible to go after them and besides most people passing by couldn't see them anyway.

And to a degree new trash is understandable, in fact, unavoidable. What can I say — there'll always be trashy people.

I once owned a restaurant and new trash/old trash reminds me of what a health inspector told me, "There's clean dirt and dirty dirt."

Maybe I shouldn't judge California without knowing the facts. Maybe money is scarce for trash pickup. I doubt there's a scarcity of prisoners sitting around, though. Maybe it can be blamed on California's population crunch. Given enough numbers, you'll up your percentage of low-lifes who throw their trash alongside the road.

I came to a plateau of sorts and noticed the entrance to a state park coming up on my left. I saw a female ranger manning the shack at the main gate. It wasn't much but thirst draws you toward any hope of water. When you've been really thirsty it's easy to understand how mirages can drive a man crazy. Luckily, this wasn't a mirage and the girl was sympathetic and had water to share.

As I drank and passed the time of day with her I noticed a stack of pamphlets lying on the counter by the window. The words jumped out at me. "Warning to back country campers: This is mountain lion country."

Great. Just what a little ole' boy from Tennessee, walking down the road alone, sleeping out in the bushes, needs. I'm being just a tad facetious. The mountain lion pamphlet didn't concern me all that much. My daylight hours were totally taken up with walking down the road and I'd never heard of a case where a mountain lion sprang from a cliff or tree onto a hiker. That's Hollywood stuff and besides with my red pack, silly safari hat, bandannas, et al, I doubt the average mountain lion would have recognized me as something suitable to chew on. I did do my sleeping in the woods and fields, out of sight, still I was never more than a few yards from the road. By no stretch could I be considered a "back-country camper." I reasoned that it would have to be a pretty desperate mountain lion to try and come so close to the road.

But then, about a quarter mile down the road it flashed on me, "Aren't all mountain lions desperate?"

If I told you that soon after the state park it was time to bed down for the night you'd say, "Hey, you were just in San Juan Capistrano and you spent the night there? And I'd have to agree that it doesn't seem as if there's much distance between beddings down. But, you're still thinking in 65 mph — Interstate terms. While you're with me on this walk we'll be doing a cool two mph.

I spent this night sleeping across the road from a campground. I know you're thinking, "Across the road? You big Dummy! Why didn't you sleep at the campground?"

Well, it isn't as if I were going to be received as royalty and shown to a king-sized bed. I would have been shown the same accommodations on either side of the road, namely, the ground. And the ground was free on my side.

I slept in the bushes just behind a pull-off area which I learned early in my walk wasn't the best place to spend the night. Seems pull-off areas are great for stopping to take a leak, chuck an empty out in the bushes, yell some obscenity, and squeal out, throwing gravel. Did I mention low-lives earlier?

Wonder if the paying patrons on the paying side of the road paid to hear what I heard for free?

The next day dawned hot, and when they dawn hot they never let up. "Nothing out there" was making me a bone to be chewed.

Thirst can make you do crazy things. Something, anything to drink had begun to occupy all my thoughts that day when I spotted a half-empty Pepsi someone had left atop a fence post. You can sit there and judge me but I know you're well-fed and well-watered. I also know positively that you'd do the same thing. It's all a matter of time. You may be able to hold out longer than I, but don't kid yourself that you wouldn't do it.

Did I mention earlier that this book wasn't going to be a travelogue? Drinking the remains of the Pepsi represents what this book is all about — walking coast to coast and everything that entails — the trials, the deprivations, the good, the bad, and the ugly.

I realize lots of people could walk the same route and write a great travelogue. I wish I could adequately describe beautiful sunsets or morning dews on flower-covered meadows but the words aren't in me. I can attest that they're there and worth the effort to see, I just can't adequately put them into words.

I think I've conveyed to you the fascination California has always held for me. In my mind far away places with strange sounding names were always romanticized, glamorized, even dramatized. Though, I realized California wasn't that far away nor that strange sounding, to a boy in Kentucky it had a mystique.

Knowing it was so different, knowing the mystique, knowing — in my mind it was even a little, downright weird didn't prepare me for — *the signs.*

I was still in the national forest and generally they are what the name implies — forests, no houses, no service stations, no grocery stores, no malls. They create, if not fear, at least a sense of vulnerability to someone walking down the road alone.

Soon after the Pepsi on the fence post I saw the first sign. At first I wasn't taken so much by the content of the sign as by the fact that it was so small. I couldn't understand how the person putting it there expected people passing by in cars to read it. It was almost as if the sign had been put there for me to read. I would be slow enough and close enough to make it out. Being in this isolated, vulnerable place and imagining it had been put there for me, made its words create an eerie feeling in me. The sign wasn't much bigger than a three by five inch post card and all it said was this, "All the men who worked on the Lake Elsinore Dam are now dead."

It just made my mind whirl with all its connotations. What did it mean? My first thought was that it was someone gloating over a doomsday prediction they had made. I reasoned that the dam had been a nuclear power project and had been inherently dangerous either in its construction, in its finished radiation disaster potential, or both. And that this person had seen those dangers, been opposed to the dam, seen all the men die and now was posting these signs to prove to the world that their prediction had been correct.

I suppose one sign would have been disconcerting enough but something you could dismiss as simply a loony being a loony. And after I saw the sign I thought about it for a few minutes, pondered its weirdness, then went on to other thoughts that beckoned for my attention as I moved on down the road.

Imagine yourself on a lonely stretch of highway and you begin seeing more of these weird signs. Another strange thing about them was they weren't placed in a logical, systematic fashion. There was neither rhyme nor reason to their placement.

Normally, if a person wanted to convey a message to the motoring public he'd put out large, easy-to-read signs close to the highway in a sequential manner, i.e., "Yard Sale 300 yards." "Yard Sale 200 yards," and "Yard Sale 100 yards." That wasn't the case with these signs. Tiny signs put there just for me? Someone else walking down the road? Way out here? What kind of audience is that? Easily scared, maybe, but influential? Able to affect change? I can picture better exposure for their message than tiny, scary signs.

Several of these signs couldn't even have been seen from a car, which thoroughly puzzled me and made me conjure up even more scary thoughts about the strange person who'd put those signs out.

It was about this time that nature called (see Pepsi on fence post). As luck would have it nature presented a nice, little dirt road shooting off to the left. Perfect.

So much the better, too, that this little dirt road seemed rarely used. In fact, bushes were pushing hard at the sides trying to reclaim what I'm sure they felt was rightfully theirs. I walked back quite a way until I was sure I couldn't be seen from the highway. I stopped in front of a nondescript tree for no other reason than it was just a tree and happened to be there and it was time to stop.

I didn't bother to take off my pack, as this was the standing *man's* version of a nature call.

In such a situation your options for directing your eyes are: down (I'd say 90% the direction of choice), straight ahead (5%), left (2%), right (2%), and up (1%). So don't ask why, with the odds stacked so overwhelmingly against me, I chose up. A 99-to-one chance against it, yet there it was. Several feet above my head the bloody beggar peered down upon me with those daunting, shivery, creepy words, "All the men who worked on the Lake Elsinore dam are now dead!"

Spooky stuff, Man!

Chapter 5
Lost and Found

Later I came upon some phone repairmen working on the lines alongside the road and after posing my well-worn food/drink question they huddled and after their collective rumination concluded that there may be a campground up ahead a few miles, and that maybe it had a camp store of sorts.

Maybes beat a blank if for no other reason than they provide hope. Hope is hope is hope and thusly good and sustaining. If what's at the end of hope turns out to be a disappointment, it still doesn't diminish its value. Hope came through this time and gave me the camp store of sorts.

Really, my needs were simple and easily met, usually by the adjectives cold, wet, and sweet.

As I partook of the camp store's adjectives I listened to a teenage boy who worked there talking about nothing in particular. He'd seen my pack, so my ears perked up when he started telling about another long-distance hiker who'd come through a while back. He couldn't remember where the hiker had started, but recalled that it had taken him two days to come all of twelve miles and he was attempting to walk to Florida. The boy said the hiker was extremely overweight and when he walked he tilted from side to side as if he might tip over at any minute. The boy expressed disbelief that the hiker could ever make it all the way to the Sunshine State. He never heard anymore about the hiker so he couldn't say if he quit five miles down the road or made it to his destination in Florida.

His story plus the cold, wet, and sweet gave me new vigor as I prepared to leave the campground.

I couldn't let some cross-country hiker person so unlikely as he'd described show me up. As I prepared to leave the story-telling boy and head off once more into the great unknown, I did something I did literally thousands of times in the following five-and-a-half-months, 3,813 miles — I put on my pack. Simple enough you say. Why tell us about it? The reason I mention it at all is that by just about everyone's definition my label would be hiker. I think that's a fair assumption for someone covering three thousand miles on foot.

And almost invariably the picture of "hiker" includes backpack. Unless you're one of those wusses who walk somewhere and have someone following you in a motor home in which you "camp" at night.

You'd think that a hiker putting on his pack would be akin to falling off the proverbial log. It never was automatic or that simple for me. Logically, you visualize putting your right arm through a strap, then your left arm through a strap, much as if you were putting on a jacket. Maybe it was stiffness born of fifty years, or the awkwardness of the pack, or some combination of both that prevented me from putting it on the conventional way.

From Day One, my system was this — at the top of the pack was a strap for short carries at a campsite or a quick grab from one of those giant circular, revolving luggage trays at the airport. I don't believe it was ever intended for the purpose I put it to. To launch my pack to the back maneuver, I'd grab that strap with my left hand and in one clean and jerk, weight-lifting movement shoot it high above my head with my left arm extended until it was straight and the pack at its zenith high above my head. Then it was simply a matter of putting my right arm through its strap. Then switch hands and hold the pack up in the air with the right hand while I slipped my left arm through its strap. It was then a matter of letting the pack slip down to my shoulders. Weird, but it worked for me.

This pirouetting ballet move gave me a split-second glance at the backside of my pack. I know you're thinking I could have looked at the back of the pack anytime. I seldom did though, 'cause it held little interest. Mine did, only because it was my clothesline. And even though I may not consciously look while I had it off, the launch to the back procedure created a situation where, without trying, I caught a glimpse of the back on its upward arc.

It was on this launch while leaving the campground camp store that I discovered my first traumatic loss of the trip.

In the months prior to leaving on my walk I'd pored over camping and hiking catalogs like Madonna ogling the latest issue of Victoria's Secrets. I found something that must have thrilled me every bit as much as those frilly, see-through, erotic, nearly-non-existent flimsies did her — blister-proof socks! Thinking about attempting to walk across the United States and you spot blister-proof socks. Could you *not* buy a pair? Could you *not* buy a dozen?

I knew blisters. Blisters and I were on a first name basis. Little did I know as I considerd the catalog's socks that blisters and I, in the following five and a half months, would be closer than blood brothers. And I came to learn that blisters can humble even the mightiest. They can reduce man, any man, to a whimpering pup. No man is bigger than blisters. Arnold Schwarzenegger isn't bigger than blisters. I knew I was the ultimate candidate to own some blister-proof socks.

However, I think the socks represented more of a psychological crutch than any real foolproof ammo in the blister wars. The catalog said "Blister-proof." I thought that was a little strong in the guarantee department knowing the adversary as I did. "Blister-proof" is an absolute. And I remembered from my high school true/false tests that anytime you see an absolute, it's probably not true. (After my walk I noticed in a later edition of the catalog "blister-proof" had been watered down to "blister resistant." And in an even later issue of the catalog they'd been dropped altogether). But for someone contemplating a walk across America they were a straw eagerly grasped.

So, you can understand the depth of my loss when the backpack passed before my eyes on its upward swing above my head and in that split second I noticed only one sock hanging where two had been.

When things got wet and they often seemed to through rain, heavy dew, not enough change for the laundromat, etc. I'd put them under one of the straps on the back of my pack.

The sun and wind were excellent dryers, but after the loss of the blister-proof sock I never put anything on my clothesline without securing it well.

I think what fed my panic more than anything was the realization that I was virtually just getting started and I had to face that great vastness with only one blister-proof sock. I hadn't gone far enough in my walk to gain any confidence that I really might be able to do this crazy thing, so the loss of the sock was a blow.

This might seem funny but I continued to wear the remaining sock all throughout my walk reasoning that half protection beat completely throwing myself upon the mercy of the blister gods.

In retrospect I think the benefits of the sock were purely mental. It didn't seem to play a part one way or the other in the overall blister scheme of things.

My next loss story wasn't so profound, but it's still worthy of note.

Once my wife and I owned a small restaurant in Gatlinburg, Tennessee. The restaurant business is very hard work with many long hours required. A lady who ate in my restaurant and was a previous restaurant owner once described it best — "Slavery." Any relief is welcome. So, it was a thrill for me one day when a young man ate with us and mentioned he was walking from Myrtle Beach, South Carolina to Chicago, Illinois. I pumped him for details until I'll bet he wished he'd stopped elsewhere. Finally the questions got around to his walking stick. I knew Moses swore by them and he'd walked for forty years, still they seemed to me as if they'd be as much hindrance as help. The walker said they were indispensable, and in fact, became like a third leg. Inwardly, I scoffed slightly at that, thinking he was blowing walking stick values way out of proportion.

Later, on my warm-up walks, I'd taken a stick and proclaimed the Myrtle Beach–Chicago hiker prophetic. It became like a wristwatch — once you get used to it, you don't think you can live without it.

It was the day after the sock loss that I suffered my second setback. And after I tell you what it is you'll think, "What a whiny-pot!"

To set the stage in my defense, imagine if you will, that instead of both your shoes having leather or rubber soles, the right one is steel on the bottom. Now wouldn't that be disconcerting? It would clang and get on your nerves, you'd slip and fall easily and you'd give anything to have two good rubber soles back.

That's sorta what happened to my third leg. In what was simply one in thousands of placements of the walking stick I noticed that the normal muted sound had been replaced by a metallic one, and that it now tended to slip. I looked and the from-the-factory, built in, rubber end of my walking stick was gone. Since as many of my steps were in the grass alongside the road as on the road itself, and since the grass muffled sound and created a better grip than asphalt, I couldn't say where I may have lost the rubber tip. I retraced my steps some but in a L.A./N.Y. walk you aren't too keen on backtracking. And, I soon saw the futility of this tip in the haystack search. I resigned myself to carrying the stick 'til I could find a hardware store and a rubber crutch tip. I didn't want to use it for fear of damaging the end.

I think people give credit to providence when they are rescued just when they need to be rescued. And, I too, am a believer in some cases. I don't think, though, any divine provider thought my walking stick loss worthy of intervention. The flip side of providence is dumb luck. And that ain't bad if it cures a dilemma.

I was on a winding road in the mountains that must have been the scene of more than a few accidents. I'd seen the remains of several burnt-out flares, the kind police jab in the ground and light to warn oncoming motorists.

At the snaily pace by which I passed any object, it was easy to digest what I was seeing. Contrast 65 miles per hour Interstates where you only think you see things. In fact, I've always contended that if you took someone from a foreign country on a New York to Los Angeles trip and stayed strictly on the Interstates they'd have no concept of what this country is all about. The planners of Interstates seemed to have made the routes as sterile as possible. Don't get me started on Interstates.

Okay, back to snaily pace.

Since flares were something I didn't normally see in my day-to-day existence I took more than a passing interest. Something was of particular interest to me, and it wouldn't have been of interest any other time, any other place, any other life. There's a hard plastic cap that must be removed to light the flares. Since they have no other purpose they are just tossed on the ground as useless. As I passed by, it dawned on me that there was some use in them for me. They fit the end of my walking stick perfectly.

The plastic cap wasn't the perfect answer. It had the same effect really as not having any tip at all…it was hard, clangy and slipped when you wanted it to grip. Yet I could use the walking stick without fear of damaging the end. At least, the flare end gave me my third leg back, even if it felt like a pirate's peg leg.

Chapter 6
The Monster Elsie

I could tell by my map I was approaching the town of Lake Elsinore. Your first sight of the lake and the town surrounding it comes while you are a couple of thousand feet above the two. They are in a valley and you are still in the mountains. It's a beautiful sight and as I stood at the scenic overlook soaking it all in, I wondered what it must have been like for the first person to see this majestic scene.

I pictured two Indians coming upon this spot for the first time. It must have been very impressive even to them. I'm sure natural beauty was more or less an everyday occurrence for them. Still, I picture each stopping and looking (Are they walking or riding painted ponies? You choose). They stop and look and even they are moved. It isn't like them to do much verbalizing. (I saw Dances With Wolves eight times). They would simply look at one another and give a slight nod. Such a simple gesture, but one that says much. We are a truly fortunate people and our God is good.

Okay, the truth. The two Indians were Wind In His Hair (See Dances With Wolves) and me. Me doesn't have an Indian name yet. Maybe at some future council they'll give me a name like "Walks With Wolves" or "Walks Far With Teepee On Back" or maybe the pack on my back would remind them of a buffalo's humped shoulders and they'd name me "Traipsing Tatonka. Wind In His Hair and I need no more than a nod, either, to indicate that we've traveled far without water and the lake looks as cold and sweet as apple juice. We start the long descent. At the bottom I look to my right and Wind In His Hair has ridden off into a mist. (I chose painted ponies.)

The lake, though pretty, no longer seems so inviting as juice. In fact, I think of something that completely turns me off when I think of drinking from it — Elsie. No, not Elsie the Borden cow.

I'm a chocolate milk lover's lover and Elsie the Borden cow would have been a great connotation had color been the issue. No, my Elsie was a sea monster. Would *you* want to drink from a lake where a monster took his baths and, no doubt, went to the potty? (Why do you think they're called "monsters?") Anyway, somewhere I'd read that Lake Elsinore had had monster sightings.

I've always had a fascination for the Loch Ness Monster. I'm a fervent believer that he, she, or it exists. I agree with the people who say it's a holdover from a dinosaur age reptile thought to be extinct. They are called plesiosaurus and look like giant sea turtles with big flippers, long necks and small heads.

If I had ten wishes and all were guaranteed to come true I'd use one to make sure that the Loch Ness Monster was captured before I die. I want proof that what I think he is, he really is. I don't want him to be harmed. I just want them to take about a hundred pictures, then turn him loose and never bother him again.

Of course, I've read everything I can about Nessie. And in some of the books and articles about monsters they included stories about monsters that are thought to exist in other parts of the world such as Lake Champlain's Champy. And, I suppose it was in one of these books that I read about Elsie. So, it was with extra fascination that I stood on the shore (not too close, those monsters have long necks) of this monster lake.

I wonder if anyone ever looked at Loch Ness for the first time and only saw a lake. Doesn't everyone, without being able to help themselves, hope to catch a glimpse of Nessie? I'm not ashamed to admit that I scanned Lake Elsinore. No Elsie. She must be sleeping or having her hair done.

Like the swallows of Capistrano I couldn't just pass through Lake Elsinore without talking to someone who'd witnessed, or could explain the legend of Elsie.

My Birdman from Alcatraz had been a poor swallow choice. So how was I to choose a monster man? I had help. A donut shop. And if there weren't any monster men present a half-dozen donuts or so never killed anyone. This donut shop was really neat. It had a shaded patio with tables and chairs out back where the beautiful California day could be savored along with your cream filleds. Workmen passed through the patio on their way to the bakery back door and the treasures within. I took a stab and said, "Excuse me" to a likely looking monster man. At my Elsie inquiry he threw back his head. Seems some of the locals think it quite amusing that their lake could contain a monster.

"If there's one in there he must be a giant mudpuppy 'cause there are times when the lake goes dry enough to walk across in places," I heard Monster Man say.

Like Elsie slipping below the surface I lowered my head back into my cheese Danish. I'd done it again — asked what I thought was a perfectly logical question only to feel like a fool when I heard the answer.

Later on the outskirts of town I came to a combination grocery/ restaurant/post office. Sounds weird, and in a big city you'd never see it, but in small rural places it isn't too uncommon. They sold postcards with pictures and I saw one that had a picture of Elsie. But this Elsie was a Chamber of Commerce brainchild to lure tourists. Seems the townspeople decided to capitalize on the monster-in-the-lake myth so they built a long, life-sized green undulating snake-like thing with three humps, pointy tail and long neck and set it out in a shallow part of the lake. I'll just quote from the postcard, "For over a hundred years, history books have recorded sightings of something in the lake." In response community volunteers built Elsie, a popular 122-foot neon-green play-o-sauras. Elsie now delights crowds throughout the year during her periodic swims around Lake Elsinore. Elsie hopes everyone will remember her motto, "Fun is never extinct!"

For our purposes let's pretend she is and move a little further on down the road.

Chapter 7
The Weapons Charge

I really hadn't gone into the post office looking for Elsie postcards.

My crossing of the mountains and forests between San Juan Capistrano and Lake Elsinore had told me something. And it couldn't have been plainer if it had been written in neon lights ten feet in front of my face. It flashed on and off like warning signs at highway construction sites. It said, "You're carrying too much crap, dummy!"

Remember my stool story? I was so proud of my stool. It seemed such a marvel of engineering. And, if you held it in your hand you'd think its weight was inconsequential. Not true. Taken by itself it presented no problem, but it was a part of the problem.

Walking with everything on your back, there comes a time for evaluation, or more correctly, re-evaluation. I decided in the mountains before Lake Elsinore it was time to re-evaluate. That pack was driving me right into the ground. And as the pain increased on my shoulders and neck I had nothing else to do but mentally give each item back there its day of judgment.

They say Dr. Mengele, by a mere flick of his finger right or left determined who was to live or die at Auschwitz. I thought of what was back there and started flicking. Tough in the respect that the items were all handy, yet it was easy to say what had to go when balanced on the "real need" vs. "pain produced" scale. One of the had-to-goes tugged at my heart almost as much as the realization that the stool had to go.

I imagine anyone contemplating an adventure similar must think to some degree about the possibility of being harmed by someone. In the months before my walk I hashed and rehashed countless times every possible means of defense I could think of. Naturally, a gun seems the logical first choice. No, "logical" isn't the right word but "first" is. It's a sad commentary on our society that guns are the first line in our defense arsenal. I never gave a gun any serious consideration, though. I could see the look of perverse pleasure on the policeman's face as he searched through my pack. "Aha, what's this?" he'd say with suppressed glee. Walking down the road, no matter how grungy looking was still, praise God, a freedom we enjoyed. But walking the same road carrying a concealed weapon was an excellent excuse to see that this grunge didn't walk down the road any longer.

Although a gun brought the most satisfaction when contemplating defense mechanisms, I didn't want to give the police that satisfaction.

I went down the list:

Knife — the kind that would be of use would be illegal, too.

Machete — It lingered longer than most after posing my defense dilemma to my buddy, Gus, and he had suggested it. "A crazy dude with a machete is not to be messed with," he wrote. Gus had spent some time in Mexico. Finally, machete, too, had to be scratched from the list — too heavy. Possibly illegal, too, if the police wanted to say it was illegal. Unlike a knife, though, you could say that it was for clearing your way through brush and snakes to a campsite, not lopping off ears if somebody messed with you.

Pepper Spray... If someone was coming after me, I wanted to stop him or at least teach him a lesson. Yes, pepper spray might stop him temporarily and would be an excellent choice, if while he was screaming and writhing and wetting his pants you could get long gone. My dilemma was that after he'd recovered from the spray I still wouldn't be that far away. And he'd be mad! I'm gonna get that S.O.B. mad! Spray — Out.

So, the more I thought the more I kept coming full circle. I decided to carry nothing. I reasoned thusly: More than likely one guy isn't going to mess with you anyway. And two would have trouble if you went nuts. So that leaves a minimum of three that it would take to do you serious harm. As I saw it, my options were:

1. Kill all three — heavy stuff and gun required, which I'd already ruled out.
2. Run — with a 35-pound pack on your back? Get real!
3. Talk like a silver-tongued devil.
4. Go nuts — see above.

After reviewing these options scores of times I realized that a person walking down the road has no defense. If evil people want to do you harm, there's little you can do.

Toward the end of my walk at a truck stop in New Jersey I started talking to a guy from New York City. I had sought refuge from an afternoon thunderstorm. The rain seemed very cold for August. I thought it was because I was coming down with something. I knew things weren't right because I ordered hot chocolate, and never since leaving Los Angeles five months earlier had I wanted anything other than cold chocolate, the colder the better.

As I sat in the booth I looked out at the rain. Really not seeing it, just lost in my own reverie.

The guy behind the counter was eyeing me and my pack. When the place cleared out, he started toward me. He stood leaning against the other side of my booth. Can you picture worn jeans, old white tee shirt frayed and sagging at the neck, scuffed running shoes, coal black hair slicked back, a cigarette in one side of his mouth and a toothpick in the other? Need help? Truck stop? New Jersey? He was a nice enough guy, though, and I was slightly ashamed that I'd type-cast him before he'd said a word.

By then I could almost lay odds as to what those first words would be.

"Where ya headed?" I knew it! If this were Monopoly, my card would say, "Proceed to Park Place — collect $200.

I've walked from Los Angeles and I'm going to New York City." I'd dropped "trying" and replaced it with "going."

His eyes bugged slightly and I thought the cigarette and toothpick might exchange places on their own.

"Sweet Jesus, Joseph and Mary!" You *walked* all the way from Los Angeles?"

With that he slid into the booth across from me. It wasn't hard to predict the subsequent questions either. By now I knew the script.

"Where do you sleep at night? How far do you walk in a day? Is that pack heavy?"

After I'd satisfied most of his questions he began talking a little about himself. "Wish I could go with you. Got a little honey there I'd like to see. Can't though, at least, not for four more years. Court order."

I didn't ask.

A little light went on. "Since you're from New York City I want to ask you something. I'm going to walk through Brooklyn and over the Brooklyn Bridge to Manhattan. I've been a little concerned (It was more than a little but I didn't want him to know that) about walking through Brooklyn. You think I'll have any problems? Will this pack make me a target?"

He grabbed for the toothpick. I guess he figured the cigarette would stay stuck to his lip but the toothpick might become a missile. With a backhand dismissal wave of his hand he said, "Naw, man, youse won't have no trouble. Just remember your personna is everything. Why, I wouldn't be afraid to walk anywhere in the toughest parts of New York City wearing a tuxedo. It's all a matter of attitude. But if you look like you're afraid, they'll attack you like a shark would an injured fish."

I left him feeling better about my prospects. I'd just have to keep my chin up in Brooklyn. I knew I was bad. I just had to let them know it. Sure.

Dang! It was hard to stay confident. I pictured gangs on every Brooklyn corner waiting to jump this little innocent from Tennessee.

I knew what the guy at the truck stop was saying. In the deep South I'd often felt defenseless and had tried to assume a certain body language and facial expression that said, "Pick another sucker, sucker!" Inwardly I knew, though, that if someone wanted to do something to me these things meant nothing.

So what was it back there in my pack that I was about to turn thumbs down on? Something I hated to see go as much as my stool. My only defense. And I was shipping it back home. Promise you won't laugh — a bag of marbles and a slingshot. You promised you wouldn't laugh! I know. I know. It sounds pretty Huck Finn. But review all my defense pros and cons:

Slingshot pros:

1. Legal

2. Non-fatal

3. Simple and easy to carry, (I thought.)

Slingshot cons:

1. Too slow if someone's intent on doing you harm.

2. You'd have to be good enough to hit a vulnerable spot. Marble on a fleshy spot would only make someone madder.

3. Weigh a bag of marbles in your mind, then picture them pulling on your neck muscles. I rest my case.

To soothe my anxiety, I tried to keep in mind something Robinson Crusoe had said, "Fear of danger is 10,000 times more terrifying than danger itself." Isn't it awesome that he lived 24 years alone on the island before Friday came along?

Alas, the stool, slingshot, marbles and another tough one — my only book, Louis L'Amour's *Education of a Wandering Man* weren't pulling their weight. I kept thinking of John Muir. Here was a walking man's walker and he only carried a blanket, a copy of *Pilgrim's Progress* (or was it *Paradise Lost?*) and the Bible. Of course, things were quite different in his day. Someone walking down the road was the rule rather than the exception. And I don't believe fear ruled everyone's life as it does now. I picture John going up to a house and asking for a bite to eat and finding people happy to share. And it was just a hop, skip and jump from bite to eat to "wonder if you'd mind if I sleep in your barn tonight." Even a non-walker can see the humor of that scenario today. Although, as we'll see a variation on that theme did happen to me a few times.

How did I get on John Muir? Oh yeah, pack weight. I figured who could you trust if not the U.S. Postal Service? So I asked the gentleman/postmaster who ran the grocery/restaurant/ post office if he'd mind putting my pack on his scales. Thirty-five pounds. John would guffaw — big time, but it's really quite light for someone on a coast-to-coast walk in this day. In fact, I can't picture anyone going any lighter than I did. I have to smile to myself when I see hikers with packs on their backs that extend about two feet above their heads. And some cross-country bikers (not the Harley type, the kind you still have to pedal) look like they're pedaling two-wheeled pickups. For Pete's sake, it should be at least a little about meeting Mother Nature on her terms without taking every single creature comfort, including the kitchen sink with you.

Still, there were times when it felt like I was pulling a Mack truck. I came to disdain the idea of carrying anything not absolutely essential. I remarked on more than one occasion that I wouldn't carry a postcard if I didn't have to. This Lake Elsinore search and destroy weight mission was mild in comparison to one I would have later in the desert of the White Sands Missile Range in New Mexico.

My next destination was a town called Temecula.

Chapter 8
Trek to Temecula

Temecula is one of those you can't get there from here places. There really is no road, as such, that goes from Lake Elsinore to Temecula, though they are only 25 miles apart and in line with one another. Technically an Interstate does, but I mean a road, not some sterile rapid-transit adhesive strip. Whoops, I'm out of the starting gate and off on Interstates again. Since my map didn't show a road, as such, I thought I'd better ask. I know you're wondering why I even assumed I could get to Temecula if the map showed no roads. Another, more detailed map did show that streets went there. Actually, it showed that they stopped before they got there, but I figured if they got me close I could make it the rest of the way.

I saw a guy working on a car in an open-air garage. Seems gaffes were part of my makeup of late, so I wasn't too surprised when the mechanic corrected my mutilation of "Temecula." I called it Tem-e-<u>cula</u>.

"Oh, you mean "Ta-<u>mec</u>-ula." He said, "Yes, this road will take you to Temecula."

Technically, it wouldn't but he did pretty much as I would have done. You want to be helpful, yet you don't have the time, nor the inclination to go into great depth.

And you know if the person has half a brain and even the least bit of perseverance, he'll find Temecula. As you get close to town the road starts to weave and bob and even change names. By this time it wasn't a biggie, though. If the first person got you close, a second person can get you the rest of the way. I did find Temecula (see perseverance/half a brain).

Not surprising in 3,000-plus miles and five-and-a-half-months, I had to ask directions numerous times and I came to learn something about the person giving them. The average person goes through life with few chances to feel big and important (not withstanding Alan Ginsberg's 15 minutes of fame). But, when you ask directions of someone you've instantly elevated them to an unearned level of importance. Suddenly they are needed.

This creates a danger of sorts. They may be too helpful — give you more information than you really need. Like the second person I queried about Temecula said, "You might not be able to get there. We had a downpour a few days ago and mud completely covered some of the roads." It was true I saw evidence of what he was saying, yet it was nowhere near bad enough to keep me from getting there.

A tendency to exaggerate? Or just too much of that elevated level of importance? Maybe either, maybe both. Directions, though necessary on occasion, must be mixed with your own good judgment. If you follow them blindly without adding some of your own reasoning, you could be as bad off as before you asked.

Just a second while I put on my padding and headgear. Okay I'm ready. I soon learned on my walk that unless I was desperate, it was useless to ask a woman for directions. Wait! Wait! Wait! Let me qualify that slightly. Granted, most do fairly well with lefts and rights, but if part of your need involves distances and you're asking a woman, you're hurtin' for certain. If she says, "About a mile," you can expect the actual distance to be anywhere in a range from one-fourth of a mile to five miles.

Traveling between Lake Elsinore and Temecula I passed something that surely would warm anyone's heart — miniature ponies, a field of them. How can you resist getting close to them? I couldn't. I walked over to the fence and extended my hand. These little angels must have invented the handout. Most of them rushed over on their stubby little legs. What have I done? Now they expect me to produce something. I wasn't prepared for this. I was usually the one hoping for a handout. I thought, "Hmm, oh yeah, I have a package of M&Ms. Hope they'll do fellas." They did. Their little lips snared those M&Ms as if it was something they did everyday. The bag didn't last long.

They began to look at each other. Who is this guy? One little bag of M&Ms? It was time for the silver tongue.

"You fellas look stout for your size. Ever get a team up and go to any of those pulls? Man, what fetlocks!"

They began to look at each other again as they inched toward the fence. I started to inch away from the fence.

"Hey guys, gotta run."

Again, that night darkness caught me out without a concealed place to put down. You'll appreciate how desperate I was when I tell you where I finally spent the night. I noticed a doctor's office with shrubbery in front of it. Some homeless person must have coined that old "any port in a storm" adage. I walked around the end of the building to see if there was a more likely spot out back. I noticed an old car parked off to the side and a little toward the back. As I passed it the light made something catch my eye. Something about the inside of the car was different. I stepped closer and was startled to see a man sleeping in the car. I quickly and quietly backed away. I'm sure he would have no reason to bother me but I felt uneasy, walking unaware upon him. Feeling certain he hadn't seen nor heard me, I retreated to my original three-foot-wide bed between bush and building. I guess the unsettling thing about coming upon the man was having a cold, stark reality rise up in front of my face. Here was someone much like me, someone without a home, so instead of being afraid of him, I should have smiled knowingly at a kindred spirit. It wasn't that kind of meeting. He represented a scary, unknown factor. Was he a homeless person living out of his car or someone on the run? I felt vulnerable. A person living in a car, whose face I couldn't see, seemed strange and foreign and I wanted no part of him.

I found Temecula to be a neat little town. Evidently it's old and has a Wild West background. At least, they seem to play that up. Whether it's authentic or merely a ploy to pull people off the Interstate, I can't say. Anyway, it looked like a gold rush town.

I'd have given Temecula a closer look if I'd known then what I wasn't to learn until much later. I read somewhere that Temecula is the oldest town in the United States. I can see those hands shooting up and all those bodies nearly jumping out of their seats, dying to inform me that St. Augustine is the oldest town. It's what I thought too, until I read differently. See, where we're making our mistake as white pilgrims is, we piously assume no humans lived here before the white folks set foot on Plymouth Rock. Yeah, in the back of our minds we know some Indians lived here but they weren't really *people*. Sad, isn't it?

The fact is that Temecula, not St. Augustine, has been continually occupied the longest. It was an Indian village before the white man came.

Chapter 9
The County Line Feed and Seed

After Temecula it was back to the country again. I grew to like an equal mixture of town (not city) and country walking. There's something to be said for both. The aforementioned cold, wet, and sweet were easier to come by in towns, and if the cold, wet, and sweet are still in that ol' fuel tank doing their job, then the beauty and solitude of the country can be appreciated. Country stays the same regardless. But if you're hot, hungry, and thirsty, its aesthetic value is lost on you. The "I'd give anything for a store right now" sorta has a way of blocking out aesthetics.

It was a relief when I spotted a sign reading "County Line Feed and Seed Store." Normally, a person wouldn't get excited about Feed and Seed holding any measure of relief. I knew from experience, though, that there's hardly any establishment, no matter its ilk, that doesn't offer some relief to a hot, thirsty walker. It might be as simple as a Coke machine, cracker machine, or a water spigot out back. If it has a sign out front, it's fair game. If you are hot enough, and thirsty enough, a sign saying, "7-11 from Hell Just Ahead," will send thrills up your spine.

If you're ever close to Aguanga, California the County Line Feed and Seed is a "must do." Feed and Seed are just a small portion of what's there. For one thing, critters of all descriptions abound. And it's never a waste of time associating with someone who loves animals. The place has a homey, general store atmosphere and you feel welcome. It's the kind of store Oliver Wendell Douglas on *Green Acres* would have loved. And you don't have to put up with the dippiness of Sam Drucker. One nice thing about the Feed and Seed is it's not some sterile store under one roof. There's as much outside as in. The hay's over by the peacocks, the fertilizer's next to the llamas.

After relating a bit of my story to the owners I asked if I could use their outside hose to shave. Nice people that they were they agreed readily.

People who love animals are some of the most well adjusted people there are. It gives them a strong, even keel. They respect all of God's creatures and treat them with dignity. Rarely do people who love animals go off the deep end. Invariably, mass murderers and other social misfits, upon investigation of their youth, are found to have set fire to cats, used pitchforks on horses, or gouged the eyes out of live fish.

Love, compassion and humor seem intertwined. I felt sure the animal lovers at County Line Feed and Seed would have a sense of humor. After shaving, as I headed back around the building I decided to pull their leg a little.

"It'd be a big help to me if you'd let me ride one of your llamas to New York. It would help him, too. When I bring him back he'll be worldly and wise."

Without missing a beat, Jim, the owner said, "Better still, why don't you ride Stinky, our goat. Then *you'll* come back more worldly and more wise. He'll show you a few things."

A sheepish (sorry) smile was my only response.

It became fairly common for people to come up with anecdotes of their own, after I told them what I was trying to accomplish. Like the boy at the camp store telling me about the hiker passing through on his way to Florida, the Feed and Seed people had a story, too. Seemed a while back a guy passed through who was riding a horse from the West Coast to the East Coast. After leaving their store, he'd gotten about five miles up the road when his horse dropped dead. And like the boy at the camp store, they didn't know if he got another horse or just gave up.

One of the nice things about my walk was looking back, after it was over, to people and places like "The County Line Feed and Seed." It represented real and warm Americana.

Chapter 10
The Bakery Mystique

I thought that the All-the-men-died-on-the-Lake-Elsinore-Dam signs was enough spookiness to last at least through California, and hopefully, much further. I just couldn't believe that my next spooky experience would be with a lady at a yard sale! A yard sale would be one of the last places you'd expect to encounter anything spooky. I'm not going so far as to say that the horse dying and the weird yard sale lady are in any way connected, but they did follow suspiciously close to one another.

What made this yard sale different? For starters, there was no yard. It was just where a side road ran into the main road. I know some yard sales contain some pretty pathetic and useless stuff, but this one was a classic.

The lady was sitting right there next to the road and I'm going by at my snaily pace, so it seemed logical to say a few words. And, really, a few were all I did say. It soon became evident that this lady's aim wasn't so much to sell her junk, as it was to vent her spleen on any person hapless enough to stop. Since we'd spoken I felt awkward passing by without, at least, fingering her wares and saying something nice about them. She never gave me a chance to get beyond fingering.

"You aren't traveling on foot, are you?"

"Yes, Ma'am."

"You wouldn't catch me walking down this road for any amount of money."

"Really?"

"The Indians around here will kill for no reason."

"Really?"

"Yes, they all carry knives and two people have had their throats cut recently. You better watch out and be very careful. I wouldn't walk for anything."

"Why do you think they're so mean?" I purposely used "mean." Her appearance and actions told me more than her words. This woman was a few bricks shy of a load. I thought by calling the Indians mean instead of vicious or murderous it would play to her childish mind.

Something else made me suspicious of her mind and all this violent Indian talk. She was wearing many things Indians wear. She had on a long, loose-fitting dress, a turquoise necklace, several silver bracelets with Indian designs, and she was wearing moccasins.

It didn't add up. Why would she malign the Indians so severely on one hand and imitate them on the other.

I would have given more credence to her Indian ramblings if she had limited those ramblings to Indians, but she went on and on about nothing and everything. Next it was the people who let kids pick up her wares, only to drop and break them. Then it was our corrupt government.

Her next and last tirade made the stop worthwhile. Every time I thought of it for days afterward the picture brought a smile to my face.

She stepped closer until all that separated us was one of her flimsy card tables.

"What's those slick little ugly dogs from Mexico that look like just-born rats?"

"Mexican Hairless?" I speculate from my limited knowledge of slick ugly dogs.

"Naw, yeah, they're ugly too, but those other little ugly dogs from Mexico."

"Chihuahuas?"

"Yeah, I hate them and I hate the people who think they're cute. They bring 'em around here and let 'em run among my stuff. And before I know it the little you-know-whats have hiked their leg on a box of my sweaters or worse, one of my table legs. It ain't hard to picture the feelin' when I go to fold up my tables and my hand runs into that stuff."

It was worth the stop. A funny crazy lady. I could smile for days at the Chihuahua table leg.

"Whew!" I thought. This woman is Disney on Parade. I mumbled something about needing to get to Warner Springs before dark and started to back away toward the road. I told her I appreciated the Indian info and that I'd try my best to catch a ride.

I did make it to Warner Springs that night, but it was another of those "just barelies." I was late for two reasons:

1. I stopped to watch planes take off and land at an airport.

2. I was deviously lured into Maggie's Roadside Cafe by that old siren, thirst.

If you thought the Pepsi on the fencepost was strange, I can tell you it wasn't as strange for me as stopping at Maggie's Roadside Cafe. But then, you don't know about my aversion to beer. Only if I'd been putting up hay on the Fourth of July, and had nothing else to drink, could I remotely see any appeal of beer. I don't like its taste or smell. I do like a couple of beer truisms I heard:

1. You don't buy beer, you rent it.

2. The reason beer goes through you so fast is, it doesn't have to change color on the way through.

Maggies was just what you might picture–a rough-as-hell roadside bar. We know, though, thirst will make you do things you didn't think you would do.

I chained my pack outside. Yes, a lock and chain made it through the extermination selection back in Lake Elsinore. I know what you're saying, "Jeez, a lock and chain are about as heavy as you can get." But, picture everything you own sitting outside Maggie's Roadside Cafe unchained and unlocked. I rest my case. As I plopped down on the barstool I tried to look as tough as the three or four guys already there. I failed dismally. In one of his books, Mark Twain spoke of a fight as being a "misunderstanding conducted with crowbars." As I sat on the barstool in Maggies Roadside Cafe that line came to mind. <u>Cafe</u> is just a slight bit of a misnomer for Maggies. Cafe denotes food of some fashion, but all Maggies had was beer and peanuts. Thirst had to be appeased, though. I squared my shoulders, tried my best not to lower my eyes, as I said to the barkeeper, "Gimme one of them Millers." He pulled the lever and the beer flowed, but stopped about halfway up the glass. He half-apologetically asked if I'd mind if he filled it the rest of the way with another brand. I muttered some answer, hoping to sound so tough that my tone would tell him I didn't care if he filled it the rest of the way with tomcat pee.

The only reason I stopped at Maggies was because my poor bone-dry body needed liquid. The beer tasted awful. I chased it with the only thing I could — peanuts.

The irony of drinking beer to quench my thirst with my right hand while eating salty peanuts with my left wasn't lost on me.

While I forced the beer down I checked out Maggies decor. It occurred to me that there must be about a thousand Maggies scattered throughout the country. Blindfold someone and take them inside any Maggies, once inside take the blindfold off and that person wouldn't know if they were in an Alabama Maggies or an Alaska Maggies. The only theme, if that's the right word, seems to consist of about 50 of those "If you'll advertise for us we'll give you this gaudy, lighted sign with some nice running horses or some rugged looking cowboy or a mountain stream with the water all white and unnatural looking." Of course, in the background there'll be a pack of cigarettes or a bottle of beer.

A guy sitting down the bar spoke and pulled me back to the here and now.

"Hey, Blue, why don't you get something in here besides peanuts? I was at a place in Baton Rouge last week and they had plates of crawdad heads on the bar. You know, the kind you suck the insides out of. Hot Cajun ones. Whyd'nt you do something classy like that here?"

"Right, Voodoo, you wouldn't know class if it bit you in the butt," Blue observed.

Most times I liked the association my pack gave me. People would ask about my pack and I would tell them what I was trying to do. My walk was a form of escapism they could envy and admire, but few could attain.

Unearned or not, I was elevated to a certain degree of admiration. But Maggies is one place I didn't feel would elevate me much because I was walking down the road. Halfback for the Dallas Cowboys, maybe; bronc rider on the pro circuit maybe, pool hustler, maybe. I was glad this time my pack hadn't been noticed outside.

Before I had nursed the distasteful beer to the bottom of the glass the Cajun guy and his two friends left to go fishing. Blue and I were the only two left and I felt relieved.

I can't say why Blue felt a need to include me in any small talk. Maybe because it was just the two of us there, he thought it awkward to not say something. Maybe he thought it was the bartender's job to entertain.

After the three guys left Blue gave a snort and said, "Crawdad heads, my behind! Calls himself Big Bad Voodoo Daddy. But he's about as Cajun as a horned toad. Lives in a trailer over at Warner Springs — keeps it sorta spooky looking, like Halloween all the time."

"I asked him if he's Cajun why he lives in a trailer in Warner Springs. Said mosquitoes in Louisiana were bigger than Brahmas and if you walk anyplace that ain't paved, chiggers tattoo your ass like a game of darts on that board over there. And besides, have you ever been downwind of a pulp mill? That dude's something else. I'm glad he comes in, though. He's always good for a laugh."

I slid off the stool and simply said, "I'd better get going."

"Hurry back," said Blue.

Maggie's beer got me to the airport. I'm not an airplane buff, per se, but I've always been fascinated by gliders, and I suppose this was a gliderport more than it was an airport. I've never really trusted airplanes, so why would I trust gliders? If you never had an engine, you won't miss the engine when it quits.

This was a Sunday afternoon and the gliderport was busy. I think rich yuppies from San Diego and Los Angeles kept their planes there.

It's a nice feeling to watch a glider soar. When man first wished he could fly like the birds, he must have pictured himself soaring like one of these planes.

I knew I had to leave because it was getting close to dark and I saw signs around the gliderport that told me sleeping over there wouldn't be welcomed. As I got on up the road the welcome was just as frosty.

Normally, a simple "No Trespassing" sign wasn't enough of a deterrent if I needed a place to spend the night. Not that I have a blatant disregard for other people's property. But I couldn't see any harm in just mashing down the grass where my body lay. Wouldn't it spring back the next day?

Really, though, I've never deep down, believed in private ownership of land. Oh, my gosh, up until now I was merely a grungy coast to coast hiker, now you'll think I'm a dirty Pinko-Commie. Just a minute, though. Think about it. Do you or I have any real right to have exclusive possession of any part of this world? Any more than a deer or grasshopper would? I believe it should belong to everyone and no one. If you run private ownership all the way to the end, why isn't it theoretically possible for some Donald Trump-type to be standing on Mars someday looking down at Earth and say, "I own all that!"

I don't remember the exact wording of the "No Trespassing" signs along this stretch of highway, but I do remember they were extra vehement — poison dripped from them. They must have been potent 'cause they worked on me and I thought I had immunity to their bite.

Since I wouldn't walk after dark unless it was a matter of life or limb, and dark was fast approaching, it looked like some make do thing alongside the road was going to be it for this night. And to worsen matters the dreaded signs were posted closer and closer to the highway. I must have had no more than the width of a couple of cars in the which to hide.

The solution? A brush fort. I gathered loose limbs, dried grass, weeds and anything else that would help to break my silhouette as cars came around the curve and the wash from their headlights splashed over me. I hoped that if I broke up my outline the people in the cars wouldn't recognize what they saw — namely, me in my tent. I deluded myself some by thinking they really wouldn't be expecting to see a tent alongside the road. If it was late and dark their eyes would just get into an argument with their brain about what they thought they'd seen. And by the time one or the other had won they'd be too far down the road to turn around to confirm it.

It was to be my first night of cold. A song from the early seventies once said something very prophetic, "It never rains in California, but, man, let me warn you, it pours, man, it pours."

I guess my image of California had also included delusions about it ever being cold in Southern California. The frost on my tent the next morning went a long way toward dispelling several myths. Waking during the night and having to steal my sweatshirt from my pillow was my first clue. Another reality bite was pulling the sleeping bag completely over my head and zipping it up until I had only a breathing hole like seals have in the Arctic ice.

The next morning as I trudged through Warner Springs I had to keep switching hands on my walking stick. The "off" hand being thrust into my pants pocket for warmth.

Warner Springs didn't seem so much a town as a company camp. More like a reservoir for workers on the Warner Ranch which, judging by the signs, was the reason Warner Springs existed at all. I reasoned that the big Warner Ranch must be owned by the Warner Brothers of Hollywood fame. I asked — it ain't.

Some of Southern California's most scenic beauty must be between Warner Springs and Santa Ysabel — lush green hills, carpeted with yellow and purple flowers which I do not know the names of, low-lying oaks interspersed with herds of grazing cattle. It's there. Don't pass up the chance to see it if you're ever close.

When I saw the name, Santa Ysabel on the map, I wondered how it must be pronounced. And, even though I point-blank asked and listened closely, I'm still unclear. I think I heard "Santa Isabel" with maybe just the slightest of "Y" sound replacing the "I" sound. No matter, it has a phenomenal bakery. By any name this rose is a rose. Regarding bakeries: They say inside every fat person there's a thin person crying to get out. I doubt anyone would call me fat, although I really believe there's a fat person living inside me. And I'm not sure that fat person really wants out. I think he's happy to live in there, making life difficult for the thin me on the outside. I'm not proud to admit that I'm a compulsive eater. There's a rice pudding in the fridge — I cannot leave it alone 'til it's all gone. I'll eat it even when I don't really want it, simply because it's there. Exercise has saved me most of my life, I suppose. I was a runner before running or country was cool. And for several years I've been a swimmer and a Nordic tracker.

In fact, in one of my letters to my buddy Gus, just before leaving on my walk, I mentioned that I thought I was a little heavy for such an attempt. In his return letter he pooh-poohed the whole notion. "After a thousand miles your pants will fall right off."

The fat person inside me has always had a weakness for bakeries.

My wife, Nancy, and I used to lament the scarcity of really good bakeries. We reasoned that they were cost prohibitive, except in places like New York, New Orleans or San Francisco where people didn't have to ask how much something cost.

To make really good bakery products you must use real butter and real cream, calories be damned, and these raise the price beyond what the average person is willing to pay.

I wasn't aware of the bakery until a biker couple stopped and queried me at a pull-off close to town. They must have wisely judged that this bakery was just what I needed.

To call Santa Ysabel a town would be to heap praise upon it. "Crossroads" is closer to the bone, which makes the bakery success story all the more amazing. Seems an immigrant baker had come to the area over 100 years ago and announced his intention of opening a bakery. Reading between the lines, I gathered this must have been greeted with much derision and some outright fun poking. Santa Ysabel is way out in the middle of nowhere, so I'm sure people joked about where the people would come from to patronize this bakery. I don't know if the guy lived long enough to see the locals eat their words, as well as his goodies, but today he could gloat plenty. It's the classic "build a better mousetrap" because you don't just walk up to the counter and tell them what you want. There are about five numbered lines and you go to the end of one of those. It's interesting, too, that there is no back room where the baking is done. You can watch the loaves and the goodies being made as you stand in line and move up toward the counter and those delectables. It was like dying and going to heaven.

Chapter 12
Ocotillo Wells Revisited
or the Sad Cactus

Remember Julian? We're going through again.

No, really, I've only spent one night in Julian ever and that was bedded down behind the "Welcome to Julian" sign.

As I walked through the town early the next morning, I only saw one other man on the streets and he seemed to be giving me that "you-aren't-going-to-stop-in-our-town, are you?" look. As I thought about it on down the road I guessed that I was being overly suspicious and he was no more than an early morning "mall walker" making do with the streets of Julian.

Remember that I'd asked the lady at the little store on the outskirts of Julian if there was any place to get eat or drink before Ocotillo Wells. I think she was slightly taken aback by another question I asked her.

I don't think it's too much of a stretch that someone walking Los Angeles to New York isn't going to be carrying any Windex. I guess it would be about 850th on your list if you were asked to name everything a cross-country hiker would need. Let's be honest. If you had a zillion guesses Windex wouldn't be one of them. It's kind of a necessity, though. If you put sunscreen on your face (you will) and the river of flowing sweat that invariably comes (it will) carries the sunscreen across your forehead and down over your sunglasses, water nor face soap will dislodge it. Then, glass cleaner is a necessity. It's one of those things that you wouldn't dream of carrying, though.

Even if you knew almost certainly beforehand that you'd need Windex you still couldn't make yourself carry it. Sitting in your living room it's hard to picture glass cleaner as being essential.

There are things you learn about the road. The "Poor Pitiful Paul" act ain't a bad tool if you can use it and still keep your dignity.

I briefly explained my little sunscreen watershed problem to the lady and she graciously produced some glass cleaner from under the counter.

You read earlier that the long descent from Julian brings you to a figurative door. And that door literally separates two worlds. When you reach the bottom of that long descending hill you are no longer in a world that looks anything like Julian. It's your first initiation to the desert, and it's a slap in your face. Julian and Ocotillo Wells may be only 35 miles apart but their appearances are worlds apart. The Julian side is a world with water, grass, trees and flowers. When you step through that door you are instantly in a world without water. Granted, you may see an occasional cactus flower but you can kiss grass and trees good-bye.

For as far as I could see it was the Ocotillo Wells world. I decided I'd stop for a break before I tackled it.

It's a sad fact that life is full of hard truths and, as I was to find out, sharp truths, too.

I'm telling you this only to save you some future pain. You just don't plop your butt down anywhere in the desert. At the sight of the desert without end I removed my pack and sat down on a bank beside the highway.

"*Yeooow!*" A cactus thorn right in the old ta-lolly!

Soon after this incident my steel-trap brain made a suggestion — sit on a towel, Idgit. Don't you hate yourself when you look back and realize you have done something dumb when a tool for change was right at your fingertips? The towel was my tool. And the cactus thorn was the switch that turned on the light.

I'd been sitting on the hot, hard asphalt, even ruining a couple of pairs of pants with tar, until the thorn made me think about sitting on the towel. Dumb! Dumb! Dumb!

A rest stop in the desert is unlike your usual idea of what a rest stop should be — sitting on a grassy spot in the shade while a cool breeze gently wafts over you. Reality check! In the desert the only part of that picture you're going to get is "sit." There's no grass, no shade, no breeze. It's just a break from walking. It doesn't mean it's a rest. When you find yourself trying to sit in the shade of a telephone pole or mailbox (I've done both) you realize how truly desperate you are.

I think a lot of people, if they could picture themselves walking across America, would envision it as being a walk of a mile or two, then relaxing under a shade tree with a jug of wine, some cheese and a crust of bread; perchance to read awhile or write some poetry.

I'd be the first to admit that it would be the ideal way to go, but then about December you'd find your butt still in Texas with that white stuff swirling about you. A truly leisurely walk was a luxury I knew I couldn't afford if I were to reach Manhattan before snow started falling. And I had no real way of knowing how long my walk would take. I knew it could not include a wine and cheese rest stop every couple of miles.

As I sat there in the hot sun there was no real comfort. I had two choices: Sit on the hot, hard ground with my head drooped between my knees, a picture of total dejection, or sit there looking outward at the endless desert all around. I did some of the former for awhile then decided to try some of the latter.

I looked up on a bank to my left and spotted something that made me sad. If there are any real men reading they're going to scoff at this. See, a real man wouldn't eat quiche, drink lite beer, or feel sorry for a cactus. And even though one of his brothers or cousins had just jabbed me in the rear, I felt sorry for this cactus. Why? The wind had blown a black plastic bag onto it. And it looked like it had been there for more than a day or two. It was Catch 22.

The black plastic must have multiplied ten-fold the already furnace-like heat. I could appreciate how the cactus must be feeling in its suffocating, black plastic prison. And, the final nail in its coffin was its thorns. The only protection the cactus ever really had, and they were going to be its undoing. Its thorns had the plastic bag in a death grip, and nothing but very careful hands could save it.

I couldn't help but feel that this particular cactus and I were kindred spirits — each must be asking, "Why me, Lord?" You may think less of me but I walked away from that cactus.

I'm not a bit proud of it. How could I feel such compassion for a mere plant and still leave it to its fate? My only defense is that it was a steep bank, I was hot and tired, and I was still smarting from the aforementioned thorn in the ta-lolly. So, at that moment all cacti were at a decided disadvantage on my sympathy index.

I celebrate the oddity that is California, both good oddities and bad oddities. California is a source of wonder in that the good and bad can exist side by side or follow one another in succession without any apparent reason.

I've talked about the beauty, the climate, the earthquakes, and wildfires. Yet on my desert walk to Ocotillo Wells I was to discover another face of California — maybe more weird than any of the others — The Plagues! My first encounter was with wooly worms. Though I came to realize they are just one of many, with some of the others being grasshoppers, hard-shelled bugs, and if you can picture them constituting a plague, butterflies.

At first I tried not to step on the wooly worms, then that became an exercise in futility when their great numbers left no worm free places to put my feet. Naturally, I had time to study the worms up close and personal, and they were busy doing something I regarded as totally irrational. Even though I may have been called a worm on occasion I couldn't relate to this particular behavior pattern. It goes without saying that in the desert one side of the road looks pretty much like the other — same sand, same rocks, same cacti. So why, I wondered did the right-side-of-the-road-worms feel compelled, even driven, to cross the road and exchange places with the left-side-of-the-road-worms? Was it the worm version of the age-old chicken crossing the road question? I saw no logic in their crossing. What was available to eat looked the same to me on both sides. And it couldn't have been a boy worm/girl worm thing 'cause they were passing each other in the middle. And for many it was their last desert journey. Worms crossing the road can't know about cars, but they should understand hot tar on little worm feet and I'd think just a few steps would convince them that the side of the road they were currently on was just fine. To a worm crossing the road it must look like that road stretches forever, but alas, most were not to be dissuaded. Grim evidence was a veritable green carpet of worm bodies in each set of car tracks heading both east and west.

Chapter 12
The Burro Bend Cafe

Try to push green carpets of worms from your mind cause I'm going to talk about eating for a minute.

The desert can sure make you long for a 40-item salad bar. Forget it. If you get anything at all it'll be a burger and fries. Funny, but when you're desperate, even a far-off sign can make your heart race and your blood sugar level elevate.

You've got nothing else to do so you squint, trying to squeeze information from a sign you can barely see. Gas station? Restaurant? Hardware store? It really doesn't matter. It only matters that it's something, anything.

Traveling in your motor home to Disney World you might occasionally desire something to drink but it really couldn't be called thirst. More likely it's just a need for something liquid to wash down something salty or sweet. You aren't really hungry or thirsty; more likely just tired of sitting.

The desert, though, brings everything into focus. You're thirsty as hell, and hungry to boot.

The sign I was seeing this time made me quicken my step. As I drew closer I saw its message: The Burro Bend Cafe. "Cafe" definitely beat out Gas Station and Hardware Store.

When I opened the door and my eyes had adjusted, I saw The Burro Bend as a throwback to the forties. It had a low ceiling, and was kinda dark inside. It had a counter and those plastic covered stools with tops that spin.

The interior of the Burro Bend was a shrine to plastic. As a cleaning aid anything that could be plasticized was covered in it.

I gave my cheeriest "Hi" to the young lady scraping the grill with a metal spatula. I was glad to have human contact after so many miles of devil sun and sand. After so many days of solitude you begin to talk to yourself. In my opinion it evolves this way: First comes humming; second is whistling; third is singing; fourth; it's talking to animals you see; fifth, it's any object, alive or dead (it's beginning to get serious); sixth, you talk to yourself; seven, you argue with yourself. It's time for the lady at the grill of the Burro Bend Cafe. I believe number seven was coming up about a mile beyond The Burro Bend. The cafe sign had saved me from myself.

The Burro Bend Cafe is in the proverbial "middle of nowhere." The girl running the place seemed to be the only one around. I thought she must be very brave or very foolish.

I was surprised when the grill lady's first question wasn't a question about where I was headed. I was caught completely off guard.

After returning my "Hi" she said, "I like your hat."

It stopped me cold for just a second. What made it so strange was that I'd taken my hat off outside as soon as I'd stepped onto her gravel parking lot. She had her back to me scraping the grill. How did she see my hat?

The hat was love/hate with me. I loved what it did for me. How could anyone not love something that literally saved their life day after day. And I don't say that lightly. I can think of any number of times the sun would have killed me if not for my hat. I hated that hat too, though. Nobody wants to walk around looking dorky.

I think she saw the look on my face.

"It's pretty hard for someone to sneak up out here. I saw you coming down the road. Even though you were walking, I could tell you were smart enough to be wearing a good hat. It looks strong, yet light."

Flattered I twirled it in front of me. "Yeah, it's a good one. Made by a company in Miami. I guess they know heat and sun, too. One of my favorite features is that it stays put. That first and second rush of air from a Semi won't budge it. Most people don't realize a Semi has a second rush but they do. It's maybe even stronger than the first."

I parked the hat and pack and threw a leg across a counter stool. "Now" I thought. "Now she'll ask where I'm headed."

I liked the girl. She followed her own script.

"We don't have any place in here but if you'd like to wash up there's a cabin around the side that used to be rented to tourists. It still has running water and there's some soap."

A salt-free face would feel great. Without comment I headed out.

She had handed me a menu (plastic covered, of course) and at the same time said, "You might picture we don't get many hikers out here."

Still no "Where you headed?"

I concluded middle of nowhere or not, cafe griddle scraper or not, this lady had class. She demanded respect and deference. The Burro Bend Cafe had nothing to do with it.

The menu said to ask about the soup of the day. I was trying to steer things toward something better than burger and fries.

"Thursday it's vegetable," she said.

"Could I have a bowl and a grilled cheese sandwich?"

While she busied herself I thought if I wasn't going to be the main character in this play, I'd let her be. "Have you always lived in this area?"

"Well, sorta, if you call Santa Fe this area. Spent most of my life there."

"Then I guess I wouldn't be the first to ask how you ended up here."

I immediately realized it sounded like a put down, and I should have worded it differently. If it hurt she didn't let on. Then she started talking.

"Failed marriages have altered lots of lives, I suppose, and as a consequence taken people in directions they never dreamed they'd take. A favorite uncle willed me this place and it happened at just the right time. I've come to love it, but I'll admit for most of my life I would have considered it a life sentence on a desert island."

"I'm glad for you," I said. "Not many of us end up even close to a place we can love, maybe learn to like, but love is rare."

Her openess made me want to be open.

"I love where I live, too, and it's about 180 degrees out from the place you love."

"Where do you live?"

"The Great Smoky Mountains of Tennessee."

"I've heard it's pretty there. Maybe someday I'll get to see it."

We talked more about her home and my home and for once I was glad that where I was headed wasn't important. In fact, during my entire walk this was the only conversation in which it never came up.

She didn't treat me any differently than if I had been in a car.

I have to admit I sometimes milked the walk to my benefit. This time it didn't seem significant. I enjoyed the Burro Bend.

There were two signs in the Burro Bend Cafe that made me smile. The first seemed to have been printed years ago to squelch a question that everyone associated with this place. It said: "Yes, it gets hot out here!" The second sign seemed to be only a few days younger. It said, "Don't stand in front of the air conditioner!"

Chapter 13
The 24 Carrot Road

Next day I came to an intersection and turned onto a road with quite a bit of vegetable truck traffic. I had no way of knowing but guessed that I'd hit upon some vegetable pipeline between Mexico and Los Angeles or San Francisco. I mention these vegetable trucks only because they, unbeknownst to their drivers, provided me with some much-welcomed sustenance. You see, a lot of these trucks were carrying carrots. More carrots than you've ever seen. Giant, open-topped loads of them. Millions of carrots on each truck. And since the trailers had no covers, naturally a few of the carrots blew out, bounced out or whatever.

And I know, like the Pepsi on the fence post, you're going to look down your nose but I saw the carrots as a source of food. And even though I didn't know it 'til I tried one, more importantly, they were a source of moisture. Maybe not so much in their own moisture content as in the saliva they let flow as I chewed on them. These were the sweetest carrots I'd ever tasted. I wondered if it was because they were the freshest carrots I'd ever eaten. The carrots I ate in Tennessee might be some of these same carrots, but how much time and processing took place before my wife put them on our table for dinner?

No one else seemed to bother picking up the carrots. Were they so plentiful around here that scavenging on the road as I was doing wasn't necessary. I didn't know. It was just a thought to occupy my mind as I munched.

An incident occurred not long after the carrot find that made me realize how really desperate I was for liquid, any liquid. It was hotter than blazes when I spotted a can of unopened beer lying in the grass beside the road.

Picture a can of unopened beer that's been lying in a scorching California sun for who knows how long, then picture where it must register on my gag reflex. I was beyond thirst. My body needed liquid.

I took off my pack, sat down and propped my back against a fence post. This was going to be worse than a dose of medicine, but it was something that had to be done. It was swallow, burp, gag, swallow, burp, gag until I got it all down.

Man, what a gastronomical treat of a day this had been — hot carrots picked up off the road, dusted off on my pants leg, and then washed down with hotter-than-pee beer.

I don't ever intend to drink another beer, hot or cold, but you can bet if I do that roadside boiling beer episode will come to mind with every swallow I take.

Chapter 14
The Not-So-General Westmoreland

I was approaching the small town of Westmoreland with visions of food and drink.

I'm a little ashamed to admit that before my walk, when I thought about the possibility of being harmed by someone, those "someones" had either Mexican or Black faces. How sadly wrong I was, as was proven several times before my walk was over.

At this point, though, I'd seen so many Mexicans I thought they should change the name of this section of the U.S. from the American Southwest to the Mexican Northeast.

I felt better when I saw on the map that I was approaching Westmoreland. You can't get more WASP-sounding than Westmoreland. I pictured a sleepy little American cowboy town. It ain't. From every indication, it is a Mexican town.

And you can guess by now what transpired. Dark began to settle in and I was caught in the middle of Westmoreland. I quickened my pace to put Westmoreland behind me and find a hiding place for the night.

I reached the edge of town but there wasn't a tree for hiding behind, nor a bush, not even a few tall blades of grass, nothing sticking up. The only sleeping spot I could come up with was an irrigation ditch that luckily hadn't appeared to do any irrigating that day. This was really that port in a storm.

I wasn't that far out of Westmoreland and the shallow ditch made for an uneasy night of seeing the lights and hearing the talk and laughter, and wondering if at any moment I'd be discovered.

A sense of security and a degree of comfort are necessary for true rest. Lying in a ditch beside the road hardly measures up on either score.

The next night out of Westmoreland one of the most unique sleeping places of the entire walk presented itself.

Funny, it wasn't private land so being chased off with a shotgun wasn't a problem. It was public land, but not in the sense that Yellowstone or The Smokies are public land.

I was in desert-desert. Synonymous with desolate. The desert has it's own beauty as much as Yosemite has its. It's like a person who isn't the most beautiful but has a great personality. When you really get to know that person, their looks have no effect on your ability to see their real beauty. Such is the desert. You need to take time to really see what you're looking at.

I have no idea if Thoreau ever actually saw the desert but he coined a phrase that captures the essence of it. He called it "The Tonic of Wildness."

The desert does have a starkness and this night the desert presented its most bare-boned self to me. I found myself on a bomb test site — both sides of the road. Had a real neat Sesame Street-sounding name, though. Its official name is the Chocolate Mountain Gunnery Range. There were big, bold signs about every 200 yards alongside the road saying, "Danger — Live Bombing Area — Unexploded Ordnance — Keep Out."

You're reading a book written by an idiot, you know! No, I didn't keep out. I suppose I could have continued walking all night but I never saw that as an option. My mind ran thusly: Those signs are just a lawsuit dodge in case someone does get hurt. There aren't going to be any unexploded bombs this close to the road.

Reminds me of something else — another warning I chose to ignore. On more than one occasion people had said, "This is rattlesnake country — be careful." And yet when nature called or it was put-down time, I pushed through the bushes and rocks like some bull. Call me stupid. I guess I just felt that if I was going to be timid or afraid of snakes or bombs then I should have stayed home and sacked groceries at Winn-Dixie.

Chapter 15
The Awakening

Since I'm still writing and you're still reading we can assume neither a bomb nor rattler got me.

When you picture the Sahara, don't you picture nothing but giant, endless sand dunes? No trees, no bushes, not even a blade of grass. Just great piles of sand?

Did you think there was any place like that in the U.S.? I didn't either. I always knew we had desert but somehow our desert didn't look quite like that.

Imagine my surprise when after the test site I came upon a real, true Sahara type desert. It has a name — The Imperial Valley Dunes Recreation Area.

Almost immediately I saw something that greatly upset me — ATVs. Here was a pristine, even exotic, nothing-like-it-anywhere area and it was being swarmed over by all terrain vehicles and motorcycles. Why did they need such a beautiful, irreplaceable place to ride? Surely there must be plenty of ugly places for them. It seemed such a desecration, a slap in the face of Mother Nature, a chanceful spoiling of something irreplaceable.

It occurred to me that the whole area should be closed except to foot traffic and the name changed from Imperial Valley Dunes Recreation Area to Imperial Valley Dunes National Park. We could be destroying a national treasure. The ATV riders might rightly argue that their wheels do no damage, that the next strong wind smoothes it all out, and that Mother Nature continues on with her grand plan regardless of the riders and their tracks.

Maybe so, but there still is a kind of aesthetic harm.

To provide for these people a campground, of sorts, had been set up. When they weren't riding they were inside their motor homes and campers.

Not too far off the main road I spotted a camper with the back door open so I took it as a foot-in-the-door to ask for some water.

Something happened that started wheels turning in my head. It was weeks later that the whole picture jelled.

Up until this point I'd been carrying a notion about water that was entirely out of keeping with the Southwest concept. Back east water is simply a given. It's taken for granted. It's just there and there is an endless supply. It's almost like air, there's so much that no thought is given to its real value.

Not so in the Southwest. At the beginning of the movie *Waterworld,* Kevin Costner is urinating into a jar. He then empties the urine into a sort of still with copper tubing, glass balls and a crank. In just a few seconds his urine is changed into a few precious spoonfuls of water. Costner immediately drinks it and even goes so far as to run his finger around the inside of the glass and then sucks the moisture off his fingers.

On my walk I came to realize the importance people who have little water place on it.

When I walked up to the door of the motor home, though, I was still living under several misconceptions.

Knocking on the door of a little tin box when the person inside can't be more than twelve feet away seemed a little ludicrous to me. I thought a questioning "hello" made more sense. You know, that hello that precedes, "Hello, anybody home?"

Isn't it kinda funny that you can turn a one word greeting into a question simply by inflection?

I felt it silly to add the "anybody home?" in this case because I'd seen that someone was home.

A woman appeared but stayed behind her screen door. That irked me some. It reminded me of when I'd had to cross an intersection where cars were waiting for a light. It wasn't unusual to hear automatic door locks being clicked. It made me want to turn to them, raise my arms, fingers curled like claws, bare my teeth, bulge my eyes to the limit and pretend I was gonna get um.

I hate what TV has done to us.

"Excuse me, Ma'am, I wonder if you could spare me a drink of water?" I hoped that my pack would get off its butt for once and relay a silent message to this lady. A message that would make her think, "Hmm here's a poor soul walking way out here. He must be very thirsty. This is a great opportunity to show what a kind and generous person I am."

There was no response to my water request at all. She simply turned and in a minute came back holding one of those small plastic cups like you might be served fruit cocktail in at a Kiwanis banquet. A couple of gulps was all it held.

It was the moral equivalent of pushing the car door lock down in my face.

I thanked the lady but felt I'd only been teased, not appeased.

Chapter 16
I *Sell* Water

If you see a dot on a map with a name beside it, don't assume that there's a town? And towns usually mean a few houses, and a store or a post office. Seems those would be the bare necessities for something to earn the dot.

When I looked at my next dot (an ocean to ocean walk involves a lot of dot connecting), I saw the name Glamis. I envisioned some form of town.

My approach to Glamis soon told me where the ATVers came for their water. It was a regular beehive of activity. And I saw Glamis for what it was — one store. I don't mean one store among other things. I mean one store. Oh well, I was happy enough; a store was my main interest anyway.

The prices! Man, they knew they had a captive audience. No matter, they had stuff, I had money.

After I'd refueled I approached the queen of Glamis. While she was raking it in with both hands I quickly said, "Ma'am, I'm traveling by foot and I wondered if you could spare me some water for my canteen."

She looked at me as if I'd just crawled from under a desert rock, and with a decided chill in her voice said, "I *sell* water!"

This from-where-they-have-water boy was so taken aback I could only stammer a meek, "Oh" as I backed away and left.

I was stung at being brought down. Hurt , humiliated and rejected, I was determined to not buy her water though the next town was Palo Verde, 42 miles away.

As I trudged away I berated myself for having no more of a retort than "Oh" for Mrs. Glamis. I was seething and wished I'd had the perfect comeback for her "I *sell* water" put down.

Then the perfect one dawned on me. It was something a rebel soldier said in *Gone With the Wind*. The rebel was part of a bedraggled column of wounded, dead-tired, soldiers just trying to drag themselves home at war's end.

They were passing close to Tara and happened to meet Wilkerson, its scuzzy overseer, whom Scarlett had recently fired. He was now what the people in the South called a scalawag, a sympathizer with the North. He was sharply dressed and was driving a fancy horse and buggy rig.

The rebel soldier was carrying a wounded comrade across his shoulder. He waved Wilkerson down and asked, "Could you spare room for a dying man?"

Instead of offering sympathy Wilkerson fairly spews contempt on the soldier. "I got no room for him nor any rebel scum like him!"

The comeback of the soldier carrying the wounded man was one of my favorites of all time. With calm demeanor and without raising his voice he said to Wilkerson, "I reckon he'd rather walk at that."

Instead of my unimaginative "Oh," I wish I could have come up with something as clever as "I reckon I'd rather walk at that" for Mrs. Glamis.

I had no idea how I'd cover that distance without water. I only knew I would put Glamis, and Mrs. Glamis, as far behind me as strength and will would take me without her water.

It was days and many miles down the road before I began to make sense of the two water incidents. I came to this conclusion: Where there is little water it's respected for it's true value. It will be shared up to a point. It isn't anyone's duty to see that you have water, though. And asking to share is asking a lot.

Chapter 17
Step Right Up,
See the Human Furnace

Forty-two broiling miles with no water! To make matters worse, the landscape was so bland. There were no distractions to take my mind off the heat. At times, the scenery didn't change appreciably for an hour or two.

I'd never been so hot. I could see me as one of the exhibits in a carnival sideshow. The barker would shout, "Step right up, see the human furnace. Touch a match to his skin and see it ignite."

I came to realize that one of the best ways to stay cool, or at least, keep the ravages of heat at bay, is to drink lots of water. What a joke! My theory was great, only it was all on paper.

I must have gone about ten miles when a car stopped that was going my way. There were two men inside, drinking beer. A Black and a Mexican. My worst fear and here I stood in the middle of nowhere.

Everyone does this subconsciously. You are confronted by a stranger. Immediately wheels are set in motion in your head. Will it be fight or flight? Does this person represent a threat to me? It only takes a few seconds for you to tell yourself yes or no. And the wheels spin extra fast if you are in a vulnerable position like I was. The adrenalin races. You feel exposed and vulnerable. You have no weapons, no escape, and your martial arts skills are slim to none.

I went through all this in about three seconds as I faced the two men.

In your three seconds of evaluation you have to do some quick acting. First, you smile whether this person is Charles Manson or Billy Graham. If laughter is the universal language, and music soothes the savage beast, then a smile must fall in there somewhere. Everyone likes to get a smile.

Then comes the not-so-easily definable part. You want to express the fact that the smile is not to be interpreted as a sign of weakness. You want to say I'm friendly and kind, but I'm not afraid and I'm not a pushover.

The fates were smiling on me once again.

"What are you doing way out here?" The black man posed the question I was to hear more than a few times.

If I had been apprehensive about the two men I wouldn't have told them the whole story because the whole story is an open admission that you're alone and vulnerable.

I found that after telling someone I was attempting to walk from Los Angeles to New York City I could count on one of two reactions:

1. An admiration mingled with awe.

2. You're crazy as hell.

Actually, the most common reaction was a mixture of the two..

I quickly got through the usual preliminary questions so I could get right down to the real nitty-gritty question, "Do you fellas know if there's any kind of anything up ahead where I could get something to drink?" That question stopped them dead for a minute.

The Mexican said, "Well, there's a border patrol station up the road about ten miles. They might give you some water. You can ride up there with us."

All during the buildup for this walk, both mental and physical, I'd vowed that I'd walk every inch. If people were skeptical as to whether I was telling the truth or not about having accepted rides, that was their problem. I knew what I knew and I was more concerned with living with myself than what they thought.

When the man said I could ride with them the "walk every inch" sign began flashing. Then that big thirsty monster in my throat tapped on my brain and said, "You can come back to this spot after you've had some water, dummy." I accepted their ride. They had a convertible. It really felt good to sit and to feel the breeze. I've hitchhiked bunches in my life and the rides I always liked best was when someone driving a pickup motioned for me to hop in the back. Let me qualify that a bit.

If it was a warm summer's day this was the best ride. You get the picture.

I was glad that the experience wasn't spoiled by my being pelting with questions. The guys seemed content with their own solitude, beer and Garth Brooks' *Ropin' the Wind*. When the ride ended their "Good Luck" seemed genuine.

They let me out at the Border Patrol Station and went on. A car was there, but I saw no sign of life. I knocked and tried the door. It was locked.

When I say "Border Patrol Station" I don't mean one of those ten-lane, Port-of-Entry facilities where they ask you if you have any fruits or vegetables. This was more like a small mobile home with the wheels taken off.

Since I couldn't just shrug and head back down the highway to where the guys had picked me up, I decided to do some investigating. I knew that it wasn't too unusual for a building to have an outside water faucet, so I walked around back. Sure enough it did. The water was as warm as bath water. My heart had been set on something big and ice-filled, but I drank my fill, rested a minute, then again drank all I could hold.

As I was walking back around to the front I saw that an officer had arrived while I was drinking. He acknowledged me by saying, "May I help you?"

Have you ever noticed that "May I help you" has two meanings? The first meaning is exactly what the words say. The second meaning is "Why are you here and what do you want?"

The gun on his hip made explaining my actions very easy.

He softened somewhat after I quickly went through my Los Angeles-New York spiel. I think he was relieved to see that I wasn't one of his usual quarries, an illegal alien.

"Did you drink from the faucet out back?"

"Yes."

A broad smile crossed his face and I could tell he was suppressing a laugh.

"Well, I suppose it won't hurt you but it's water for flushing the toilet," he said. "May give you the trots, though," he added. And this time he didn't bother to suppress the laughter. "Come on in, there's a water cooler inside," he said.

As I drank I pumped him about the illegal alien business.

Occasionally a car would pull to a stop in front of the building as directed by the large signs as you approached the border patrol station. He'd go out and almost immediately reappear inside after waving the car on through.

"How can you tell so quickly that that car was ok?" I asked.

"After awhile you know." I concluded he had a sixth sense about such things; much the same way that a good cook throws ingredients in without measuring.

I was pleased with the water at the Border Patrol Station. It had all the ingredients I loved — cold, wet and plentiful.

But the water was in one of those five-gallon upside-down jars with those small, white paper, cone shaped cups. They hold about a fourth of a cup and I ran to the water jug many, many times before I felt satisfied.

It was getting on in the afternoon and I told the guard I needed to be getting back to the spot where the two men had picked me up.

I walked about a hundred yards down the road and stuck out my thumb. It wasn't too long before an elderly Mexican gentleman gave me a ride. His English wasn't the greatest and my Spanish was zilch. Yuma, I assume, sounds pretty much the same in either language and I guessed that was what he was saying was his destination. His cut-off to Yuma left me several miles short of my goal.

My next ride was with a county sheriff's deputy which was okay. I was "clean," he was nice, and everything was cool.

Naturally, I had explained my full story to the deputy. It's been my experience that it's best to come clean. "The man" hates gaps if he discovers them because you've conveniently forgotten them. I had no gaps so I told the deputy the unvarnished truth. On more than one occasion he was nice enough to slow down and let me size up the landmarks as I tried to study exactly where I'd gotten in with the guys in the convertible. Oh, I knew it was at the gold mine. The gold mine was huge, though. At what point along the mine was it?

Before the two guys had picked me up I'd been studying and trying to figure what the mine actually was. It was a big operation with dozers, huge dump trucks, giant metal buildings, a very high don't-even-think-about-coming-around-here, fence and layers of dust everywhere. There was a sign on the front of the fence but one of those non-commital ones like GNA Industries or Vulcan Tech or some such.

Soon after I'd gotten into the convertible and before we'd gone beyond the company's fartherest stretch of fence I asked the guys, "What's that place over there?"

"It's a gold mine."

Silence from the back seat.

"Not what you thought they looked like, huh?"

The Treasure of Sierra Madre is one of my all time favorite movies. Gold mines are picks and shovels, those pans you swirl gravel around in, sweaty, gritty guys in sweaty, gritty shirts and Bogie leaning against a burro with a hand-rolled cigarette that dangles but miraculously does not drop from his bottom lip. *That* was gold mining.

This operation was the mining of today, not of yesteryear. The guy's tone told me, too, that this was a hush-hush, no nonsense business. You didn't mess around it. Gold mining today had become high tech. Claim jumpers had better bring some heavy duty artillery to back them up.

I didn't want to try the patience of the deputy. When we came to the fartherest end of the fence I said that's where I'd get out. I had to guesstimate where I'd gotten into the car with the black man and the Mexican. I wanted to err on the side of fairness so I probably went back just a little further than necessary.

Chapter 18
The Nudist at the Windmill

The next day I walked back to the Border Patrol Station. Though this was my second trip through in less than 24 hours, hitting that glass jug water cooler had been on my mind all morning. A different crew was on duty and one of the officers came down the road in his jeep while I was still about half-a-mile from the station. I knew what he was thinking — he'd caught one!

As he slowed and stopped beside me I wanted to quote an old Sonny and Cher song; "It ain't me, Babe. It ain't me you're looking for." I think he saw that I didn't fit the M.O.

While I was sucking on that five-gallon jug for the second time, the officers scored a hit on a carload of Mexican young men.

I went outside to observe. The border patrol officer never raised his voice and I didn't detect any malice.

Really, it seemed more like a game of catch, or fox and hounds. At times the officers must feel like the little Dutch boy with his finger in the dike. And if you asked them who was winning they might say, "We are," but follow it with a wink.

Back inside the officer told me he couldn't help but feel sympathy for the people trying to come to the U.S. "They're only trying to find a better life," he said. "I'd probably do the same."

"Ever get any bad guys, desperate guys, guns?"

"Desperate guys? I guess you'd say they're all desperate. They may live in cardboard and tar paper shacks but somebody they know has a television, so they get the impression that the U.S. is all *Lifestyles of the Rich and Famous* and if you see that you want that. It's only natural. And it isn't rocket science to figure out you aren't going to get it making $1.75 an hour picking peppers."

He moved to a back window of the trailer, away from any action out front and stood looking out at nothing. He had coffee in one hand and a cookie in the other, but seemed not to be aware of either. He was looking far into the distance with a there-but-for-the-grace-of-God-go-I look on his face.

Somehow I felt a little sorry for him. I got the feeling it really wasn't in him to be a thwarter of dreams. Who among us would relish that role?

Before I left I asked where I might find my next food and water.

"Palo Verde, about 20 miles away", was his reply. Then he said, "There is a windmill about a half mile off the road about ten miles up. You'll come to a crossroads. Watch closely 'cause the crossroad is only dirt."

I came to what I thought must be the crossroad but couldn't see a windmill. It was a nice walk along a rolling, dusty road. The most enjoyable walking was when I didn't have to worry about traffic — like along service roads, or when there was a sidewalk.

I didn't want this windmill search to be a dry run. I hadn't relished backtracking to look for my lost walking stick tip, and I didn't want to waste steps and energy looking for a windmill. I had 3000 miles looking me in the face, and the idea of backtracking or taking side trips, especially fruitless ones, wasn't very appealing.

At about the time I spotted the windmill I also noticed a white van coming slowly toward me. It had come from the windmill. As the van drew alongside me it stopped and I could tell the driver wanted to say something to me. I walked up to the open window on the passenger side. The driver was a man in his sixties, I'd guess, and he was naked! For him it must have been his business as well as birthday suit.

With no explanation for his condition, and without a salutory greeting, he met my surprised look with, "If you take a bath stay on the wood lattice work. If the wind's blowing, the windmill pumps all the time. The wind dries the very top of the ground and makes it look solid. But if you step on it you'll go straight up to your thighs. And there'll you'll be till someone comes and gives you a hand. Not too many people around this time of year, so be careful."

He blurted this out as if it were his duty, and just as he started to scratch where I wish he hadn't, he caught himself, and jerked his hand back as if he'd suddenly remembered that there was one additional part of the required script and every bit of the message demanded decorous and proper presentation. With more bearing and proper head carriage than I thought necessary under the ridiculous circumstances he added, "Some wells around here are sulfureous and will tie your gut in knots, but this one is as sweet as your first kiss. Drink all you want."

My pack had again told my story, and accurately this time. If I had appeared too seasoned the man may not have felt the warning necessary and then where would I be?

I loved the old Johnny Weissmuller Tarzan movies when I was a kid. The little theater in my town was simply called The Griffith. The director, D.W. Griffith was a native son. Admission was 20 cents, popcorn and cokes were ten cents each.

Seems like every Tarzan movie had a quicksand episode where at least one of the bad guys went under.

Naturally, none of the bad guys stumbled onto the quicksand and immediately disappeared.

First it was to the knees, then his hips and since all bad guys are whiners and squirmers by nature, they paid for the squirming by being sucked deeper and deeper. I'll bet the Titanic went fast once there was nothing left above water but the tip of her stern. Not so bad guys in Tarzan movies. One hand was always left sticking out and was still grasping as it slowly sank below the surface.

Death by quicksand left an indelible scary mark on me.

I didn't visualize anything that serious back at the windmill. I could see how being stuck, really stuck, might get serious if no one came along, though.

After the man in the van had issued his warning, he eased into a kinder, gentler role. He put on his old history professor cap.

"The windmill's been here since pioneer and gold-rush days. It's one of the few instances where the Whites and Indians didn't fight. It was a perfect democracy. No one felt it belonged to just them. As long as both sides showed respect if one or the other was using it at the time, everyone got along fine. I've often wondered why they could peacefully co-exist at the windmill and had to be at each other's throats the rest of the time."

I wanted to appear friendly and appreciative of his concern so I thought I'd interject an innocent, interested question. As soon as it left my lips I wished I could reach out and grab it back. It was so obviously stupid.

"You live around here?" As if he jumped in his van naked every morning and drove down from Colorado. If it sounded as stupid to him as it did me he was kind enough not to show it.

"Yeah, I live over on Sand Mesa Road. But you probably don't know where that is."

"No, I don't."

"I don't have running water so the windmill is my kitchen and bathroom. You kinda have to watch if you take a bath because cars can drop over that rise before you know it. Wind's against you here. Actually I'm only a snowbird to this area — only winter here. Montana's my summer home."

I could see by the leather look of his skin, *all* his skin, that he followed the sun year round.

Then he asked a question I thought was really odd. He asked if it bothered me that he was naked. I truthfully answered no. In some situations it may have, but he was seated behind the steering wheel and didn't seem inclined to change that. After a few more pleasantries he eased off down the road toward what I assumed was his home although I couldn't picture a dwelling within 20 miles.

It felt nice to take a bath at the windmill and to drink all the water I could hold. I just about had all my clothes back on (that wind almost made *me* the nudist at the windmill) when a couple came with several plastic jugs to fill with water.

This windmill was an oasis in the truest sense.

Chapter 19
My First Crossing and the Measured Mile

When I came to a town that had a restaurant I didn't want to get there at breakfast time. What I needed most was fruits and vegetables, not bacon and eggs. But after 42 miles of little but dust and oppressive heat, Palo Verde looked good even at bacon-and-eggs time. When I had left Glamis and set out in that waterless huff, I wasn't even sure I could cover 42 miles out here without a water refill. I just knew it would be right, left, right, left until Palo Verde or something else appeared, i.e., windmills and kindly border guards. I was surprised that on the third morning I had barely started walking when the first visible structure of Palo Verde appeared on the horizon. I had no idea what time it was, just that it was early.

I was so glad to see Palo Verde. If every man, woman, child, dog, cat, horse and Gila monster had lined up in a row I'd have given each a hug and kiss on the cheek.

Palo Verde is a pretty name and it makes you wonder how such a pretty name got wasted on just a few houses, a gas station and restaurant.

I went into the only restaurant and ordered the Country Boy Breakfast — two eggs, sausage, hash browns, grits and three pancakes.

"I like to see a man eat." the waitress said. I smiled and hoped she didn't *smell* the man eating.

Blythe, California rated a larger dot on the map. I was coming to the first town of substantial size since leaving Los Angeles, and I began noticing an occasional storage area for hay. The hay bales were stacked outside, and must have reached three or four stories high and 100 yards long — a veritable Homeless Hilton.

Ever since I'd gotten out of the grasp of Los Angeles and into the countryside, there seemed to be more cattle and horses than there was pasture to sustain them. Had I stumbled upon the equine King Solomon's Mines just outside Blythe? From nearly the beginning trucks loaded with hay kept the highway hot. I couldn't picture where they were coming from or going to. The giant hay Hiltons shed some light on things.

Most people passing by would see the hay storage areas as, well, just hay storage areas. To someone on the lookout for a place to spend the night it was nirvana.

I went around to the back of one of the huge stacks and made myself a fort.

One of the things that made my walk interesting was how quickly scenes and events could change. Day after endless day of Arizona desert or Louisiana swamp or Georgia pine could suddenly and unexpectedly give way to bright lights, big city. And that meant supplementing my chips, candy bar, and chocolate milk diet. Buffets are what attracted me most. A missile couldn't hone in better than my stomach could on an all-you-can-eat buffet.

Buffet restaurants rely on an average to make money. There are people they lose money on and people they make money on. The make-money people are little old ladies in their eighties. The lose money people are field hands and cross-country walkers.

For their sakes I hope the Western Sizzlin' in Blythe had their average index geared high the day I was there.

Early in this book I stated my dislike for Interstates. They do a good job for what they were intended — moving people from point A to point B quickly and safely. But why more quickly? More safely cannot be attacked. No argument can be made against safety. We erred when we first thought we had to get there more quickly. It moved us from one realm of living and thinking into another. Interstates changed our pace forever. They caused us to become scurriers. Our lives would be better if we didn't think we had to get there quicker. And they consume so much farmland and trees. If an interstate is to be built in a certain spot, then whatever is there now can be damned. It's illegal to walk on them. Not that I want to, they're much too dangerous. And weirdos seem to prefer interstates — any questions?

There are a few instances, like on the road east of Blythe, when you have no choice except to walk on the interstate. So you are constantly looking over your shoulder for a policeman or a weirdo.

While I was poring over Rand McNally planning my route, avoiding interstates was a primary objective.

From day one, however, I knew there was one 30-mile stretch there wasn't any getting around. It was heading east out of Blythe. You have no choice. Interstate 10 *is* the road!

I know you're thinking I could have walked on the median or well off the side of the road. And I agree that's possible in most cases but not here — too rugged.

This day brought joy, even if it did have to occur on an Interstate. Just east of Blythe, the Colorado River forms the border with Arizona. It wasn't that I was happy to be leaving California, because California will always hold a special place in my heart. Mark Twain said it best, "California is like Heaven only without the boring music." I was happy to be crossing into another state. It was a high point in my walk each time it happened.

More rewarding was leaving one geographical area for another. When the desert started giving way to trees and grass was probably the best.

Along an Interstate there are more straight stretches. I decided I'd see how many steps it took me to get from one of those little green mile markers to the next. I gathered up several small stones and put them in my left pocket. At the end of 100 steps with my left foot I'd take a stone from my left pocket and transfer it to my right. I counted for several miles and it averaged about 2,200 steps in a mile. That equates to about a 29-inch stride. Not very long by most standards, but I tried to walk just as I normally would. With the distance I had to cover trying to lengthen, shorten or quicken my stride would be folly.

If I averaged 2,200 steps in a mile, and I walked 3,813 miles then on the entire trip I took 8,388,600 steps.

I know what you're thinking. I thought it was roughly 3,000 miles coast to coast, but he's saying he walked 800 miles more than that.

A few years after I'd finished my walk curiosity got the better of me as to the exact number of miles I really did walk, so one year on my vacation I borrowed my father's Isuzu pickup truck and Alyce and I re-traced the entire route. I kept close, written records of the odometer readings. The extra 800 miles is due to the fact that I didn't walk as the crow flies. I had a touch of *Gone With the Wind* syndrome and wanted to walk through the land of Rhett and Scarlett. In fact, at one point I was only about 15 miles from the Florida line.

I think the fact that I made such a big loop through the South raised more than a few eyebrows. No one ever came right out and said it, but I knew anyone who walks coast to coast is a little suspect. If you're dingy enough to do a 3,000 walk, why not go a direct route?

When I say I walked 3,800 miles and took 8,388,000 steps, that's really an under-estimate. That mileage is measured in a truck. It doesn't take into account the hundreds, maybe even thousands, of side trips I took. For example, no grocery of any type was passed. And you don't just step from the highway into their front door. It requires a walk off the road and back. Finding a place to sleep also required X number of steps that add to the total.

When I was counting the steps between mile markers on the interstate just east of Blythe, I was struck by how far a mile really is. I'd done more walking than most people, still I was guessing way short when I tried to pick out a prominent landmark that I thought would be one mile away.

Since the average American does about 99.9 per cent of his traveling by car, I thought it would be fun to see how close he could come to a mile if he tried to guesstimate the distance on foot. I feel sure if you took 100 people and said, "Okay, start here at the X and begin walking down the road, and stop when you think you've gone a mile, that no more than five would go a full mile before stopping. I think the average person would stop somewhere between two-thirds and three-fourths of a mile.

Since there weren't any groceries along this 30-mile stretch of highway, what did I eat? Have you ever seen what's called garlic pizza? It's a pizza crust without sauce or meat. It only has garlic butter and cheese. Two pieces laying in the emergency lane. Don't look down your nose at me. You'd do it, too, given time.

My chance to escape the interstate was Highway 60 to Wickenburg. It meant going out of the way, but I didn't care if it meant being on a sane road again. It created a little nostalgic longing in me to think that US 60, on which I was walking, also ran close to my boyhood home in Kentucky.

It was only a mile or two until saw a green sign indicating I was coming to a town named Brenda. But all I saw was a trailer park named Black Rock Recreational Park. I think there was a movie once called *Bad News at Black Rock,* but this Black Rock was good news for me. After 30 miles of nothing but yucca, mescal, prickly pear, dust, sand, heat, desert near, mountain far and only two pieces of gritty garlic pizza, Brenda had to be a beauty.

As I walked by the trailer park I noticed a garden hose beside the combination office/living quarters.

"Ma'am, I'm walking cross country. I was wondering if I might have a drink from your water hose?" I said to the kind looking Black Rock lady who answered my knock.

Without suspicion or hesitation she said, "Sure." Such is the Old West at Black Rock. Trust and giving. We can all pay attention and learn.

And if there's a Mrs. America contest somewhere for mature ladies I'd like to nominate my Black Rock Brenda Beauty.

As I was filling my water jug I heard something behind me, turned and there was Mrs.

Black Rock Brenda with a heaping plate of fried chicken and accompaniments. I could have kissed her.

"My husband and I just finished eating and thought you may not mind leftovers."

Mind?!!

Before leaving I wanted to show my appreciation. In the Recreational Park Parking Lot I twisted and shaped her garden hose to read;

I LOVE YOU, BLACK ROCK BRENDA.

Chapter 20
I Lose My Head in Salome

There were a few places on my walk that I truly liked. They were the tiny, rural towns that time and Wal-Mart had passed by. Salome, Arizona was just such a place. Salome is a true western town. Straight out of the forties, it isn't pretentious and doesn't have horses tied in front of the stores next to Volvo wagons or Jeep Cherokees, or have wooden planks for sidewalks. And not everyone is wearing cowboy boots and a ten-gallon hat. It's just a small country town that happens to find itself in the west. I imagine everyone knows everyone else's name.

Salome offered my favorite things — chocolate milk and Gatorade on the way in, a small Mom-and-Pop restaurant in the center and a soft, sandy, secure sleeping place on the way out; all in the few short blocks that was Salome, Arizona. Salome had been such a treat that I enjoyed her too long. The local banter in the restaurant made enjoyable listening after so many nearly solitary days. When I stepped outside I saw that I wasn't going to make it far before the sun set.

In Salome I first encountered a phenomenon I was to see several times in the desert. Actually, I'd heard it a few times in the days past and wondered what it was.

My bed was in the sand at the eastern edge of town next to the railroad tracks. While spreading my sleeping bag out I heard what sounded like a semi running — a really *big* semi running. Surely no one would leave it running all night. They did.

It wasn't until days later that I realized it was actually an engine about four times the size of a truck engine, and it was pumping irrigation water out of the Ogalala Aquifer. And at a tremendous rate.

It's long been a bone of contention between environmentalists and the people doing the pumping. I concluded that the farmers from Nebraska and other states in that area contend that the farmers in the dry states of the Southwest are pumping too much water from the aquifer to irrigate their fields. The huge pumps drain the aquifer faster than it can be replaced. The Southwestern farmers position is that it's just underground water spread over a vast area and should be free for the taking. The Nebraska farmers counter that the huge quantities taken by the Southwest farmers is being stolen from everyone who uses the aquifer.

I hasten to say this is *my* concept of the problem based strictly on what I heard as I passed through. The aquifer is huge. I don't know that much about it, but I think it's like an underground lake (it may be in rock veins rather than looking like your normal lake) stretching from Nebraska to Texas.

Chapter 21
Timbuktu and Beyond Hope

I think all my ranting about the desert and its heat has given you the impression that my life was an endless unmitigated burning hell. Yes, it was, but not 24 hours a day. There were good times too. For sleeping, the desert can't be beat. It is cool, sometimes even cold, and both feel delicious when you are inside your sleeping bag and you let your mind do a re-wind back to about noon.

There are no insects, at least none of the biting variety. There is no humidity. For a few days you might notice a dryness in your nose. That is more than offset by the ease of breathing. You realize how heavy the air is where you come from.

I never fully understood why people wanted to retire here or why doctors recommended the Southwest for patients with breathing problems until I became conscious of how nice breathing was here.

And you can be assured that during certain months it isn't going to rain. No need for a tent. Just scoop out a depression in the sand for your hips and shoulders and a better bed doesn't exist.

And the stars. I guarantee you've never seen that many stars. The sky is so clear, and the multitude so large, they seem to be meeting you halfway.

Being able to see great distances makes for some beautiful sunrises and sunsets.

About mid-morning on the first day out of Salome, I spotted a low-lying white building with a windmill out in the desert. It had sharp, angular features that spoke "business" rather than "household." When I got close enough I saw the sign: Timbuktu Garage — Auto and Light Truck. It was the only thing in sight. I had to smile at the "insight" of its name. I knew meeting the person who named it would be a worthy addition to my trip.

The back of the garage was largely open-air so I strolled right in. I followed the sound of hammering and found Harry installing a muffler. I wondered where Harry's clientele came from. There were three possible answers:

1. Harry was the best there was around — period.

2. Harry was the *only* one around.

3. Harry fixes and refixes the same car like some sorcerer's apprentice.

Harry was rolling around on his back on something known in the trade as a creeper. He must have been used to that "there's nobody within a hundred miles" feeling because I walked right up to where he was and he never noticed. I decided to give the generic, working man's greeting. "Hey, how ya doin?" He gave a push with his foot against an axle and came shooting out from under the car like a cake of soap squirting between wet fingers.

His grin was as wide as if I'd been Ed McMahan with a check in hand instead of some clown he'd never laid eyes on.

Harry jumped from the creeper and was on his feet surprisingly fast for a man whom I was sure would never see 50 again.

At his neck I counted three heavy shirts layered one atop the other. Even three shirts couldn't conceal what was obvious about Harry. Probably not politically correct anymore but in my younger days we'd have called Harry "stout." In my youth there was a local legend in my little town that Harry reminded me of. The man had a job picking up milk from dairy farmers; milk destined to be bottled and sold in stores. At that time farmers shipped their milk in ten-gallon cans. The cans were steel, thick and heavy even empty. Most people could hardly budge a full one. It was widely circulated that the man could grab a full milk can in either hand and hoist them onto the back of a truck.

When I saw how tight the three shirts were stretched on Harry I thought of the milkman legend of my youth. So, don't mistake "stout" for "chubby."

Usually people who do the type of work Harry does have someone around to lend a hand with heavy things — "Hey, Roy, grab the other end of that crankshaft, will ya?" It was obvious Harry had no Roy. Harry was *both* ends of any carrying to be done. "Both Ends" can be parents to some pretty hefty offspring. "Stout" is usually the eldest child. "Hernia" the youngest.

My eyes must have settled a little too long on Harry's three shirt collars.

"It's only supposed to get to 90 degrees today. I'm freezin' to death."

Did I detect a bit of facetious put on? I'd already felt an occasional drop of sweat slide down my back and into the crack of my bottom.

It was impossible to miss my pack, now leaning against my leg.

"What? Are you walking? Where in God's name from? And where to?"

Harry gave a perfunctory swipe at the top three layers of grease on his hands and extended one. I grasp the two remaining layers with my sturdiest I'd-like-to-be-your-next-dogcatcher vote soliciting handshake.

"My name's David (my last name wasn't important and few people know what I've said when I say it anyway), and I'm attempting to walk from Los Angeles to New York City."

"You're kidding me!" (not his exact words but this is a family book.)

I half-laughed and said, "I always emphasize the word "attempting."

"Well, you've got a danged (again, my word choice) good start."

Harry seemed eager for human contact, respite from the muffler, and a chance to talk. He directed me to take a seat in the customer lounge — a seat from a school bus bolted to two boards across from his desk. He leaned back in his swivel chair and propped both feet on the desk.

As required (I think there are laws on the books) by the Mechanics and Garage Owners Code, his desk was stacked about a foot deep with old work orders, each with greasy fingerprints plain enough that a fourth-grader with a Jr. G. Man detective kit could pin Harry to any crime. There was an assortment of calendars, some current, some not, all with pictures of I'll say "scantily"(but what's a word that means less than scantily)-clad young girls with melon-sized breasts leaning over checking their oil or gauging their tires. And, of course, Harry had the mandatory ashtray that looked like a miniature Michelin Radial.

"Where you from?"

"Tennessee." I watched Harry's face to see if he could grasp the concept of someplace lush, green and moist.

"The Smokies or somewhere else in Tennessee?"

"Yeah, I live in a small town called Gatlinburg, right at the entrance to the Great Smoky Mountain National Park. You been there, Harry?"

"No, but my brother and his wife have. They tell me it's a lot like where I'm from."

"Oh, you're not originally from here?" (I do wish I'd stop pre-judging people.)

"Naw, I'm originally from green and wet Washington State. When we had to move here to be close to my wife's ailing mother I thought the Lord had cast me into Hell without even giving me a chance to plead my case. That was 22 years ago. It took some adjusting of both mind and body, but I like it here now. Can't picture going back to Washington and getting rained on every day. People think we must feel deprived all the time living way out here. I've been to Denver, Phoenix and, of course, Seattle and after seeing that mess, believe me, I don't feel deprived."

"Is the lack of water the biggest problem," I said.

"People think we don't have water but there's plenty two or three hundred feet down."

"I saw the dish on your roof. Hey, at least you've got cable."

"Yeah", he smiled. "I guess the worst part is having to drive so far for groceries. And it's a little scary if you need to get to the doctor quick."

I liked Harry. He was an okay guy. I spent about an hour with Harry and then I thought it best to move on and let him get back to his muffler.

Incredible as it seems I didn't bum any water from Harry. He assured me there was a place to eat in Hope.

"You'll be there in no time, it's only six miles," he said.

When I finally dragged my carcass into Hope I couldn't believe Harry had said, "You'll be there in no time." It might have been six car-miles, but my barking dogs said it felt closer to 16 foot-miles.

I learned one thing about the people and their cars out west. They don't think in the same terms, distance-wise, as people east of the Mississippi. To the people out west, a hundred miles isn't a long trip. I guess that it's so far between places, if they let their minds dwell on it, they'd never go anywhere.

The spot on the map that they gave Glamis, California should be taken away and given to "spotless" Hope, Arizona. Hope has no dot and it has lots more to offer — campground, filling station, *and* restaurant. When I told Alyce what I ate in Hope she made a face.

The memory lingers sweet and clear — tuna sandwich and a chocolate milkshake. It doesn't sound particularly tasteful now but in Hope it was grand.

Hope, Arizona is about as wide as your back yard and as you approach there's a little green sign about as big as two business-sized envelopes taped together saying simply Hope. On the other end of town there's the big brother of the little sign. The proud citizenry of Hope have erected an impressive eight feet tall structure of brick and wood that would make Frank Lloyd Wright pea-green with envy. In big, bold orange letters, complete with an artist's rendition of a roadrunner chasing a rattlesnake, are the words "You're Now Beyond Hope."

Chapter 22
The Stage to Wickenburg

I was entering the land of the saguaro cactus. They're impressive. Big dudes. I was curious as to their consistency. I picked a strong he-man type about fifteen feet tall, walked over and gave him a sharp jab with my walking stick. Arnold Schwarzenegger never had abs that hard. It was like a concrete cactus. It had no give at all.

I've always been a sucker for roadside historical markers.

You can digest and enjoy them at your leisure if you are on foot. When you're in a car it seems they're always in the wrong place, there's no good pull-off, or the kids are having screaming fits to get to Wally World.

My next destination was a town of moderate size called Wickenburg. About five miles before you get to Wickenburg there's a historical marker and I almost wished I'd had a car for this one, not for enjoying, for getting away quicker. I'll admit it's the Cadillac of historical roadside markers. It's a multi-colored stone obelisk but without the sharp point, standing about six-feet high and atop it there's a metal cutout silhouette of a stagecoach being pulled by horses. I was surprised that no one had vandalized or stolen it. There's a plaque embedded in the stones on the side: Wickenburg Massacre — In this vicinity Nov. 5, 1871 Wickenburg — Ehrenburg stage ambushed by Apache-Mohave Indians. John Lanz, Fred W. Loring, P. M. Hamel, W. G. Salmon, Frederick Shoholm and C.S. Adams were murdered. Mollie Sheppard died later of wounds.

Just then I longed for a car. But I hoped the Indians still had only those little, painted ponies.

Wickenburg has one of those 100-year-old bakeries that no passer-through should miss, but I won't bore you with another bakery story.

There is another historical point of interest, though, The Jail Tree. Seems that for many years, 1863 to1890 in fact, the town couldn't, or wouldn't, afford a jail so outlaws were chained to The Jail Tree. It was unclear to me whether they stayed out there 24 hours a day or not. Ironic that we do that to our dogs and they're our best friends.

That night was another one spent in the great outback of desert Arizona — nothing but me, a few forlorn cacti, a bunch of hot rocks and God. God could leave whenever he wanted. The rocks, cacti and I weren't so lucky.

At some point during the night I was up like a shot! What the hell was that coming for me? My ears were screaming at my brain. They heard mighty legs churning rock, sand and dust, iron hooves flashing fire, flared nostrils spewing hot breath, eyes wild with rage. All were bearing down on me. There was no time, or place to run. My eyes strained to separate the shroud of darkness, desperate to make some sense of what I was hearing. I was scared — super scared! I stood there like a concrete statue. What in God's name was tearing to pieces so violently this quiet Arizona night?

I just knew this desolate southwestern desert was where I was going to die. It was getting louder and closer. Just as I was sure the end was upon me the clashing of metal on rocks and the heavy snorting veered and shot to my left.

I had nearly been run down by a herd of wild mustangs. Wild mustangs may be a tad theatrical but they were horses, *running horses.* If you're run over by a bus you don't care if it's Greyhound or Trailways. I sat down weakly and took the first breaths I'd had in several seconds.

I was in their territory. I was sleeping again in a gulch, or is it more correctly a "wash?" Back home we'd call it a dry creek bed.

The surrounding countryside may be made up of mostly flat, dinner plate sized rocks and cactus but most of the time the dry creek beds would have a nice sandy spot. They were soft and required no work for site preparation. I found if it was rocky countryside, lifting one rock usually set a chain reaction in motion. Four or five neighbors were waiting to move into the vacant property created by the removal of one rock. And then there was Mr. No Shoulders, our rattler friend. I had to be especially careful in failing light when I put my hands among the rocks.

In most cases a wash continues under the road through a culvert, and if the culvert was big enough for Mr. Horse to slip through and play with Neighbor Smith's mares,then a fence was built across the entrance to the culvert to discourage such amorous escapades. Sometimes the fence was set back far enough away from the entrance to the tunnel that I could make my bed in the No Mare's Land between fence and culvert. And sometimes not, like this stampede night when I had to sleep on the stallion's side of the fence.

The fact that the clear Arizona night returned to absolute quiet didn't mean it was a pleasant, restful night for me. My ears stayed cocked for the clash of hoof on stone.

When I was planning my route I saw that there was no way to avoid Phoenix. I wasn't too wild about the idea, either. I purposely planned my route to avoid big cities. Phoenix was the only really big city I couldn't avoid. I would have to cope somehow.

Highway 60 took me through Del Webb's Sun City, a suburb of Phoenix, probably one of the biggest retirement communities in the US.

Golf carts, the vehicle of choice in Sun City, zipped around, back and forth. I didn't see anyone younger than 65 and had the feeling anyone under 40 would be shot on sight.

Highway 60 goes from the fortunates of Sun City to the seamy unfortunates as it gets closer to the heart of Phoenix. I didn't care at all for where Highway 60 was taking me but was swept along nevertheless.

It took me two full days from one side of Phoenix to the other. Having Tempe and Mesa jammed up next to Phoenix made it seem even bigger.

For the second time since I began my trek I stayed in a motel. I was a little concerned that I'd be turned down flat so I apologized for my appearance and explained my mission.

This was the first time I'd had a chance to see my old body up close and personal. I looked in the mirror and thought it was my dad looking back at me. My belt was in its last notch and still not doing well what belts are supposed to do.

This might gross you out: After I'd gotten my room at that place where they leave the light on for you, I walked up the street to a 7-11. Back in my room I opened a jar of Smucker's Hot Fudge Sauce and ate it all. Alyce asked me why I didn't try to find something better. I told her it wasn't that kind of neighborhood — the zoo was right across the street.

Something happened the next morning that doesn't seem possible. It's like absentmindedly leaving the baby in the car seat all day or looking for your glasses when they're on top of your head. I had left my motel room and was already out on the street when it hit me. I'd forgotten my walking stick. It was still in the room. With a little embarassment I explained to the desk clerk. He produced his master key and we retrieved my stick. When we were out of sight and sound of the desk clerk I heaped apologies on my friend and humbly begged forgiveness.

Mesa seemed as if it would stretch forever. Luckily, I found an abandoned motel in Mesa and slept behind it.

Just to the east of Phoenix are the Superstition Mountains. I had plenty of time to look at them as I passed slowly by. I've always had a fascination for the Lost Dutchman's Mine. Could it be right where I'm looking? Or there? It was distracting and fun.

Chapter 23
Superior

There's an old fable about three blind men who were asked to describe an elephant. One man was led to the elephant and touched the elephant's tail. Another man touched the leg. And the third man felt the elephant's trunk. Each man's description of the elephant was completely different and way off base considering what an elephant really is. The moral being that it's all in how you look at it.

The same thing would happen if you asked three people who'd never been here to describe the United States. Let's say you fly three Frenchmen (Yeah, I know — Three *Frenchpersons!*) Okay, three Frenchmen in a plane and they've never been to the United States; know zero, zip, zilch about this country. You parachute one into Times Square, one in Rabbit Hash, Kentucky (if he can hit it) and the third into Pocatello, Idaho. Next day you pick them up and ask their impressions of the US. For our purposes we'll forget that the Frenchman who landed in Times Square was relieved of his wallet before his feet touched the ground, the Rabbit Hash man landed in the middle of a tent revival and the Pocatello man landed on the street during a Shriner's Parade. The point is each man would have a different impression of this country.

It would be the same way if three people walked from Los Angeles to New York. They'd each have their own unique experiences and impressions. I'm telling you about mine but that doesn't mean yours would be anything like them.

I haven't told you my over-all impression of the US. I'm saving that for later. All this is leading to an event that happened to me east of Phoenix. It could have been an elephant experience and, if taken out of context, affected my over-all impression. The advantage of hindsight tells me it was just an isolated incident.

Yes, I thought Phoenix and its satellite, velcro, wanna be Phoenix cities of Sun City, Tempe, Scottsdale and Mesa would go on forever. They look like groupies clinging to a rock star.

But finally, I was out in the country again. I came to one of those ersatz Old West Trading Posts. You know, the head dresses, Taiwanese spears, rubber Jim Bowie knives, Lash Larue whips, rattlesnake eggs. It was a man and woman operation. I won't say Mom and Pop, that's too warm and cozy for this place. As I always did, I made a beeline for possible chocolate milk.

The man was watching the Celtics in a waist-high enclosure in the middle of the store. I thought it a little odd that he'd use valuable retail space for that purpose. I didn't go inside the enclosure, but enjoyed the game just behind his shoulder. He knew I was watching, but abruptly got up and turned off the television. I thought it a little rude even if it was his television.

I strolled around looking through the store and when I'd finished my chocolate milk I bought an Eskimo Pie. The store had a section where they sold "genuine" Indian moccasins. In this section they had carpeting so you wouldn't get the moccasin bottoms dirty when you tried them on. Since the moccasin "try on" section contained the only chairs I saw I decided I'd sit and enjoy my Eskimo Pie.

I'd only been sitting a few seconds when the owner came over and asked me to not eat on the carpet. An innocent and logical request coming from his standpoint, but I felt a little hurt that I wasn't to be trusted. That, along with the television being turned off in my face, made me feel like I was getting the bums rush.

It's one of life's in-your-face stark realities that not everyone in the world likes you. Not that "moccasin Pops" was my first introduction to that fact — not by a longshot.

In the Southwest it's not unusual to see signs along the road saying "Warning. This is a flash flood area!"

It's easy to yawn and wink at the signs when you are an ignorant Easterner. You look at the earth, you look at the sky. They look just like the day before, and the day before, and the week before that. It doesn't look like it ever rained.

After so many endless days of the same skies, the same cloudless skies, the signs become the boy yelling wolf. You just know it isn't going to rain.

There hasn't been enough white stuff in that sky to hide a white handkerchief behind, much less enough gray stuff to produce rain.

The danger lies behind those cloudless skies and that parched desert. They lull you into believing it won't rain ever.

Contributing to the danger is the fact that the cross-country walker likes to sleep out of sight, and out west a great out-of-sight place is under the road.

Where washes or arroyos come down out of the hills and run under the road (it does rain), there's usually a large culvert made of steel and shaped like a giant tube, or a concrete structure with a low, flat concrete roof and concrete sides. They are appealing because they have a dry, sandy bottom and are cool. Sounds like a perfect snake hideaway, too, although I never saw one.

I slept in these places many times oblivious to the disaster I was courting. I told myself it just wasn't the rainy season. The chances of a flash flood were slim and none.

One time I had walked a few hundred yards up a dry creek bed. I couldn't find a suitable sandy place to make my bed. The creek bed was all stones. I finally spotted a large hole in the creek bed that looked like it had been dug by a backhoe. It was about big enough to put two VW mini-buses in. The hole had a sandy bottom, though. I climbed down and made my bed. I also did something I rarely did in the desert, I slept in my tent.

I don't have to tell you what my chances would have been if a flash flood had come and I'd been in a deep hole in a creek bed in a zipped-up tent.

The night after staying behind the abandoned motel in Mesa, I slept in a culvert under the road at Florence Junction. Not far from my culvert home was a small grocery store, an unusual but welcome addition to this sleeping spot. I went up and field-tested a pint of chocolate milk. I wanted to see if chocolate milk was to be my fill-up drink for the night, or if this was going to be a Gatorade or iced tea night. The chocolate milk passed muster so I bought two quarts (yes, quarts) a bag of Doritos and some candy bars and took them to my little squirrel-away under the road.

I wish everyone in our great nation would walk to their city limits and continue on for another hundred yards. If they pay the slightest attention to the right of way along the highway, they can't help but see that there's a whole bunch of people out there that need their butts kicked. We're so trashy. It's beyond me why people can't keep their trash in the car 'til they get to a proper receptacle.

During my Los Angeles to New York walk, I think the only thing I didn't see beside the road was a kitchen sink. I'd be a rich man if I could turn old work gloves and used pampers into cash. I saw lots of useful and interesting things, and would have sent more home if it hadn't meant carrying them to a post office.

I was approaching the town of Superior, Arizona. I think it's odd that there's only a mere handful of towns I truly liked on my walk and three of them are in Arizona. Superior was the second. Odd that it was one of my choices because it's a mining town and "mining" and "nice" aren't usually found close to each other. And there isn't any flat ground in Superior. It's built on a hillside. Then why was Superior one of my favorite towns? The people were nice and it was Wal-Mart free. Untainted by "progress."

On my approach to Superior I found the first item I thought worthy of sending home. I may have let it lie, too, if I hadn't known I was close to a post office. It wasn't something I needed at that time, that's for sure. It's 100 degrees in the shade and what do I find — a down vest. How it got out of someone's closet in the heat of summer and found its way to the side of the road I'll never know.

When I got into town I went behind a convenience store and found a suitable box in their dumpster. In the store, I bought tape and a magic marker. As I was paying the lady I asked, "Would you please tell me how far it is to the post office?" As soon as I said it I realized that a normal request would be worded "where is the post office," not how far. Distance was the important consideration for me, whereas "where" might be the main concern for the rest of the world on wheels.

"Hmm, let's see. How best to tell you? Are you familiar with Superior at all?"

I shifted the pack on my back and started to give a blank "duh." Then I remembered my upbringing. As sweetly as I knew how I said, "No Maam, I'm just passin' through."

"Well, that street out there (she's pointing) is Shamrock."

"Shamrock!, I say to myself. There hasn't been a shamrock within a thousand miles of here — ever!"

"Go north" (Whoa! I've already explained about women and their directions. I didn't want to hear any north, souths, east or wests).

"You mean right?"

"Yeah, right. Then go down to the Citizens Savings Bank and turn left, then three blocks to Bryant's Chevrolet and the road sorta forks.

"Yadda, Yadda, Yadda."

My shoulders must have visibly slumped because at just about the thirteenth "then you" the guy standing in line behind me who, no doubt, had been shifting from one foot to the other spoke up.

"I'll be glad to take you there."

I explained my "walk every inch" philosophy, and that I'd have to come back to this exact spot.

I guess all things considered, he figured he could take me, wait for me, and bring me back quicker than the convenience store lady could finish her Shamrocks, Regals, Glen Oaks, Mesquite Ways, norths, souths, rights, lefts, forks and "watch out fors."

Once again I saw that for every Mocassin Pop in our great land there are several Post Office Petes.

Chapter 24
Charades in Reservation

The towns of Superior, Miami, Claypool, and Globe, Arizona were all nice. In addition to the fact that they were all ducks in a row and had names that flowed gently from the tongue, they had a common thread running through them. They were all in the mountains and relied on mining for their very being.

After Globe the mountains gave way to flat land and desert again.

The Wickenburg Stage Indian Massacre was still a fresh memory so my spine stiffened when I saw the San Carlos Apache Indian Reservation sign.

Driving through in a car you might think it quaint. I don't see how any Anglo-Saxon Paleface walking down the highway could not have some thoughts, though. I don't care if it is the 21st.century — "My" people wronged "Their" people. Maybe not everyone can forgive and forget.

One Saint who has forgiven found me, as I'll explain in a minute.

The Southwest is dotted with Indian reservations and though I haven't seen many, the conclusion I've drawn is that they lie on land the white man had no desire, or use, for. "Give it to the Indians," must have been the catch phrase of the day. For a free-roaming people who were one with nature and sensed where they fit in the scheme of things, the American Indian, for the most part, has been reduced to a pitiful caricature of his former greatness.

Forced to live on land that, in most cases, is no more than a desolate piece of dust, their houses are often third-world looking. Sad, really. Did the Indians have any say at all in the matter? Was it their homeland, and meaningful and desirable for them?

I know Indians lived and roamed all over the US, but I can't picture them actually living and staying in a place as stark and desolate as the San Carlos Reservation

My map told me I wouldn't be crossing the San Carlos Reservation in one day. Now there's the added specter of a *night* on an Indian reservation.

I heard something that night I'd never heard before and it did nothing to calm my nerves. And if it had been combined with what I heard the next day (I'll explain in a minute) they'd have had to carry me home in a basket. That night I slept about a quarter mile off the road in a dry creek bed. It was well into night when I was lifted from my bed (no, not aliens) by an unmistakable sound. It went, "Yip, Yip, Yip, Yeow." That's as close to the sound a coyote makes as I can come. It was unnerving. I didn't need any strange noises while sleeping on an

Indian reservation. I laid awake for awhile, ready to fight off a snarling, man-eating pack of coyotes.

Finally I slept. Fatigue won over nerves.

If the howling pack of coyotes wasn't enough, the reservation had more to shake my nerves and rattle my brain. The next day I started walking, but I was feeling skittish about the coyotes, the Indians, and the whole reservation scene.

I was crossing a bridge when off in the distance, down the dry riverbed I heard Indians chanting as if preparing a war party. They were rhythmically beating a drum and chanting just like in the movies. "Hi, ya, ya, ya — Hi, ya, ya, ya." Well, you get the picture. Me, the only non-red person within 50 miles and I'm going to be caught in an Indian uprising.

The standard army marching cadence is 120 steps per minute. My cadence for the next few miles was about 500.

The next day I came to a dirt-poor village on the reservation called Bylas. I saw an old Indian man walking along a railroad track and tried to ask my eat/drink question. It was hopeless. It may have been a combination of culture clash, his hearing, both our accents, or whatever, but I got nowhere. I acted as if I understood him, thanked him, and returned to the highway.

I was passing a long row of very shabby houses. I would say "poor" houses, but my high school English teacher would have said, "Houses haven't the ability to be poor, Mr. Stoess." Trust me, they were poor.

From over my left shoulder and about 75 yards back I heard a booming voice calling me. Of course, it wasn't my name. How did I know the voice was calling me? I just knew. I didn't acknowledge the first two yells. I could tell by the sound that this was a man's man. No wimp could have this voice. And I wasn't sure I wanted to be involved with this voice. The third yell was so commanding it made me turn and acknowledge. By this time I was well beyond the range of conversation, so he began making hand signals.

If you've ever played charades you remember the gestures for movie titles. You hold your left hand up slightly to the left of your face, and with your right hand you pretend to be cranking a movie projector. When I finally turned to look at the shouting man, it looked to me as if he were doing the movie title charade. I was half-curious and half-apprehensive. I screwed up my courage and started back. As I got close to his house I could see he'd gone inside. I was just ready to turn around and continue back down the road, half-glad that my problem was solved. He came out the front door carrying a plate of food and a large drink.

There was an old kitchen table and chair sitting in the dusty front yard. He set the plate and glass down on the table.

"I thought you might like something to eat."

At that moment my faith in humankind had been better fed than any bodily good his food would do me. I was so taken aback I could hardly do more than mumble.

"Sure would."

Hunger did play a big part in my "sure would", but I felt the glory shouldn't go to the food but to this magnificient man.

I attacked the plate of fried chicken, peas, mashed potatoes and "light" bread accompanied by a large glass of Kool-Aid.

I was surprised by the next thing he said. His first question momentarily stopped my fork in mid-air.

"Don't you have a home?"

Boy, I really must look the part, I thought. I knew I didn't look like I'd just stepped out of G.Q., but a homeless bum? I tried to stay decent looking. I bathed and shaved when water presented itself. Even though I hated the laundromat chore I stopped when I thought I needed to stop. But I had to admit that here in Bylas on the San Carlos Apache Indian Reservation, yes, I could easily be mistaken for a homeless bum.

With a smile I replied, "Well, I can see why you might wonder but yes, I have a home. It's in Tennessee." I told him why I was passing in front of his house.

There was a chair leaning against a tree. It looked even more rickety than mine. I cringed as he dragged it up to the table. This was a stout man. The other stout. Instead of pulling the chair to the opposite side of the table, he pulled it just diagonally across the table so that our knees nearly touched. He tilted his cap back and leaned forward on his elbow, chin in hand, his face hardly two feet from mine. Under different circumstances I would have felt threatened by this invasion of my personal space. From the beginning, though, this man had dispelled any fear. His body language said, "Hey, this is going to be the most exciting, interesting thing likely to happen to me today. I want to soak up every word."

Picture yourself pulling up a chair close to Mark Twain or Abraham Lincoln. No, no, no, I don't by any stretch insinuate that what I was going to tell this man would be as much as a wrinkle in either of those guys jockey shorts. I'm just saying that is the look he had.

After seeing his expression, and partly to help pay for the chicken dinner, I elaborated fully on my story. I didn't embellish, I just filled in most of the blanks in my "attempting to walk from Los Angeles to New York City" story.

He hardly moved and his breathing seemed shallow. I was pleased when I finally ground to a halt and he ran his hand across his face.

"Man, Oh, Man."

I wasn't the only show in town. Here I sat inches away from a real Apache Indian. What emotions that evoked. In the not too distant past, with apologies to *Dances With Wolves* my fear might have been that this man was going to have me *for* lunch instead of *to* lunch.

As we talked I wondered how relationships between races can become so convoluted. When you talk one-on-one at a kitchen table in a dusty, chicken-scratch yard with no posturing or threatening, it becomes pretty clear that we're all brothers; with differences maybe, but still one nation, one world of man. It's hard to slice it any other way.

As delicately as I could I broached the subject. I didn't think it in good taste to just blurt out, "Do you have a job?"

"What do you do for a living?"

"Jobs are pretty hard to come by around here."

You'd have to be dumb as a box of rocks if you couldn't come to that conclusion after sweeping the horizon of the San Carlos Reservation.

"Let me show you one way we make money." He got up, walked across the yard and stepped onto the porch; then gave a gentle knock on the screen door. I heard some muffled talk between him and someone in the house. In a minute his wife and daughter came out carrying several tiny, beaded dolls, some no more than an inch tall. They were cute and the workmanship was intricate and clearly good.

If this was a livelihood, to whom would they sell? Probably any number of people in a 50-mile radius did the same thing.

Before I could ask he volunteered, "We sell them at fairs, craft shows, and flea markets."

It couldn't amount to much. It was painfully obvious when you saw his tiny, cinder block house, badly in need of paint and repairs. I didn't see any evidence of a car. I wondered how these dolls got to market.

"Do you like living here?" I asked.

At that, he threw up his hands in a whatta-ya-gonna-do gesture.

"My wife thinks we'd be better off in a city. I'm not so sure. Indian is Indian as much as Black is Black. Here we have some government benefits. If we moved off the reservation we'd be on our own. We're with our own kind here. People help each other when they can. I'm afraid we'd have to fight that "old Indian" thing if we moved away."

He let it trail off as if he were burdening me with something that wasn't my problem.

I, wanting to be understanding and sympathetic, nodded my head but I think we both knew the realities. I might look like the homeless one but I could leave the reservation, bathe, shave, put on a suit and go back to cappuccinos and golf.

I was so proud of this man. There have been few things in my life that have given me such a warm feeling. By every visual measure this was a poor man, yet I saw one of the richest hearts and souls I'd ever hope to meet.

After finishing the meal and our talk, I profusely thanked him from the depths of my heart. I know my pack felt lighter as I continued on through Bylas and the San Carlos Apache Indian Reservation. I wonder if he knew his manna fed me spiritually as well as physically.

Chapter 25
Home of the Fighting Horned Toads

As I walked away from my benefactor's reservation home and through the last 50 odd miles of Arizona I thought about the odd charade-like arm signals he had been making. Then I caught on. He had turned his body 90 degrees to me and was pretending to eat from a plate held close to his mouth — not doing movie titles.

"Creepy" would be the best word for my next adventure. Even though I was in Arizona, the incident was typical California. Is there anyplace in the world as enigmatic as California? Where else could you have a plague of butterflies?

About ten miles east of Bylas I spotted something black crossing the road far in the distance. I was almost upon it before I could make sense of what I was seeing. It was a tarantula! I thought you'd only find those in a boatload of bananas from Guatemala. Since he was on a course 90 degrees from mine I practiced my live and let live philosophy.

"May the road rise to meet you Mr. T. May the wind be always at your back. Just don't alter your course."

Wouldn't you think if you were on the Apache Indian Reservation, and coming to a town named Geronimo, that that town would be the best the Indians could come up with? All I saw at the town named Geronimo was one old dilapidated, abandoned building, grown up in weeds. Not much of a memorial to the man.

Although Geronimo was a disappointment, my next town was the third jewel in my Arizona Triple Crown. If you saw Fort Thomas you'd say, "What the hell does he mean "jewel in Arizona's crown?" It's an individual thing. Everyone would pick different towns for different reasons. Mine are small, country, seemingly forgotten towns that haven't been raped by developers or anyone else for that matter. They've retained the same character for a hundred years. The people all know each other and swap good-natured jokes and barbs.

The town of Thatcher was the next to fall to my Shermanesque march. I had to smile at the banner stretched above the road. It said: Welcome to Thatcher and the University of Southern Arizona — Home of the Fighting Horned Toads. The San Diego Chicken likes to whup up on everybody elses' mascot. But I'll bet the University of Southern Arizona mascot could kick some big, yellow, chicken butt.

I've told you I looked strange on this walk; weird safari hat, pack on my back, long-sleeved shirt, bandannas around my hands, walking stick, sunglasses, big ol' boots. It was about this time I did a couple more things that added to the montage.

Back in California every item in my pack had suffered through an inquisition as to whether its usefulness outweighed its weight. Even after all that the pack still caused me lots of misery.

It reminds me of an old barroom betting game — Bet someone (whatever you can afford to lose) that they can't hold two coke bottles straight out from their sides for two minutes. Everyone who tries it will think there's nothing to it; that they could stand there for half a day if they wanted to. This lasts for about fifteen seconds. After a minute it feels like some giant invisible hand is pushing down on those Coke bottles. The same principle was working on my pack. You'd think you could carry it all day — no sweat. I can tell you that giant, invisible hand likes backpacks, too.

Since I never had anything to do but walk, look, and think, I got to thinking about how I might be able to lighten my burden even further. Then one day I was passing through a town and saw a lady walking down the street wearing a fanny pack. That's it, I thought! Wouldn't it help if I transferred some of the small heavy stuff like lock and chain, toothpaste, shaving cream, nail clippers, coins, etc. from my shoulders to my hips? Although I'd never seen a man wearing a fanny pack I figured the heat, the desert, the constant neck and shoulder ache won hands down over any fashion statement. At the next K-Mart I bought two.

There are a few things you must have in the desert Southwest. They aren't luxuries, even necessities doesn't adequately describe them. They are vital — lifesavers. One is a hat and the other is sunglasses. Okay, some calloused, grisly old cowboy who has cataracts and is half-blind at 50 may pooh-pooh sunglasses, but they are a lifesaver if your eyes mean anything to you.

In addition to a hat and sunglasses there's a third item I considered just a step down on the vital scale. If you don't want to wind up looking like those leather skinned old ladies in Miami Beach, you need sunscreen. The kind that doesn't show when you put it on is the best kind. You may look a little greasy but people will think you're just sweating. And even if you read labels carefully you might be fooled by their double-speak and carry out the kind you don't want.

When I bought my two fanny packs I also bought more sunscreen. But I was tricked by deceptive labeling into some white, non-vanishing cream that looked like clown makeup.

Now I really looked strange walking down the road. To the silly hat, the sunglasses, the bandannas, and the walking stick, tack on two fanny packs resting across my stomach and a face that looked like I'd fallen into a flour barrel. It was just too much. And I didn't want to attract attention.

In a laundromat in Safford, Arizona I gave the white stuff to the change lady.

Chapter 26
The Right Side of the Tracks and the UFO

I was about to experience my second "state line rush." The Arizona/New Mexico border lay just ahead. It wasn't the same as leaving California. There the Colorado River created something tangible. You walked across the bridge from Blythe and entered Arizona.

Not so on the other side of Arizona. The only way I knew I was in New Mexico was because there was a sign: Welcome to New Mexico.

A lawyer once told me the definition of a property line was "six inches either side of a line between two properties."

"What do you mean by a line," I asked.

"Just a line," says he.

I wanted something more tangible than that.

"Doesn't a line have to have some physical properties like height, width, depth?"

"No," says he, "it's just a line."

I wasn't satisfied but let it drop.

It's this way with Arizona and New Mexico. They share a line you cannot see or feel. You just have to have faith that it's there. Arizona looks like New Mexico, New Mexico looks like Arizona. Nothing has changed but the rules.

A simple weigh station greets truckers at most state lines. Not so in several western states. The weigh station becomes a Port of Entry. A tad self-indulgent, I'd say.

Port of Entry connotes water, though you won't find enough here to float your rubber ducky. I wasn't about to express my sentiments though. I knew they had water and I needed their water. There was a nice officer there whom I suspect was a little bored. He was glad to trade water for my story. Only later did I realize what a benefactor he would be.

From my pre-walk planning I knew that in addition to the interstate east of Blythe there would be another section of highway that would present a problem. Between Lordsburg, New Mexico and Deming, New Mexico Interstate 10 is the only road. That old interstate bugaboo. Unlike the highway east of Blythe, though, where Interstate 10 is the only road, there is an alternative (sorta) between Lordsburg and Deming. There's only one catch — it's way the hell out of the way. You must go up to Silver City, which is about 50 miles north of Lordsburg and then drop back down to Deming. Not a thrilling thought.

In the course of our conversation the officer at the Port of Entry (snicker) asked what route I planned to take east out of Lordsburg. I explained about interstates being such a wad in the underpants of a country walker. I told him I couldn't see any alternative to walking north to Silver City and back down to Deming. Without hesitation he said there was another possibility. I was open for suggestions. He said there was a railroad track that ran beside the interstate and beside the tracks there was a dirt road used by railroad maintenance crews. And he was sure there were stock watering tanks with windmills where I could get water. Food might be a problem. There were, however, a couple of interchanges with service stations where I could, at least, get Coke and crackers.

It sounded Spartan and risky. Sixty miles and nothing was certain. I did like the idea of the dirt road beside the railroad tracks. The food/water part might be scary but walking, free from traffic worries looked good.

And it was nice. Nice in the respect that I didn't have to worry about J. B. Hunt bearing down on me, or Billy Bob, through accident or purpose, beaning me with his empty Budweiser bottle.

To be able to enjoy the sky above and the earth below, and to have the time to truly contemplate our place in the universe is something we humans rarely find time for in our hurried world.

This wasn't to be a walk through a lush, flower-carpeted meadow, though. It was still the desert.

An occasional train came by and it was good to see there were still guys riding the rails. They may be homeless, hungry and thirsty, still there was an adventurous romanticism about them.

I came upon a train that had stopped. A couple of guys were beside the engine throwing rocks at a sign. They were the guys driving the train, and were on a siding waiting for another train to pass.

I saw a chance to break the monotony and have some human contact. A spot of water, if they had any, would go down nicely, too. We exchanged "Heys."

"Not often we see a hiker out here."

"Well, I don't consider myself a hiker in the sense of someone who goes for an afternoon walk in the woods." I knew "woods" wasn't a good word choice out here so I quickly added "or the desert." "I like to think of myself as a walker. I'm trying to walk from Los Angeles to New York City."

The other guy gave a snort, "Hell, I'd call you a hiker *and* a walker *and* a few other things if you weren't around to hear me say 'em."

He finished with a smile and I knew this was my chance to slip my little walking toe ever-so-gently but firmly into the crack of that old water door.

"Sure, we got water!" And he proceeded to climb up an iron ladder on the side of the engine, one I wasn't even sure train engines had. I guess I always thought the engineer *just appeared* inside the train engine. It never crossed my mind how he got there. As he came back down the ladder I could see three frosty half-pint bottles of water cradled within his left arm," I hadn't pictured refrigeration on train engines either. All I ever pictured up there was a tiny door that was always open with fire shooting out. And a sweaty, beefy guy with no shirt on shoveling coal furiously through the fiery door. There was always another guy dressed in gray striped overalls and the standard engineers cap. He'd be chomping on a stubby cigar, one hand on the throttle, the other propped on an open window of the train. He'd be yelling over the din of the locomotive, "Faster, Charlie, we're down to 120 pounds."

No, these train guys weren't those train guys. They wore jeans and casual shirts with collars that looked like they'd been ironed by their wives that morning.

In the little town where I grew up was a sweet spring so faithful that an enterprising German immigrant started bottling it and delivering it to the surrounding area.

And as it is with most successful small enterprises, a bigger enterprise made an offer that couldn't be refused.

The train man handed me the bottle and I noticed it was spring water. Naturally, I read the label.

If the little German man had lived he'd have been rightfully proud. Water from his little spring had made it all the way to a train engine in the deserts of New Mexico. The distinctive taste of the cold spring water carried me fondly back to my boyhood.

We were too poor for "bought" water, but we had a train depot in town that kept a five-gallon jug with those tiny paper cones just like the one at the border patrol back in California.

Passengers got off the train and entered a waiting room. That's who the spring water was for, not us little street urchins. Whenever our roamings about town took us close to the depot we dropped in for a spot of sweet Anita Spring water — often under the baleful gaze of the ticket agent.

I was curious about the guys "ridin' the rails" and what the drivers might say about them.

The glory days of rail travel were a little before my time but I did hop aboard and ride across Wyoming once in a railroad snowplow. This snowplow was the rail equivalent of a highway snowplow. The snowplow has a giant fan. If there's a track closed somewhere by snow they back into it. Rather than push through the snow they blow through it.

On a hitchhiking trip from Kentucky to Montana I saw a train stopped at a siding, pretty much like this train. Way out in the country and easy to step aboard. I could see the plow had a ladder up the side and there were seats inside. I suppose the seats were for someone to sit and see if the plow was doing its job. I'd always had visions of running hard beside an old freight, and just as I thought I couldn't keep up, throwing my bundle aboard — then flinging myself after it. This wasn't the classic run to catch an open boxcar.

"Back where I'm from you don't see guys riding the rails much anymore. I've seen several out here in the west. How do ya'll feel about that?"

"It doesn't bother us, but the "suits" still frown on it. Charge 'em with criminal trespass if they catch 'em. Of course, if they do get caught they can't make bail and don't care. Jail is "three hots and a flop" for them. Pretty soon the wheels of justice realize it's the old 'Please, Brer Fox don't throw me in the briar patch.' Course they go through the formality of setting a court date which is a standing joke. Everyone concerned knows when the date comes these guys will be riding another train somewhere in Idaho."

"Did ya'll know during the early thirties Clark Gable was a rail ridin' hobo?"

"Hmm, it's a good thing he didn't get caught. You didn't get any free meals then. The yard detectives just dusted your head good with a night stick. I doubt they would have picked him for Rhett with several teeth missing."

I was relieved that these spring water benefactors of mine were content to let the guys ride the rails, and go in peace. They were okay guys. The train guys peppered me with the usual questions. Then, as I was leaving, they made a statement that pleased me.

"Just about ten miles ahead you'll be crossing the Continental Divide. It'll be all downhill after that."

Were those wry smiles I detected?

"Oh boy, it'll all be downhill after that!" NOT! I couldn't tell any difference.

I found the life-sustaining windmills and their accompanying stock watering tanks. They keep everything going for miles around. Every desert creature is there at one time or another. Cattle, horses, birds, rabbits, coyotes, terrapins, snakes, butterflies and even ants share the life-giving water.

All the above creatures use the stock tanks for a single purpose. My superior (ha) homo sapien brain saw a dual purpose. Picture the smiles and waves from the passing train engineers as I stood in my birthday suit bathing at a stock tank.

The railroad, without knowing, helped me out too. At any significant wash there was a trestle to let the water, when it did come, pass under the railroad. These trestles gave me a cool, sandy, shady place for respite from the unrelenting heat. You had to stoop to get into most and I'm sure the average person would say, "Cool, sandy, shady? Ain't that what rattlesnakes are looking for, too?" I suppose that's logical. But I don't have to suppose that most people would knock me aside to get back in there first. Consider yourself introduced to the New Mexico Sun.

Is it my imagination or do 90% of UFO sightings occur when people are alone. Don't they feel stupid with no one around to confirm what they thought they saw? And people smile and wink at each other when they try to explain what they've seen. Don't they feel like the boy yelling "wolf" when the wolf really did come? They saw it, it's the truth, and no one believes them.

I suppose any coast-to-coast walk worth its salt would have to have at least one UFO story.

I've already told you that other than a railroad, a couple of Interstate interchanges and the Interstate itself, there is nothing between Lordsburg and Deming, New Mexico.

In a place so remote, desolate, and hot, your choices of what to do are very limited. I want to say walk is one of your choices. But that isn't a choice, you walk or die. You can look at the scenery, sing, whistle, throw rocks at any number of things, bemoan your lot, or reminisce about old girl friends, chances taken, opportunities blown, or praise the Lord for saving you from yourself.

One bright, sunny midmorning I noticed a silver object off to my starboard bow at about a mile elevation. Naturally, my first thought was airplane. Then I noticed that it wasn't moving. It just looked like a silver object tethered up in the sky. I could have run with that thesis and gone with the pat "weather balloon" answer if I hadn't known that there wasn't a line that long. Maybe that long, but it would have to be big enough in diameter for me to see if it were restraining something at that great height. I had all the time in the world to figure out what I was seeing and yet study it as I may, I couldn't make sense of it. There may have been a logical explanation but no one was around to provide it for me.

Chapter 27
The Wages of Ignorance or the Boots From Hell

On the map, the black letters of the city of Las Cruces are only slightly smaller in size than the big boys of Albuquerque and Santa Fe. I was coming to a town where Gatorade and chocolate milk flowed like wine. In fact, for the last 60 miles I'd had a Gatorade fantasy. The unforgiving heat was working on my brain. My mirages were even filled with Gatorade. I'd dived off the high board into a swimming pool of Gatorade with my mouth open going down and coming back up. I cavorted under a Gatorade fountain in the reflecting pool. For a few seconds I'd lie in the pool, then I'd jump up and run under the fountain, holding my head back and mouth open until I was Gatorade saturated.

One of my fantasies was obtainable, though, and I resolved to do it. In Las Cruces I would get a motel room. But first I'd go and buy about a gallon of Gatorade. Once in the room I'd take the ice bucket and go fill it up with ice. I'd fill the ice bucket with Gatorade, then get buck nekkid and stand in the shower with the cold water on full blast. I'd just stand there for hours if I wanted to, satiating my parched body; my innards with cold Gatorade, my outards with icy jets of water.

As so often happens in life reality doesn't quite turn out like your fantasies. I did drink my fill of Gatorade and I did feel those icy jets but they didn't occur at the same time.

It's funny how quickly you can forget what a pain is like if you have some way of alleviating that pain.

Got my first pizza of the walk in Las Cruces. I guess my stomach had shrunk because I couldn't eat it all. It was silly of me to think it would keep, but I carried the leftover pieces out of Las Cruces and into the hell that is the White Sands Missile Range. The next night I brought it out with hopes of having it for dinner. It was a barely-recognizable-as-pizza mess. Need I tell you that the coyotes, prairie dogs, and mice experienced their first taste of pizza that night? I hope it didn't make them sick.

Whenever I was getting low on money I'd call Gus in Kentucky and he'd mail some to a post office in a town I knew I would be walking through in a few days. It was always a juggling act deciding where to have the money sent. It had to be a town that I wouldn't have already passed, and more importantly, a town not too far beyond the point where my money had run out. If I had come to the agreed-upon town and the money hadn't arrived, it meant either waiting or walking ahead and hitchhiking back. There were a few times when I did have to hitchhike back. It seemed more logical to go on and come back because I'd either have to get a motel room or camp around town, neither of which appealed to me.

Las Cruces was to be a money drop. And a drop of another kind of which there were only three the whole trip. The boots I started the walk with hadn't been new. Hindsight tells me that was a good thing, as blisters were not a problem. But now they had gotten thin on the soles, and the hot asphalt was causing some discomfort.

Before I started my walk I'd read that a respected hiking magazine had rated a certain boot "most comfortable."

I ordered a pair, planning on their being my replacement pair. I had been lulled by the magazine's description. When they arrived I looked at them, but never tried them on. Beeg mistake! As with so many SNAFUS, one problem leads to another problem and a snowball effect is set in motion. The fact that I didn't try the boots on was the first link in a chain reaction of foot misery.

When the lady working at the post office gave me my boot box I was excited. Now when I looked down I'd see new boots. And my feet would love the new look and feel. What a cruel joke.

What to do with the old boots? I had two choices. Either I could throw the old boots away or ship them back home. These weren't just any, old worn out boots to be unceremoniously tossed on the dead boot trash heap. Far from it. These boots would have a rather unique tale to tell. And they couldn't tell it if they wound up at the Las Cruces landfill. I wanted to show these boots to my grandchildren.

And this time, in this place, with this box, was my only hope of preserving this little bit of history.

I sat down, put on the new boots, put the old ones in the box the new ones had come in, slapped a new label over the old, and walked back to the mail person's window and mailed them back to Kentucky.

They say hindsight is 20/20. Man, do I ever see now what I should have seen then. It was a grave mistake, sending those old boots home as soon as I put the new ones on. I should have carried both pair; alternating wearing old and new until the new ones were broken in.

You'd assume anyone on a Los Angeles-New York walk should have more than one pair of footgear, right? I agree that's the ideal scenario. But the weight and volume of more than one pair of boots was a luxury I couldn't justify. What I had on my feet was the court of last resort, good, bad or indifferent.

I hadn't walked from the post office more than a block before I realized something was seriously wrong. "Most Comfortable Boot" kept pulsing in my brain and each pulsing signal was followed by about three king-sized question marks. What the hell do they mean, "Most Comfortable Boot?" My big toe is digging into the front of the boot and my heel is burning like fire in the back.

I tried my best to rationalize it all away by telling myself that everything would be okay after they were broken in. I tried not to let the fact that I'd been "caught out" creep into my mind. I'd sent my old comfortable boots home. These boots were it. Case closed.

The closer I got to the edge of Las Cruces the harder the panic was to suppress. Once I left town there was no alternative — I walked in these boots. Walking barefoot isn't an option on the White Sands Missile Range.

To my great relief I spotted a K-Mart. I went in with the idea of getting a second pair of shoes to give me relief until I could break the boots from Hell to my will.

I figured some cheap running shoes should do the trick. I bought a pair of twelve dollar wonders. It wasn't until I got outside that I realized they were *plastic* running shoes. Of all places on earth this is one where you need shoes that breathe, not plastic shoes.

I rationalized I would only be wearing them long enough to break the boots in.

In the K-Mart I also bought Band-Aids, moleskin and lamb's wool. When your feet hurt you pull out all the stops.

I once heard about a professional football player who had been stranded outside in a snowstorm with no way to make heat. When he was rescued a reporter asked him why he hadn't built a fire. He replied that he had nothing to burn, but if he'd had a stack of thousand dollar bills he'd have burned them without hesitation.

Cold and blisters have a lot in common when it comes to seeking relief. If you have money, you'll spend it.

Outside the K-Mart I tried on my plastic running shoes. It was too early to tell if I'd get relief or if I was just going to boil the blisters I already had.

Only if your feet currently have several quarter-size blisters and your big toenail is solid black from being rammed into the front of a shoe can you have empathy when I say I hobbled into the next town after Las Cruces. It's pain you can't even imagine or remember. Sorta like childbirth, I suppose. You have to be living it at the moment. What they say is true: "When your feet hurt, you hurt all over."

About ten miles north of Las Cruces there's a tall, for lack of a better word, "geological" structure. It's too short, thin and wiry to be classified a mountain. Impressive, though, it looks like the pipes of a giant organ. I confess to not seeing them as organ pipes until I approached the town sitting at the base of this giant structure and saw the green town sign that said "Organ".

I wonder why the town fathers didn't expand on "Organ" a bit, though. Seems it would be more aesthetically pleasing to the ear if they'd gone just a little further and named the town "Organ Pipe," "Church Organ," or "Heaven's Organ." When they stopped short and named it simply "Organ", it left the town wide open for anatomical association. When you look at the rock formation the town is named for, the musical instrument isn't necessarily the first thing that comes to mind.

Yes, Organ has a grocery store. And no, thank goodness, it isn't called "The Organ Store."

It was late afternoon and I was purchasing my "tear the bag, rip the wrapper, twist the cap" dinner, when I heard a lady's voice behind me.

"I saw you this morning between here and Las Cruces, where are you going?" Her boldness stopped me for a second.

"I'm attempting to walk from Los Angeles to New York City." My usual generic comeback. I was almost all the way to New York before I dropped the "attempting."

After a few more pleasantries the conversation turned to how and where I spent the nights. Again the reply was simple and straightforward.

"I have a tent and I usually just sleep off the road somewhere."

Something about this woman said "nurse." Was it my keen powers of observation or could it have been because the only thing not white on her was a tiny black band around that semi-circle, cardboard-looking hat on her head? Yeah, either this was a nurse or else someone who *really* knew how to dress for this incendiary Organ sun.

Nurses, by nature, aren't shrinking violets but I was a little surprised at how bold her next statement was considering there were other people in the store. And by "bold" I don't mean "forward." I mean brave. What she said would make 98% of American women recoil in horror. Ninety-eight percent of American women watch too much television, though. Not every strange, or more correctly, "new to you" man is Ted Bundy. Meeting new people is a big part of what growth and a true appreciation of life is all about.

"You're welcome to put your tent up in my backyard," I heard Organ Voice say. Holy organ music to my ears, Batman!

I moseyed around the store while she paid for her groceries. Her banter with the clerk and other customers told me she was brave *and* boisterous. And boisterous nearly always accompanies a sense of humor.

So I felt at ease posing a question to her as we jounced in her van along the dirt streets of town. Her van looked like it had just come back from the crusades, dust and rust were its mantle if not its armor.

"Since you're a nurse I guess it doesn't bother you but do people ever get embarrassed when they have to say they're from Organ?"

She chuckled.

"Well, within, say a 100-mile radius no explanation is necessary but beyond that I've learned to quickly add that there's a really big rock formation nearby that resembles the pipes of a church organ. Sometimes if you're quick, you can beat the quizzical "Organ?" look. And really, about half the people picture Bach's organ anyway. You learn to spot quickly which way their minds are headed. It's actually kind of a fun game, trying to judge which Organ face they're going to present."

Driving to her house I was able to better see Organ. It's kind of hard to imagine how it ever came to be. But many other towns in the U.S. could make you ask yourself, "Why here? Why a town at all?"

If you can picture a child playing in a sandbox, deciding to start a town of their own, you can pretty well grasp what Organ is like. It's as if two or three people happened upon this spot at the base of the giant organ pipes, got their hands on a dozen and said, "Let's scrape some of this sand off the side of the mountain and level it off so we'll have a place to sit and look at the pipes."

I couldn't think of a single more logical reason for Organ's existence. I saw no object in Organ, man-made or natural, living or dead, moving or stationary not coated with that old New Mexico, Land of Enchantment, sand.

I once heard a fella who'd lived briefly in New Mexico say, "The 'enchantment' soon wears off when you spend most of your time sweeping it back out the door."

During our meal that night I related my foot woes to the nurse. She said she'd take a look later.

Later, when I presented my feet, she hesitated for just a second. I thought, Jesus, they even stopped a nurse cold. She sized them up, then said, "They showed us some pretty gross stuff in Nursing School to see if we could cut the mustard. I might just nominate your feet for a training film. You should see a doctor. You could ride back to Las Cruces with me in the morning."

There was that word again — "Back."

That hurt nearly as much as the blisters. I knew I'd either have to wait for her to get off work and bring me back to Organ or I'd have to walk from Las Cruces to Organ *again*!

I knew, too, that nurses seldom work a normal eight-hour workday.

I told myself I'd just tough it out with what lay ahead. Going back wasn't an option.

"Is there anything you can do for them?, I asked.

She brought out some antibacterial ointment and band-aids.

"This really isn't adequate but it's all I have."

I enjoyed my night in her back yard. Standing, my blisters howled piteously, lying, they mercifully only whined. The security of her back yard made the night enjoyable. If you are homeless a safe, secure place means more than a soft bed.

The next morning as we rode back out to the highway I was a little surprised when she offered me some advice.

"Since I'm a nurse it's in my heart and training to offer hope but I can't give you much encouragement between here and Alamogordo. Prayer is my suggestion. You'll have to cross the White Sands Missile Range and I'd say only Death Valley is hotter and drier. If you think there's any way your feet will make you quit, I'd quit now."

I couldn't come up with any response, only numbed silence.

Then in a lighter tone she added, "At the store they have great breakfast burritos. I'll treat."

Breakfast? Burrito? Surely that's a contradiction in terms, I thought. I'd never heard of such. I couldn't picture the combination of morning and burrito being very complimentary.

"Breakfast Burrito sounds like an oxymoron to me," I said.

"Maybe in Tennessee. Not out here," she said.

The factual burrito was better than the one I had pictured in my head. Outside I thanked her for everything. I had the feeling that the burrito was usually "carry-out" for her and she needed to get going.

It wasn't very long before I saw why my nurse-friend could offer me little encouragement for what lay ahead between Organ and Alamogordo. It wasn't her fault. It was landscape straight from the twilight zone. For once the government used good sense in taking land suitable for nothing else and created a missile range on it. Fifty-six miles of desert, the likes of which existed few other places in the world. Only later did I learn the early Spanish considered this area one of the harshest deserts in the west. They called it *Jornada del Muerto*, The Journey of Death.

It was a good thing I was already on the dance floor before I knew the name of the tune.

The nurse said I could expect to find water at only one place and that was chancy. The guard at the White Sands Missile Range would have water and might share.

Even though the nurse had done what she could for my blisters, my feet were a pitiful mess, red and swollen beyond my own recognition, with broken blisters oozing clear liquid. Each step was labor.

I tried a system of foot relief, hoping against hope, that the new boots would get broken in. At each mile marker I'd sit down on the hot road and change shoes — a mile in the plastic shoes, followed by a mile in the boots from hell. The plastic shoes were only marginally less painful than the boots. I'd see the mile marker in the distance and wonder if I could hold out until I reached it. I looked forward to the exchange of shoes although I suspect it was more for the rest than relief from the present pair of shoes I was wearing.

I was about half-way across the 60 mile stretch between Las Cruces and Alamogordo. I was both physically and mentally drained from my game of blister hopscotch.

I was sitting on the side of the road, sockfooted, my head between my knees. The personification of total dejection. Other than the occasional car, I saw nothing. As well as nothing to see, there was nothing to hear either, except the occasional high-circling hawk or far-away plane.

As I sat dejected by the road I was startled by a slight click. I looked in the direction of the click and was surprised to see a man on a bicycle not five feet away. "What are you doing here" was the first question on both our minds. I've forgotten who posed it first. Strangely enough, my answer made more sense, at least to me.

"I'm attempting to walk–Yadda, Yadda, Yadda. What are you doing out here," I asked.

"I'm spending the summer birdwatching throughout the Southwest. I just happen to be doing it by bike."

For a minute there was silence as we pondered the magnitude of both our acts.

"Do you think there's a judge anywhere who wouldn't have us committed?" I asked.

"We could hope for a jury of our peers. They'd be the only ones who might cut us some slack."

"I don't know. Anyone out here of their own free will would be peerless, in my opinion. The only 'peers' we have are coyotes, prairie dogs and rattlers."

The biker sat well out into the highway. He was off his bike and was sitting on the bikes crossbar. There was no way a car could sneak up on you out there. He snorted a slow laugh and kicked at a flattened cigarette butt, thrown from some car. The snort and kick told me he agreed about our peers.

"What have you got to drink?" asked birdwatcher. I offhandedly showed him my canteen resting beside my feet. The bottom line was I had some hot water and I told him as much. I could tell by the way he posed the question that he was more curious as to what I was drinking than whether I had any to share.

To my credit I had learned the water I was drinking hot would go down easier if I mixed in some pre-sweetened Kool-Aid. And the water was always hot.

But when I needed it most, the Kool-Aid hadn't been available back in the small Organ store. Drinking hot water in a hot place is not a cool experience.

The quantity seems to make little difference. You can have all the hot water you want and you still feel as if your thirst hasn't been appeased.

One of Ann Landers pet phrases is; "If life gives you lemons, make lemonade." Sorry, Ann, this desert lemon has no water or sugar.

The water I was carrying was a contradiction. It's molecular make up of two parts hydrogen and one part oxygen made it the most beautifully composed and constructed element I could possess in this place. Next to the air, nothing could be more precious.

But this was hot, flat, and tasteless.

"This might help some," the cycling birdwatcher said as he tossed me a couple packets of powdered Gatorade.

There's no way I can adequately describe what Gatorade meant to me. It's like they say about the Mona Lisa, there's no value that can be placed on it. You'll think I'm just being dramatic but my defense is the same as the one I used to justify my drinking of the Pepsi atop the fence post. Unless you've been there, there's no way you can understand. If I say there's literally no amount of gold I would have taken for my Gatorade you just smile because you're well-fed and well-watered. It's the old "mile-in-my-moccasins" thing, though. Stop for just a minute and picture yourself dying of thirst in the desert. A genie offers you the key to Fort Knox or that gallon pitcher of Gatorade filled with ice. Sitting there in your living room with that two-liter Coke and a bag of chips you might say, "Hell, I'd take that key and try to find something to drink somewhere else on down the road!"

Reality check! Your body don't work that way. Self-preservation is the strongest instinct. Your body wouldn't let your mind come up with any off-the-wall stuff like that. After I've said all this, you'll think I'm really strange when I say Gatorade can be the best of drinks or it can be the worst of drinks. If you aren't really thirsty, or the Gatorade isn't really cold, it can be ghastly stuff. But if you *really* need it, it's nectar of the Gods.

I had once read that a person needs a gallon of water a day. That was hard for me to swallow (I'm sorry). I'd try to visualize one of those big glass jugs. I'd tilt it over in my mind and picture the amount of milk or water that would flow out.

No way, man! Some sissy might *think* they needed all that water, but anyone with a will of steel like mine (insert small chuckle here) could tough it through on half that amount if need be.

Of course, these thoughts were formulated on a winter's day during a commercial break on Oprah. I'm lying on the couch sipping hot chocolate and the refrigerator is only seven steps away. I hadn't field-tested my theories during July in the American Southwest.

It only took a few days in the desert for me to see that whoever came up with the gallon-a-day rule had done some testing.

In a way I suppose we were both right. They were correct in that a gallon is the correct amount if you want to keep your body and nerves functioning at anywhere near the level they did back in Peoria.

And I'm right if you want to be macho and stupid. You can drink the recommended gallon a day or you can endure the day, feeling like every pore in your body has had a faucet installed and every one of them is turned on. Every ounce of your body moisture has been drained into the dry Arizona air. Your day will be consumed with visions of Gatorade plums dancing in your head. You'll spend the day looking at your feet saying, "left, right, left, right. I didn't even have the capacity to carry a gallon of water if the gallon had been available in the first place. I only had two water containers, one held two quarts and the other held one quart.

Through my own convoluted system of survival I came up with a plan. If I was on the edge of one of those "Hell, there's nothing for 40 miles" places, I'd drink all I could possibly hold. My sides probably looked like a lion's after a zebra kill. After I'd gorged myself I'd fill my water bottles. I'd try my best to take only sips during the day. Then at night just before I went to sleep I'd make a ritual of drinking all the water I had. I'd take a big mouthful and just hold it. I wouldn't swallow until I'd swished it all around my mouth, splashing it against my teeth, sending it to the roof of my mouth to do a big ocean curl. I'd even lift my tongue making sure the area under it could enjoy the glory for a moment.

These times were cause for special celebration if I happened to have Gatorade. Every single drop was savored as if it were liquid gold. Every effort was made to not spill a drop. And if any did I felt like I could cry if I'd had any moisture for tears.

The reason this system worked best for me was I found that I could continue to walk during the day if I was thirsty but if I was thirsty at night I couldn't sleep. It's a terrible feeling to toss all night because of thirst.

I know you're thinking if I drank all my water what did I do the next day? Well, if the distance to be covered was close to forty miles, my system would work because I could cover the first half by just taking sips, then drinking it all before bedtime, and then I could force myself to walk the second 20 miles if I kept that Gatorade carrot-on-a-stick a few feet in front of me. Knowing something existed at the end kept me going the second day.

And if it was more than 40 miles? Believe in the power of prayer, Brother!

I think the cycling birdwatcher could see I had reached the lowest depths of my spirits, and I'll always be grateful to him for sharing something so valuable and irreplaceable in this hot, lonely place.

It was a kind, humanitarian gesture. The best kindnesses are the ones given with no thought of reward or even discovery. We never even exchanged addresses so unless he buys this book or recognizes himself on a future episode of *Touched by an Angel*,, he'll never know the depths of my gratitude. And though I can never be sure, I believe he was the cause of another incident that brought me immeasurable relief. I'll explain later.

The birdwatcher rekindled my desire and determination. His kind act made my foot agony seem bearable when I was beginning to think I couldn't trudge another trudge.

Remember early in my walk I had given every item I was carrying its day of judgment? Did its end justify its means? Was its value worth more than a pain in the neck? I thought I had been stern but just, giving every item a fair and impartial trial. I had sent so many things home I figured I was as bare-boned as a cross-continent walker could be.

That night as I lay in a sandy ditch beside the road running through the White Sands Missile Range I looked at my feet. They throbbed as if they had a heartbeat all their own. Blackened toenails with a side of blisters were "the catch of the day." The tools I had at hand offered no relief for my feet. The only break I could give them was to lighten their burden even more.

If my previous judgment was a fair and impartial trial, this White Sands Missile Range judgment was a kangaroo court. I hastily, and with some malice, threw things I thought weren't carrying their weight (sentiment had no place here.) I was fast, clean and harsh. I had to somehow survive this place and I was grasping at the only straw I could see.

I tried not to look at the pile I had created for the coyotes. I knew if I did I might weaken and drag something back.

Next I turned my attention to the boots from hell. Was there anything I could do to soften, stretch or make them conform to my feet? They say Eskimo wives chew their husband's boots to soften them and I wasn't above doing that but I figured Eskimo, form-fitting, seal skin boots lent themselves to the tooth more readily than my steel-shanked, rubber and cowhide ones. My walking stick seemed to be the only softener I had. The boots were too short. They were blackening my nails. I held the boot between my feet. I rammed the walking stick down into the toe with both hands. I looked like an Indian woman turning grain into flour. Wham, Wham, Wham for about two minutes — then, I tried the boot on. It was impossible to tell. The only proof would be moving down ol' Highway Number 70 the next day.

Then I attacked the heels flailing like a washerwoman with my walking stick. I was so mad at these boots I didn't care if they flew into a hundred pieces. I was going to break the backs of these rock-hard blister producers.

The next day the scoreboard said it all. Boots from hell, one. Cross-country hiker, zip. I hadn't fazed their cussedness.

Forward was the only direction now. Going back wasn't a choice. There's an old saying, "What cannot be cured must be endured." I was definitely cured of these boots, but still they had to be endured. I was so low I could have sat on a nickel and still kicked my feet.

Then I came to the rest area. (Excuse me while I suppress a laugh.) Everyone is familiar with rest areas. You know, nice brick building with restrooms clearly designated: Buoys — Gulls; Inboard — Outboard. And large grassy areas for walking Fido. Trees, picnic tables. Yes, everyone knows rest areas.

But, (Big But) have you seen desert "rest areas?" I didn't think so. Here's the picture: A gravel pull-off with one porta-potty and a dumpster. That's it, finis!

At least the dumpster offered some shade. I leaned my pack against it, then my back rested beside the pack.

I must have looked pretty pitiful to the Mexican family that pulled up to the porta-potty. After everyone had visited the single potty and they were ready to pull back on to the road, a teenage girl came over to me.

"Would you like a chicken sandwich?"

Naturally, there was only one answer.

Well, we know cold drink was what I really wanted but I didn't want to sound ungrateful.

"Yes, I surely would!"

Drink may have been first on my list but food was running a close second.

The Mexican family was barely out of sight as I washed down the last bite of my sandwich with birdwatcher Gatorade.

As the Organ nurse had said I would, I finally came to the guard shack at the entrance to the missile range. And who was to be my benefactor: the pre-walk-dreaded black man. This man gave me two precious gifts, one tangible and one intangible. You can guess the former was water. The second was just a few words on his part, but they were of no less value than the water.

When I told him I was attempting to walk to the Empire State Building he gave me a simple, off-hand reply, but one that meant so much to me.

"Oh, you'll make it all right," he said.

Those few words of quiet confidence on his part buoyed my spirits so.

Words couldn't dissolve blisters, though, and I was hobbling badly as I approached Alamogordo. Just a few miles before you reach town you get to view the missile range's namesake, The White Sands. It's a sight to see. If you can picture the Sahara and its mile after mile of high undulating dunes, and you can imagine those dunes being sugar instead of sand, you've got a pretty good idea of what the White Sands Missile Range looks like. To man's credit he preserved this part and called it White Sands National Monument. Hooray for man!

I was glad to see Alamogordo for three special reasons; food, water and my map told me it might be big enough to have new boots.

On the outskirts of Alamogordo there's another border patrol station. I'd always assumed the border patrol was located on the border and here was one that must have been 75 miles inland. I queried the officer about that as I mooched from his cold water jug. He explained that the border patrol stations were situated on main highway arteries, or the convergence of main arteries that came into the country. And even though the station may be far from the border, illegals had to pass through there or else walk through the desert which he implied and I knew would hardly be a viable alternative.

"We get few customers on foot," he smiled.

I'm sure I looked a tad sheepish as I lowered my eyes into my water cup.

"Why are the white sands here and no where else?"

"Well, strange as it seems, this was once a large lake, thousands, maybe millions of years ago. Today it all looks like salt but it's really gypsum that has leached down from the surrounding mountains. When the weather changed to hot and dry, and the lake evaporated, it left all this white stuff on the lakebed. Pretty but not much use to anyone. Pumps a few tourist dollars into the place, though."

He continued, "Doesn't affect our business much. The people we're concerned with don't have any bucks to spend and I wouldn't exactly call them tourists."

He was a nice guy so after we'd talked awhile longer about the desert, the white sands, and aliens I wasn't altogether surprised when he said, "Hey, I think the wife is having her classic meatloaf for dinner tonight. You're welcome to join us. And, if you can stand my wild five and seven-year-old daughters you're welcome to spend the night."

Even though I stammered a delightful acceptance I felt this had all moved too fast. Surely there was more here than met the eye. I wouldn't have been surprised that a bachelor would invite me in, but a man with a wife and small kids? It all seemed pre-arranged.

It wasn't until days later, when I had time to ponder as I walked that I began to piece the puzzle together.

I couldn't be sure, but I believe the cycling birdwatcher gave me a second gift. I think he rode on ahead to the border patrol station and asked them if they'd be on the lookout for me. I believe he was a truly compassionate person who saw me at my ropes end and direly in need of help. The border patrol officer's invitation made me think how refreshing it is that there are still people who haven't been brainwashed by the news media. There's so much bad stuff on television and in the newspapers that has warped most people's sense of reality. But the person who uses his head knows not everyone walking down the road is an axe murderer.

It rubs my fur the wrong way when I think how our slavery (yes, I stand by that word) to the automobile has made us suspicious of anyone going from point A to point B and *not doing* it by car. Americans have been dependent upon, and in love with, the car for so long that they think anyone not using a car must be suspect.

Sometimes I'd look at the faces in the cars that passed on my walk. I couldn't believe that look that said I wasn't normal. I expected to be noticed for my weirdness. I just didn't want people looking at me like I was a criminal.

I ask you, (be fair) which is more normal: a 3000 pound metal contrivance, or two good legs? I loved my wife dearly, but I used to fuss at her for driving the car 100 yards to the mailbox.

I didn't have to wait long for the border patrol officer's shift to end and we drove (Ha! We didn't walk) to his house.

I mean nothing disparaging when I say he was the typical American with a house in the "burbs," two-point-four kids, and a dog and cat, but we already know he wasn't typical because he invited a stranger to his house.

His wife was a real gem.

"If you'll get your dirty clothes I'll wash them for you."

She said this not long after we arrived so I suspected the spring from my Irish Spring was wearing thin. The washer invite was quickly followed by a shower invitation. I was not at all surprised. After dinner (since all my socks were in their final spin cycle) I thought I'd get their advice on swollen, blistered feet.

I detected a collective gasp when I showed them my poor swollen feet. They weren't a normal pink but a decidedly red color, and dotted with nickel and quarter sized blisters. If I hadn't already seen them, I'd have gasped, too.

They wanted to be helpful but I could see it was beyond them to come up with anything new to try.

After relating the boots from hell story, the border patrol officer volunteered, "There's only one real possibility for finding boots in Alamogordo. I'm off tomorrow so we'll go to the only hiker's store I know of."

The next morning, the store clerk said they had one pair left but they were a half size larger than what I'd requested.

I hesitated but I knew I had no choice, so I bought them. As it turned out it was one of the best decisions of the entire trip. Those boots never hurt my feet and I wore them all the way from Alamogordo, New Mexico to Blakely, Georgia.

Someone up there must have wanted to see how this trip was going to turn out. Without the new, pain-free boots I don't see how I could have continued. After I'd purchased the new boots the border patrol officer graciously took me back to the border patrol station so as not to compromise the intregrity of my walk.

The border patrol family were such nice people. People like them were a big part of what the trip was all about. A walk consisting of just places would be just a walk. Add people and you have an experience.

Chapter 28
The Meadow in the Clouds

"The Boots From Hell?" I went to the post office and sent them back home. Bet you thought I'd walk the streets until I found a tree-trimming crew with one of those chippers and let them have their way with those devil boots. An entertaining thought, if there had been any trees.

Brace yourself. Today I wear them without pain, but strictly on a casual basis.

My feet being swollen so badly must have been the reason they caused so much pain. And I think it was a big dose of hardheadedness. I'd read on more than one occasion that hiking boots should be one-half size larger than your street shoes. I had "pooh-poohed" that. What did they know? When I looked down at my feet I wanted to see little princess feet. Adding a half-size wasn't going to help. Live and Learn.

As you leave Alamogordo heading east, you leave the flatlands of the Missile Range and start climbing into the Sacramento Mountains and the Lincoln National Forest.

Now I was switching off wearing my plastic K-Mart running shoes then my new one-half-size larger hiking boots. I could tell things were going to be better although it still wasn't a stroll on the beach.

The Sacramento Mountains kinda reminded me of the beach, though. You often see tall, brown, majestic columns of rock stretching skyward that look like sand castles that have been swept over by incoming surf or pelted by an afternoon rain.

After several hours of steady climbing the mountains leveled off a bit and I came to the hamlet of High Rolls. The high rolls on my hams should be so pretty. This is one of the most pristine, beautiful places I passed through on my walk. I call it Hamlet because it must have a population of 50-counting goats. And those 50-odd goats and people would wring my neck for saying this but if you're ever in south-central New Mexico, drive, no, walk, through High Rolls. I guarantee you didn't know such clean, pure, delightful air existed anywhere. To placate the lovely residents of High Rolls (goats, too) I hasten to add I don't want you to stay. If everyone stayed it wouldn't be clean nor pure nor delightful for long. Just savor as you pass through. As the saying goes, leave only footprints.

Nearly as beautiful in sight and sound is the next town. Could any place whose literal translation means "Meadow in the Clouds" be anything but beautiful? Cloudcroft, New

Mexico is a smaller, less discovered version of Flagstaff, Arizona. High elevation, evergreen trees, a cool crispness to the air. It truly is the closest thing to a meadow in the clouds you're likely to find.

Cloudcroft is the big brother of High Rolls. A little more touristy with western storefronts, schools, churches, fire hall, yuppies, and like Flagstaff snow remains much of the year in places where the sun doesn't easily reach.

You can imagine what a change it was for me, being only two days from the White Sands Missile Range. The cool air, the mountains with their beauty and lushness provided by the rain and cold air, versus the hot, dry austerity of the desert.

Cloudcroft was so mountainous it was hard for me to find an out-of-the-way spot level enough to pitch my tent. I walked far back into a ravine surrounded by spruce trees and spent a glorious, cool night in my sleeping bag and tent. There are few pleasures greater than a night on a bed of spruce and pine needles in the mountains.

Chapter 29
How Sweet It Is

Now the walk was becoming more like it had been in my dreams. It was supposed to be fun. Up until Cloudcroft it had been about ten percent pleasure and 90 percent pain. Cloudcroft had shown me there could be beauty and a climate that felt good to my skin. Oh, there had been beauty before Cloudcroft. But it had been "tough love" beauty if you will. It required peering through searing heat and pushing past ravaging thirst to see. Cloudcroft's beauty required no such effort. It was there for the taking. It surrounded and gently enveloped me. The cool air, fresh greenery of the mountains soothed, invigorated and restored. My step was lighter. The pack less heavy. The road less traveled. Cloudcroft was a tonic.

The new boots were proving to be just the ticket. Switching back and forth between the plastic running shoes and my new boots became less frequent.

Finally, I decided to cut the cord. With some ceremony, I placed the plastic running shoes atop a culvert beside the road. They had been faithful servants. They hadn't asked to be plastic and made no apologies for it. They had delivered as promised. I couldn't just trash them. They deserved some dignity and respect. Maybe someone else would come along and find them and they could continue to serve.

This was still New Mexico, and deep down somewhere I knew the cool and green wouldn't last forever. I just wanted it to. After Cloudcroft it was the return of mesquite, cactus, rock mesas, sand and that old nemesis — heat.

I mentioned that in 1965 my wife and I rode bicycles from Louisville, Kentucky to Daytona Beach, Florida on our honeymoon. As you might imagine, eastern Kentucky is a seemingly endless series of up hill, down hill and around a curve. Even in a car you think you aren't getting anywhere. Bicycles seem to intensify that feeling.

For miles and days we saw billboards advertising Carter's Country Store, "Stop and See The Ham Tree." It became a running joke with us. At each billboard we'd look at each other with that "What-the-hell-is-a-Ham-Tree" look on our faces.

On a bike trip you are confronted with heat and thirst, though not to the degree a walker crossing the desert is. It's keen enough to make you anticipate any upcoming grocery or service station, though.

Carter's Country Store created visions of cold drink in our minds. The Ham Tree was only a mild curiosity.

Much to our disappointment the only drink offered at Carter's was cherry cider. By the gallon! We didn't want cherry cider much less a gallon of it. But negotiating the hills of Kentucky by leg power can do some heavy convincing. It's surprising how fast cherry cider becomes unpleasant when you pass a gallon jug back and forth. After about a quart we didn't care if we ever saw cherries or cider again. Jug in hand, we moseyed around until we found the Ham Tree. We had to laugh when we saw it. We hadn't expected it to literally be a ham tree. It was the trunk and limbs of a tree that had been stripped of its bark and painted white. From each limb hung a country ham. What did P.T. Barnum say? There's a sucker born every minute.

I reminisced about that trip as I fought the return of the desert and the discomforts it brought. The taste of the cider itself wasn't pleasure evoking but the fact that it was cold, wet and sweet was.

The heat and thirst of the desert were soon grinding my cherry-cider memories under their heel, as well as any nostalgic feelings about Cloudcroft and its coolness and plenty. I was back in the real New Mexico.

Chapter 30
Dear Dead Deer

Water is at such a premium in the west that it is exalted and given titles it hasn't earned. "River" is one. A New Mexico river would be called a creek or branch in Kentucky or Tennessee.

I stopped at Mayhill, the next town east of Cloudcroft, and ate in their lone, but proud, eatery. Naturally, in small places like Mayhill I was a curiosity. In most cases there's someone brave enough to ask who you are and what you're doing. Maybe not so straightforward as that, but still they find ways. And usually it's the young or old who ask. The young haven't yet found out about the propriety of asking questions of strangers or, more likely, aren't as concerned about niceties as they are curious. And the old aren't afraid to ask because they think they have "right-to-know" privileges. An elderly man asked me where I was headed. After I told him he said something that sounded very good to my ears.

"You're out of the mountains now and you'll be going downhill for a long way. It'll be nice walking because there's a river running beside the road."

"River" is a little strong for this "body of water." When I can step across it I call it a branch. When I can bathe in it I call it a creek. I never saw a river. I didn't drink from it. Too many cattle drank and bathed there. The old man said he didn't drink from it but people did and didn't die from it so I could if I was brave.

The further I walked down the road the more I saw that the river running beside it was a life-giving source; in much the same way a watering hole in Africa provides sustenance for many creatures. I learned this by piecing together a puzzle. Other than cattle, I never actually saw that the river was benefitting any other creature. The puzzle pieces were of bone. To be more exact skeletons, skeletons of deer. The roadside was littered with them. Nearly every hundred yards was another one. It took a lot of miles of to figure out why there were so many deer carcasses and skeletons along this stretch of highway. Finally I pieced it together: The river ran in the valley to the right of the highway. To the left of the highway were hills with trees where the deer spend their days. At night they come out of the hills, cross the highway, and go to the river to drink and graze along its' banks.

Herein lies the problem for the dear deer. You've heard the saying "like a deer caught in the headlights." That saying must have originated just outside Mayhill, New Mexico. There was so much sad evidence of deer, headlights, frozen wonder and death.

Chapter 31
How Sweet It Is — Part 2

I was hot and thirsty. The fruit and vegetable sign I saw about 50 yards ahead was welcome. Even if I didn't want fruit or vegetables, a sign meant there was someone there and that someone would need water to drink. Maybe they'd share. Water wasn't always given in the form I'd like — in copious amounts with glacial quantities of ice. I can't even say it was always given with a cheerful heart, but given it was.

I walked up to the open air stand and my eyes swept over and past the cucumbers and squash to the back of the stand where, for me, the really interesting stuff might be. I only saw one liquid, and you guessed it — cherry cider. At least it was sold in half-gallon jugs instead of gallons. Surely this person running the fruit stand doesn't drink cherry cider as the drink of preference. At least not after the first few hours of the first day on the job. But the stinging rebuff of the I — sell-water lady in Glamis was still fresh in my mind. People who have things to sell aren't too keen on giving them away. Twenty-five years had dulled the memory of the Ham Tree cider, and this cider did look invitingly cool with its beads of cold condensation on the jug exterior. This cider offered something else that water lacked. Something this cross-country walker always craved — sweet.

I bought a half-gallon jug of cherry cider. And this cider was pretty much like the Ham Tree cider of that long-ago honeymoon bike trip.

Economics 101 and the law of diminishing returns came floating back across my mind.

I think my teacher gave ice-cream cones as an example of diminishing returns. Your first cone is great. The second one is good. The third is fair. The fourth is poor, etc. I wasn't sure how that related to Economics, but I saw how it related to cider.

The first long pull on the jug was great. The second good. Third fair. You get the picture. You can guess that after about the sixth swallow I was looking for a place to pitch that jug of cider.

You know how eating something sweet makes you want to eat something salty. After I left the fruit stand I was stuck with that sickening, sugary taste in my mouth and no way to rid myself of it. And the real kick in the head was that I was still thirsty. Trust me — don't trust cherry cider.

Chapter 32
Sleeping Over
at Mr. Skunk's House

That night I found myself in flat lands that contained practically no plant growth other than Ocotillo cactus. Ocotillo is a sorry looking plant. At their base they look like a bunch of spindly beanpoles stuck in a washtub. Picture the old snake charmer in India but instead of one cobra rearing up there are about 25. And all 25 look like they've been on the Slim-Fast Plan for about ten years. So, it ain't much for hiding behind. When they bloom they redeem themselves some but you aren't likely to see them in *Better Homes and Gardens*.

It was time to put down for the night and I was scanning the roadside for the healthiest, full-bodied Ocotillo to hide behind. I spotted the Arnold Schwarzenegger of Ocotillos on the distant, dusty plain. It was quite a way off the road but that was okay. With what little protection it provided, the further I was from the road, the better.

I climbed the fence and struck out for Mr. Macho Ocotillo. As I arrived I noticed a hole in the ground a few yards away from my designated cactus. I dismissed it as merely the front or back door of a prairie dog's home.

It was a warm and clear night, requiring no tent, so I spread out my ground cloth and sleeping bag. I lay on top of the sleeping bag with my hands folded behind my head, my right foot crossed atop my left. I lay there just resting, thinking and waiting for the sun to go down and the stars to come out, lost in my own reverie.

It was dusk and I was just turning from my hands-behind-my-head , feet-crossed-thinking position to my drifting-off-to-Never-Never Land-lying on-my-left-side position, when out of the corner of my eye I caught movement at the hole. I raised up on my left elbow just as a black and white prairie dog was launching himself from the hole. Whoa! Either I just saw the world's first black and white prairie dog, or this was something of a different stripe I didn't want to see. The critter was now completely in view. I was face-to-face with Mr. Skunk. He had a determined, no nonsense manner about him much as if he was off to the third shift at the skunk perfume factory.

We eyeballed each other. Either he realized he'd forgotten his lunch or didn't like my smell because he did an immediate about face and scurried quickly back down the hole.

I saw my chance and grabbed it. Though we'd met and parted on good terms. I knew that Mr. Skunk could change all that at his slightest whim. I grabbed a few large rocks and jammed them down the hole. I meant him no harm and knew he probably had another door somewhere. I'd remove the rocks the next morning as I left.

Lying there by the skunk hole waiting for sleep to come I smiled at what must have been the conversation going on underground as Mr. Skunk rushed, all breathless up to Mrs. Skunk.

"Fifi, there's a big, ol' stinkin' goat settlin' down for the night just outside our front door!"

"Go on with you, Pierre. You've been at the bottle again! There ain't no goats for a hundred miles."

"No, for sure, he nearly took my breath! Come, I'll show you."

The curtain descends as Mr. and Mrs. Skunk bang their heads on rocks someone has put over their front door and they too, float off to Never-Never Land.

Chapter 33
The Man Who Drank
All the Chocolate Milk
in Hope, New Mexico

Remember the crossroads of Hope, Arizona? The town so small the "Welcome to Hope" and "You Are Now Beyond Hope" messages were written on the front and back of the same sign? Just kidding, Hopians, Hopefuls, Hope-persons.

Does every state have some kind of a Hope? Even, New Mexico has its own version. Small, really small. I arrived in Hope, New Mexico on a Sunday afternoon. I guess all towns are a little quieter on Sunday afternoons. But Hope couldn't be any quieter and still retain its dot on the map.

Hope was all I'd asked for. I didn't need tall buildings, libraries, museums, or Wal-Mart. I didn't even care if the streets were paved. Hope's gas station/grocery was my oasis. What existed in the surrounding sand was of little consequence.

And my desires were well-defined and well-honed. Once they locked in on the station/ grocery they carried me in their arms as they zeroed in on the drink cooler in the back. I blocked out everything except for my two preferred items — number one was chocolate milk, number two was Gatorade. It only took about three-tenths of a nanosecond for me to scan the entire cooler to determine if either, or (joy of joys) both were present. Sad to say there was no hope of Gatorade in Hope, and the milkman doesn't deliver on Sundays. Two pints of chocolate milk were all that peered back at me in Hope. They say a short horse is soon curried, and so goes it with chocolate milk in Hope.

The boy's lackadaisical reply to my Is-there-anymore-chocolate-milk inquiry told me I'd inhaled all there was to be had in Hope, whining wouldn't help.

Chapter 34
Scalpels and Dust Devils

Isn't "Artesia" a nice name for a town? Doesn't it sound like the neatest, cleanest place? Wouldn't Artesia have a large fountain in the town square that gushed thousands of gallons daily of the sweetest, coolest, purest mountain spring water? And Artesia would have a large, green, well-manicured park and everyone's lawn would be flowery and healthy and look like the seventeenth tee at Augusta. Artesia is like girls named Rebecca or Heather or Shawntel. You just know they're going to be pretty even before you lay eyes on them.

Artesia didn't quite deliver. An oil refinery is smack in the center, and it towers over and blankets Artesia with the awful pall of smoke and smell that goes cheek and jowl with the word refinery.

But Artesia's like the plain girl who is so sweet you love her nevertheless. I have fond memories of Artesia, refinery and all, and especially fond memories of the La Fonda Mexican Restaurant. I can't recall precisely what I ordered for the main course. More than likely it was the Big Hombre Sampler, or some such platter that had at least one of everything. I do remember downing mountains of tortilla chips with salsa.

I believe that the practice of placing a glass of water on the table in front of the diner at restaurants today is just a carry-over from a bygone day. But the custom must be on the way out because I've seen little signs on the tables, or small disclaimers at the bottom of menus that say, "Water served upon request." Even those restaurants that automatically bring water bring it in token-sized glasses.

So, it was refreshing to see how The La Fonda Mexican Restaurant in Artesia, New Mexico dealt with the water/no water situation. On each table was a giant pitcher of ice water. The La Fonda hierarchy obviously understood the elements in play here in eastern New Mexico.

On one side of their door you have the great New Mexican outdoors — 'nuff said. And on the other side of that door is a Southwestern Mexican restaurant. Each table has a giant pitcher of water on the table – any questions?

There was one person at my table and one full pitcher. That was at the beginning. At the end there was still one person and one pitcher, but no water. And water wasn't even my drink with that meal. Iced tea is what I drank. I lost count of the number of glasses.

Just outside Artesia I had a strange dust-devil experience. Most everyone has seen them, tiny tornadoes of dust. When conditions are right they occur even in cities. They're much more prevalent in the desert Southwest and they can get pretty big, too. I doubt they'd suck a person up but maybe a cat. And you could definitely lose your hat. Or in a really big one the cat in the hat (just a joke.)

I sat down beside the road one afternoon to rest and write some postcards. I had no warning. Suddenly there was a rush of wind, my eyes filled with dust and just before I was blinded I saw my postcards and one of my precious bandannas being whipped high into the air. They were being carried across a barbed wire fence and far out onto a cattle range. I watched as best I could through gritty eyes, thinking if they came down in a reasonable time and distance I'd go retrieve them. It wasn't to be. This devil ate my bandanna and postcards.

If you've ever walked down the highway for any distance you know that you're always finding things. Sure, 99% of it is trash, but occasionally you'll find something worthwhile. The day after the dust devil episode I found something I carried for the rest of my walk.

I noticed something shiny lying about five yards off the road. I went to check it out and discovered they were blades for a surgeon's scalpel. At least that's my opinion. I've never really seen a surgeon's scalpel and can only guess that the blades are replaceable. They were sealed in aluminum foil. I hadn't started out carrying a knife on my walk but I could see how one might come in handy and these blades seemed just the ticket. They were compact and sealed so I thought them worth taking along. They served me well on several occasions and I never gave them much thought until I had to ride in a police car (Don't start imagining things. It isn't what you're thinking.) I'll explain when we get to that point.

Chapter 35
It Had to be Told — The Baseball in the Bottom

I was closing in on Texas and the heat was becoming oppressive. I wondered if Texas held something more devastating, more ravaging than even California, Arizona and New Mexico had.

Standing on the threshold of Texas I was reminded (several times on this walk I was reminded) of a story I read in a book called *The Walk West* by Peter and Barbara Jenkins. They walked from New Orleans to the coast in Oregon.

It's my favorite "It was so hot in Texas...How hot was it Johnny?" story.

Barbara told about going into a laundromat in Texas. She was desperately hot and felt sweaty, gritty, and dirty to boot. The laundromat restroom had a toilet, but no sink nor any other water. Barbara was desperate beyond caring. She screwed up her courage, flushed the commode several times, then scooped the water out of the bowl with her hands and splashed it on her face.

I told you that, yes, you too, would drink a half empty Pepsi from atop a fence post and eat garlic pizza off the road. And whether you believe it or not, you'd splash water on your face from a toilet bowl.

I never bothered people I saw puttering around in their yards unless I was forced to by extreme thirst. I knew I was harmless, but they didn't know that. I knew they'd be standoffish and reticent and generally not in the mood to mess with me. So, I only forced myself upon them if driven by thirst, and on that rare occasion hunger.

I've talked a lot about the heat. And I feel like the boy yelling wolf sometimes. I'm afraid you'll become hardened to my heat miseries. So, I'll back off a little. It gets worse, and when the time comes I want you to feel the torture of Texas.

Let me say one other thing about the heat, then I'll move on. In addition to the discomfort that heat causes, it robs your body of moisture. Most people know that, but can't really identify because they've always had adequate liquid to offset the dehydrating effects of heat. When you don't have that liquid your body shifts to code red. That's the situation I found myself in between Artesia and Hobbs, New Mexico.

This area is dotted with oil wells.

Remember those plastic birds on long legs in the backs of car windows, the kind that always seem to be bobbing for a drink of water? That's what came to mind when I looked at oil wells. Up and down, never ending. Some were almost silent and others had a rhythmic click or clang or squeak. Depending on your mood, the rhythmic clicks or squeaks were either soothing or as nerve-rattling as a barking dog.

It was normal to see men travelling the highways whose jobs were to maintain or perpetuate the oil gathering business. They included men in the white-collared shirts, men in the blue-collared shirts, and men in white T-shirts without collars. The "T-shirt men," were covered with the oil and grease. Most of the men were Mexican. They traveled in trucks with uncovered flat beds strewn with tools needed for the jobs and assorted old parts covered with the oil and grease–always the oil and grease.

In the late afternoon one of the trucks that was going the same direction as I slowed and stopped. The driver said they'd seen me on their way to work that morning. After the usual, what-are-you-doing-way-out-here questions, the driver said, "We've got some baloney and cheese sandwiches left over from lunch, would you like to have them?"

If you've stuck with me this far, I don't need to go through how I felt. The workers were on their way home to Hobbs, New Mexico after a day in the oil fields. They were gracious and interested in me but I could tell they wanted to be on their way.

After they had left I sat down on the sand beside the road and as slowly as I could make myself do it, enjoyed the bologna and cheese sandwiches chased with three cans of root beer.

Yes, heat does two things to your body? First, and most obviously, it causes burning discomfort to your skin. Everyone has experienced it and it needs no explanation. But heat has a second effect on your body. One less obvious, but maybe more insidious than the burning discomfort. Heat causes you to sweat (duh) and if you don't drink enough your body becomes dehydrated. Obviously a dangerous situation if not corrected in a reasonable time.

It was that night, just before dark, that I realized I was in a state close to dehydration.

Soon after I'd finished the sandwiches and root beer I came to a large culvert running under the road. It was the usual dangerous but inviting place to spend the night–concealment and a soft place for a bed, in exchange for the danger of flash flooding, rattlesnakes, scorpions, and tarantulas. I read somewhere that the creatures of the desert Southwest include twelve snakes, the Gila monster, the scorpion, and a couple of spiders. Most could make you sorry you invaded their turf or culvert, as the case may be.

Some of these culverts are quite large and like this one only require a slight bend at the waist to enter.

I had made my bed and was about to call it a day when nature called. And this was the more serious version of the nature call if you get my drift. No sweat, I thought, just my body saying it needed to make room for those bologna and cheese sandwiches. I went outside the culvert, dropped my pants, and squatted — nothing. I strained — nothing. I strained hard — nothing!

It didn't take long for me to see this was serious business. I felt like I wanted to go, needed to go, but nothing was happening.

This will sound gross, but I believe under the circumstances anyone would have reacted as I did. I felt to see what the problem was. It was apparent. There wasn't enough water in my system to lubricate and moisturize. My lower bowel was dry and impacted.

What to do? I was pacing back and forth in misery, my pants at my ankles. It hurt — hurt bad. My body was giving me the pain signals to make me do something for it.

So, (here comes gross again) I did the only thing I could think of under the circumstances.

The circumstances being I was alone in the desert, under the road in a culvert, miles and miles from anywhere. I took my finger and tried to pry the impaction out. No luck. It felt like I had a baseball stuck there. I tried straining and prying at the same time until I realized if I didn't quit something else might give way and burst and then I'd be in even more trouble or dead. I gave up and lay down on my "bed." Finally the pain relented some and I drifted off to a fitful sleep.

Maybe during the night the three cans of root beer realized that they had a humanitarian mission to fulfill and went to work. The next morning with a push worthy of a mother hippo giving birth, the problem was solved.

Chapter 36
Texas — The Bigger Apple

The next day I experienced something few people will experience in their lifetime. It was an eerie thing, producing feelings of awe, vulnerability and a little apprehension.

Picture yourself being the only person on earth. It's a bit disconcerting, isn't it? A little frightening. It makes you realize we are social creatures. We may get really tired of people, but pretend there aren't any other people. It can bring to play some strong emotions, can't it? And those emotions ran quickly through me on my last day in New Mexico.

There's one big difference between what I experienced and what I asked you to picture, though. I asked you to picture everyone gone as if they really were.

On a small rise in the New Mexico desert everyone was gone, but I knew they really weren't.

I suppose I should define "rise." That may be a southern term like "grits." A rise is a very small hill. Maybe "hump" would be a better word. If you wanted to get a 360 degree look at the surrounding countryside a rise would do the job nicely.

On this New Mexico afternoon, I topped a rise and could see in all directions for as far as my eyes would let me. There was no evidence of any other human on earth. No house, barn, car, electric lines, airplanes, man-made noise. I felt as if I was the only person on earth.

But what I felt wasn't a rush of desperation at the thought of being the last person on earth. What I felt was vulnerability. I may have felt alone but I knew there were 260-plus million in this country to keep me company but I still felt defenseless. What if someone came along with thoughts of doing me harm.

A few hundred yards later, the evidence of man prevented itself. And even though I'd chosen to take this walk alone, I was glad for the company once again.

"Welcome to Texas." Boy, that sign created one emotion quickly followed by another. At first I was elated to have reached this milestone of another state line, and one so significant as Texas. Secondly, though, thoughts came to mind about Texas and its bigness that I'd heard since childhood: "We drove for days. I thought we'd never get across!" When people talk about Texas they feel it's their right and privilege to stretch the truth. Haven't we all seen that postcard with the cowboy riding the giant jackrabbit? It goes with the territory. Stretch or not, there had to be a grain of truth to it. And it hit me harder when I looked down I didn't see a gas pedal. All I saw was a couple of ol' size 9s.

There was a convenience store on the state line so I went in for my obligatory chocolate milk celebration.

I told the man behind the counter that this was a big moment for me, and I knew instantly we weren't on the same wavelength. By now I was used to that what-are-you-some-kind-of-nut look.

He got to use that look a second time when I followed with "Are there anymore eat/drink places on up the road?"

People seemed to take delight in saying, "Eat or drink?!" Hell, threre's nothing for 40 miles!"

There was *something* up the road that lifted my spirits — a real rest area with trees and grass. It had been forever since I'd seen either.

I grew up in Kentucky and was accustomed to hills. At age 39 I moved to Tennessee and lived next to the Great Smoky Mountains National Park so I got used to mountains. Well, they're called mountains by Tennesseans but someone from Colorado might dispute that call. Danged big hills, though, I'd say.

If you've known hills all your life and travel to a different area, say Kansas, and that place has no hills, after about three days you begin to feel weird, and at first you can't put your finger on why. It's a feeling that something's not exactly right. Then it dawns on you: there aren't any hills.

It would be true in reverse, too. I've heard of people who lived all their lives in Kansas, and they felt uneasy when they visited a state that had lots of hills. They feel hemmed in, even claustrophobic.

So, it was nice to see grass and trees in Texas. Kind of a cruel joke, though, because the rest area had the only greenery there would be for many weeks.

This may seem an insignificant thing but it buoys your spirits to be walking toward a town with a nice sounding name. It connotes pleasure.

My first two Texas towns were Seminole and Lamesa. Wouldn't you feel better about walking toward Seminole or Lamesa than walking toward Sylvester, Georgia or Dothan, Alabama?

Poor Seminole couldn't escape the clutches of Sam Walton. I shrugged and decided to go in and see if I could replace the bandanna the dust devil had eaten.

It was nearing dusk when I came out and since Seminole was to be a money drop anyway I decided not to leave town. I slept behind the Wal-Mart.

The next day I visited the post office. The money hadn't arrived yet so I headed out of town with the intention of hitchhiking back in a day or two when the money arrived.

For the past several nights I had been awakened during the night by thunder and lightning far in the distance, but it hadn't rained. At one of my chocolate milk/Gatorade stops I'd mentioned it to the lady clerk.

"Oh, it's just "heat lightnin'."

I wasn't sure what she meant, but assumed it was a local or regional phenomena that wasn't that unusual.

That night I was about halfway between Seminole and Lamesa. Since I'd left Los Angeles the only rain I'd seen was about 25 drops in Alamogordo so it was easy for me to be lulled into a misconception about electrical storms. It's dumb, I know, but I just supposed they had "heat lightning" but it was far off and never brought rain.

As was often the case in the Southwest the nights were so warm you could sleep outside with no more covering than the clothes you'd been wearing during the day. So, this night my bed simply consisted of my ground cover, my sleeping pad and my open sleeping bag at my feet in case the air got chilly toward morning. My sleeping bag would unzip all the way and make a blanket.

I was awakened again by distant thunder and lightning. I ignored it and went back to sleep. Sometime later I felt a drop, then two, then ten. I still dismissed it and didn't bother to get up and put up my tent.

I think you get the picture. I've snapped the shutter and the print is ready to come out of the developing tray. The heavens opened and I went into my heat conserving fetal position in a futile attempt to keep warm.

Before I could employ defensive maneuvers, I was soaked to the skin and then some. And I'd violated that supreme survival law about always having one dry outfit as a safeguard against deadly hypothermia.

What could I do? Everything was soaked and I had no idea how many hours it was until daylight and some hope of heat from the sun. Then I remembered — my ground cover was really a space-age survival blanket designed to keep body heat in. It wasn't big so I had to twist and tuck to get it around me. And "survival blanket" means just that. No one ever said toasty and dry. It not only keeps your body heat in, it also keeps your perspiration in. So you stay survival warm, but also wet and clammy.

We all have nights when you sleep so well you feel your head has no more than hit the pillow before the alarm goes off. Then we all have the other kind. If you can't sleep for some reason, the night can seem endless.

Dawn is dull, gray, cool, and windy. Inside is the only place to be. There were no "insides" for this walker. I realized it wasn't something that could be shrugged off or toughed through. I *had* to find someplace dry and warm.

Black, Mexican, Mexican, Black; it happened again! I can only say I started the walk apprehensive of Mexicans and Blacks, and yet 90 percent of the kindnesses shown me were by Mexicans and Blacks. Prejudices had blurred reality. It would be such a better world if we could see past our prejudices and just see a fellow human being. As Michael Jackson said in one of his songs, "To make a change, start with the man in the mirror."

I was caught in the vast Texas outback alone, wet and cold with only one way out. I walked to the road and stuck out my thumb. Reality is serious and powerful stuff sometimes. It can push fears and prejudices way back to the back of the picture. If Godzilla had stopped and offered me a ride, I'd have kissed his scaly feet. I was in dire straits and knew it. Hypothermia will not let you take it lightly.

The car that stopped held two Mexican men. Words can't adequately describe my feelings of joy. Though I felt a twinge of remorse as I saw what my muddy shoes were doing to the back floorboard of their Oldsmobile.

If they'd been wearing T-shirts that said, "Serial Killer" and "Ax Murderer" respectively I'd still have been glad to be sitting in that warm dry car. But they were wearing suits and this was a Sunday morning. The Bible lying on the dash helped, too. I pictured preachers, churches, prayers and peace.

The two men said little to me. It was as if picking up someone on the road was the natural thing to do. Was it just them or God again rescuing this fool? Let's give credit to both.

I sat numbly enjoying being in that car. Too soon we came to the town of Lamesa. I knew I had to get out though I wanted to ride in the car until it was warm and sunny again.

Luckily, just around the corner from the convenience store where I chose to get out, there was a laundromat. I stripped down to the barest modicum of decency and threw everything in the dryer.

In most parts of the country the rain scenario usually plays out thusly: A steady buildup of clouds during the day, followed by a thundershower of a relatively short duration in the late afternoon. But Texas hasn't read the script. And I suppose Texas has to live up to its Bigger-Better billing. Nothing just *happens* in Texas. They don't just have an afternoon shower. In Texas they have storms. I'd bet if you could harness the energy released by one Texas storm you could light Dallas for a month. Texas storms seem out to get you. With Texas lightning it's personal. It booms and crashes right over your head. And it goes on for hours and sometimes days. I had never known such storms as I saw in Texas.

When I came out of the laundromat it was still raining. I just didn't have the heart to fight the rain and start back to the point where the Mexicans had picked me up.

I spotted a motel across the street. A port in a storm. I deserved to take a day off. Texas would win today. I'd lick my wounds under the security of a real blanket and roof. Let the storm fight with someone else.

It was escapism at its best. A bed with covers, a shower, even a television. Not that it was the Ritz. It was a thirteen dollar motel room with an overgrown bush outside the door that made it necessary to take a giant step to cross the threshold.

There were a few cars out back that looked as if they were being used to attempt more desert travel against their wishes. Hoods were raised seemingly in an effort to resurrect life, but the cars looked old, dusty and very tired. I noticed that the gutter sagged in more than one place. Just one more of the walking wounded in the great Texas storm wars.

When the owner took my thirteen dollars he said, "I've had the exterminator in, but if you see any bugs let me know." Translation: You're liable to see anything in any quantity, so be forewarned. It was luxurious to me but you have to understand this is from a man who had only slept in two beds since leaving the beach in California. I'd say ninety percent of the American public wouldn't set foot in the door. It was a $13 motel — not a $113 motel. It fit my needs perfectly. It sheltered me from a classic Texas storm.

It wasn't until the next afternoon that the skies had cleared enough for me to head back to the point where I left off. I walked to the edge of Lamesa and extended my thumb.

It took a long time to get a ride out of Lamesa. And the two young dudes in the pickup truck who stopped surely didn't look like preachers.

I decided to go all the way back to Seminole with them to see if my money from Gus had arrived. I rode in the back of the truck, they rode in the front. When they stopped to let me out in Seminole, they had combined their monetary resources and some groceries and shoved them all at me as they pulled away. With the gifts there was a wish that God would bless me. Seventeen dollars and food for someone they hadn't spoken a word to or would ever see again. God is good. All is right with the world and Texas.

It had taken most of the day to hitchhike back to Seminole, go to the post office to pick up my money and walk to the edge of Seminole to try and catch a ride to the original spot between Seminole and Lamesa where I'd gotten soaked and all this mess started.

It was getting late and if dark caught me my chances of getting a ride would take a sharp nosedive. Just as I reached the outskirts of Seminole a place to spend the night presented itself. Of course, I had seen it on my first walk through Seminole a couple of days before but it hadn't registered because I wasn't looking for a place to stay just then. This time it jumped out at me. Most people could pass it a hundred times and never consider it a place to spend the night. Some nights I wouldn't either. I know you're wondering what difference it would make what night it was. Let me give you an example of why some places are good on certain days of the week but not on others.

If it's your business to be on the lookout for a place to camp each night, and that place has to be free, halfway comfortable, and as out-of-sight as possible, then you look at things with a practiced eye. You see things in an entirely different light. You soon learn that churches, better yet, country churches, fill all your needs. They aren't without catches though, and "day of the week" is their catch. Let's take Saturday night. That's out because even though there may not be anything happening at the church on Saturday night, there sure will be on Sunday morning. And though most likely you'll be up and gone before anyone arrives at the church it's a chance you can't take. Sunday night most country churches have some kind of service. Monday — great, perfect. Tuesday — ditto. Wednesday — prayer service, so you can forget Wednesday unless you want to sit in the woods until all the cars are gone. Thursday — probably the best church camping night. Friday — iffy, but if it's cold, rainy and dark, worth a chance. And more than likely you'll be gone before that good parishioner shows up on Saturday to mow the lawn anyway.

But it wasn't a church I was eyeing as I approached the outskirts of Seminole. And it wasn't the first time I'd stayed at one of these places. I'd learned about them on other expeditions. It was a drive-in theater. Picture it. (Sometimes I can't help myself.) Not only are most not open every day but lots of them are out of business, period. They all have a big fence around them to discourage freebies and you know there'll be grass somewhere. How do you know it's going to be closed on the night when you're standing there eyeing it with sleep on your mind. You have to be there at the right time of day. Too early in the afternoon and you have no idea unless "closed" is on the marquis. But if it's dusk, you know there's going to be some activity if there's going to be a movie tonight. Lovebirds will be arriving or the popcorn popper will be there.

I admit the signs aren't as easy to read for drive-in's as they are for country churches, but if you're looking for a place to spend the night they must be read in rather short order. I was convinced this drive-in was closed.

The next morning I was given a ride back to the spot between Seminole and Lamesa where this all started. I got a ride with one of the last American cowboys. You know the type — ten-gallon hat, high-heeled boots, jeans and a belt with a big silver buckle, a chaw in the jaw, and a rugged, lawless manner real or imagined. No horse, though. The horse has been replaced by a Cummins diesel and 18 wheels.

This trucker was an "independent." Independents own their rigs and aren't shackled to a big company and its tight structure. Company policy may forbid picking up hitchhikers but these guys are their own bosses.

As we bounced along I thought it was a good opportunity to get an opinionated rise from my benefactor.

"Do you view yourself as the last American cowboy or just a vanishing breed?"

A quick roll down of the window, a snap back of the head, and a stream of amber Red Man was sent out to moisturize the Texas countryside. The window glass bore streaked evidence of many ill-delivered attempts.

With the window back up and a clear throat the driver sat for a second as if I hadn't said a word. But I could see wheels turning.

"Oh, the big boys'll squeeze us independents out eventually. We're sort of a burr under their saddle. We've got the desire but as in everything the clout goes with the money. They'll find a way to regulate us out of business. The companies can make up margins with volume. They can shave corners that would kill us."

"What'll you do if you can't make it trucking?"

"I grew up ranchin' but with cattle prices the way they are those guys are hangin' on by their fingernails, too. You ask what I'd do and it's really kinda scary to think about it. My uncle's got a hardware store in Lubbock and he'd probably find a place for me but I'd hate the thought of hardware and the city, too."

I kinda felt sorry for opening up the wound.

The trucker was a proud man, happy at what he did. I got the feeling that the thoughts I brought up were often brought up by the trucker himself when he was alone and had nothing to keep them at bay.

When he stopped to let me out, I thanked him with real meaning. But I did that each time someone showed me a kindness. This time I added something to the thanks. As I shut the door I said, "I wish the best for you." And I meant it.

I enjoyed my double-clutchin', gear-jammin', spittin' out the window cowboy-philosophizing ride back to my gotta-start-walkin-again spot between Seminole and Lamesa.

The end of the rain, the warm but not-yet-hot sun, made it feel good to again be walking. Late that afternoon I passed through Lamesa for the second time. I smiled as I passed my thirteen dollar motel.

I felt I was descending the comfort ladder as I prepared to make my bed that night between Lamesa and Snyder, the next town to the east. First it had been the soft bed at the motel in Lamesa, then it was the grass behind the high fence of the drive-in theater at Seminole, and now it was going to be a rock-pile.

The countryside between Lamesa and Snyder was flat and featureless and finding a place to hide seemed like it was going to be a problem.

At first I couldn't make out what the big pile was beside the road. Apparently it was rock for roadbuilding. I'd say if you stacked, no, not stacked but dropped ten Greyhound buses from a giant helicopter, you'd approximate the size of this pile.

When I first walked over to the pile my thoughts were to use it only as a shield from eyes passing by on the road. It was then that I noticed that the rocks were black, smooth and rounded, not jagged, gray rocks like gravel roads are usually made of. Still the idea of spending the night on the rocks didn't occur to me until I had the boyish notion to climb to the top. If I was going to spend the night on the ground behind the pile why not have some fun playing on it while I was waiting for the sun to go down? On my way to the top I noticed that the rocks moved and conformed to the shape of my foot as I stepped on them. I'd long known if you were going to sleep on the ground you could gain comfort by scooping a shallow depression for your shoulders and hips. The rocks molding to the imprint of my foot made a light go on in my head. This would be just like sleeping on a waterbed — a hard waterbed — better than the hard ground. The rock pile turned out to be one of my favorite sleeping memories of the trip.

The next day I was walking through Snyder, Texas when a cub reporter stopped me. Snyder was big enough to have paved streets, sidewalks and of course, the ubiquitous McDonald's and Wal-Mart. Must have had a newspaper too because the reporter asked my opinion about a recent incident that had been reported in the paper. When I explained my *raison d'etre* he filled me in so I could voice my opinion.

Seems a spouse abuser had been shot and killed and the abusee had been given five years probation as a sentence. This must have caused some community uproar else why would the reporter be out soliciting opinions?

I told him without all the facts it was hard to pass judgment and that anything I said would only be opinion but I did believe that without just cause a person who takes another's life should pay very dearly. I'm sure the victim's life was very dear to them. There are lots of extenuating circumstances but I feel murder isn't justifiable in most cases of abuse. Murder is only justifiable if the person being abused can stand before God and man and say they thought they were going to be killed. Otherwise they should flee the abusive situation. I did add that anyone who takes someone's life with careless disregard, drunken driving being a good example, should lose theirs also.

The town square in Snyder has a life-sized statue of a white buffalo. Next to it was a historical marker. I'm a sucker for historical markers and my interest was piqued by the white buffalo. What it said was historical — but depressing and not very humane. In essence the marker said that near Snyder a rare Albino buffalo had been killed along with 22,000 (who was counting?) other buffalo. One man (I don't remember his name) was the doer of the deed.

I respect the fact that an albino buffalo is rare and mention of it is worthy. But, is the fact that one man killed 22,000 admirable? Small wonder the millions that once roamed the United States were reduced to a handful before some intelligent and brave person said, "Enough!"

Chapter 37
The Near Fatal Slip
and Thunder in the Hogshed

East of Snyder was farmland. Really the first I'd seen since California. Big fields? The county I live in would fit in one of their fields. Not literally true but I want to impress upon you that these were <u>big</u> fields.

It must have been between crops because the land had been plowed and disked and nothing was growing for miles. This created a problem for me in two ways: First, if it was dry the Texas wind (Yes, it's Texas-sized too) whipped across those fields and started dust clouds rolling. The red dust was thick and looked like a boiling pot. The thought of one engulfing me was scary. Secondly, If it wasn't dry it had to be wet (duh) and wet created a problem, a big problem for me. At least once it nearly took my life.

I was east of Snyder one morning when I began hearing that rumble that no hiker ever wants to hear. And just like everything else in Texas, they were big rumbles. I looked over my shoulder and the sky was ugly and black. I didn't see that I had any choice but to keep on keeping on. This was Texas farmland. There were no trees. And I got the feeling if you wanted to build a house, a barn, or even a doghouse you'd better have a good reason. Farmland it was and farmland it would stay. Deviate from that and you could well be handed a ticket to Fort Worth.

The first drops didn't concern me much. I figured I'd just have to walk on through the rain. It was definitely warm so I thought I'd just pretend I was a kid again and my mother had let me go out and play in the rain. I stopped and dug from my pack the only rain defense I had. And a pitiful defense it was. It was an Army poncho I had bought at a yard sale for fifty cents. Though I came to hate this poncho for it uselessness, I have to defend the military equipment on the whole for its quality, dependability and forethought. From my Navy days I knew that the American Fighting Man wasn't asked to put up with any garbage. Military equipment is good stuff — one man's opinion.

I have an idea how the equipment may have gotten good: an overprotective mother.

My first clue was when I was in Navy boot camp in San Diego. Our boot camp instructor told us that everyone had to go through the chow line. You didn't have to eat but you did have to go through the line. From bits and pieces of what he said I concluded that somewhere in the Navy's past, some whiny kid had complained to his mother that he was hungry, or the Navy wasn't feeding him right or something silly to that effect. And that mother had whipped off a scathing letter either to her congressman or maybe even the commander-in-chief, expressing her horror that her darling was being deprived of the nourishment he so rightfully deserved.

But what is, or isn't, the relationship between little Johnny's precious stomach, good military equipment and crummy ponchos? Well, I just think somewhere along the line some other mother complained that her son's shoes, rifle, airplane, underwear, _____ (fill in the blank) was substandard and that she'd fight tooth and nail and start a letter-writing campaign to end all letter writing campaigns if her son wasn't provided with the best equipment known to man.

How did Army ponchos slip through the cracks? I can only guess that the right sniveling little brat hasn't written to the right overprotective mother.

What's wrong with Army ponchos? First, if you haven't beaten the first rain drops by at least a minute your butt is as good as wet. It takes at least that long to figure out how to put it on. And even if you get it on in time you're still gonna get wet. It's the rare rain that isn't accompanied by wind. And wind renders the poncho virtually useless. Even a moderate wind can whip the poncho around like a sail and it's as likely to be on top of your head or wrapped around your neck as hanging down around your body where it should be.

That black Texas storm bearing down on me must have been rubbing its hands with glee. "What an innocent, tasty little morsel this is going to be." it must have said.

Before I put on my poncho I had thought about just walking this one out. At that time I was warm and the drops hadn't begun to multiply and things didn't seem to be too bad. All that changed and soon I was wet and worried. Just ahead I spotted a culvert under the road. I investigated and it seemed big enough for me if I stooped over. This wasn't one of those big round, corrugated metal culverts. It was a square concrete one with a concrete floor. I dropped down the road bank and walked back into the culvert.

"This was a God-send," I thought.

No matter if it sloped off to the other side of the road at about a 30 degree angle and I had trouble keeping my footing. It was dry and I could wait out the storm here.

I mentioned that this was the land of gigantic fields and one of them was on the side of the culvert where I had gotten in. The elevation of the field was just a little higher than the road. After I'd stooped and entered the culvert I turned around to look out at the storm. It was then that I realized this one culvert must serve as a sort of storm drain for the humongous field, which was just fine loose dirt. Nothing alarming registered at this point because I thought that this would be a short-lived rain.

Instead of easing, it seemed to strengthen and in only minutes the rivulets of water coursing their way down through the muddy field were converging and heading for my culvert.

As the water came in and covered the soles of my shoes I propped my walking stick at an angle behind me to brace myself from the steep, downward angle of the culvert. It was hard to get a grip on the now wet concrete. Some mossy growth, now with water rushing over it, was making the concrete floor as slick as, well, moss-covered concrete.

My mind flashed back to a kayaking adventure I once had back in Tennessee. It was at the end of a day's paddling and I was going ashore to camp on the bank. I'd pulled alongside a concrete boat ramp, the kind you back your car down to launch the boat. By design and necessity part of the ramp is always under water and algae and other mosses love it there. I sidled my kayak up to the ramp thinking how nice it was going to be getting out on concrete instead of mud. No sooner had I transferred my weight to that outboard foot than I was looking straight up at the blue Tennessee sky. When I finally re-oriented my head, butt and feet, I put my foot down again; thinking this time I'd be careful. Big — 175-pound splash. Quicker than I could even begin to think what was happening I was looking bottom feeders in the eye.

Finally I put the kayak's bowline between my teeth and prayed no one was around to see me as I crawled inch by inch up the ramp on my hands and knees.

So I knew the potential for slippage on this water-covered concrete under the highway.

But even when the water had risen over the tops of my boots, my only thought was for my boots.

At first water wasn't racing through the culvert. I could judge its speed by the occasional twig or broomstraw that floated toward me.

Soon though, the water began to pick up speed and its color darkened as more dirt was being carried down from the field. Now the water had a definite rush about it, and the sound began to alarm me.

My back was killing me from having to stay bent over. When the water had been only shoe-top deep, I could squat and give my back some relief. Now that it was groin deep I was forced into a navel contemplating posture. If I tried to squat I was in danger of losing my balance and toppling over backward.

Soon my crotch was forming a small dam for the rushing water. It couldn't get around or under me fast enough. There was definite pressure against my legs and lower body. I looked out about four feet in front of me and saw a giant black spider twirling out of control but still on his feet atop the brown water. A quick triangulation of speed, direction and force told me this creature was dead on line for my fly. I knew spiders ate flies! Sure enough, he grabbed hold with all eight legs at the point I least would have wanted him to grab. I froze. But after a second I realized he had his own problems. Survival topped eating at this moment. I couldn't spare a hand to swat at him and my spit sailed right past him and was lost in the swirl. After I'd spit and missed several times it dawned on me how ludicrous the act was. If you, or a spider, are clinging to life, a little spit is not going to dislodge you. It occurred to me how helpless I'd be if he gained enough foothold and started climbing toward my face.

My prayers must have been answered. Just as the spider sensed he'd latched on to something solid and instinctively started his upward journey, a surge, from where I do not know, suddenly rose and caught the spider, loosening his grip on me, and sending him roaring past me.

I braced my back against the side of the culvert so I could look behind me and see what was happening to all the water rushing under, around and through me. I was still wearing my pack that was covered by the poncho, and when I tried to turn my head the hood of the poncho blocked my vision. I couldn't pull it away because both hands were doing bracing duty with the walking stick. When I was finally able to see behind me I was aghast. All the water was rushing down the slope and creating a churning cauldron at the lower end of the culvert.

It took me less than a second to realize that if I lost my footing, or the water rose much more, with this heavy pack and a poncho over my head, they'd find me a week later, face down in the pool at the bottom of the culvert. That is if someone got curious about all the buzzards. I knew I had to get out of this culvert. I also knew I couldn't do anything rash. I had to slowly, deliberately inch myself out. If I slipped the prognosis was gloomy.

It wasn't easy forcing myself out against waist-deep rushing water on slippery, angled concrete. I knew every move had to be slow and measured. If I pushed against the walking stick it was imperative that it was solidly planted. The boat ramp in Tennessee had told me how quickly my feet could go out from under me and there were much greater stakes here than the embarrassment of falling. No one would see me under this culvert.

The water was chest deep now and making each movement count and controlling the urge to panic were vital. The culvert that had been a savior was now a death trap.

I braced hard with my walking stick then tried to move one foot forward. Each slow step covered no more than six inches. I was scared. I'm not ashamed to admit it. It's sobering when you realize whether you live or die is entirely in your hands.

Finally, I was out in the open again and clawing my way back up the bank to the highway. Texas lightning never looked so good.

But I wasn't out of the woods yet. I was totally soaked, the wind felt cold, and lightning cracked all about me.

I tried to remember where I'd seen the last house or barn. I thought there had been a house not too far back. I decided to start back thinking something known, even far back, was better than the unknown which lay ahead.

I walked up to the door of the farmhouse and was greeted on the porch by a collie with a passel of pups. The dog never barked. She seemed glad to see me. It's as if she was saying, "No one pays me any attention and these pups are driving me crazy." I knocked politely several times. Nothing. Then I banged impolitely until it was obvious the dog family was the only family home.

I walked around back to check out the barn. I was thankful the dog family stayed on the porch. I was the only one I wanted to cope with just now. I slid the door back on the metal shed. The noise the door made brought shuffling and grunting noises from inside. Sounded like hogs to me, but if it had sounded like water buffalo or hippo or striped hyenas, it wouldn't have deterred me. Again, on this walk I found myself in a desperate situation calling for immediate action.

I was pleased to see that the hogs didn't have the run of the whole barn. They had a section of their own. I noticed a door to the left and opened it. Behind the door was a room that looked like it had been a fort or playroom. I'm sure that wasn't its original intent but probably a father who remembered his boyhood and forts of his own had acquiesced to his son. It looked as if the son had long ago gone off to college or on to other barns and sons of his own.

Dust and the smell of the hogs was everywhere. Cobwebs and brown dust from the fields lay thick over everything like a scene from an old horror movie.

I guessed that the boy lost interest in his hideaway room not too long after he tacked up the pictures of the pretty women. They weren't particularly daring or revealing but indicated that the boys unasked for but inevitable and unstoppable stirrings within him were on the verge of taking him in the directions of drive-in movies and back seats of cars and away from "forts" in a barn.

If not warm, the room was at least dry, so it looked like I could wait out the storm in relative comfort. The comfort quotient was greatly increased when I noticed a large, square piece of thick foam rubber lying in one corner of the room.

I even got help from the military. *With God and the military for thee who can stand against thee?* Hanging on a nail was a dust encrusted, torn but dry and functional army field jacket. A dry, soft bed with covers — my cup runneth over.

I lay under the field jacket on top of the foam rubber bed for what seemed hours feeling totally immune to the still raging Texas storm outside.

I dried out, thought, napped and without wanting to, listened to hogs jostle, chomp, slurp and squeal. The drying, thinking and napping came and went, but the chomping, slurping and squealing seemed to go on forever.

I kept expecting the farmer to come into the barn to check on the hogs. If he did come in, there was no way I could show myself without startling him. One way or the other it would have to be done, though. So, I was really glad no one ever showed up.

The crazy storm continued unabated through the afternoon and all through the night. Occasionally I'd get up and look out the door to see if there was any sign of letup. I just couldn't believe it could go on for so long.

Luckily I had a little water and a few snacks, so it was almost enjoyable. It was dirty and smelly but after the culvert experience, dirty and smelly were easily offset by warm and dry.

It must have been two or three o'clock the next afternoon before I felt the rain and accompanying lightning and thunder were over.

I had a pen with me and scrounged around until I found a piece of cardboard. As legibly as I could, I wrote an explanatory note to the farmer. I know you're wondering why I would bother to leave a note when no one would know I'd been there. I guess it was because I was so happy his barn had been there when I so desperately needed it, that I felt I owed him a thank you.

My boots hadn't really dried out. So I just knew when I started walking they'd fall apart, or at the least produce some classic blisters. I was really happy when it became evident that neither was going to happen.

Within a few hours I came to a roadside park. It had a high chain-link fence around it.

The wind was blowing like crazy. The sun was out, though, and since most of my clothes were wet I decided I'd have to tackle that dreaded drying out process.

It never bothers you too much if your things are wet during the day. Unless, of course, you get cold and reach for something to put on. But when you really want things to be dry is when it's time to go to bed.

So often you have to pack things away wet in the mornings because of a rain during the night. Even a heavy dew can soak them more than you'd think. So it wasn't unusual to have to let them dry at the warmest part of the day. It was a bother, but it had to be done.

At the roadside park I pulled all the wet stuff from my pack and started spreading it out on the ground. It didn't take long to see that the wind wasn't going to let me do that. It would catch my clothes and roll them in a wad or spin them along the ground till the chain link fence stopped them. When I saw a shirt plastered to the fence it occurred to me that it might be the best solution after all. The wind was blowing so hard that all I had to do was spread a piece of clothing out close to the fence and the wind immediately grabbed it and plastered it against the fence. It was better than Maytag.

Chapter 38
The Possum Kingdom

In the weeks and months following the completion of my walk there was plenty of time for reflection about it. It was fun to reminisce about the good, the bad and the ugly in our dear ol' land.

I thought about all the towns. Which ones I really liked or disliked and why. It was odd that in all those cities and towns I could only come up with five or six I thought were neat. I don't know if it says something about me or about the towns. First, few have been able to resist strip malls, fast food joints, and the overpowering, all-encompassing discount stores. These things erase neat and interesting quite well for me.

In my opinion for a town to retain its beauty, grace, and charm it has to sometimes say no to progress. You'd think in 3,800 miles there'd be more than a handful I'd like. The day after the drying fence, I came to one.

If the opportunity presents itself take a look at Albany, Texas. I'm not going so far as to say Albany is still a virgin. It isn't frozen in the forties. It's just managed to hang on to more of the good qualities.

I've always associated the color white with neat and clean. And Albany still has white picket fences, a white church and steeple, white milk trucks, and white houses. I even went into a small grocery in Albany and the man behind the counter was wearing a white apron.

Albany had another quality that qualified it for my hall of fame — it was slow. A town can't be slow unless a certain percentage of people are out of their cars and walking. Of course, you'll see people walking in every town but the key word is percentage. How many hundred cars do you see for every person on foot. It warmed my heart to see a high percentage of people strolling about Albany.

My dream town also has to be friendly. Do those people walking down the street bury their chins in their chests, or do they greet each other with a genuine "Hi, how are you? Some weather, huh!" And the *real* test of a genuinely friendly town was if they greeted me with the same attitude.

Albany had one other small thing that helped secure its place in my mind: a sno-cone wagon. Where I grew up the only time you saw sno-cones was at the fair. But they aren't that uncommon in Texas and throughout the deep South. Seems all kinds of enterprising people, both young and old, have them a little shack or "rollin'-cone" (little shack on wheels) out next to the road. I passed by one in Albany and, though I wasn't in the mood at the time,

I read the big sign that listed all their flavors. One of the flavors was "dill pickle." Albany must surely have the pregnant lady market cornered.

As I walked on "dill pickle" was souring my enjoyment of the unique little town of Albany. I couldn't erase the thought from my mind. Finally I said, "I gotta go back." How many times in your life are you going to get the opportunity to experience a dill pickle sno-cone? Picture taking the juice out of a dill pickle jar and pouring it over crushed ice. I say, "Expectant mothers — Bon Apetit!"

A good place to put down hadn't presented itself, and it was getting dark. I came to a campground and, although it was my policy to not pay to sleep on ground that would be free just a little further down the road, tonight it seemed there was no alternative.

I saw no sign of life at the campground but noticed an open beer joint next to it. There was a sign saying, "Check at the tavern about campsites."

There's always life at a beer joint if your expectations aren't too high. As luck would have it the tavern owner was also the campground owner. As ingratiatingly as I could, I told my story.

Climbing aboard a stool in a bar was so foreign to me that I felt like a child at a 40's soda fountain. I knew the guy expected me to order some kind of beer but I said, "You don't have any coke, do ya?" My resolve nearly melted when he gave me that "What a weenie" look.

"I got some root beer, he half-heartedly said.

"You have any thing to eat?" I meekly asked.

"Pretzels is it," he replied but his back was already half turned to an episode of Cosby on television.

I sat with my pretzels and root beer in silence, except for the television.

After Cosby was over he flipped off the television and turned as if to see if he could milk any entertainment from me.

"You aren't from around here, are you?

"Well, no, I'm attempting to walk blah, blah, blah."

I was glad to see a spark ōf interest and some degree of softening in his eyes.

"No____!" he exclaimed. "You've got a danged good start," he said as he pushed back his sleeves and moved closer. "When did you start?"

"I left Huntington Beach at Los Angeles April the eighth.

Man, today's just June 15th and you're already halfway across Texas!"

He was relaxed now, leaning back against the cash register, arms folded, one foot propped up on a metal beer keg.

"When do you think you'll get to New York?"

"That's a tough one," say I. "These old dogs have given me a lot of trouble. I guess it depends on whether they hold out or not."

"I wish you all the luck in the world, but you wouldn't catch me walking down that highway. Not for a million bucks would I be out there."

"Why is that?"

"I think any bartender would tell you the same thing. Ninety-nine point nine percent of the people who come here come in a car. Odds are that nearly 50 percent of the people who leave here are going to be driving a car. I know there's a big push these days to make the bartender responsible for the wrecks caused by drunks, but that's just plain stupid. Sure, I'm not gonna sell liquor to a falling down drunk. But you've got people who'll want to stand up and lead the rest of the bar in a version of "When Irish Eyes are Smiling" after three Budweisers, and then you've got guys who could down a fifth of Vodka and quote you the Gettysburg Address. How the hell am I supposed to know whose capable of driving and who isn't? But I know for a fact, enough of them leave here driving in a condition that would scare the hell out of me if I was walking down the road like you are."

I wanted to ask how he felt about being out on the road in a car. Did he feel safe then, knowing what he knows? Weren't a large percentage of people in cars killed by drunk drivers, too?

Instead I shook my head in agreement and smiled sympathetically. I didn't want to argue any points with him. The only reason I came in was to try and secure a campsite. I intended to show complete agreement and not rile him in any way.

When he'd finished I said, "Yeah, you're right. I realize there's danger out there. I guess my only hope is to stay alert and be ready to jump."

He smiled and in a lowered and softened voice said, "Anyway, I admire you and wish you the best. You're a better man than me."

I could see it was advantage cross-country hiker, so I decided to try for match point.

"I usually just sleep off the road somewhere but it got dark on me tonight. Groping around trying to find a place isn't much fun. How much are your campsites?"

"Shoot, this time of year the campground doesn't pay its way nohow. Just go out there and pick you a spot. You don't owe me a thing."

Cha-ching. The Poor Pitiful Paul routine came through again.

By this time it was fully dark. For the first time in my walk I was approaching country that had a few lakes, and darkness meant it was time for the mosquitoes to report for work.

In the 50's there was a show called "Beat the Clock" where the contestant had to perform all kinds of kooky stunts within a certain time limit and always with a blindfold or both legs in a sack, etc.

That night I felt like a "Beat the Clock" contestant as I tried to put my tent up in the dark with one hand while fighting off a cloud of mosquitoes with the other.

Most people in the US have water near them — an ocean, a lake, river or creek. It's so natural you don't give it much thought. It's just there. No big deal.

In the Southwest, from the California coast to central Texas, people don't get excited about water either. But for completely different reasons. It's hard to get excited about something you've never seen. The concept is lost on them.

As I neared central Texas I began to sense some water excitement.

Campers pulling trailers with boats atop began to appear with more and more regularity as I moved eastward. They were filled with smiling, waving kids and inflatable rafts and umbrellas.

Billboards about cars or tires or cigarettes were replaced with billboards about jet skis, Mercury outboards and suntan lotion. Everyone on the billboards were laughing like they'd stumbled onto Shangri-La.

I knew something was up.

Nothing I'd seen thus far could elicit such joy. I looked at my map. Sure enough, I was approaching my first body of water you couldn't step across or drink at one sitting.

Why, though, with so much to celebrate, had the people given the place such a silly name? An object this precious should be called something golden, beloved, heavenly — not

"The Possum Kingdom Resort." Maybe in central Texas folks hold the possum in high esteem like the people in India do the cow.

Even so, you can imagine how nice it was to see my first big lake.

The lake came right up to the road. It was great! I was walking beside water for the first time since the Pacific Coast Highway.

I noticed a large steel-piped rack just off the road on the lake bank. I'd never seen anything like it. It looked as if it held up some kind of shelter. I decided it was a kind of drying rack. It had lots of ropes hanging from it, thick ropes, darker toward the ends, and from nearly all the ropes some large, strange object was hanging. If this hadn't been broad daylight with lots of traffic, this rack thing would have made me edgy. Looking as hard and long as I wanted I still couldn't make out what I was seeing. I was almost upon the rack before I could make it out — giant catfish heads!

I don't mean big catfish heads. These were giant catfish heads. I supposed they were hung there by proud, very morbid fishermen.

There were two men nearby on a little platform. It had a railing around it and a roof. It also had a waist-high shelf running the length of the side facing the lake. As I got closer I saw that this was the fish cleaning facility — "Possum Kingdom Catfish Auschwitz!"

One of the men was slicing a filet from the side of a large catfish. I felt so sorry for the fish. The man wasn't slicing down the side of a fish without a head, tail or guts; this was a live fish with a head, tail and guts trying its best to squirm away on the slimy, bloody, killing table. I hated to think of the sound if fish had the ability to make sound. It was an inhumane way to treat anything. It wasn't a tree or a rock. It was a living, breathing creature with nerve endings.

I turned away and headed down the road. I knew it was best not to voice my sentiments. Maybe I should have but I knew I was walking down the road alone.

Don't misunderstand. I'll eat a fish sandwich as quickly as the next, a hamburger, too, still I think if we are going to set ourselves up as lord and master over all other of God's creatures (a title I'm not sure we deserve) then at the very least we owe them a swift and dignified death.

Since the catfish can't make sound I'll speak for him and quote something I read that was spoken by a Jewish person as he stood facing certain death at the hands of a German officer during the holocaust: "You can take my life, but you can't take my dignity!"

Chapter 39
French Onion Chips, Skunk Cabbage, and Cow Manure

The next day I saw another example of one of God's creatures being robbed of its dignity.

I stopped at a small combination gas station/grocery store. I noticed a box of rattlesnake rattles on sale for fifty cents each. I thought that cheapened an animal that deserved better. No matter if you fear and hate them I didn't think they deserve to be degraded. Killing them for their rattles at only 50 cents each seemed a senseless waste when the good they do in rodent control far exceeds any harm they cause man. And selling their rattles at any price encourages people to kill them. It legitimized senseless slaughter.

No doubt I'll catch it from several sides for siding with rattlers. I want to think I'm defending the dignity of all life. I never could understand man's belief that it was his divine right to ride roughshod over the Earth and anything on it.

Texas seems to relish its reputation as bigger/best. After completely crossing it west to east I conclude that some of it is real, and some is imagined.

Muhammad Ali once said, "If you can do what you say you can, it ain't braggin'." And if a Texan says, "It gets hot here," it ain't braggin'.

At the time my experience with dehydration was limited to the time...well, you know. I didn't realize there were things happening that were pointing to dehydration.

One afternoon the heat was almost unbearable. It felt like a weight pressing down upon me. I thought it was just an extraordinarily hot day, now I know it's one of the early signs of dehydration.

That same day I began experiencing stage two of dehydration. And again I didn't recognize the signs. I was terribly thirsty and stopped at a little convenience store and drank my fill of Gatorade and chocolate milk. I drank till my thirst was completely appeased and my stomach looked like I'd swallowed a bowling ball.

But an hour down the road, the raging thirst was back again. Much too soon for me to be that thirsty again.

It was late afternoon in central Texas and all the signs were there. I'd drunk my fill and in no time I was extremely thirsty again.

I came upon a junkyard that was as classic as they come — rusted hulks of cars discarded after their glory days so they could be replaced by younger, prettier faces. Weeds living among the dead cars because they knew they weren't welcome in polite society, and the ever-present, always scratching, scroungy dog.

A man was working on something in the center of it all. Normally this scene would be no more than a curiosity, but thirst can make you do things you normally wouldn't do. Nothing to be ashamed of. Any and all of us would lie, cheat, and steal if our throats told us to. I veered off the road and headed straight for the man.

I expressed my need for drink and the junk yard owner sent his son (oh yes, every junk yard has rusty cars, horseweeds, itching dog *and* little dirty boys) to see if the "old lady" had any tea (the official junkyard drink) left from supper.

The boy came down from the house at a trot, jostling tea from a giant plastic glass. The boy had a serious look. Either he did exactly as he was told by his father with no nonsense allowed or my face and thirst said something about my need for liquid that I wasn't aware of.

I downed the tea pretty fast and as soon as I'd drained it the owner sent his son back up the hill for a refill, assuming without asking that I wanted more. I didn't really, but felt I should drink the second glass after making such a show about being thirsty.

As a courtesy and payment for the generosity I listened to the junk man, sitting on an inverted bucket, explain what it was he was working on. Seems he enjoyed buying, selling and tinkering with old one cylinder engines popular during the early part of the century. I think they ran combines or some other farm machinery. Probably they filled the gap between real horsepower and modern multi-cylinder engines.

"What's the favorite one you ever owned?" I asked.

"A 1932 John Deere, four stroke," he said. "Are you familiar with old John Deere engines at all," he continued.

"Yeah, a little I guess. I once had a 38-acre piece of ground back in Kentucky and I bought an old 1952 B John Deere to mow with."

He stood just long enough to pull out a knife and cut a plug from his tobacco. He slid it back in his lower jaw with a grease-blackened finger, arranged the car mat over the bucket on which he was sitting, and when he'd settled again said, "Then you know that sweet putt, putt, hesitation, putt, putt, putt sound they make when you idle 'um down."

"Oh yeah. When I was a little boy about ten or twelve I used to hang around on a farm owned by a friend of our family. He had an old "B" from the 40's with a hand clutch. Used to let me drive it to get the cows. I loved it. It was the reason I bought one after I married. There's nothing else like that sound."

"Yeah. I found this one in a box at an auction of old farm machinery up in Wichita Falls. It was in a hundred pieces but in mint condition. I think I was the only one there who had any idea what it was. Only one other guy bid, and I think he was buying it for scrap. I got the complete engine for 25 bucks. I couldn't wait to get back home and start puttin' her together. Jeez, she had a sweet sound."

"Still got it?" I ventured.

"It hurts me to say it but I sold it. Back in '84 the wife needed hip replacement. A guy over in Lubbock told me once if I ever wanted to sell it to give him first refusal. I called and told him my situation but that I wouldn't take a penny less than $2,500. Next day he was here with the cash."

Though I hadn't been at the junkyard that long, darkness was approaching and it was time to begin my daily search for my home for the night.

Why didn't I ask if I could spend the night among the junkyard horse weeds? I have slept and would sleep about anywhere, but this place was rugged, even for me.

As I left the junkyard I sensed that it would be a clear night and rain wouldn't be a problem. A couple of miles up the road I saw an open-air cattle barn about 100 yards off the road and thought it would be just the ticket.

As I got closer I saw it was a barn only in the respect that it had poles and a roof. Its western and southern sides had been enclosed to give some protection from the winter wind. It wasn't so much a barn as it was a staging area for cattle being gathered to ship somewhere else. There were cattle around but there was a fence around the barn so they couldn't get in. Toward the back of the barn next, to one of its walls, was some higher ground with fewer cow tracks. I call it "ground" but since it was almost dark I can't say for sure if it was really ground or just more layers of cow potty. It was dry, sheltered, and relatively flat and I'd spent nights in worse places.

For several days I'd noticed a plant growing alongside the road. It was a low-lying plant with long runners and big leaves that reminded me of the plant upon which yellow, crookneck squash grows. But it smelled to high heaven! I named it skunk cabbage.

It was just my luck that my barn home had skunk cabbage all around it. And some of the runners had ventured into the barn itself. I had to sleep with it right under my nose, but bad smell or not, I wasn't moving.

I had been asleep for about an hour when I was awakened by a pain in my stomach. It felt like a blender had been turned on in there. I had no idea what it was but I thought I could ride it out. About two minutes later I gave up that idea as I was being driven out of my sleeping bag by what felt like a dam about to burst. In the next fifteen seconds not one but two dams did burst. I was bent over going at both ends. The problem was compounded by not being able to escape. If I moved forward I was caught by vomit, if I moved back, it was diarrhea. When I felt like surely all the fluids in my body had gone over and through the dam, I made a giant step to the side.

Have you ever been sick to your stomach and had someone mention a fried egg? You never forget the feeling.

After the junkyard iced tea, I'd arrived at my barn home and had my supper — the only thing I had with me — French onion chips. Like the thought of a fried egg I was surrounded and trapped by the taste, smell and thought of French onion chips, skunk cabbage and cow manure. Just when I thought my stomach and bowels were completely empty, I'd get a whiff of manure, or skunk cabbage, or the taste of those onion chips would cross my mind and I'd be overtaken again by waves of revulsion. It went on all night. Nearly every hour I was up on my feet doubled over. I searched my mind for the cause. It had to be the tea — Montezuma's junkyard revenge!

Chapter 40
The Human Water Pistol

Why me, Montezuma? Maybe I wanted your gold but I didn't try to get it. And I had no interest in making slaves of your people nor violating your maidens. So why are you doing this to me?

Though I kept walking down the road the next day, the "running at both ends" situation didn't get much better. It became challenging to find a spot for doing what I had to do at the precise moment it had to be done. There was little warning and no putting it off. In cases like this, when nature calls, you pick up on the first ring.

To make matters worse, I was losing vital moisture from my body in two ways now. Not only was the devil Texas sun sucking it out through every pore, but Montezuma had his suction pumps attached to my stern and bow. And it's a physiological fact that if you don't have enough water in your system to create perspiration, you are going to overheat.

Either I was getting weaker or the sun really was beating done with new intensity. I knew I'd look silly, still I wished I had an umbrella as some sort of sun block. As I walked I began searching the ditches and roadside for something to block the sun. I had no delusions about finding an umbrella, I was just hoping to find something I could rig up. First I found a black plastic garbage bag. I couldn't figure out how to use it but figured it was worth carrying until something else came along. An hour or two later I found a car radio antenna. I was ready to try anything between me and that hellish orange ball.

I slipped the radio antenna up one side of the open end of the garbage bag. On the other side of the bag I ran my walking stick. To see if this project would be worth it, I held the tautly stretched bag between me and the sun, then after a few seconds I'd take it away to feel the difference. Yes, it worked. There was a definite difference.

It took both hands to make my sun shield work and it was tiresome holding both hands up in the air for any length of time. In my weakened conditioned I wasn't sure I could hold it up long enough to be of help, but any relief was welcome.

I didn't know where Montezuma was getting the water from. It seemed like every hour, on the hour, I was off the side of the road, hiding as best I could with my pants at my ankles. And each time I dropped my pants and bent over, I shot a stream straight and long for several feet behind me. I was like a water pistol — one you wouldn't want to get hit with. It was so powerful and directable I could have scored very well on any dartboard.

The diahrrea was saddling me with another burden I didn't need. Throughout the walk

I'd tried to maintain a respectable appearance. I thought looking weird wasn't too bad but there was little excuse for looking unclean. My mother used to say, "There's no disgrace in being poor, but you don't have to be dirty. Soap and water are cheap." Of course, she was using Kentucky, not Texas as her yardstick for water.

I didn't know how I was going to get close to anyone. Every possible below-the-waist article of clothing had suffered from less-than-successful trips made off the road. I had to run sometimes and that seemed to loosen valves not too tight and secure at best.

Feeling dirty or looking dirty is bad enough. Smelling dirty is worse. But it's really embarrassing and degrading to smell *that* way!

I thought about how I might remedy the situation before I had to face anyone. The best idea I could come up with was to lay everything out in the sun to dry. I thought the smell might seem less acute if it were dry.

But the churning inside my stomach and head precluded much concern about offenses I might create for others. I felt awful, light-headed but heavy-bellied. It didn't feel any better sitting and holding my head. It felt no worse to be walking so I might as well cover ground.

The road I had been walking on since I'd entered Texas took a straight shot across the state through Dallas, and continued on to Louisiana. I was approaching Dallas and would have liked to have seen where President Kennedy was assassinated. I had no desire to tackle Dallas. I just wanted to stand at Dealey Plaza and take in that one spot.

I was so tired of sand and mesas and treeless terrain. It must have shown in my voice a few days earlier. I asked a state trooper who had stopped to talk (If he had other motives he didn't let on) when I'd get to some civilization. I could tell by his tone that he was offended by my insinuation that his part of Texas had no civility. But I was sick of the West and wanted things familiar to me, things that meant comfort, solace and relief.

He said I couldn't expect much until I got to Dallas. I didn't want to walk through Dallas, though, no matter how badly I needed civilization. I could forego it for a while longer.

It must have been something Freudian that made me sleep in a cemetery that night. No, it wasn't any "meet my maker" thing. I'd long known that in addition to country churches, country cemeteries were good places to spend the night. But first, you've got to overcome the Childhood Campfire Ghost Story syndrome. And even though I was able to put those thoughts in the back of my mind, I still slept next to the fence. I consider sleeping on graves too spooky and a sacrilege to boot.

It didn't help my nerves when I was visited that night by another storm.

Up until now it wasn't unusual for me to walk 20, 30, or 40 miles between eat/drink places so when I saw on my map that I'd be walking through three towns that were only four or five miles apart I was glad. Maybe I could replace some of the liquid I'd lost. And even though the thought didn't appeal to me I knew that I should try to get some decent food down.

The first town was Strawn. Strawn was a literal pinpoint on the map. It seemed that the railroad was its only reason for being. I saw a man working in his yard. I made a point to stay out on the road and downwind. His yard had a sycamore tree. Sycamores were common back home and it was good to see a familiar face. When I told the man it was good to see a sycamore again he seemed to want to take a few steps back. So I quickly added that I'd walked from the shores of California and any tree looked good to me.

Yes, Strawn had a laundromat and a restaurant, and the Sycamore man provided the necessary "lefts and rights" to get me there.

In any other time and place my stomach would have taken precedence over clean clothes, but we already know these were desperate times.

I was so thankful to be the only one in the small laundromat. I wanted every article to be washed. I had no way of knowing how long I'd be alone so I took a big chance. My hooded sweatshirt and nylon jacket hadn't taken any direct hits so they were the freshest articles of clothing I possessed. I took the arms of the sweatshirt and tied them around my waist, letting the body of the sweatshirt hang down over my bottom. I did the same with my nylon jacket, only this time I spun the jacket around so that its body was down the front. For the top I chose my cleanest dirty T-shirt. I knew if someone showed up I'd die of embarrassment, but I also knew in a court of law twelve men, good and true, could only find me innocent of indecent exposure.

I didn't even bother drying one pair of underwear and one pair of pants. As soon as the washer stopped spinning I grabbed them and headed for the restroom.

Don't ask me why I chose fried chicken as my first solid food. It was late, I was about the only one eating, it was the special and I didn't want to upset the cook. The fried chicken, peas, mashed potatoes, rolls and tea were about what I expected. But good, bad, or indifferent, I just couldn't get past Murphy's upset stomach/fried egg law. The tea, potatoes and rolls went down pretty good, but the more I chewed on the fried chicken the bigger it got.

Waves of revulsion were pouring over me when I stepped out into the hot sun again. I walked about a block, took off my pack, and sat propped against the side of an abandoned brick building. You've had the feeling—you think if you are perfectly still your stomach will calm down. In a way it's partly true. How long can you do it, though? Unless you're home with nothing to do and nowhere to go you can't do it for long.

Sitting with my back against that building, my stomach doing a Mary Lou Retton gymnastics routine, I longed for home and to have nowhere to go and nothing to do.

Home was a million miles away. And I couldn't expect to be rescued. Nothing to do except pick myself up by the seat of my nearly dry pants and start trudging toward the second part of this three-town Texas trilogy — a town named Mingus.

Mingus may have been the only town between Los Angeles and New York that didn't appeal to me as far as food/drink were concerned. And that's saying something.

Hindsight tells me it wouldn't have mattered. I learned early in my walk that Sundays were chancy in little towns. Even if there was a place to buy something it could easily be closed on Sunday.

Sunday in Mingus is dead, dead, dead.

The third town was called Gordon. And Gordon wouldn't have been much more exciting than Mingus, except that I happened upon a man and his wife working in a business that they hoped to turn into a poolroom. A few local boys were playing at the lone pool table. I could see that the couple had a way to go before it would be finished. But they were going to be the only game in town and patrons were standing by. The pool lady graciously gave me water.

The next day, about ten miles north of Stephensville, I was waylaid by another of Texas' patented storms. Black clouds reached all the way to the ground, crashing thunder and violent lightning seemed to have my name on them. My eyes searched rapidly. No hog barn to rescue me.

Just as I thought the next lightning flash would turn me into a lit Christmas tree, I spotted a man coming out of his house to do something in his carport. I noticed he had a low, metal utility shed behind his house. I headed for the carport and as I got to the man I blurted out something about walking Los Angeles to New York and could I take shelter in his shed. I sensed or thought I sensed, or wanted to sense approval and immediately started a dash for the shed. Then I heard, "Wait!" The man was calling me back to the carport. I could tell he'd had second thoughts.

Standing under the carport I was something that he could see, measure, calculate and evaluate. Out of sight in the shed I was an unknown. I might scour the shed for an axe and come back to the house swinging, with blood dripping from my fangs.

We talked on the carport. I was happy to have shelter even if lightning was cracking close on two sides. He said he was going back to the house for awhile. I asked if I could sit in the cab of his pickup truck. He said okay, and I fell asleep. After awhile, I'm not sure how long, he came out with sandwiches. He said he and the wife had to go to town but she had made some sandwiches for me. I got his meaning. The wife said in some fashion that it was time for me to go. The sandwiches were her part and the getting rid of me was his part.

The storm hadn't passed yet, but I knew my welcome had run its course. I dreaded leaving the limited shelter of this carport in a storm. It was security and leaving meant vulnerability in the storm again. I bit the bullet, and after thanking him I headed down the road.

Just a couple of miles down the road from my carport experience I was to benefit from someone else's shattered dream.

I'd been given the bum's rush at the carport. (Not that I was bitter. It was more than some people would have given and I was thankful.) The storm was still in full bloom, though, and I was still searching for shelter more substantial than my little tent.

I noticed a building that looked empty. There were tall weeds all around and the large plate glass window in the front was dirty. The building was relatively new and in good shape. It looked as if something had happened just at the moment the building was completed. Divorce? Death? Bankruptcy? I'd never know.

The building met all my requirements. And even though the storm wouldn't have made me "break and enter", I saw no harm in spending the night if it wasn't locked. I suppose you'll think I was splitting hairs if I told you technically it wasn't locked. Someone had taken measures to try and keep anyone from entering the building by piling lumber in front of the door on the inside. It took a little huffing and puffing but finally I blew the door open enough to squeeze through.

I now had a dry, warm, secure place for the night. There was even some flattened cardboard boxes that made a bed fit for a king.

While I was lying on my cardboard bed in the abandoned building, I had a few hours of daylight so I got out my map and looked at the names of some of the places I was going to be walking through: Chalk Mountain, Glen Rose, Rainbow. With names so appealing surely I must be approaching civilization at last.

With nothing better to do my eyes began to wander to names of other Texas towns — Cut and Shoot, Gun Barrel City, Muleshoe, Sour Lake, Bangs, Spur, Earth, Happy, Scurry, Idalou, Deaf Smith, and the best sounding one of all, the one I'd been searching for since I began this Texas odyssey weeks ago — Comfort.

I knew Stephenville was big enough to have umbrellas and even though I'd sworn before that I wouldn't carry even a postcard more than I was already carrying, the Texas sun was more persuasive than a Mafia don. I did have criteria my umbrella had to meet. I wanted one of those black (not even the Texas sun could make me carry one that was pink with daisies on it) collapsible executive-types like a Wall Street broker might carry in his briefcase. One of those giant golf ones would have been nice, but I'd felt the Texas wind and I'd seen *Mary Poppins.*

I had trouble finding a place that had any left. Ironic that the rain was the reason so many had sold and I wanted one for the sun. I had to walk a long way out of my way to a drugstore for the last umbrella in Stephensville, Texas.

Remember I've recommended towns along the way that I thought were worth the effort to visit? Okay, Chalk Mountain, Glen Rose, and Rainbow are roses that do not smell as sweet.

Chapter 41
The Dueling Widows
and the Pitiful Kitten

I was entering the town of Hillsboro and the map told me I was almost directly south of Dallas. And things were beginning to look a little more civil — an occasional tree, a patch of grass.

The man in west Texas must have been right when I asked him when I could hope to see some trees, grass and water again.

"You'll have to get to Dallas and off this cap rock before you can expect much of those."

I didn't want to seem so obviously dumb so I didn't pursue "cap rock." I had plenty of miles to chew on it and came to the conclusion a cap rock was a giant rock plateau, thousands of square miles in area, lying just under the topsoil in west Texas.

Something happened in Hillsboro I always made every effort to avoid. Dark caught me in town. The Lord provideth. I spotted an old abandoned garage. Not a private garage. This looked like it may have been an auto dealership in the 40's or 50's. Grease, oil and dirt told me that after the auto dealership left, someone turned it into an indoor junkyard with some of the merchandise spilling out into the yard. I guessed about ten years prior the city fathers decided they'd had about enough of this eyesore and the owners were politely or not so politely asked to leave. I sensed bad blood, with the junk men gaining one-upmanship by pulling out in the middle of the night leaving grease, rust, old car seats, grimy rags and assorted pieces of junk.

This is all conjecture. Now it was a dry, abandoned building that would be a very adequate home, thank you, for a weary traveler this night.

I dragged a couple of car seats to the back corner wall, not for sleeping on but to serve as a sort of duck blind. The addition of a few old, oil-stained, cardboard boxes made for a nice fort to hide behind and help make the cavernous garage seem smaller and more cozy.

It had gotten fully dark and the day noises of passing cars and kids yelling had given way to night sounds — yelling kids and cars passing. Frequency and volume were the only differences.

I was in my fort somewhere in the twilight zone almost asleep yet still vaguely aware.

Between a tire squeal and a kid yelling I heard, no, actually, *felt*, close to my ear what seemed like someone pulling a very loose guitar string and letting it go. It didn't make sound so much as it made airwaves, if that makes any sense.

It wasn't long before the string was again plucked close to my ear.

I had no choice. I had to deal with it. I reached for my flashlight aimed it in the direction of the phantom guitar.

The beam revealed something I didn't want to see. Really! My headrest was right next to a giant black widow spider's web. And Mrs. Widow was shaking her web like a gorilla rattles the bars of its cage. Was it frustration because I was too big to eat, or a spider jumping for joy at the prospect of having a year's supply of food right at her eight leg tips?

Wham! Hiking boot meets garage floor! Not this time, Mrs. Widow. You've killed and eaten your last man. In a way I felt bad having to do it. I'm a live and let live guy for *all* creatures.

Am I crazy? Not five minutes after lights out for the second time the guitar twangs again. I sweep the flashlight beam again. I couldn't believe it — another big web, another big spider, more killing fields.

I gave the area a more detailed search this time. Up, down, around, under until I was satisfied I'd wiped out the entire spider string section.

It still wasn't to be a quiet night, though. The garage was located in town and right behind it were houses and mobile homes. It was well into the night when I heard it for the first time. It was the plaintive cry of a tiny, starving kitten. It's a heartrending sound. The cries of any starving creature would be pitiful. The young and innocent tug at your heart really bad. The kitten seemed to be aimlessly wandering, crying for help. More than anything I would wish for me, I wished at that moment for a can of Friskies and a big bowl of warm milk.

Before my walk when trying to think of every possible thing I'd need to take, it occurred to me that earplugs would be a good idea. They didn't occur to me on the first day of planning or even the first month of planning. But when I needed them I was grateful I hadn't overlooked what to most people would seem like a small detail. This kitten was crying for its mother's love and for food. As badly as I wanted to I could provide neither. All I had were a few Doritos Tortilla Chips and a Payday. It hurts to turn a deaf ear or a blind eye to innocent suffering. All I could do was plug my ears to try and make it go away and next day as I walked down the road tell myself that some other kind soul had been the Friskies and milk fairy for the poor deserving kitten.

Chapter 42
Blooming Grove Bravado

People, places and things were coming at more frequent intervals now. The two guys I'd asked about civilization had been right. Depending on which way you're going Dallas can either be the gate to a fruitful landscape or the threshold of desolation. Believe me, for the hiker, in Texas, it's "Go east, young man!"

"You got any ID?" It ends in a question mark but it's closer to a command. And it means, "I don't like your looks and this uniform and badge give me the power to, at least verbally, push you around."

The question/command in itself didn't surprise me too much. I'd been "asked" it several times. But this was gentle-looking Blooming Grove, Texas. You wouldn't expect anyone to ever be rude or raise their voice in a place called Blooming Grove.

"You got any ID?"

It was the abruptness of it. I was taken aback. I just wanted to strike up a pleasant conversation as I approached the officer. I admit my real motive was to see if I could get his blessing to spend the night somewhere in his fair town. Sometimes small towns have small city parks. My plan was to open my act with my usual, "I'm attempting to walk from Los Angeles to New York and I was wondering if I could...?" (Fill in any walker request you like) Just as I was about to open my mouth I was hit with, "You got any ID?

I think one of the saddest things in life is realizing not everyone likes you. Did *everyone* like Albert Schweitzer? Joan of Arc? (somebody had to light the match).

In defense of the policeman, I don't think it was anything personal. I think he felt it was his duty to keep Blooming Grove, well — Blooming Grove. Sorta like a nightclub bouncer keeping things from getting out of hand. He might be as wild as any there but it's his job to act otherwise.

After running me through the national computer and finding no outstanding warrants his demeanor toward me improved and my story took on a little more interest for him.

Yes, I could stay in Blooming Grove's city park. This was great. A protected, safe place to spend the night under the watchful eye of the local constable.

I found a nice, sandy spot among the swings, seesaws and slides to put up my tent. I threw up a friendly hand to the policeman making his rounds as I sat eating my dinner of cheese curls and Gatorade.

Why shouldn't this be one of the best nights of the trip? All the good signs were there. Those boys walking and occasionally shouting will all go home after dark. What else is there to do in Blooming Grove after dark?

It was dark and I was lying on my back in my tent just thanking my lucky stars that I'd found peaceful Blooming Grove and how good life in general was.

To quote a once popular song, "The boys are back in town." I didn't realize that one possibility, besides walking the streets and shouting before dark, was walking the streets and shouting *after* dark. These boys hadn't read the script. They were supposed to be at home watching TV.

Maybe they wouldn't have mattered to most people. They mattered to me for two reasons:

1. It was impossible for me to sleep.

2. Did what they were shouting have anything to do with me?

I lay there and listened, listened hard. Yes, something about their talk did have something to do with me. You've seen a cat approach something strange. At first it's very cautious, ready for flight at the slightest sign of danger. Then if the strange object doesn't move the cat becomes braver until it will touch the strange thing with its paw. If there's still nothing the cat will exert more paw pressure until its curiosity is appeased.

I can't remember the exact words but lying on my back in that tent I got the distinct feeling when cat caution had given way to cat bravado I'd feel paw pressure of some kind. I decided I wouldn't wait around to see what these cats' curiosity led them to.

I got out of the tent, slipped the poles out of their sleeves so I could compress the tent. Then I put my pack on, reached down and in one fell swoop gathered tent, sleeping pad, sleeping bag and assorted clothes in one big bundle in my arms and started back toward the main highway.

It was a terrible time to be looking for a place to sleep.

An old used car dealer once told me: "Never go look at a car after dark." And to this used car axiom I might add: "Nor sleeping places."

Again, I did as I had done when I had almost been flushed like a sewer rat into that swirling cauldron. When I got back to the main highway I headed in the direction from which I'd come. It may not be the best direction, but it's a known direction. When I had gotten some distance from Blooming Grove I threw my stuff over a fence, climbed it and struck out across a cow pasture. Naturally, I came upon a herd and startled them. Cows don't have the curiosity of cats and their first instinct is to run. And when one runs they all run. Great! A thundering herd to draw the farmers attention.

I looked all around and didn't see a house. I struck out for a low stand of what I thought were bushes with some of those big, rolled hay bales lying nearby. I was 50 percent right. Yes, the hay was hay. No, the bushes weren't bushes. The "bushes" were stinging nettle.

There's no reason to go further with this story. The ending is rather short and not so sweet — tellable in a few succinct words:

1. Shaking head.

2. Stamping feet.

3. Bawling.

No, not the cattle — Me! See "Stinging Nettle."

Chapter 43
Nutty As a Fruitcake

If someone asked you to name the fruitcake capitol of the United States wouldn't you guess someplace in the South, maybe Atlanta, Charleston or Savannah? Me, too.

When I was poring over the Rand McNally planning the route I was going to take on this walk I never would have dreamed that it was really in central Texas.

It's Corsicana. There's a bakery there that makes 4,000,000 pounds of fruitcake every year. The bakery wasn't directly on my route and I would have missed it if a proud Corsicanian hadn't suggested I stop for a free sample (two of my favorite words).

The fruitcake story is unique and interesting. After reading about it in a pamphlet I couldn't help but see the similarities between it and that great bakery way back in Santa Ysabel, California.

Both bakeries were started by German immigrants in unlikely locations and have been immensely successful.

The Corsicanians might be wild about their fruitcake, might eat it three times a day but if the bakery makes 4,000,000 pounds of fruitcake a year you can bet somebody in addition to Corsicanians is eating fruitcake. The explanation is that the rich and famous have heard about the fruitcake. Who better to have on your side?

Seems the Ringling Brothers Circus came to town years ago and experienced the cake. If word-of-mouth is the best advertisement who better to spread your word than the circus? They must have spread it good — 4,000,000 pounds good.

I must admit that fruitcake isn't on my short list of good cakes, so weigh that when I say I wasn't *that* impressed with it. And there was no way I was going to buy a whole cake, so my critique is based only on a sample. Who am I to dispute the weight of 4,000,000 pounds.

Chapter 44
My First Taste of Six-Legged Hell

The next day I encountered an animal whose behavior made me wonder why man thinks he's the only creature capable of forethought or feelings.

I was walking, facing traffic. The grass was about six or eight inches tall alongside the road. I saw it parting about eight feet in front of me in a zigzag motion. Something was coming toward me. Before I had time to comprehend what was happening the zigzag was only about two feet in front of me. A snake's head raised above the grass at about the same time my foggy brain grasped what was happening. For half a second we both froze, eyes locked on each other. I don't know what he saw, or what he thought. Maybe I'll spend one of my three wishes someday and find out. What I saw was a look of preoccupation. A look that said, "Now did she say pick up half a dozen fresh frogs, or was it check the banks of that new bog?" Nevertheless, the look on his face said he had more important things to do than bother me.

I didn't know it was possible but there it was on the snake's face — a look that said, My time and my life are just as important to me as yours is to you so just keep on truckin' and I'll do the same.

I stepped to the right a few steps and Mr. Snake continued on his grassy way down the side of the road. He respected my reason for being, I respected his.

Down the road I spotted the hiker's Eden — a stream running under the road. There are so few streams in the West that actually have running water. Clean, cool running water, a place to hide and frolic came along so rarely in the Southwest that each time it did I felt like a child. Naturally, by the time a stream appeared I was long overdue in the bath department. But first I would wet a bandanna and drape it over my head. I read once that no matter how thirsty an elephant is, when he comes to a water hole, before he'll drink he takes water in his trunk and sprays his ears. The many veins running close to the surface over such a large area are his "wet bandanna."

As I half slid, half stumbled down the bank I was smiling to myself in anticipation of the coolness to come.

I took off my pack and set it on the bank beside my feet, dipped my bandanna in the water and draped it over my head. Total baptism would come in just a few minutes. First I wanted to feel the delicious coolness of the water dripping from the bandanna. It brought such blessed relief. Next, it's cool trip down my spine ended in that spot that made me involuntarily shiver and twist as the water followed the path of least resistance, finding its way right down the crack of my old talolly.

When my head heated the bandanna, I jerked it off and swished it through the water, replenishing its cool strength. Then I slapped it back on my head and relaxed with a silent, "Aah."

I finally realized that this bandanna spa couldn't go on forever if I ever hoped to reach New York. I reached for my pack. It was time for soap to bring a sweet smell to the next phase of "wetted bliss."

Just as I reached for the zipper on my pack my hand stopped in mid-air. I felt something on my foot and instantly knew the soap could wait. I looked at my foot and was aghast. Both feet were covered with tiny ants. I couldn't comprehend why. I knew it would take more than a casual slap to rid myself of so many of the little beggars so I just swished my feet in the water sending the ants to the next county downstream.

I thought the incident odd but it didn't overly concern me. I dismissed it as a freak thing and my thoughts returned to my bath as I again reached for my soap compartment. As my eyes followed my hand to the pack, and just before my hand reached the zipper, I saw that my pack had hundreds of the little devils crawling all over it.

Swishing my feet in the water was no more than an inconvenience but now these little varmints were attacking my pack, too. This was WAR!

Poor, innocent child that I was. Declaring war when I hadn't the faintest notion of the strength of the enemy. At the time I didn't realize this was David and Goliath only David is a 97-pound weakling and Goliath is Conan on steroids. And I learned that David ain't gonna win this one even if his slingshot is super high tech and armed with an atomic warhead.

When I picked up my pack and started brushing the ants off I had no way of knowing I'd taken my glove and slapped the face of my enemy. If I could have seen their little ant faces I'm sure their pincer jaws were spread antennae to antennae in a wide grin. They must have been saying, "Aha! A fool who wants to fight!"

As I began brushing the ants from my pack I knew these weren't your typical ants. I'd heard of fire ants but had never seen any. I just assumed they were red, about an inch long, and had pincers that could pierce a Toyota and maybe even lift it off the ground. All I'd heard was that they were cussed creatures but had never seen any. Beneath that bridge in eastern Texas that day the fire ant said, "My world and welcome to it!"

I was so naive. I thought I could win this war. Looking back I see how funny that must have been to the ants. Sure, I could brush the ants off my pack if I wanted to use my hands for that purpose instead of knocking the ones off my feet and legs. And I can guarantee that you pay more attention to the ones on your feet and legs than you do the ones on your pack. Somehow you don't feel that fiery bite as keenly on your pack as you do on your legs. And the bite is way out of proportion to the size of the ant. Judging from the bite, you would think there were giant pairs of poisonous, knifelike (Did you see Edward Scissorhands?) pincer jaws attached to those tiny little bodies.

There were ants everywhere. I was way in over my head. It was like being attacked by a swarm of bees with legs instead of wings. Cool bath or not, I wasn't going to stay under this bridge this day.

And Mr. Elephant, wetting his ears, couldn't stay either. With his tough hide, you say? But, even elephants have tender parts, say I.

Fire ants, especially roused or mad fire ants are invasive, persistent and can throw more bodies at you than a Mongol horde. They'd find the chink in Mr. Elephant's armor — up his trunk, in his mouth, his eyes, ears and even the discreet body openings on the other end.

Between arm flailings I gathered my stuff as fast as I could and scrambled up the bank and back to the road.

I honestly can't say if fire ants bite or sting or both. My money's on both!

Further on in my walk in Louisiana I was discussing the hellish fire ant with a man who told me about a local happening: An elderly lady had fallen on her back porch and hadn't been able to get up. It was a few days before anyone discovered her. Fire ants had covered her and invaded every body opening. She lived but I couldn't help but think of the terrible pain and anguish. I've heard that one of the Indians favorite tortures was strapping a man across an anthill after they'd smeared his body with honey.

On the road again it was quite some time and distance before I didn't feel or see any more ants to slap away.

I had plenty of time to reflect on what had happened and it was a little unnerving. It made me feel slightly uneasy to think of the absolute power of the ants. They really *owned* the territory under that bridge — and man is a bloody fool if he thinks *he* does.

Hundreds of miles later across several Deep South states, and after numerous other run-ins with fire ants, I came to a conclusion. You're going to think I'm delusional but it's my story and I'm sticking to it. I say this without humor and I fully believe my mind is sound: They say there are more stars in the heavens than grains of sand on every beach in the world. I can carry that theory one step further: There are more fire ants than there are stars in the heavens.

You'd have to be a coast-to-coast walker, sleeping out in the fields and woods 22.4 miles (average) from the place where you slept the night before to fully appreciate how pervasive fire ants are. They are literally everywhere from east Texas to central North Carolina.

I truly believe that if a Hitler type fire ant came along and could organize all the ants they could take over the world. Man would be a puny adversary in my opinion.

Chapter 45
Those Six Little Words Again (Oh, You'll Make It All Right)

I thought the under-the-bridge incident was simply a freak of nature. If fire ants did occur in large numbers, man would find a way to control them. If man can go to the moon, he can do anything he sets his mind to. After my walk I saw the naivety of that thinking. The bottom line is the fire ant has beaten man — at least midway through the fourth quarter. A man told me experiments in genetic altering were being tried i.e. somehow making the queen sterile but that's nowhere near practical yet.

After the bridge incident, it was time for the daily search for a place to put down. I spotted a small house that looked like an abandoned real estate office. Nice. There was a hay field behind the building that I could sleep in. The hay had been cut and was dry. I could gather some and make a nice, soft bed.

About an hour after dark I was awakened by little feet scurrying around and over me. I turned on my flashlight and those little feet scurried away. They weren't fast enough to escape detection though — fire ants! I jerked aside my sleeping bag, pad, pillow and anything else I thought they could be hiding under. The slow ones got smushed between my thumb and tent bottom. I caught as many as I could but saw nothing to do but turn out the light and try to sleep again.

You can guess how that night went. After the light had been out for about 15 minutes the cycle started over. And so it went all night.

The next day I tried to reason how the ants had gotten into my tent. Size wise my tent was little more than a body bag with some screening for breathing. To enter it I had to get on my hands and knees and back in. It was a glorified tube sock. Forget sitting up in it. The roof was only about 18 inches above my face when I lay on my back. Changing clothes in it was like a butterfly coming out of its cocoon. But if you weren't claustrophobic, its size gave a sense of security. More imagined than real. Still it was completely enclosed with no-see-um netting and zipper closures that met snugly together to help create a feeling of protection. It was the old ostrich defense to the 'nth degree, strictly an illusionary security blanket. A cruel joke and childlike in its innocence. I'll tell you how the little beggars could get in. I must have carried some of them in with me on my clothes or pack. At first I wanted to blame it on the hay I gathered to make my bed soft. I also learned that they like to travel along the outside bases of buildings and I had put my tent as close to the rear wall as I could. I must have brought two warring factions together (the city ant from next to the building and the country ant from the hayfield) and I was caught in the crossfire.

"Would you like some peach cobbler?" Thank goodness for a world where good people and peach cobbler *as yet* still reign over the fire ant.

I had just savored, if all too quickly a delicious home cooked meal. I had enjoyed this meal in a slightly unusual place.

Late in the afternoon I had stopped at a never-pass-one country gas station/grocery. The nicest retired couple, Kelly and Jessie, owned the place. As almost always happened the conversation eventually got around to why I was there. It worked that way almost everywhere, but it never failed to happen in the South. "Strange" (I had it in spades) creates interest anywhere, I suppose.

Nice people of curiosity and intellect welcome "strange," though. They realize it might broaden their horizons, and a smart person never lets the opportunity pass them by. I was strange, and an opportunity, though I'm not sure how much "broadening" I could offer.

After I'd gone through my Los-Angeles-to-New-York song and dance, the grocery store owner hesitated. For a minute I didn't know what to expect. His face told me nothing. To him was I just someone completely full of it, or was he dumbstruck that I'd already reached central Texas on foot?

For a few seconds it was a puzzlement. I felt awkward. I'd said all I could. The next move was his.

I blinked as his voice boomed in the small grocery.

"My God Almighty! Randy, go over to the trailer and get Jessie. She'll want to meet this man."

Randy hightailed it out the back. I just sat, the air thick for lack of conversation. I was about to be put on display. I was beginning to appreciate the monkey's perspective at the zoo.

Kelly and I both turned at the slamming of the door, glad that it meant relief from an awkward predicament.

As soon as Jessie's eyes adjusted they pounced on me.

Kelly began, "Jessie, this fella..."

"Yeah, Randy couldn't wait. He told me already. For us you're celebrity stuff, ya know."

I dropped my eyes and squirmed slightly, but I'd be a liar if I didn't confess I was soaking it up.

Jessie and Kelly pelted me with questions.

"When did you start? Where do you sleep? How far each day? Aren't you afraid? What does your mother think?" Et cetera, Et cetera.

Finally, every ounce of curiosity must have been satisfied.

"Hey, our daughter-in-law is bringing dinner over for us tonight, you wanna stay? She's a great cook," Jessie said.

"Sounds wonderful to me," say I.

It was the first truly home cooked meal I'd had since I'd left Tennessee. I'll spare you the pain and won't list the offerings. Picture Thanksgiving dinner at your grandmothers.

The dinner fed my body and my soul. The food was wonderful and was topped with the best peach cobbler I'd ever eaten. Even in my perpetual state of half-starvation I was just a tad gun-shy when they mentioned cobbler. Any cobbler has always been near the bottom of my dessert list. The wonderful meal and the cobbler made my eyes light up and my stomach say, "Howdeee!"

Remember back at the White Sands Missile Range I said how much my spirits had been buoyed by the guard's words, "Oh, you'll make it all right." Only two times was I to hear those uplifting words — there, and here in central Texas from the sweet cobbler lady. I still had not let thoughts about making it or not making it enter my mind. I resolved to just get up each morning and walk until dark. I knew that after X number of days of walking I'd somehow feel if New York was attainable or completely out of the question.

Since theTexas/Louisiana border looked sorta halfway, I figured if I reached that point I could, at least a little, believe I might be able to complete the walk.

As you can imagine there were a lot of times when I could have used those "Oh, you'll make it all right" words. Yet I heard them only twice. Both times they were such an uplifting force given at the best possible time. The first was when I needed *anything* to lift me out of the inferno called White Sands, and the second was here, in Texas' heartland. I was close enough to my halfway point to have some confidence. I had survived the desert Southwest? Isn't it surely the toughest half?

Those words remind me of what Frank Kennedy said to Scarlett in *Gone With the Wind*. Even though he was being buttered up by Scarlett because she needed his money to pay the taxes on Tara, he still said, "Scarlett, you work on me just like a tonic."

That's what those "Oh you'll make it all right" words did for me — worked on me just like a tonic.

Chapter 46
Spurs at the Rodeo

I was approaching Palestine, Texas. I was mildly excited because I would be getting on the highway that would take me all the way to Savannah. That meant I wouldn't have too keep looking at the map and asking if I was on the right road. One road, one number all the way to the Atlantic — a comforting thought.

Why do we always assume our way is the right way, the only way? Where I come from Palestine is pronounced as if the last four letters rhyme with "nine." I had to smile to myself when a Palestinian (Texas variety) corrected me.

"We call it Pal-es-teen," she said.

I thought to myself, "That's silly. These people *live here* and still mispronounce it."

Who among us hasn't been to the beach and had the lovely experience soured because of a sandspur? The plant version of the fire ant, in my opinion. I never gave it much thought but since I'd never seen them except at the beach I just assumed that was the only place they grew.

Did you hear my squeal of delight? That was me seeing them growing alongside the road in Texas. Texas has it all! Grass spurs and fire ants. Who could ask for anything more?

I blessed their ancestry as I passed them, every time I passed them. There are things on this earth that make you wonder if God didn't delegate some during those six days.

I noticed a sign with an arrow saying Bethel Baptist Church (Name changed to protect my innocence). It was quite some distance off the road and by the time I got there I was wondering if I'd made the right decision. It was a country church, off the beaten path (way off), and it was the right day of the week for churchyard camping but was it worth this long walk out of my way?

Every night, after campsite selection, I closely inspected the exact space my tent would occupy (especially since the fire ant incident!). I suppose it goes without saying why a close inspection was necessary. I'll say it anyway. It was my tent, my home. It would make no sense to let something poke a hole in my home simply because I was too lazy to inspect the ground I was putting it on.

I'd venture to say there are very few reading this who know what it feels like to not have a home. And unless you are one of the homeless, you can't appreciate the feeling.

I've talked about heat; I've talked about thirst. And you nod your head as if you understand but you don't. You might understand the heat and thirst you felt when you mowed the grass. It isn't the same. It's the old mile-in-the-moccasin thing. You can't really appreciate hunger, thirst or what it feels like to be without a home until you've been there. But you have to be taken there by your body. Trying to visualize it isn't enough.

And it's strange how little it takes to create a feeling of home. My tent was just a little slip of a thing not much longer, wider or taller than my body stretched out on the ground. But inside I felt protected. It really did feel like home. Of course, it wasn't protection in any real sense of the word. The secure feeling came from being able to hide, to withdraw into a world of my own. We see or hear of people living in cardboard boxes and pity them. But I contend their box still gives them the feeling of "home" and they feel a sense of warmth and security inside it.

So, I did everything in my power to protect my tent home, every stone, every stick to even the tiniest was pitched out of the way. No precious baby's bottom was ever treated more delicately. A puncture meant loss of security, and loss of security for me meant devastation.

I want to emphasize that I was a pseudo-homeless person. I had a home. It may have been thousands of miles away and purely mental at this point, but that's two-thirds of what a home is anyway. You may say, "That's silly, a home is a physical thing." If you've ever been without a home, though, you realize that it's much more than that. It's a safe place to go. I had the ability to buy some security, real or imagined.

Security was part of the reason I hated the grass spurs. (Sandspurs are just grass spurs that have enough money to go to the beach.) I knew they could puncture my tent with a hundred little holes. The other reason I hated grass spurs was that they hurt like hell.

My first concern when choosing a site for my tent was the "lay of the land." Let me qualify that a little. Avoiding fire ant hills was a primary objective and took precedence over how level and aesthetically pleasing the campsite was. Also important was whether my head was going to be lower than my feet — a sure bet for a sleepless night. I could count on spending the night constantly pulling my body back up the hill and onto my sleeping pad if I'd neglected to study whether my site tilted up or down or yawed right or left. And, lastly, if I failed to diligently inspect my campsite I could count on that partially hidden tree root finding my eighth vertebra.

Here I was on a late Thursday afternoon inspecting the back yard of Bethel Baptist for sticks, stones, hidden tree roots, and — God bless Texas — grass spurs.

Yes, there they were. Bless their little gizzards, waiting with baited breath and needle spines to pierce my tent floor, sleeping pad, sleeping bag, underwear, epidermis and finally talolly nerve endings.

I may have been the weak sister in the battle with fire ants, but I had some firepower against grass spurs. I think the difference is roots. Quick legs, monster jaws, possible venomous stinger, but no roots to slow them down, made fire ants a formidable and elusive foe. Roots were the Achilles heel of grass spurs. And I'll bet they cursed their ancestral roots as I jerked them out of their earthy home with zest and glee, flinging them well out of tent territory.

Late the next afternoon as the black clouds got louder and closer, and the neon marquee was flashing "Another Texas Storm," a vacant rodeo arena looked like Trump plaza with a smiling doorman awaiting my arrival. Even Texans were looking for a place to hide from this one so I felt sure no one would see me hopping the rodeo fence.

It was a large dirt arena covered by a high metal roof. There were no sidewalls. That was okay. I knew nothing short of a hurricane could reach me if I plopped myself down in the very center.

It was too early for sleep and there wasn't much to do except watch the storm play itself out, so I thought I'd catch up on some long neglected sewing. And from the elevated judges' box I could sew for awhile and maybe judge some steer wrestling and bronco busting between stitches.

As night approached I inspected some loose hay lying to one side of the show ring. The fire-ant-infested hay I'd used back at the abandoned real estate office was still vivid in my memory. Here I had time and adequate light to avoid making that mistake again. I reached down and grabbed a handful of hay to inspect it closely. Yeow! Stabbed by a grass spur. My life flashed before me and instantly I was a little boy hopping on one foot, yipping at the beach. I dropped the hay and stood cursing my luck.

In my tent that night I got to thinking about my spur-induced Irish jig at the beach back those many years. Then I thought about the pain when I reached to pick up the hay here in the arena. It occurred to me that if spurs could penetrate a ten year old boy's heel, a heel that was used to being shoeless and had been hardened by a summer of pointy sticks, bottle caps and gravel roads, what must they do to the tender insides of a horse's' mouth? Either horses had a sixth sense about grass spurs and knew which hay to eat or somewhere there are a lot of horses doing an Irish jig.

Chapter 47
Your Pants Will Fall Right Off

I wish you could see the post office at Maydelle, Texas. Or that John Steinbeck was here to paint with words a picture for you. But I'm the best you've got, so here goes: Although the flagpole looked homemade and was about two-thirds the height of its post office brothers and sisters scattered throughout the land, it still dwarfed the post office in Maydelle, Texas. And the blue drop box on the front porch left just enough room to slide by and enter the front door. The neat, white building was so small that the "U.S. Post Office, Maydelle, Texas 75772 covered most of the front of the building. In square footage the post office and three Volkswagen Beetles parked side by side would cover the same ground.

Maydelle, bless her heart, wasn't much at all. Vacant buildings nearly equaled in numbers the ones that people lived in. There was one building, though, that made Maydelle worth the effort to see — a country store and the "C" should be capitalized. No matter what you asked for, no matter how rare or weird it might be, the storeowner was likely to say, "I'm sure I've got it if I can only find it."

Where is John Steinbeck when you need him? Now, if he'd just step over and tell us what we'd see at the Maydelle Country Store.

Again you'll have to do with my inadequately drawn picture. You can't be there, and I sure ain't no Steinbeck.

Antlered deer heads covered the walls, deer hides covered the rocking chairs. The local paper was draped over the chair arm in case someone came in who hadn't read it. An old galvanized coffeepot spouted steam atop the wood stove. Wood shelves were brown from generations of Maydelle handprints and countless years of scooting and shoving wares onto them. Soot from the wood stove in winter, and dust from the Texas summer, had mixed and taken its resting place over everything.

The merchandise told a story about the rural people who lived in and around Maydelle and what they needed. Not many frills at the Maydelle General Store.

The magnitude of stuff necessitate that the shelves be close together, and walking between them meant some twisting to one side. Toward the back some squinting was required because there weren't any windows, and the sheer volume of merchandise created surfaces, corners, angles that caught and absorbed most of the light from the lone, dusty bare bulb. There were tins of products no longer in vogue, that had been replaced by something new and better. The people of Maydelle were much too conservative to simply throw something out because it was out of fashion. The rear part of the Maydelle country store was a testimony to their frugality. There, items are still sold in quantity and unwrapped — grass seed, dried beans, pickled eggs. You reach in and take what you want. The health and sanitation rules may have reached Maydelle but aren't they such a bother sometimes?

Most of the things pushed to the back were farm-related, low ticket items, harness, cream separators, calf scours medicine, bag balm, hog ringer with rings, rakes, shovels, and in a barrel, chicken feed.

The fast money was in those things the motoring public jumped out of their car for — videos, a two liter Coke and a bag of chips, a half-gallon of milk, a loaf of bread, a quick candy bar and a magazine at the check-out. And in the case of the Maydelle store, a couple of strips of gator or buffalo jerky and a Little Debbie.

No, you won't find these items at the rear of the store. They are the little princes and princesses of the country store. They've earned their place on the throne at the front of the store where it's warm and the lighting is good.

All along I'd tried not to think about whether I'd make it all the way to New York. But it was impossible to keep the thoughts out. If they came on a bad day, doubts could fuel a multitude of negative thoughts.

But now I was beginning to see how making it all the way might be possible. My system of "Day One: Get up in the morning, walk 'til dark. Day Two; repeat day one" was working. It's every bit as much mental as physical. Not that occasionally my feet and legs didn't stage a labor revolt against management brain. When the make it/not make it thoughts couldn't be driven away I'd settle it all by drawing a mental line in the sand. The line was to be the Texas/Louisiana state line. "Cross that point, then you can start thinking thoughts about making it. Don't bother me 'til then."

I was in Rusk, Texas and even though I had 70 miles to go before I reached my psychological over the hump mark, I was doing a little premature celebrating. It was hard to suppress.

I had a fairly good idea how far it was to Mt. Enterprise, which was relatively close to the state line, but out of curiosity I wanted a local's opinion.

I saw two ladies running a fruit stand by the road. In response to my Mt. Enterprise question one of the ladies shot back, "You aren't going to try to walk all the way to Mt. Enterprise, are you?" I tried to keep the smile inside but they must have seen it. After I told them where I'd come from, they saw the humor in their question.

I have to admit it gave me a nice feeling when I saw the look on peoples' faces when I told them about my walk. I tried not to tell anyone unless there was no avoiding it. Or if it was useful as a foot in the door. I knew the ground I'd covered already would be impressive to most people, still I figured if any bragging rights were earned they'd come at the Empire State Building, not at a fruit stand in Rusk, Texas.

It's been said that everyone has 15 minutes of fame. I found my walk was giving me more than my allotted time. My fame was being stretched across the country. It was like adding oatmeal to the hamburger when you're making meatloaf. It was fame extender.

In one of his songs Frank Sinatra says "Ridin' high in April, shot down in May." I don't want to give you the impression that everyone fell all over themselves when they learned how far I'd walked. Many seemed indifferent. It wasn't too long after my "ridin' high" at the fruit stand that I was "shot down" by a man shooting hoops.

On my way to Mt. Enterprise, I developed a sizable thirst for something better than the hot water I was carrying. No roadside stores came along, so Gatorade and chocolate milk remained fantasies. The next best thing was a *cold* drink of water. That seemed attainable. I thought I'd hit upon a sure cure for my thirst when I saw some boys and their dad shooting hoops in their driveway. As I walked up the driveway to them the game stopped and the father walked toward me.

"Excuse me, Sir, I'm attempting to walk from Los Angeles to New York City. I'm thirsty and I was wondering if you could let me have a cold drink of water?" I put a definite emphasis on "cold."

I was still high from the exaltation at the fruit stand and just knew that my coast-to-coast walk proclamation would send him running to the refrigerator for a tall glass of water, chock full of ice.

The man's response was civil but short, "You can get a drink out of my garden hose."

Whoa! Here I stood a revered coast-to-coast walker. I admit I was strange looking but I deserved more respect than something that just escaped from the circus. Didn't he know that a garden hose lying in the sun produces hot water? So much for the respect due a living national treasure.

I could see he wasn't the least bit impressed by me nor my walking accomplishments. He'd fulfilled his humane obligation by not turning me away.

I drank deeply from his garden hose, thanked him heartily and hummed a little Frank Sinatra on the approach to Mt. Enterprise.

It hadn't been more than three or four days after I left Los Angeles that I noticed my pants were getting loose and I had to cinch the old belt up a notch. By the time I reached Hobbs, New Mexico there were no notches left and the seat of my pants was sagging badly.

It was time to check into the Hobbs Goodwill. I looked at all their belts. Most were Ralph Lauren types, much too delicate for my line of work. Finally, I found a good ol' construction worker's model with a big square buckle, real leather, and best of all, it was about two inches wide with notch holes halfway around to the back. No way was I going to run out of notches and still have strength enough to walk.

The degree and rate of weight loss was a surprise to me. Naturally, before I started my walk I expected some loss. It was the nature of the beast — limited food and drinks, and daylight-to-dark step aerobics.

Before I was to begin my walk I was mildly concerned about my weight. I wouldn't say I was fat. I just didn't feel "fighting trim". In a letter to Gus I expressed my concern about my weight. His philosophical reply cheered and amused me.

"Don't worry," he said, "after a thousand miles your pants will fall right off."

I was sitting outside a grocery in Mt. Enterprise having my standard lunch — tortilla chips, Snickers and Kool-Aid.

I know you think I existed on nothing but junk. Actually, I consider myself a healthy food disciple. I'm not a yogurt-and-carrot-stick kind of guy, but I do believe in the food pyramid and, when available, try hard to eat something green and yellow and have two pieces of fruit every day. But on a Los Angeles to New York walk, vegetables and fruit don't jump out at you around every bend. And my eating habits took it on the chin even more because I carried no stove. At times I felt like I had to have something decent, and I'd buy a can of spinach or peas or mixed vegetables. But eating them right out of the can is tough.

Money wasn't a problem, so when they showed themselves, Chinese buffets and Pizza Hut salad bars took a terrible beating. On the whole, I suppose I stayed fairly healthy, even though much of what I had to choose from was pretty sad.

One of my favorite recipes was for "Roadie Kool-Aid". This was my formula for "Roadie Kool-Aid": Buy a ten-pound bag of ice. I know it's overkill, but it's the smallest quantity you can buy. And, yes, eighty percent of it is wasted. But having all the ice you want is part of the formula for "good drink".

Next, I'd fill my canteen completely full of ice. Then came the pre-sweetened (the heat in the South and the heat in your throat don't allow for patiently waiting for sugar to dissolve) grape or orange (my personal favorites) Kool-Aid. Then water to fill all the spaces between the ice cubes. The cubes' volume should greatly outnumber the water's, so that each water molecule can snuggle its little body right up next to a slab of ice and be chilled to the utmost.

As I sat on my tuffet in front of the small grocery eating my organically grown Snickers and whey and dreaming of border crossings to come, a man came up. Though he may have taken a different tack, his course and port were the ones I'd become accustomed to. Where had I come from, where was I heading? I didn't mind. I even enjoyed the attention and conversation. It was more fame extender. Especially nice were questions containing a hint of envy.

The man owned a drugstore next to the grocery. I suppose it was a mixture of small town curiosity, lack of customers at the moment, and downright boredom that brought him out and over to find out my story.

"I have a hotplate in my store and I was just fixing some fiery rice, would you like some?" Even though I was already in the middle of my Snickers dessert course, I was on my feet in the same nano-second. I think the quickness of my movement startled him.

Strange thing about being social animals. We never give any thought to needing contact with others until we are deprived of it. If you're ever alone for any length of time, you realize why "solitary" is the worst form of punishment that prisoners have. Toward the end of my walk I commented to more than one person that I wish I'd had someone with me if only to argue with.

The fiery rice must have loosened my tongue as well as my tonsils because I spent over an hour chatting with the drugstore owner. Normally, I was too anxious to be on my way to indulge in conversation of that length.

It's been my experience that there's something about everyone that'll surprise you.

I advised my daughter when she went away to college for the first time to grasp the experience for all it was worth — try to learn from people and things as well as books. I told her not to devote all her time to the best looking boy there. Other people have stories to tell. Even the village idiot can teach us something. Each of us has many faces. We are all part pretty, part ugly, part smart and part dumb. It's in seeing those faces that we learn about people and life.

I wanted to see the pharmacist's other faces.

"As you can see, walking's my thing. What do you like to do?"

"Hmm, I guess I'd have to say I have a weakness for BMW motorcycles. The kind that have those funny cylinders that stick out on each side."

I suppose my look couldn't be suppressed because he quickly added, "A long time ago I sorta got the feeling the townfolk didn't think their doctor, lawyer, preacher or pharmacist should be riding motorcycles, so when I wanted to ride I headed away from Mt. Enterprise. People are more tolerant now that they've seen that my love for motorcycles hasn't affected my ability as a pharmacist. People will usually come around once they get to know the real you and not their first impression of you. I don't believe many people give it much thought anymore."

Over our lunch the conversation turned to weight.

"How much have you lost?"

I told him the belt story.

"I've got some electronic, computerized, nuclear (or some fancy sounding words like those) scales if you'd like to find out how much you've lost."

He had no way of knowing that for the last twenty years I'd have sooner stepped on a dog foaming at the mouth than step on a set of scales. I hadn't wanted to know how much I weighed. But lately, the seat of my pants flapping in the breeze had piqued my curiosity. Surely I was below the point of embarrassment.

I agreed and stepped on his scales. It sounded downright skeletal. 147 pounds!

I was amazed! I hadn't seen a 147 pounds since the 50s when I was wearing white bucks and ducktails.

When I walked away from Mt. Enterprise, Texas I felt good. Maybe the advice to my daughter had been pretty good after all. If you don't reach out to other people you're going to miss a lot of motorcycle riding pharmacists.

Chapter 48
Thirty Days Hath Texas

Crossing the Sabine River with Logansport, Louisiana on the opposite shore. I was tempted to stop in the first shop and buy a T-shirt that says, "I Survived Texas In The Summer of...!"

Standing on the far side of the Sabine River bridge knowing my next step would take me into Louisiana and out of Texas, I could at last turn to the big brute and say, "I *walked* you, I survived you, and now I know how long it takes to do you on foot!"

You've read the book, you've seen the movie, now meet the man!

Now when I appeared on Jeopardy and the category was Transcontinental Walking and the answer was: "It's the length of time required to cross Texas," I could buzz in and correctly ask, "What is 30 days, Alex?"

You can understand why crossing each state line was a thrill. It's your best measuring stick of what you're doing out there. And as nice as the feeling was at each state line, there was another marker that gave more pleasure. State lines were infatuation compared to the "true love" of realizing you were leaving one geographic area and entering another. I've alluded to it several times. When I asked the policeman when I could expect to see some civilization, it was really a longing for a different geographic region. When you are walking you have more than enough time to first like, then maybe love a new region. And then there's still more than enough time for either continued love or the other possibility — loathing.

Maybe I'm being a little overdramatic, but after you've walked in one geographical area for weeks, possibly longer, you're definitely ready for a change of scenery. When you're sure that the sight of one more creosote bush will bring a bilious taste surging up into your mouth, it's definitely time for a geographic change.

Louisiana! Oh boy! Mardi Gras, delicious cuisine, the French Quarter. Good-bye sand mesas, heat, thirst, storms, grass spurs — Hello, refinements of civilization.

As I stood on the Sabine River bridge about to enter Louisiana, I turned to take one last, long look at Texas and pay honor to her, a big entity, a majestic being of sorts. Texas deserves respect and I don't believe anyone could appreciate that more than someone who has walked all the way across her. I couldn't help but admire her.

I read somewhere that El Paso is closer to Los Angeles than it is to the eastern border of Texas. That puts the enormity of Texas in good perspective.

Chapter 49
It Ain't No Joke!

Mansfield was the first town of any size in Louisiana and a few days earlier I'd called Gus and asked him if he'd send me some of my money to Mansfield.

You'd think that it wouldn't be too tough to hit a post office between nine and five Monday through Friday, yet somehow I'd done it again — Sunday in Mansfield. I said it before, just going on and hitchhiking back seemed more desirable than hanging around Mansfield all day.

The next morning I walked back about a quarter of a mile from my campsite to an abandoned 7-11-type store I'd passed the night before. I wanted to change into my cleanest dirty shirt before hitching back into Mansfield. I'd noticed that the door had been kicked in so my crossing the threshold would be only semi-illegal. It had been a convenience-type store and I was surprised it hadn't survived. Most of these stores flourish no matter where they're stuck.

After hearing about some of the places I spent the night you must be wondering why this abandoned convenience store wasn't the Ritz-Carlton to me. But, I'd peeked in the broken door the night before.

Early in my walk I learned that near-highway "pull-offs" were not a good place to spend the night? They're just places to use the bathroom, make-out, get loud, or sit and play music at mega-decibels.

And this had all the qualities of a pull-off. It looked like a magnet for alcoholic beverage consumption. And what always seems to follow is foul loud mouths, foul loud music and worst of all, loud imagined bravado.

My quick study told me this was what I called the Big Double A. Abandoned and Abused. People had trashed the inside of the place. One person wouldn't do so much damage. The joy comes in showing off how much havoc you can wreak. And this store had been wrecked. There was hardly a place where you could see the floor. Broken items of nearly every description covered the place — glass, plastic, cardboard, metal all strewn everywhere like a tornado had struck.

Add to the desolation the reek of urine.

I managed to teeter on a piece of plywood long enough to change my pants and shirt and get the hell out.

And getting the hell out got me right back in hell. Standing in front of the store waiting for a ride, it felt like the county I was in had been draped with a big wet washcloth and some giant was up above waving a blowtorch across the surface. Lord have mercy.

The Southwest heat had felt like a colossal hand pressing down on me. Now that hand had been replaced by a moist, hot hand squeezing me from all sides with a few fingers reserved for gripping my lungs.

I pulled out my umbrella. I knew standing there on a perfectly clear day with an umbrella over my head would nearly kill my chances of getting a ride. A shrimp at a Japanese restaurant had a better chance of escaping those flying knives than I did to get a ride. I found it just too miserable to try to stand there in one spot with the sun boring into me without trying to get something between it and me. And it didn't help that I was in a rural area. About all that was passing me were big log trucks.

It seemed like hours and I was beginning to think I had two choices: either start walking all the way back to Mansfield, or drop to my knees facing the road with my hands clasped in prayer.

Finally, one of the log trucks stopped. No longer was I surprised when I saw my benefactor was black.

It was quiet a few miles back into Mansfield so I had time to tell my story to the log truck driver. I found that working people weren't as impressed by my walk as the leisure class was. Just having the time to walk across the United States is so completely out of the working man's realm as to be more like a fairy tale. There was sort of a look of incomprehension when I told a working man what I was doing. Of course, he understood in the same way he understood that man had gone to the moon. But that was far removed from the world he traveled in.

My target in Mansfield was the post office. I had no way of knowing where it was and when I saw the Piggly-Wiggly a few blocks after we got into town I told the truck driver I'd hop out there. Those hours in the sun had given me a thirst that took precedence over the post office and money.

In the Piggly-Wiggly I made straight for the dairy case. I grabbed a quart of chocolate milk and downed it on the spot. I reached for another quart and drank it as I went to investigate the chips aisle. My body soaked up a half-gallon of milk like a sponge in a period of less than five minutes. I walked up to the checkout and put the two empty quart containers on the counter. The young boy picked up one of the cartons, and feeling its lightness, gave it a jiggle. Then he picked up the other carton — same message. He looked at the cartons, then at me.

"Is this a joke?"

I sheepishly told him that I was pretty thirsty. I'll bet he still wonders how someone my size managed to down a half-gallon of chocolate milk before reaching the checkout.

Luckily the Piggly-Wiggly and the post office were in the same zip code. It was a short walk made jollier by two quarts of cold chocolate milk sloshing around like they were the inside of a Maytag washer.

As usual Gus had been efficient and prompt and the sweet green stuff was waiting for my arrival. I counted out those crisp new bills and mentally calculated the money/milk conversion rate.

Now I had to get from Mansfield back to the trashy, forsaken store chore. Not without a court order was I going to walk it twice. That left one choice – Thumb. Who should stop to give me a ride — Saint's among us! — The same black man who gave me the ride *into* Mansfield. A definite candidate for sainthood.

Chapter 50
The Mardi Gras Bubble Is Burst

Louisiana was one of the states I was most looking forward to. I'd been to "Nawlins" several times and just naturally assumed it and Louisiana were one in the same. New Orleans is one of the few really unique American cities. Walking down one of the narrow streets in the French Quarter you're just as likely to have to step over a homeless person as see someone you'd swear must be a Mafia Don or movie star. It's a carnival, anything-goes atmosphere where class, good taste, and the unique exist cheek and jowl with weirdness and depravity.

I just assumed as I started into Louisiana that I'd be greeted with all the things I'd experienced in New Orleans. My days would all be like Mardi Gras. And if not that garish and wild, at least there'd be great food, southern hospitality, and general frivolity. How could I lose?

I lost! And I was quick about finding it out. I didn't see anything that suggested New Orleans, Mardi Gras, or any other grand vision of Louisiana to me. From my vantagepoint on US Route 84, Louisiana was made up of pine trees, red dirt, and log trucks. A quick reality check told me I'd better adjust to the real Louisiana and forget my dreams about New Orleans.

It seemed that forever on this walk one adversary was being replaced by another. Never was there a shortage of things — be they animal, vegetable or mineral to bug me.

The Louisiana "insect du jour" was the chigger. Not to say that King Fire Ant had been dethroned. He would regard the lowly chigger as no more than a bump on the butt.

My first chigger connect-the-red-dots infestation came while I was waiting for a cemetery to clear.

That statement needs a bit of clarification.

We have already learned that the edges of cemeteries are good places to spend the night. Remember, we're taking a coast-to-coast walk here, not a family trip to Disney World.

It was late afternoon and the large cemetery on my right was inviting — in a metaphysical sense. All but the backside could be seen from the road. And I didn't want some passer-by seeing me heading in there with a pack and jumping to the conclusion that I was going to spend the night nestled atop Grandpa. So I kept trucking on up the road until I thought it was safe to double back and come out on the backside of the cemetery boundary.

I topped a small rise where the surrounding woods met the manicured grass of the cemetery and stopped suddenly. As quickly as I could, without drawing attention to myself, I eased back into the brush thicket out of sight.

Four or five people were standing nearby in a loose circle, talking in muted tones among themselves. I had no idea what about but my steel-trap brain told me instantly it must have something to do with a recent guest.

I figured no sweat. Cemetery talk by its nature is short lived (I had to say that). I'll just slip over into the woods where I can hide among the trees and observe until the coast is clear.

I observed and observed and observed.

I was getting danged tired of standing in one spot. What could be all that fascinating to talk about in a cemetery? Finally, I couldn't wait any longer. I had to find a campsite before the rapidly approaching darkness settled in. I headed back to the road. I found a place to sleep a little farther down the road, but it was disappointing to lose the level, mown grass and what was a given at a cemetery — peace and quiet.

A couple of days later I learned the price of standing in the woods next to the cemetery. I was "eat-up" with chiggers. I don't know why the area fascinated them so, but between my thighs and navel you couldn't put the end of your little finger on a chigger free spot. Under the belt must be the chigger Club Med. They must feel secure in such a tight spot. Or they simply have a high threshold for sweaty, smelly places.

It was double dark by the time I found my cemetery alternative. By the outline of black shapes against an only-slightly-less-black sky, I could tell it was a business of some type sitting toward the rear of a large lot. Only the next morning did I find out what I'd picked. Before daylight I was awakened by truck tires and shoes on gravel and the sound of men's voices.

I was in a trucker's staging area of some kind. For the sake of my hide, I knew I'd better be up and out of there quick. I got dressed, packed away clothes and sleeping gear, took down and stowed my tent and was walking toward the road in about ten minutes.

There was no way I could reach the road without passing a group of about ten truckers talking. Never have I felt smaller or more out of place. I was somewhere I had no business being and had no one's permission to be there. I had to say something. I picked a likely looking person in charge and walked up to him. "Excuse me, I didn't have a place to spend the night last night so I hope you don't mind that I slept on your lot."

It was a hurried attempt to spit it out and get the hell outta there so I doubt if it was that logical or clear sounding. I purposely avoided the words "Walking from Los Angeles to New York." These looked like tough guys. "Out of work" they might understand, even "homeless" may provoke a spark of sympathy but I knew cross country walking wouldn't be on their short list of activities they'd feel compassion for or camaraderie with. The man mumbled something that made as much sense to me as my speech must have made to him. I was just happy that nothing came out of his mouth that sounded like, " Grab his ass, boys! I'm calling the law!"

Chapter 52
A Night in Police Custody

One day while writing this book it occurred to me that I was spending an inordinate amount of time telling about my nighttime adventures.

I think I know why they outnumber the day.

A person on the average adventure is in a car. Since he knows he has the money and ability to spend the night in a motel, his nights are taken care of. Nights aren't much of an adventure for him.

Hikers have the nights in sharper focus because having a safe, secure place to spend the night isn't so certain. The difference lies in the word "certain."

When it's certain that you will have a home your thoughts and actions can be directed toward your daytime activities. And since by its very nature walking precludes safe, secure places, you must deal with the inevitable nightly problem.

You're smart. You know I don't mean to give the impression that the day of the walker is nothing but fret and worry about where there're going to spend the night. I only want to inform and enlighten.

How you deal with all this is in direct relationship to how you handle other aspects of your life. If you let stuff get to you, you're going to get paranoid every time you see those afternoon rays start to slant.

I guess I'm a "something'll turn up" kind of guy. It would cross my mind a few times during the day, but I knew from past experience that it's rare for something not to turn up. A practiced eye is a big help. And too, a generous helping of Harry Truman's old saw about staying "out of the kitchen if you can't stand the heat" applies to long-distance walking. If thoughts about where you are going to spend the night completely take away from your enjoyment of the day, you need to hang it up. The road ain't for you.

I suppose we all have things in our lives that we've heard more than once and, on that basis, have accepted as fact. Hearing something once doesn't guarantee that we'll take it as a certainty. But, invariably, if we've heard something at least two different times, from two different sources, it's true.

If Bob said it it's probably true. It *might not* be true but Bob's usually reliable. If Mike also says it, it's fact. Reality and logic don't have anything to do with it.

We all have lots of those kinds of fallacies stored inside us. One of mine was to come into play as I walked into Winnfield, Louisiana on July 4th.

It was late afternoon, and if you've ever spent a summer in the South you know, likely as not, afternoon will work itself up into a frothy thunderstorm. And if a game show host said, "For a new car, tell me what day of the year is the most typical, hot, summer day in the South."

"I'm gonna go with — July 4th!"

I don't know if you won the car, but I do know it's a good answer.

As I got into the heart of Winnfield the sky over my right shoulder was getting dark and ugly.

If I had been out in the country on either side of Winnfield I could have quickly put up my tent. (We've talked about the old ostrich defense before).

I was in the heart of town, though, and couldn't see anywhere to go. I could have ridden out the storm in a doorway somewhere but it was so late in the afternoon that by the time the storm blew itself out it would be dark, and I'd be stuck in Winnfield with no place to put down.

Just at this time one of my two-different-sources-at-two-different times "actualities" popped into my head.

This one was awakened in my memory by a sign, "Winn Parish Courthouse and Jail." It all fell into place. There was the storm, the night, the jail.

Hadn't I heard more than once back somewhere in my hidden past that "knights of the open road" were given a spare jail bed to sleep in if the bed was vacant and the knight was gentle and skillful in the asking?

It seemed logical. Why should they care all that much? The bed was there. It wasn't *their* bed. Why not give it to some deserving person just for that night?

A young lady sheriff's deputy was behind the desk. I'd turn on my charm. I'd be her knight.

My story had never been told more sweetly.

Nothing! Not so much as a glimmer of hope radiated from Miss Winn Parish Sheriff's Department. Evidently, she hadn't heard the same stories I had.

"You might try the police department next door."

Noticing big, fat drops already hitting the sidewalk out front and figuring I had nothing to lose. I ducked next door.

I decided to alter my approach this time. On my way over from the jail I'd noticed that the police department building had a large, covered parking area. This time I wouldn't be so bold as to ask for a bed.

Bending the truth only slightly, I said to the lady dispatcher, "The lady over at the jail said you might be able to help me." It was a half-truth and it helped soften the blow — sort of a verbal foot in the door.

Just at the precise moment I'd finished my twice-told tale of walking and need, in my best "sugar wouldn't melt in my mouth" manner, the phone rang and it was the chief on the other end. After he'd finished telling her why he'd called, the lady dispatcher said, "Chief, there's a guy here walking across the country, blah, blah, blah. He wanted to know if he could sleep, blah, blah, blah."

I held my breath. This could go either way. And if I'd had my druthers I'd have taken my chances with the dispatcher. She could see the hurt in my eyes, hear the pleading in my voice. To the chief I was another nameless, faceless, bum looking for a handout.

I was sure the dispatcher would either say, "He wants to talk to you," or "Okay, Chief, I'll tell him." Meaning my chances of getting refuge from the storm were slim and none. To my amazement there was no hesitation at the end of the conversation. She hung up, looked at me and said, "He said it was okay."

Tell me why mosquitoes would hang around the outside of a police station all night? Flies are a no-brainer (all those powdered sugar droppings from all those doughnuts.) But mosquitoes? Policemen get out of their cars and dash into the station, and then dash just as fast from station to car. Where is the mosquitoes window of opportunity?

Though the mosquitoes relieved me of several pints of blood, they surely can't depend on the extremely chancy and gaunt trans-continental walker for their "bread and butter."

As the night progressed I realized the police hadn't been so magnanimous after all. Really, all they'd given me was a slab of hard concrete with fire ants living in the cracks, a cloud of killer mosquitoes, and an endless stream of police cars coming and going all night. It looked great as long as the storm raged, but the calm after the storm made this place lose a lot of its luster. The next morning I felt like the dogs had had me under the porch.

Chapter 53
Tell Us About Tullos

Tullos is one of those places where "Welcome to Tullos" and "Please Visit Tullos Again" are written on the front and back of the same sign. I fully expected Tullos to be a forgotten blip on my walking radar screen as soon as I was out of sight. What about Tullos could possibly be memorable? There were so many other people, sights, sounds, tastes and even touches to remember from this walk. Poor Tullos. It was America's stray dog. Not a prayer for a visit from the Good Morning, America show, a "rest of the story" from Paul Harvey, or even an ultra-conservative zinger from Rush would ever grace poor Tullos, Louisiana. And yet, for me Tullos will always shine as bright as Venus in the early evening sky.

Asked to name the top ten memorable experiences of five-and-a-half months and 3813 miles of walking, Tullos would stand as straight and tall, bright and polished as a member of the Queen's guard. What did Tullos do for me to deserve such a place in my memory? Actually, my initial impression of Tullos was drastically different from the glowing assessment I've so far given it.

I'd only been in town a few minutes when three black men in a pickup stopped beside me. These three men *could* have made me come away from Tullos with entirely different memories.

But these three men weren't the "few bad apples" they were the finest fruit on the vine.

"We saw you back down the road. Where you headin?"

Their manner, tone, and apparent honest interest was cause for me to launch into a short version of my I'm-attempting-to-walk-from-Los Angeles-to-New York speech.

When did you start?"

"How far do you walk in a day?"

"How much longer do you think it will take?"

"If you're walking from Los Angeles to New York why are you way down here?"

Questions of real interest can't help but boost a person's ego. These guys were graduates of the finest Swedish school of mental massage. My 15 minutes of fame was purring like a stroked pussycat.

Their questions weren't the best of what I took away from Tullos, though. Nice as they were, I'd heard them all before. What I remember most was an act of complete selflessness by one of the men.

These weren't rich men. The truck, their clothes, their fingernails — Tullos itself said as much.

The driver reached deep into his front pants pocket. He didn't just grab whatever was on top. He scooped, then scooped again like a backhoe. When he was satisfied he had it all he held out his cupped hand to me.

I could hardly express my thanks. The few crumpled bills and assorted change didn't mean that much to me, I had money. It was the act, the gesture. The man's actions spoke so much louder than any words he could say. Here was someone without that much to give — giving from the heart. It was a picture larger than life. This is what humanity is supposed to be. A generous heart and a loving nature. The man has a lesson for all of us.

Chapter 54
Good Pine / Bad Pine

Just down the road from Tullos is her sister city, Good Pine. I couldn't help but see some irony in that name. From what I'd seen of the worship of the pine tree in Louisiana, I wouldn't have been surprised to hear that the legislature had proclaimed New Orleans now to be "Good Pine."

Why waste a name of such reverence on this little Tullos look-alike?

As truck after truck after truck filled with pine logs zoomed past me, I couldn't help but feel that either consciously or subconsciously, directly or indirectly, every life in this state was affected by the pine tree. And I don't mean just human life. From the burrowing groundhog to the soaring red hawk and every fire ant, armadillo, rabbit, and deer in between. Somehow the pine tree played a part in their lives. For better or worse, richer or poorer, in sickness or in health, they were all affected. Louisiana was strapped to the back of the pine log. Its fate entirely in the pine trees' hands. In fact, every wheel turning in the Deep South was either fueled or greased by the pine tree.

I saw so many log trucks running the roads I wondered if there were any butchers, bakers or candlestick makers or if everyone in the south was on one giant pine processing assembly line. Was everyone either a planter, a grower, a cutter, a hauler, a processor or a consumer?

And have you ever been close to a pulp mill? Some outsider, with his unaccustomed virgin nose, might twitch it, make a face and say, "Oooh, how do you stand the smell?" While the guy who has three kids and has been looking for work for six months says, "Smells like money to me!"

So it's hard to come down too hard on the logging industry in Louisiana. She's putting gravy on the table and shoes on the feet.

All of the logging has made a moonscape of much of the South, though. So many areas had been clear-cut. Giant wheeled trucks and metal tread dozers went in and took the trees from the cutters and the end results looked like a battlefield. Nothing remained but churned earth, fire ants (always the fire ant) and the occasional, spindly branch not worthy of the effort to cut it.

Unpleasant as these areas were to the eye, I found myself forced one night to put down in one. I walked back over a rise, out of sight of the road, and in complete darkness put my tent up.

I knew from past, painful experience that this was bad business. Like Custer, blundering onto a gathering of Sioux nations at the land of greasy grass on the Little Big Horn, a person setting up a tent in the dark in fire ant hunting grounds could easily be scalped before daylight.

Sure enough, about two hours after "lights out" I felt the first bite. I wanted to say it wasn't possible. Not again. I'd made sure nothing touched the ground but my feet, and I'd even brushed off the bottoms before getting in.

How did they do it? Nothing to do but drag out the flashlight and investigate. To my amazement, there was an unbroken line of ants that looked as if they were imitating elephants in the circus, grabbing with their trunks the tail of the ant in front of them.

My light did a reverse sweep over the circus parade. Where were these fire-breathing devils entering the big top? The light came to rest in one corner of my tent, next to where my head had been lying moments before.

Those Jackasses! Those six-legged, mega-bite Jackasses! They'd chewed a hole through my tent!

Ants too slow or dull-witted to grasp what my light and heavy breathing meant got smushed.

My batteries would only allow for the briefest of damage control at this time. Real repairs would have to wait for more light and a safe port.

I balled up a sock and jammed it into the corner.

The next day when I thought I'd put sufficient miles behind me to be out of harm's way, I stopped at a country church and sat down on the steps. I pulled out my tent and inspected the hole. I ran all my meager repair possibilities through the computer. The answer came back: smooth stone and dental floss. I searched the churchyard for a suitable stone. At the minimum it had to be about half again as big as the size of the hole. And actually, that was the maximum size, too. I wanted it to adequately cover the hole but be unobtrusive. You want to keep rocks in your tent as close to the molehill, versus the mountain as you can.

I stuck my selected rock in the center of the hole, squeezed the tent fabric down around its sides 'til it was all bunched at the rear of the stone. Then I took my length of dental floss and did several rodeo "calf-ropin'" whip stitches around the bunched material completely sealing off the hole.

Would the ants be desperate enough, or dumb enough, to chew through granite to get to me.

Chapter 55
Lightning Strikes Twice

There really are saints among us. And it's nice that there's no roster in a program that lists them. It would spoil the spontaneity that characterizes saints if they were readily recognizable. They really only materialize when a person is in need. You don't find them, they find you. They're out there, looking like ordinary people, toiling away like everyone else, ready to spring into action when the situation dictates.

You've followed recipes that say "add a pinch." You take the quantity that can be grasped between your thumb and forefinger, then you shift your finger and thumb across each other distributing the ingredient into the mixture.

That's how I picture God distributing saints among us. As He shifts His giant fingers up in Heaven, the saints drift down to Earth and are scattered so that no one area has too many or too few. There are just enough to enrich our life here. It was wise of God to not give the saints any special features, or clothing or signs saying, "Resident Saint."

Through their deeds, we'd find out who they were. It might be that lady who works at the 7-11, the clerk at the post office, that farmer who keeps those pigs that smell to high heaven, or even that guy who irritates you by writing a check in the express lane at the grocery check out.

They only need a catalyst to reveal their true sainthood. If the opportunity to comfort, help, serve, or support presents itself, the saint is revealed.

One day when God was sprinkling saints down it must have been humid because two stuck together and landed really close together near Tullos, Louisiana.

It had only been a few days since my last saint encounter — the one where the black man had given me all the money in his pockets. Little did I know I was about to encounter another saint just down the road.

On my walk there were times when I'd sit at a "proper" resting place, like a bench in front of a grocery store or service station, or a picnic area at a roadside park. But then there were times I was so weary I dropped wherever there was a place to drop.

I was out in the country a few days out of Tullos. I was hot, thirsty and weary. The desire to see anymore of Louisiana had left me. All I was interested in was relieving my shoulders of that two-ton pack, and sticking my feet in a tub of ice water — shoes on or off, it made no matter.

I came to a curve in the road. There was a house with a fairly large front yard that ended at a dry, shallow ditch beside the road. Luckily, shade from a tree in the yard reached the ditch. I could sit on the edge of the yard with my feet in the ditch and still be under the shade from the tree.

I shed that killer pack and sank heavily to the grassy bank, too tired to even inspect for fire ants.

As I sat there I must have been the picture of heat-induced pitifulness. I had no water so I just sat. The grassy bank offered only partial relief.

I heard a sound coming from the direction of the house. I looked over my shoulder to see a man coming toward me. In each hand he was carrying a large glass of ice water. When he was about ten feet from me he said, "I thought you might be thirsty."

See, he had no fear of me. He saw someone in need and sought to relieve the pain. He knew I had no knife or gun. He even knew there was no desire in my heart to do him harm. He had the vision God grants all saints.

It's really kinda sad that we've let ourselves as a society evolve into such a fast paced, run away, "Me" machine. There's such a hard scramble just to keep the wolf from the door that it seems there's little time left for any really deep thought or concern. We should take more time for our fellow man.

But I found on my walk across America that there are still people who refuse to get caught up in the machine. I like to think of them as "People- People". To them it's still a world of people, not things. They realize we're all in this together and they practice the Golden Rule.

The kind man and I talked. I could see he was interested in my story about walking across the U.S. In fact, he had no way of knowing there was a "story" attached to the guy sitting dejectedly on his front lawn. To him I was simply one of God's creatures in need.

Thank you God, for the saints among us. Not only are they saviors, they are a beacon, a guiding light for us to follow.

Chapter 56
Oh Dear, I'm Caught in the Headlights

A cardinal rule of distance walking: Don't get caught out after dark. You feel like you're swinging the pinata stick at a birthday party. You can't see and flail out in any direction hoping to connect with something. Not good tactics if you're a stranger in a strange land.

I did everything I could to prevent it happening. In spite of the best-laid plans of mice and men, it still happened.

Seldom did I get caught in such a situation if I was out in the country, but I might suddenly find myself entering a town with no indication of its size. If it looked like it was going to get dark, did I stop, turn around and walk back out of town or take my chances and try to reach the other side before dark? Not once did I turn around and go back. My guess is, it didn't have anything to do with darkness or towns or sleeping. The thought of the dues I'd paid to reach this point, and the enormity of what still lay ahead made it virtually impossible to take one step backward.

Jonesville, Louisiana. I breathed a small sigh when I double checked the green sign at the edge of town and confirmed it was Jones*ville*, not Jones*town*. The town was nice, but dinky. Not dinky enough that I could stretch the remaining daylight all the way across its borders, though. By the time I'd reached Jonesville's eastern limits it was starting to get difficult to make out shapes, forms, and distance. I knew that the very first opportunity for a campsite must be grabbed.

I spotted a possibility. It was chancy. Something I wouldn't have considered under the best of times.

I saw a gravel lane winding back to a large, two-story farmhouse way off the road. About halfway back I noticed a barn. It looked like it belonged to the farm. The distance and failing light made it hard to tell exactly but it looked like the little lane ran up to the barn, then turned sharply to the left, skirted around the barn and continued back to the farm house.

I studied layout and sight angles for a moment and hastily came to the conclusion that if I positioned myself just right I could sleep so I couldn't be seen from the house.

Of course, anyone coming off the highway headed toward the house would expose me big time. They'd come within a few feet of where my tent would be and their headlights would play on my tent for several seconds before the sharp turn to the left. I'd be the proverbial sitting duck.

It was almost dark, though, and I'd be gone by first light. The odds were in my favor. The farmer was probably already watching the evening news with his pipe and slippers, and not likely to emerge again unless the dogs made a racket.

I remember in the book *All Creatures Great and Small* the Veterinarian, James Herriot made the observation that whenever he called upon a farmer concerning a sick animal he always went straight to the barn rather than to the house. No self-respecting farmer would be caught in the house during working hours.

His was kinda the reasoning I used as I stood contemplating the breach of this farmer's sanctity. It was nearing dark, and hadn't the farmer put in a day's work? From the looks of the place, this was a real working farm. Even if Jonesville had any nightlife to offer, he was similar to James Herriot's North England farmer. Duty and decency required he be home with wife and family after dark.

It was with some faith that these unspoken codes wouldn't be broken that I gingerly walked back the lane and put up my tent. I never gave any serious thought to sleeping in the barn. I thought it would be cooler in my little screened tent. And I figured if I did get caught, just mashing down grass would plea bargain better than "breaking and entering."

You'd think that after walking since daylight, my head would hit the pillow with a thud and I'd be out in ten seconds. Seldom did it work that way. Like most people I'd have a few minutes of reflective thought before I dropped off. Thoughts about the day, folks and friends back home, now in their nice beds, with full stomachs and moist throats. And a few thoughts and moments devoted to girlfriends — past, present and future.

I'm not sure what stage I was when I was jarred back to reality by the simultaneous sound of wheels on gravel and flash of headlights lighting up the inside of my tent.

As Scarlett would have said, "God's Nightgown! I'm caught!"

I just laid there. I didn't know what to do. I knew this situation wasn't going to just evaporate into the Louisiana night air but I wanted more time to think. What defense would I use? Maybe this wasn't the farmer. If luck was with me I was about to be taken aboard a spacecraft and examined gently by kind aliens. It could happen!

Then there was no sound just the lights easing slowly closer and closer to my tent. If it was the farmer was he going to extract his revenge by slowly crushing me inside my tent?

The bright lights continued to inch forward. Finally, they stopped no more than three feet from my head. I decided whatever the outcome I had to face the music. I threw back the zipper and popped out. Surely I looked like a prisoner of war emerging from an overrun bunker.

I could see nothing but blinding light, or hear nothing behind that light. I only knew there was *something* behind the light and silence, something I had to give a good accounting to.

I blurted out the only thing I could come up with, "Sir, before you pass judgment could I plead my case?"

Silence. Nothing from behind the headlights.

"I'm trying to walk from Los Angeles to New York. It got dark on me before I could find a suitable place to spend the night. I noticed your barn."

It sorta trailed off at this point like the last few sparks of a brilliant burst of fireworks on the fourth of July. It was short, booming and brightly colored but fizzled to nothing quickly.

The first sounds that came from behind the lights were the *second* best I could have wished for. The first would have been, "Hey, no problem, Buddy, have a good sleep." And the icing on the cake would have been those six little words I loved best during my walk: "Oh, you'll make it all right." (Yes, I realize "you'll" is a contraction and technically two words but humor me on this.)

What I actually heard was, "Yeah, I saw you earlier passing through Jonesville."

Praise the Lord, it wasn't, "I don't give a flying cow cookie!"

My relief was enormous. We talked and, even though there were no words to this effect, I sensed something of a kindred spirit. I caught just a hint of envy in his voice. But being a hardworking responsible farmer who wouldn't dream of being in the house during daylight hours, he probably couldn't admit to a desire to do anything as frivolous as what I was doing.

"When you get up in the morning come on down to the house and have breakfast with us."

A night that could have been spent tossing and turning, worrying about getting caught, became one of peaceful rest, secure in the fact that I was safe and accepted at this spot.

Do the words "cheese grits" mean anything to you? Grits are a staple in the southern diet. Breakfast simply isn't breakfast without grits. But I had never really tasted cheese grits until I experienced them at the farmer's house. And these cheese grits were loaded with garlic. Mmm!

The next morning, sitting there as the farmer's wife prepared breakfast, many warm thoughts of the good life came rushing back. It had been months since I'd experienced a really soft chair, the smell of bacon frying and conversation with people who didn't look down their noses at me.

Like all good cooks she had a meal on the table much quicker than you'd think possible.

"How'd you get so fast? Did you do your internship at McDonald's," I joked.

"No, just 37 years of three-meals-a day practice," she said. "When you have three young boys and a husband standing around like hungry hounds you learn to dish it up pretty quick."

"Unless you've walked from Los Angeles I don't think you can fully appreciate what a meal like this means. It's really great," I said.

So as not to give all my attention to the cook I turned to the farmer and mostly as a courtesy asked, "What do you have to do on the farm today?"

"Well, I've got beans that need dusting."

I'd grown up in a rural area and knew what bean dusting meant. Still it was fun to picture a weather beaten old farmer wearing one of those cute little French maid aprons standing out in a field of knee-deep soybeans, feather duster in hand.

I thought I'd use this opportunity to pick the brain of a local regarding fire ants. Did they agree with me that the potential was there for them to become the master race?

"Fire ants have bedeviled me for a long time. How do y'all cope with them?"

In their voices I detected a hint of hatred, yet resignation. Much like any other population that has been overrun and conquered by an enemy.

"Of course, we hate them too, but you learn to cope."

Then he said something I'd painfully learned weeks before but wasn't sure other people were aware of.

"No one really knows why but they seem to congregate and travel along the bases of buildings. You have to keep that in mind if you work around the outside of your house."

"Yes Sir," I said. "I'm well aware of that. Back in central Texas I had a run-in with them when I slept next to the rear wall of an abandoned building."

"Then I don't have to tell you what demons they can be," he said.

"No Sir, We've had many battles."

"Something else surprising is that they like to swarm around anything electrical. They can ruin an air conditioner. That's another weird thing about them that has everyone puzzled."

Take note fellow citizenry. Think! Wouldn't a simultaneous and total blackout of all electrical power be a logical first step for an invasion and takeover?

Chapter 57
Struggle in the Churchyard / Struggle in the Stockyard

It was hard to leave cheese grits heaven. If breakfast was this good, what delights lay in store at lunch and dinner?

I wasn't invited, though. And even if I had been something was tugging at me. Actually, two things were tugging at me. There was that ever-present, strong magnetic pull coming from the island of Manhattan. And the second tug was coming from The Father of Waters just a few miles to the east of Jonesville. I could almost smell the Mississippi. Crossing state lines thrilled me, and the Mississippi River represented even more. When I crossed it I would have walked halfway across the country.

Something happened in this section of Louisiana that still has me puzzled. I should have asked someone to explain. But I suppose the event always occurred out in the country and by the time I reached town my thoughts were, as always, channeled down the Cold, Wet and Sweet Tunnel.

It's a little difficult to explain because I never saw it, I only heard it. Here's my best explanation: You know those small cannons they fire at Civil War re-enactments? The same ones that some colleges use when their football team scores a touchdown?

If you were walking down the road and at exactly thirty second intervals you heard one going off over in the woods, out of sight, wouldn't it pique your curiosity? Of course, the first shot jars your skin loose, the second has you checking your body for holes and after the third, you strain to hear a rebel yell.

I had more than enough time to try and figure out what it was. I have no way of knowing if I'm correct but here's my theory: Cotton was once king throughout the South. Times and needs change, the land gets weary, so other means of livelihood need to be found.

New Orleans, Gulfport, Biloxi, Mobile are all relatively close. They need seafood don't they?

It's said that most rich and successful people are the ones who saw a need and filled it. Perhaps the cotton farmer thought there was more money in supplying crawfish, catfish and frog legs to restaurants along the coast. And after the farmers started his ventures, he realized birds liked young crawfish, catfish and frogs too.

I'm still speculating. Nets or screen over the ponds are too costly and laborious. Loud noises scare birds.

Rig a noisemaker that blasts every 30 seconds when no one was around.

I have no way of knowing if this is true. Aha! I must be on to something. I was looking at the map to see how much further it was to the Mississippi when I noticed the name of the very next town — Frogmore!

All this thinking made me weary. That and that infernal pack on my back. I needed a break. The old abandoned church yard seemed just the ticket. Since I could easily be seen from the road I decided to go around back.

By this time on my walk, even my dull mind knew to watch for fire ants. I knew I couldn't sit down, and that I'd best prop my pack in the fork of a tree instead of putting it on the ground.

I stood there just looking at the surroundings enjoying a few moments of relief for my neck and shoulder muscles.

I heard a noise that wasn't loud, yet it seemed out of place. It sounded like leaves rustling. I paid close attention to see if I could determine direction and distance. After all, this was rattler country. I hadn't heard any buzzing or rattling but this was unnerving. Finally, I zeroed in on the noise It was coming from a worm — one of those big, green, hairless ones, the size of your index finger.

No, silly. The sound wasn't coming from the worm's mouth. The worm was thrashing about in the leaves. Why? I bent to take a closer look.

Then it was obvious. He was thrashing for the same reason you, or I, or a water buffalo would be thrashing. He was being attacked by ants.

Now I have no affinity for big, green worms. Neither love, nor distaste, nor revulsion do I feel for big, green worms. One thing was clear in my mind, though. I had a distinct and unequivocal hatred for fire ants.

I suppose if you can look at it with a detached eye it was no different from what occurs a million times a day in the food chain. It was only nature taking its course. Maybe the fire ants had no animosity toward the caterpillar, no more than we do the cow, or the tomato. The fire ants were only doing what nature told them to do.

Somehow it's different with fire ants, though. I'll bet if you had a magnifying glass you'd see smiles on their faces. We might enjoy sitting down at McDonald's, but I doubt anyone relishes our victory over the cow. Nor does the lion smile at having overtaken the antelope.

Naturally, I felt sorry for the worm. I would have felt differently if it had some defense, but some anemic jerking was about it.

This scene may be repeated a hundred times within a hundred yards, but I just couldn't let this happen. Not when I had the power to change the outcome. I picked up the worm and brushed the ants off. They didn't fall away as if they knew they were doing something wrong. When they could, they scurried to the other side of the worm. And when cornered, they clung tooth and nail to the worm's sides. They weren't going to go down without a fight. And I'm sure if my finger flicks hadn't been fast enough they'd had no compulsion about attacking me.

When the worm was finally an ant free area I placed him on the limb of a tree. If it's possible to say a worm looked exhausted, he looked exhausted.

And knowing fire ants, there was a better than even chance I had only postponed the inevitable.

I thought it best to *git while the gittin* was good, before the enemy had time to regroup. I grabbed my pack and put my feet on the only safe place I knew of–the hot asphalt of Highway 84.

Late the next afternoon I realized I was about to be caught in a squeeze play. I rounded a curve and above the treetops in the distance I could see the green steel girders of the Mississippi River bridge. The thrill of accomplishment running up my spine ran headlong into the caught-on-the-bridge-in-the-dark chill that was going down my spine. Would dark catch me in the middle of this very long bridge, playing a game of twilight pickle? Should I play it safe, stay on the Louisiana side or try to make it to the Mississippi side before dark. With a smile I envisioned me running back and forth across the Mississippi River bridge. Louisiana darkness, glove and ball in hand, was on one side chasing me. While on the other side of this narrow Field of Dreams, high above the river, Mississippi darkness waited to catch the ball and tag me out.

Maybe if I shifted into overdrive I could make it across before dark. Naw, too "iffy."

As I stood there on the Louisiana side of the bridge debating whether to dash or not to dash, I noticed a stockyard across the road. The longer I looked, the more it looked like the Hilton? I ventured closer. I didn't see any cars or trucks. And I didn't see, and more importantly, didn't smell any animals. It looked like a stockyard that had seen better days. But I guess a stockyard is one of the few businesses where smell is a measure of prosperity. The worse a stockyard smells, the more business they've been having. This one didn't smell terrible, so I knew it had fallen on hard times.

I hopped a few fences and soon was deep in the bowels (I had to say that!) of the stockyard. This was going to be great — a walker's dream come true. There was plenty of fairly clean, loose hay lying around and shelves about eight feet off the ground. I could pitch my tent up there and even if some beast I hadn't seen wandered in, it couldn't reach me. For a fleeting moment, the ant of fire crossed my mind.

"Naw!" "He has his pick. Why would he pick the smell and the mess?"

I started gathering arm loads of hay and pitching them up on the tiers. This was great. It would be one of my best campsites ever. After I had a soft bed of hay, I pitched my tent on top of it. It was a typical deep South night–hot as Hades. So why was I sleeping in my tent?

Have you forgotten about the Louisiana State Bird — The Mosquito? When I had my tent put up, I decided to celebrate my stockyard windfall. After all, not often did I find a spot that offered isolation, security, comfort and protection from the weather. Usually, just one of these was cause for declaring a campsite adequate. All of them being present at once earned the spot a Hikers Five Star Approval Rating. In fact, if you could blot that stain of "stockyard" from your mind, it was almost as comfy as home.

Alas! My euphoria, though beautiful of face and strong of body was destined to die much before its time.

Since I just happened to have the two ingredients essential to celebrations on the road — tortilla chips and pre-sweetened Kool-Aid, I sat down and dangled my feet over the edge of the tier; broke out my chips and decanted the grape *champagne*.

Aah! It doesn't get much better than this.

As I sat crunching chips (in mouthfuls too big) and washing them down with grape Kool-Aid, I noticed I wasn't alone after all. Not too far from me was a huge bull in a small pen. I was surprised that I hadn't noticed him before. It must have been my excitement at finding this place. Or he was quieter than the one who got into the china shop.

Watching him, I noticed he seemed quiet and sad. There didn't seem to be another animal around, and he constantly paced back and forth in his small prison. I felt sorry for him. I was reminded of something a farmer told me when I was a boy growing up in Kentucky. We were discussing farm animals, and he made the comment that he never kept just one of any kind of animal. He didn't elaborate but reading between the lines, I gathered he thought it a heartless thing to deprive any creature of the companionship of his own kind.

The bull took little notice of me so I wasn't concerned about his proximity to me. His life seemed to be taken up not with thoughts of getting at me, but with pacing and wishing and longing.

I realized I had been sitting for quite some time, not chewing nor drinking, just contemplating the bull, and his and my loneliness. We had something in common, really. He had no one to talk to, to laugh with, to touch. Neither did I. His life was pacing back and forth over a short distance. My life was pacing in a straight line for long distances. It occurred to me that I had become that solitary farm animal.

I'm not sure what brought me back, back from the fields, back from the longing, back from the bull. It was more than a feeling, it was a presence. There was a "force" in the midst of the bull and me. Something certainly bigger than me. Bigger even than that great bull.

Oh well, intangible inner flutterings would have to take a back seat — Doritos and Kool-Aid awaited. Without looking I reached for another handful of chips.

Something wasn't right. Not only was I grabbing something, something was grabbing me. My eyes followed my arm to the point where it disappeared into the bag.

Sweet Jesus, Joseph and Mary!

Suddenly the intangible presence took on a very palpable property.

My arm, hand, chips, bag and legs were swarming with fire ants. They hadn't bitten yet. They were just enjoying the nacho chips picnic.

I was about to experience a quick reversal of fortune. I knew as soon as I threw the first punch the party would be over and the fight would begin.

This reflex was impossible to control, though. Your first instinct is to start lashing out at the hordes from hell. No other course of action is even thinkable.

I started flailing, they started biting. They bit with a vengeance born of a party ruined.

"What peasant dare spoil the king's picnic? Off with his head!"

Oh, to have my friend the bull bust out of jail now and come to my aid with giant hoof and horn. I fought with speed and strength I didn't know was in me. My mind flashed to the song *The Battle of New Orleans.*

"We fired our guns and the British kept a comin', There wasn't nigh as many as there was the time before."

Yes, I was winning but at what price? I sustained many bites and was forced to relinquish my beloved chips to the enemy below on the stockyard floor. When I was satisfied I had beaten back the enemy, I looked to see how they could have invaded so quickly. I thought the eight feet of air between me and the ground had created a safe haven. Fire ants were the be-all and end-all of adversaries, but even they couldn't fly. How did they reach me? If I hadn't seen about a hundred clinging to the twine it never would have occurred to me.

Someone had casually draped a piece of baling twine over the tier, apparently just to get it off the ground. It was just touching the ground. If the person tossing the string had exerted just one more infinitesimal particle of energy, it would have raised the twine one more inch, and the ants wouldn't have had a super highway straight to my chips.

What to do now. Here I was, caught in a hotbed of fire ant activity. My tent was up, it was almost dark. It was next to unthinkable to venture away from this place in the dark. Here I knew my only enemy was fire ants; away from here it could be them, plus a multitude of strange and frightening possibilities. But my tree house wasn't so safe and secure anymore.

Their sheer numbers would insure that at least one fire ant would come up with a way to reach me, and direct the others to it. They'd either climb the walls, cross the rafters and dive bomb me, stand on each others shoulders until they were tall enough to reach me or come up with a tiny ant version of the hot-air balloon.

I knew these suckers. They'd be back.

I searched my brain for a defense, anything would be considered. I remembered I had mosquito repellent in my pack. Maybe, just maybe, they'd find it repugnant enough not to cross. After all, they already had my food. I wouldn't let the possibility that it may have been *me* they were after enter my mind.

I sprayed the repellant around the outside bottom of my tent. When I'd made the complete circle of the tent I stood back to admire my ingenuity. I looked closer. Oh, my Lord! The mosquito repellent was creating some sort of chemical reaction on my tent. The nylon was crinkling like cellophane held too close to a flame. The fabric of my tent felt slimy and weak like it had lost its desire to live. I needed an antidote for the venom now and fast. Again my mind raced, going over everything I was carrying. Mentally my bar code scanner covered the entire package that was me. My eyes came to rest on the grape Kool-Aid. This was a stretch but what else could I do. I soaked my washcloth with Kool-Aid and began wiping the repellent from the bottom of the tent. What a mess. It was slimy, burning, icky, hay encrusted, and purple.

The mess I created must have confused or disgusted the ants because I had no more problems that night.

Chapter 58
May and June

Once again fire ants had spoiled what promised to be a pleasant experience. As I zipped my tent closed atop the stockyards tier, I thought about the locals here and the struggles they must have with them every day. The poor natives–none but the rich with their power of money, and the homebound old and infirmed had any hope of avoiding them.

Next day, Natchez.

In all the vastness of what we call The South, in what must be hundreds of thousands of square miles from Louisiana to North Carolina and Tennessee to Florida, there are only a handful of truly southern towns.

Before I get pelted with rotten eggs and pine cones let me explain: I'm talking towns that fit the concept of the *old* south — places where white columned mansions, and manicured, flower-draped lawns with giant magnolia trees lining the driveway are the rule, not the exception. The places where you wouldn't be surprised to see a matched pair of fine bays hitched to a carriage at the front door and a sign on the lawn saying, "Twelve Oaks barbecue here today." The places you would have expected Rhett and Scarlett to live. Places that are genteel and have grace and charm.

Here is my short list of true towns of the old South: Atlanta, Charleston, Savannah, New Orleans, Mobile and Natchez.

I can't say why, but with the exception of Atlanta, a common thread that they all have is water. Did being situated on water have anything to do with the development of the ideal southern town? Maybe a proximity to water created commerce and commerce created wealth which led to mansions and all that went with them.

When I chose to walk through the old South rather than take the crow's route through Kansas, Indiana and Pennsylvania, I pictured it all being like New Orleans and Savannah with magnolias, azaleas, camellias, mint juleps and shoofly pie.

Well, the scrub pine, the log truck, and clear-cutting have smudged my pretty picture of the old South.

But at least I had Natchez to enjoy for awhile.

It's funny that one of the things I did while in Natchez was so far removed from our concept of the old South. Just a few short years ago it would have been foreign anywhere in the US. I wonder what Scarlett's reaction would have been if told that one day you could sit down in Atlanta or Natchez to a Chinese buffet?

I'm afraid I upset our trade balance with the Chinese this day. The small amount of money I gave them in no way was equal to the amount of food I took away nestled next to my gizzard.

During my third egg roll I had slowed enough to take a look out the window and noticed that a nearby business was a pest exterminator. I thought it would be the perfect chance for me to ask if there was any way to get this fire ant "monkey" off my back.

After lunch (When I was a boy we called it "dinner." And I think "dinner" is closer to what I had than "lunch.") I dragged that overstuffed sack of lo-mein called my body over to the exterminator.

Well, yes, they'd be glad to help but they'd never been presented with the fire ant problem in this cross-country-walker light. It required some thought and a little head-scratching.

Finally, their answer was surprisingly close to the one I'd tried back at the stockyards. Go to the hardware store and get a large sheet of black plastic, one that will extend beyond your tent floor at least a foot all around. Buy a heavy-duty ant killer and spray all around the tent on the black plastic. And just as importantly, inspect your campsite carefully for ant mounds, no matter how small, before erecting the tent.

I detected another underlying bit of advice: Sleep with your fingers crossed!

Something that surprised me from the beginning of this walk was how fast my clothes got dirty. I mean, why should they? All I did was walk down the road. I ruined a few pairs of pants (Why do we speak of pants in "pairs?" Pants have a pair of legs, but taken as a whole pants are singular. Shirts have a pair of sleeves, but you'd never ask someone, "How many pairs of shirts do you have?")

Oh well, as I was saying, I ruined a few pairs of pants because I sat on the road to rest and got tar on them. I'm surprised I had enough gumption: (Did the author of *Forrest Gump* mean "Gump" to be a play on words?) to make it from Los Angeles to New York if I didn't have any more sense than to sit on hot tar.

After a few hundred miles it occurred to me to grab a piece of paper or cardboard from alongside the road to sit on. And after a few hundred more miles my pea brain took another quantum leap forward and pictured my resting place beside the road being even mo' better if I folded my towel and put it between the paper and my bony butt.

So, if the worst thing I did was sit down on my towel beside the road why did I get so dirty? Did cars passing by stir up dust I couldn't see? And did the dust mix with my sweat to create mud on my clothes?

I found I couldn't hold out much longer than a week before going to a laundromat if I expected to be accepted in polite society.

Brookhaven, Mississippi was coming up and the dot on my map said she would be big enough to have a laundromat. Brookhaven didn't really sit directly on my beaten path, and though it pained me to deviate, I knew it had to be done.

About a mile off Highway 84, on my way over to Brookhaven, a car slowed and stopped beside me. I wasn't uneasy because it was a man alone, wearing a suit, driving a car (versus a pick-em-up truck) and he didn't pause long enough to give me time to conjure up any bad thoughts.

He immediately launched into the familiar "I saw you walking back down the road, where you headin'?"

I was always glad for the interest and attention. And by now, I thought I was a good enough judge of human nature to tell the good guys from the bad guys.

It boils down to two choices. Either you can go out and greet the world, cope with it on its own terms, make up your mind that you're going to have fun or you can bag groceries at the Piggly-Wiggly, come home at night and bury yourself in the vast wasteland of television and one day wonder how you got to sixty so fast.

We talked and I grew more confident that this guy was all right. I gathered he was an insurance salesman who longed for something more challenging and exciting. After we'd talked a few minutes he said, "There's a Western Steer just up the road. Are you hungry?"

Picture my sly smile here.

"Good, I'll buy."

Over the All-U-Can-Eat-Buffet (Will these people never learn) I found out he had dreams, too. A dream maybe even more exotic than my Los Angeles to New York dream.

I had only managed a few bites when the man said his name was Robert.

"You know what I'd like to do? Do like the pioneers did and take off out West in a covered wagon. Eventually, I'd cover all the western states. Before I was married I used to frame houses so I can work with tools. I'd just load the wagon up with all my tools and I'd make ends meet by doing odd jobs as a handyman. I'd go on the backroads, pull up to a farmhouse and offer to make any repairs they needed done. They could pay me or simply feed me dinner and let me pasture my mules for the night. I could sleep in the wagon."

I could tell his story needed telling. I knew the excitement that had built inside him. During the entire telling he'd hardly taken a deep breath and his fork remained suspended between his plate and mouth.

It was good meeting and talking with a kindred spirit. The enthusiasm made him beam. Maybe we all dream but to what extent are we willing to act on those dreams? Rationalization is easy.

I figured some encouragement would be kind on my part, if only to help pay for the meal. Later, I thought my first words may not have seemed kind nor encouraging.

"I knew you didn't see covered wagons on every used car lot so I said, "Where would you get a wagon?"

I was stopped cold when he said, "Oh, I've already built the wagon. It looks just like a covered wagon from a western movie except it has rubber tires instead of steel. It has taillights and turn signals; a fold-down bunk that fastens to the wall during the day and it even has a seat with springs. And to complete the rig I've got the prettiest pair of matched mules you ever saw — May and June."

By now I was caught up in his enthusiasm and was only slightly joking when I said, "If you need a tool gopher I'll volunteer."

One of the first things we'd talked about when he'd stopped beside me on the road was my need for a laundromat, so I was happy and not all that surprised when he said, "If you'd like you can go home with me and have supper. I'll show you the wagon and introduce you to May and June. You can shower and use our washer for your clothes."

His place was way out in the country. Where I come from there are three levels of land ownership and they are:

1. A certified farm from which you make a living.

2. A house with a lot or yard. This can be in the city or country.

3. That nebulous quantity in between which can be anywhere between one and fifty acres called "some acreage."

I'd say May and June's dad had "some acreage." By the time I'd been shown around the place, been introduced to Carol (his wife, not a mule), May and June, seen the other critters, and had a thorough indoctrination into the joys of building and owning a covered wagon, it was dinnertime. And this wasn't any grab-something-out-of-the-freezer-and-pop-it-in-the- microwave dinner. Carol went out into the garden, picked several different kinds of vegetables, cleaned and cooked them on the spot. (I didn't see the chicken meet his demise, so I can't say if it was done, or more correctly "done in," on the spot).

I couldn't believe my luck. The Western Steer All-You-Can-Eat Buffet and a home cooked meal both in the same day.

Over dinner I expected to be pumped further about my walk. I was surprised by what Carol said first.

"You'd have to be a mother to understand where I'm coming from, but I'm curious as to what your mother had to say about all this. Worrying and motherhood are one in the same."

"I guess she worries, but I think she learned a long time ago not to be too surprised at anything I might do. She told me once that she was afraid when I got my first motorcycle, but she told herself to trust in the Lord to take care of me. I think that policy has served her well through some episodes concerning me," I said.

I learned the lady wasn't too keen on the handyman out west adventure. I was surprised because I thought all this had been worked out. My impression was this had been talked about and planned for years, so I just assumed that the trip West was with her blessing, or at least she had acquiesced to the idea.

The nice thing about dreams is they are unisex. One size fits all. There is no right or wrong dream. Everyone has them. The sad inequity of dreams, though, is that they are often only comprehensible and rational to the person they were born to. And never was the disparity greater than the gap that exists between the dreams of the sexes. So often women's dreams don't make sense to men, nor do men's dreams hold any logic for women.

I sensed this thing was going to fester until the day Robert came home from work and announced that he was finally going to hitch up May and June and head out. Then the fester would erupt and spew hurt all over the marriage. It would get loud and ugly and ultimatums would be given that would be regretted later.

When Robert went out to make his final check on the cattle for the evening I decided to give Carol my philosophical, walking-down-the-road, grain-of-salt, sage advice.

Both Robert and Carol had made me feel more like family than just someone off the street. I didn't feel I'd earned any right to speak my mind but somehow I didn't feel discouraged from doing it either. Oh well, I thought, I mean well so I'll just say what I think about this going-out-West-in a-covered-wagon thing.

"Carol, I think there's more "little boy" in men than there is "little girl" in women. And if women care about pleasing their men and if they realize that in giving that pleasure they get more in return, then they should cater as much to the little boy as to the big man. I feel that for the sake of your love and marriage you shouldn't fight his going. In fact, I think you should encourage it. Setting your foot down and forbidding him to go only sets the bit between his teeth. You'll gain more in the long run if you don't create an atmosphere of bitterness and resentment. It's overused and maybe even kinda corny but there could be a lot of truth in that old saying about if you love something set it free. If it loves you it'll come back."

The irony was if she wanted the dream to go away, she needed to encourage it to happen in the first place. Little boys might dream about adventure, but after a taste of it they often realize how much home means to them, too.

I wondered how all this serious stuff was coming from my mouth. Who was I to be offering advice?

I decided to end my counseling session on a lighter note. "Anyway, Carol, how many times have you heard stories about little boys who start to run away from home? Most times they're back around suppertime."

If indeed, Robert launched this great adventure, he might be gone for a few months. But one day, if he really loved her, the novelty would wear off and he'd realize what he really wanted in his life. And if he just kept going, it was the wandering life he really loved and not her anyway.

I was invited to spend the night in the covered wagon. It was the first bed I'd slept in since my thirteen-dollar motel room way back in Lamesa, Texas.

While I laid in the covered wagon it was no longer the 1990's. It was 1849 and May, June and I were headin' for Californy to strike it rich. No odd jobs for us. We were going where the streets were paved with gold. And along the way we might even fight off a band of Indians or two.

Little boys have such fun.

The next morning, after breakfast, I was taken back to the exact spot where I'd been picked up the day before. Before I got out of the car, I did my best to convey my heartfelt thanks. I left Robert with a wish that his dream might come true.

Chapter 59
The Best Gift of All

I'd thought that after reaching the civilization that began at Dallas, my days of thirst and hunger would be over. Wouldn't the South be dotted with gas stations and small groceries every few miles. When I looked at the map and saw that the next town after Brookhaven was 20 miles away, no warning flags went up as they would have in the desert Southwest. This was the deep south of Mississippi. Wouldn't there be Mom and Pop groceries every few miles or so?

I learned a "deep south" lesson between Brookhaven and Monticello. If you walk it and don't prepare, you can count on heat, thirst and hunger. Do not count on Mom and Pop. My only relief in those 20 miles was a cool stream running under a bridge along the road. I got "buck-nekkid" and laid flat on my back on the streambed. I don't know of anything city folks got that's quite as delicious.

We all have a day of the week we like best and a day we like least. The day varies for different reasons.

If you took a nationwide survey, I'd say Saturday would top the list and Monday would be at the bottom. You don't need me to elaborate, it's obvious. One is "Oh boy, I don't have to get up and go to work!" The other is "That can't be the alarm, I just laid down!"

Cross-country walkers have their favorite days, too. But since walkers don't have alarm days, other factors come into play.

You might think that, since Saturday is generally a carefree, let's party, day without lots of pressure, the joviality would carry over to the cross-country walker. "Joviality" is the operative word here, however. Joviality denotes some degree of reckless abandonment. And it seems often as not people think they can't be jovial without alcohol being a part of the picture. That's where it gets hairy for the guy walking down the road. Alcohol and reckless swagger seem to go hand in hand. Saturday is also the most likely day to have an empty beer bottle whiz by your head. And Saturdays are a breeding ground for show-offs. I've read that, statistically, one out of every ten cars on the road on Saturday night is being driven by someone legally drunk.

No, Saturdays are not good for walkers.

You may be a little surprised at my favorite walking day. Actually, it's a tie. Tuesdays and Thursdays are equally good. They are both solid, run-of-the-mill, white bread days. For most people they aren't cause for celebration or depression so there's less chance that any emotions will likely boil over and affect the walker. But if Tuesdays and Thursdays were my favorite what was my least favorite day? No, even after all I've said, Saturday wasn't my least favorite. It's the non-work, do-almost-what-you-want, first cousin to Saturday called Sunday.

Let me give you a little background. I carried no stove, no refrigerator, and my pack was about twice the size of those book-bags kids use. The pack had to contain my wardrobe, my rainwear, my vanity closet, my medicine chest, my food and drink, and my gear for sleeping. In short, everything I needed, all in a space about two feet square.

Even though there was some space for food and drink, there was definitely no room for any reserve. I had to be constantly on the alert for sources. It was extremely rare for me to pass a grocery or convenient store. Yes, I ate like a bird — double my body weight every 24 hours.

I was like a wild animal on the prowl. It was a constant search for food. The range of my hunting grounds was very limited, really.

I was heavily dependent on businessess. They were at the top of my food chain. For me a 7-11 was the equivalent of the zebra for the lion, the mouse for the hawk, or the little fish for the big fish.

Picture the sinking feeling when you are tired, hungry, and thirsty and see a sign in the far distance that meant food, only to find when you got there that it was closed.

Sunday was the day the walker's prey was most likely to elude and escape him.

It isn't of that much concern to the non-walker. You just jump in the car and zip to someplace that is open. Zipping is a little tougher on foot.

I was passing through Prentiss, Mississippi on a hot Sunday, a blankety-blank hot, "closed" Sunday.

Do you remember my reluctance to turn and acknowledge the Indian that was beckoning me on the Apache reservation back in Arizona? I felt especially alone and vulnerable and those three little words, "Indian," "Apache" and "reservation" didn't exactly add up to "I Love You." I hoped that by ignoring the Indian, what he represented would go away.

Prentiss, Mississippi gave me the same feeling. I was just beginning to return to country walking after passing through the town of Prentiss. On my left I noticed a group of what must have been ten tough looking men milling around on a carport of a house I was passing. I don't have to tell you my eyes remained front and center, my shoes came down on the pavement without a sound, and my pace and heart quickened, even if I was the only one who knew it.

After I had gone past the men and was just ready to release the breath I'd been holding for the last thirty seconds, I heard a woman's voice: "Would you like a drink of cold water?" Like the Indian's booming voice back on the reservation I could tell the woman's voice was directed at me.

"Cold water" are words probably used on a hot Mississippi afternoon by many hungry spiders to lure many flies. On most Mississippi summer afternoons you couldn't have a better bait. Just like on the reservation, I wanted to pretend I hadn't heard her. Wasn't she being held prisoner? Didn't the men have her chained to a post? Weren't they using her siren voice to lure people to within their grasps?

Even "cold water" was having trouble washing away my fears.

The Indian had persisted until I couldn't pretend any longer that I didn't hear. It was happening again.

It's funny how social expectations control us. We do things that are expected of us, even when we don't want to. Strong forces are at play here. Be really honest. You do certain things every day, either consciously or subconsciously, just because it's expected of you. Example: Are the clothes you wear on a hot summer day what you'd pick if you were free, without any social restraints, to choose. Instead of a business suit, wouldn't a white bed sheet with a hole for your head and two for your arms be more logical? For better or worse, we are controlled. Maybe it's necessary for a functioning society to run smoothly.

I turned and headed back toward the men on the patio. I couldn't turn my back on a kindness, or the offer of a kindness. You don't always have to accept a kindness, but you can't disregard the offer.

I could go back and politely refuse the water but go back I must. It's one of those unspoken, unseens of our society.

I've read that Ted Bundy ingeniously used our tendency to "do the right thing" to lure his victims. He'd wear a cast on his arm, then ask a young girl to help him with a task. Something inside the girl might say she shouldn't be going out of sight with this man, but that old unspoken, fear of hurting someone's feelings was even stronger.

I walked up the drive and as I got to the patio I detected, from the men assembled, a range of feelings about my presence. Some greeted me with a smile and an indication of interest, some didn't seem to be interested one way or the other, and some had a look of displeasure as if to say, "It wasn't me who called you back."

I was relieved when one of the smiling faces asked me about my story. I didn't see the woman and was beginning to feel a little awkward standing there. The telling of my story brought an array of reactions from the men. For the most part, I could place the vocal reaction with the earlier facial one. The smiles I had been greeted with earlier became oohs and aahs. The "It wasn't me who called you back" faces read something like "You over-inflated sack of dog droppings!"

I was glad to hear the screen door slamming and see the approach of "cold water" lady with promised nectar in hand. I could tell she'd be an "Ooh and aah" and would tip the scales in my favor.

After a couple of refills and a few more pleasantries, I sensed it was time for me to move along. Before I left, I wanted to pose an important Sunday afternoon question to the kind lady.

"Are there any places on up the road where I might get food and drink?" I asked.

After a few moments of "yes, no, maybe" she finally said, "I think there's a small place about four miles away."

Though indecisive, she had tried to come up with an answer to my question. I thought it would be impolite to press for further details. My thanks for her kindness was from the deepest reaches of my heart.

After all, what did she owe me? It would have been so simple just to let me pass. She may have been black, I may have been white. But this noble person wasn't concerned with black or white or even shades of gray. Humane people like her don't see distinctions. If they see need, or hurt or misfortune, they do whatever is in their power to relieve it. It's as natural as breathing.

As wonderful and sincere as this lady was, the concept of mileage was lost on her.

Even though it was Sunday and I was leery of maybe-yes, maybe-no grocery stores, there was still hope in my heart. The lady had been so kind, so sweet, surely she wouldn't give me false hope. But the further I walked the more I wondered. Napoleon said an army marches on its stomach. It seemed like I'd been marching forever on nothing but her water. I felt both hopeful that the store was just around the next curve, and worried because it was Sunday, my "leastest" day. I was hungry, hot, thirsty and a stranger in a strange land.

"Where is that store?" I was awash on a sea of self-pity. My gait must have looked like Frankenstein's by now, stiff, plodding, tilting side to side.

Without looking, I could tell a car was slowing down behind me. No, not now. I didn't need this on a Sunday afternoon.

Had I been seen leaving the wrong house? Had some twisted mind construed that to mean whatever was convenient for it?

I thought about slipping out of my pack as fast as I could, jumping the fence and making for a pine thicket, doing my best evasive zig-zag maneuver, but did you ever see Frankenstein run? Me either.

I turned to acknowledge. My guardian angel had re-appeared. And she was holding a barbecued chicken sandwich out the window.

"I got to thinking," she said, "maybe that store is closed on Sundays."

I couldn't believe it. Mother Theresa did stuff like this, not an ordinary woman in Mississippi for a stranger walking down the road.

She'd taken the trouble to come find me, give me sustenance of body and, most importantly, restore my faith in humanity. Her only reward was the inner warmth that comes from having done the right thing.

After she'd gone I ate the sandwich, but it was only by rote. I couldn't enjoy it as it should have been enjoyed. I was touched by the experience — still shaking my head in disbelief. No matter how hungry I was the sandwich shouldn't have been eaten. It should have been bronzed!

Chapter 60
People Get Shot —
The Dark Side of Humanity

When I saw the name Collins, Mississippi on the map, something told me I was going to like the town. There's something about the word "Collins" that says good things to me. Maybe it's the apparent balance of the word itself. I know, I know — "apparent balance" doesn't make a bit of sense to anyone but me. But when I picture the word "Collins" lying across the tip of my finger, it doesn't fall off, it balances.

All right. Picture Schenectady. Does that balance? I think not. Besides balance, Collins has a creamy smoothness to it. Schenectady is buttermilk compared to Collins. Collins has good flow and pleasing aesthetics. Schenectady is bumps and bruises and angles and halting jerks.

This was before I saw the physical Collins. When I laid eyes on her, I knew it was, as Old Blue Eyes said, "My kind of town." And as Rush would say, "It was the way things ought to be." It was of the same mold as Julian, California; Salome and Superior, Arizona; Artesia, New Mexico and Albany, Texas. Like them, Collins was, in a word, "quaint." It hadn't been overrun by progress.

Collins is unique in that the stores along Main Street are still like they were in the 40s. I'd say about the 70s some marketing genius said all storefronts should be set back off the street. It simply wasn't cool to just step from the sidewalk right through the front door. Either Collins was one of the five percent who never got the message (as they say in the military) or more likely, were smart enough to say "Hogwash" and left their storefronts just the way they were, thank you. There was one progress sin I had to forgive Collins for — Pizza Inn Buffet.

Someday when the world becomes too much, sneak away to Collins. See the way things were before they became so crazy. Tranquility, peace, and good sense await.

It isn't unusual for roads leading into or out of town, any town, to be four lanes, when just a mile or two either way, the same volume of traffic is making do with only two lanes. I don't know why. Maybe we're talking some kind of Engineering/Physics law of movement and space and volume here, the crux of which is lost on me.

Maybe the town is just saying, "Look at me. I'm sophisticated." So what if the little green sign on the edge of town says, Escatawpa, or Itta Bena, or Ethel, or Kosciusko, or

Noxapater, or SoSo, or Yazoo City, or even Hot Coffee. "I have something to offer. Stop. Look me over."

In my book, Collins would have been classy with or without a four-lane highway sticking out her sides. In fact, I wish she'd passed when they were giving out four-lane highways. She was a beauty queen to me. Four lanes she had, though. Even out into the country she had four lanes.

Leaving Collins, I was on the four-lane, divided highway walking east. The cars meeting me were headed west. I considered facing traffic the only sane way to walk. If an empty Bud Light bottle was going to say "Howdy" to my head I wanted to see it coming. And the hurler in this Bud Light Olympics might be just a tad less likely to bean you if he thought you might be able to finger him in a line-up later.

I passed an old house, nothing remarkable, just and old and small Mississippi house. The South is dotted with them. Usually low slung, perched on blocks to escape either the water that stands after a rain or an unusually high water table. Whether they are gray or not, a lack of paint gives that appearance. And rich house, poor house, it makes no matter, invariably there are the old oak trees huddled up close, drooping with Spanish moss. There's a dirt driveway and always a big front porch. Nowhere so much as in the South do people like to sit on their front porch.

The house I was passing caught my eye for two reasons. First, there was a Mercedes in the driveway. This little house and a Mercedes did not go hand in hand. And I noticed a big man sitting on the porch in a suit and tie, another inconsistency. Curious as they were, the man and car slipped from my mind before I'd gone as far as a couple of city blocks. Dual forces kept them from lingering: heat because this was Mississippi in July, and thirst brought on by ten pieces of pepperoni and sausage pizza back in Collins.

Then I came upon something else that seemed out of place. It was a small used car lot. You've seen them. About ten cars on a gravel lot. And even though you might notice an occasional ding in a fender, or a low tire, or a missing hubcap, invariably they will all have written in big white letters across their windshields, "Loaded," "Nice," or "One Owner." There's always those little triangular, gaudy-colored banners stretched on a string across the front of the lot. And a sign on the little shack of an office, proclaiming your credit to be good there. Buy here, Pay here, it says.

The cars were the least of my interest on the lot. The ten pieces of pizza, though, made something stand out that was of supreme interest to me. There was a water spigot just on the front edge of the lot. I didn't see anyone around, and I saw no harm in helping myself. Pizza thirst can be bad. I turned on the water, let it run a few seconds to give the sun-heated water and any fire ants that may be in there drinking or bathing a chance to flush out. Then I immersed my head. Remember the elephant who always wets his ears before he drinks? When my head was cool I turned and let the spigot run into the side of my mouth.

I had just turned the water off and straightened up when I was nearly scared out of my skin by a car going down the highway the wrong way. It slid to a stop, not four feet from me. It was the man in the Mercedes.

I couldn't imagine what could be so urgent that the man would come flying down the highway on the wrong side and screech to a halt right next to me. I was soon to be enlightened.

"WHATYADUIN!!!"

"I was thirsty, Sir," I said, and finished the sentence more with a weak pointing of my finger in the direction of the spigot than any actual words.

"People get shot goin' on other people's property 'round here!"

Pulling my pack closer to me as a visual aid, I hoped he would get the message when I said, "I only wanted a drink of water, Sir."

"You got no right to be over there!"

I saw no advantage to be gained by my repeating, for a third time, the fact that it was solely water I was after, so I just stood there. If it didn't win me a reprieve I didn't know what would.

After a few seconds of stewing, the man gave one of those harumphs like Mammy gave Scarlett when she announced she wasn't going to eat a bite before going to the Twelve Oaks barbecue. I got the feeling he wished he could come up with some valid excuse to shoot me. Going on his lot was sufficient in his book, but it might look bad in court.

It was a standoff. All he could do was slam the Mercedes in reverse and head, well actually tail, back up the highway. This time he was going the right direction but pointed the wrong way.

Although I mentally drew a hand across my sweaty brow in relief, I was somewhat annoyed by the ridiculousness of the whole thing. It was nothing more than a power play on his part. He needed to feel big and I was a means to that end. Obviously, the suit and tie, the Mercedes, weren't working.

I didn't sweat it for long. I felt guiltless and thought I was actually the party who'd been wronged.

It didn't seem possible that the lady who brought me a barbecue sandwich just a few miles back and this man who wanted to shoot me could exist in the same world and here they were in the same county.

Chapter 61
Purple Hull Peas

If before I actually started shufflin' these number nines on this walk, someone with a turban and strange mystical powers had said, "Oh Ye of stunted brain, on this elephantine trek, friends of which you were unaware shall give you water and other sweet drink," I would have replied, "Yes, I can see it, Oh Great One."

If he had said, "And birthday cake," I would have replied, "Weird, but maybe." But, if he'd said "Purple hull peas" I'd have said, "Are you crazy, Swami-Dude?"

And yet on consecutive days in eastern Mississippi, I was given all three.

The water and sweet drink wasn't all that unusual. A young couple coming back from a picnic stopped because they'd seen me on their way to the picnic. They had water and soft drinks left over. We exchanged our stories. I expressed my thanks for their thoughtfulness on a hot afternoon, Bon Voyage was expressed among all and each continued on.

The second day and the fulfillment of the second prophecy of birthday cake was a little more strange.

Again a young couple stopped. Seems the vast majority of "Stoppees" (or is "Stoppers?") were young. It's one of the many nice things about being young, you are still adventurous, bold and daring. Bad experiences haven't jaded you yet. This nice couple was in a pickup. (I'd be interested to know which has the greater percentage of pickups, the South or the West) And as was almost always the case, they'd seen me earlier.

It was a brave person, indeed, who made contact with me the first time they saw me.

I've read that sharks rarely attack any large creature, without first making a pass by. The theory is they first want to make sure that what they think is food won't just as likely think *them* food.

I found it was rare for people to formulate and execute on the first sighting.

These kind people weren't sharks. They even had Gatorade. And for Gatorade in July in Mississippi, you'd tackle a shark.

In other times, and other places I had been brave (or was it foolish?) and ventured to try other flavors of Gatorade, besides my "de rigueur" ones, lemon-lime and orange.

I may have said this before, but Gatorade can be the best of drinks, and it can be the worst of drinks. It depends entirely on the circumstances. Are you hot? Are you thirsty? If you can feebly shake your head in the affirmative, Gatorade is great. If you are watching the

Super Bowl in January, and snow is swirling outside, Gatorade is the last thing you want. In fact, it's downright ghastly.

At first, Gatorade only came in lemon-lime (still the choice of the "old guard"). Now they have lemonade, grape, iced tea, (Get real) and something blue. Real men are offended by light beer, and real Gatorade aficionados are offended by what the couple in the pickup offered me — Fruit Punch.

I was sure Fruit Punch was wimp Gatorade. It wouldn't taste like real Gatorade. It would taste perfumy.

But, God bless Texas, that was great Gatorade! I couldn't imagine any other flavor Gatorade, nor the fruit of any other vine, being as wonderful on this summer south Mississippi highway.

It just shows how far removed from snow, January, and the Super Bowl I was.

They said they'd like to talk longer but were late for a birthday party. Everything seemed fairly normal to this point, then they said something that surprised me.

"We'll bring you some cake on the way back."

I knew that their intentions were good, but that their offer could fall through the cracks for any number of reasons. Their resolve could evaporate over time. It might be dark when the party was over and I'd be off the highway by then. I might happen upon an eat/drink place and be inside when they passed by. Or I might be behind a tree for a nature call. If they and the cake found me I'd be happy and thankful, I just wasn't putting much hope into it.

Sure enough, though, two or three hours down the road they rolled to a stop beside me.

So many things happened to me on this walk that if I could have seen a movie of it before I started (Of course, Robert Redford would play me) I would have shaken my head in amazement.

Only in the movies would a person be given birthday cake one day and purple hull peas the next — or so I thought. I never even knew there was such a thing as purple hull peas.

There was an old grocery on the extreme western edge of Waynesboro, Mississippi that had been abandoned. It was one of those places that had been deserted so long it looked like it was built that way, as if it were a movie set. Had it ever been a thriving business with people bustling and doors slamming and money changing hands. It looked dead but what concerned me most at this moment was it had a stoop. I needed to sit. I needed to sit badly. My dogs were barking. Ever see a pack of young hounds who've "treed" a coon? If you've seen it, you've heard it, too. It's one heck of a racket. If my feet could have barked they would have matched, decibel for decibel, any number of coon-frenzied hounds.

I sat on the grocery's stoop, took off my boots and socks, and let the blessed breeze have its way with my feet. "Delicious" is the only word to describe the feeling as the breeze darted in and out between my toes.

I knew I looked like a Norman Rockwell Saturday Evening Post cover. I didn't care. Vanity and hot, tired feet cannot exist side by side. As I sat there, looking at feet I wasn't sure were really mine, I wondered how far feet could expand before they exploded.

I was shaken back to the world of the living by the crunch of tires on gravel — another young couple. I wasn't overly enthusiastic. I was so tired it was easier to wallow in self-pity than to seem interested in what they had to say. They were super-nice people so I tried my best to perk up some.

Air Jordon-ites, Computer Geeks, Mall Rats, Soccer Moms and "Couch Potatoes" may have a little trouble identifying with my next reaction, but my ears raised and my head tilted like a Cocker Spaniel when I heard the words, "Would you like to come to our house for dinner?"

You must wonder how I accepted invitations into people's homes so readily. These people could have been ax murderers! Yes, but it was a two way street. The chances of being sliced and diced and thrown in the bilin' pot were no greater for me than for them. On some sliding scale of human encounters, we all make instant evaluations every day. Whether you want to or not you form opinions in the first few seconds. Is this person nice, is this person not nice? Do I want to spend more time with them or distance myself from them? It's no different on the road. The need to evaluate just comes more often, and your decisions carry more weight.

Though a mustard seed more of faith and an extra dose of gumption are required on the road, the evaluation process itself is no different on the playground, the church steps, the first day of school, a new job, or on the gravel parking lot of an abandoned grocery in Mississippi. You see, you listen, you evaluate. You go with your gut feeling.

I got into the couple's car willingly and without fear. I'd made my assessment and had no reservation about the decision. I'd stake my life on it and I did.

They lived in a mobile home a few miles from Waynesboro. We had to stop by the sitters and pick up their two little girls. Though never ill at ease, I was now completely calm and assured. These were two beautiful little girls that they obviously loved very much.

Maybe I was arriving at conclusions by coming from the wrong direction, but I figured if they trusted me enough to bring me into their house and expose their two innocent little girls to me, then conversely, I shouldn't feel any less trust for them.

"What line of work are you in?" I asked the man.

It wasn't just space filler. I wanted to gather all I could about these people, so as to see if there was a profile of the type person who would pick me up and take me into their homes without fear. Such people should be the subject of a detailed study by qualified professionals.

Yes, professionals should submit a report to the President.

"Mr. President, it is our considered opinion that there are people among us who actually "do unto others as they would have done to them."

"I'm an off-shore oil rig worker, but I'm on disability right now because of a back injury. I got a little piece-a-land and I'm trying to raise some purple hull peas to bring in a little money. I have a running battle with the deer. They love 'em and conduct nightly raids on my pea patch. Of course, it's legal to shoot them in Mississippi if they are eating a cash crop, but who can stay up every night with a shotgun across their lap? Tall fences, they leap with ease. Bright lights keep them away but only until they discover that the lights make the peas easier to see."

"I've never heard of purple hull peas. Are they anything like black-eyed?" I said.

"Sorta, but without that wang that turns people off about black-eyed peas."

I knew the "wang." And was more willing to try purple hull peas after his assurance.

"Since Joyce has been forced to go back to work because of my back, I've been doing a lot of the cooking. I'll fix us some for supper. You feel brave enough to give my cooking a try? The kids say it ain't bad."

"You kidding? I could eat the hindquarters off a road kill skunk right now," I said.

"While I whip up supper you're welcome to use the shower and Joyce'll throw your clothes in the washer." I hadn't mentioned dirty clothes. Was my smell preceding me?

In the hands of this gifted cook, the purple hull peas took on qualities I'm not sure they would possess in other hands. They rose to heights that betrayed their humble beginnings. They were good.

There was a supporting cast of great fried chicken, mashed potatoes, gravy, light bread and the South's ever present iced tea. It was brought up that the next morning would be pea pickin' time. Since I'd already been invited to spend the night, been given a meal like nothing I'd had for hundreds of miles, and the lady had even insisted on running my malodorous clothes through the washer, and since I'd been generally treated like the Grand Marshall of the Purple Hull Pea Parade, I thought it only fair that I volunteer to help pick.

There was a hide-a-bed couch so any embarrassment over lack of sleeping space was avoided.

A full stomach, a hot shower, a real bed, a safe place — Yeah, I'd pick peas for that.

The next morning in the patch, there was some head-hanging, mumbling, and moving of dirt clods with the toe. The drawn corners of the mouth said it had been a deer and not a dear night.

My untrained eye couldn't tell last nights hoof prints from the ones left on previous nights, nor that slightly brown edges of half-eaten pods meant it was damage from a deer picnic. These people were regular Indian scouts when it came to deer signs.

I could tell this had been a bitter and protracted war with many casualties on both sides. I felt sorry for both the people and the deer. With maybe a slight edge of sadness going to the deer. They were only doing what came naturally. I'm sure the peas were a real treat for them. It must have beat scrounging and foraging for a living. But they were lambs being led to the slaughter by the pea and the dollar.

It's a story hundreds of years old. An animal stands in the way of profit. Has the animal ever won that war? Man has always found a way to win if a profit margin was at stake. I knew that eventually a way would be found to keep the deer from the peas.

There's an old saying, "Find a job you like and you'll never have to work a day in your life." Labeling my coast-to-coast walk might invoke several words, some of them not very pretty, but one I wouldn't use is "work." If I had to put any labels on pea picking, "work" would be in the top three. "Back breaking" would be right up there, too.

I was relieved when it was decided we had enough peas for the day, and I was taken back to the abandoned grocery.

Chapter 62

Coyotes and Alligators in Ala-Freakin-Bama!

You've noticed the trash beside the road as you drive along. You can't miss it. I don't care if your mind is in never-never land or you're tapping your fingers on the wheel to the beat of the Kentucky Headhunters and mentally undressing that cute little thing you met at the Alibi Social Club last night. Somewhere in there, it's got to be registering — look at all this crap along the road! Only if youre blind, dead drunk, or just plain dead could you not see it. If you can see it that well in a car, imagine how up-close and personal it must be for someone passing it at two miles an hour. It's a national disgrace, really. We as a nation should be ashamed.

There's a simple solution, really. And right now, that solution is probably watching television, or working out with weights, or playing cards. I refer to our national bird — the jailbird. Our universal dead-beat brother-in-law. Someone tell me why our roadsides can't look like the eighteenth green at Augusta with so much cleaning power at our fingertips.

On this walk, I became convinced if a person could overcome the smell and the mess and find an economically feasible way to recycle used disposable diapers he'd become a rich man. After all, we get a workable, serviceable, methane gas from cow manure.

It isn't hard to see why used Pampers are prevalent alongside the road. Understandable, but not justifiable. But what is so hard about keeping a beer can or a pretzel bag, a pop can or a candy wrapper inside the car until you find a trashcan?

I wouldn't call this a major contributor to the trash picture, but something struck me because of its volume — work gloves. I formulated a theory on the disproportionate number of work gloves beside the road: Billy Bob, for whatever reason, be it necessity or boredom, realizes he has to get a job. He may be a tad dull, but he knows without a skill the job will involve a lot of hands-on training. And his hands are soft from long periods of nothing more harsh than grasping the remote and a beer can. He gets a pair of gloves. Then the gloves end up on the side of the road for one of several reasons:

1. Billy Bob realizes he just isn't cut out for work and, as a symbolic severing of the cord, tosses the only material thing that he associates with work out the window. "Begone ye devils — I cast out the demons of work!"

2. Billy Bob gets fired because he won't work. Gloves go out the window. (See Reason Number 1)

3. Billy Bob fails to grasp the dynamics that a sixty-mile-an hour-wind exerts on gloves carelessly left on a truck fender.

There are two other items that dot the landscape and, though technically trash, are much more interesting than pre-owned diapers and work gloves. These items are girlie magazines and full bottles of beer. It was on a walk previous to this one walk I formulated theories for this odd phenomenon. Here are my ideas why you find a disproportionate number of either on the sides of the highways: The male human is fascinated with the female body, especially if there's an element of mystery about it.

I suppose men and boys fall into two categories. While most men don't find it necessary to spend hard-earned money to look at the female body, there are those who do. There's a small problem, though. A certain percentage of these are either happily married men, or boys too young for their mothers to let them have such "trash." But these two types may be the girlie magazine publisher's best friends. They can buy the magazines, they just can't take them home. So they drive down the road, check the rear view mirror, look at what's ahead, then roll down the window, and heave the forbidden magazine. That way they don't get caught with the evidence.

Ditto with young boys and beer.

Before my first nighttime howling coyote experience back on the San Carlos Apache Indian Reservation in Arizona, I'd never heard a coyote howl. Like a lot of people, my idea of what a coyote sounded like had probably been supplied by Disney. I bet if we could pinpoint a lot of our perceptions of the world, for better or worse, they could be traced back to Disney. If we didn't know better wouldn't we just assume all stepsister's looked and acted like Cinderella's?

We are swayed by countless influences throughout our lives. Disney being just one of those influences. Probably our parents shape our thinking the most and that's how it should be. And peers influence us second most. We form opinions and concepts from hundreds, maybe thousands of sources in our everyday life. We are constantly bombarded by stimuli that we shapē and form and store in our heads.

Somewhere in my past I had formulated my classic coyote howl profile.

And until this point, the only time I had heard actual coyotes was on the Indian Reservation. I thought surely that New Mexico and Texas would have some coyotes. But coyotes in Alabama? Coyotes are "out West" critters not "South" critters. (I was wrong about the armadillo, too).

You can see I was in for a shock when I bedded down in a farmer's field in Isley, Alabama. You might think I was mistaken. In Alabama it must be a dog or a fox or something besides a coyote. But if you've ever heard a coyote in the middle of the night, you'd know there's no mistaking it. Logic may say it couldn't happen in Isley, Alabama, but the chill that skittered like a water flea down my backbone was sending a whole different message.

That night a shaggy head groomed only by the wind and rain held fierce, deep-set eyes, black as the moonless, Alabama night; eyes that strained to pierce the darkness, eyes fine-tuned by thousands of years of hunting. And the head had lips that moved slowly back and forth over sharp, yellow teeth. And the body had stiff hair that bristled along the spine in anticipation. Strong, musky odors lingered like a shroud.

Oh, my gosh! I just described the picture of me that stood ready to fight off Mr. Coyote. If he thought for a minute about having hiker hors d' oeuvres this night surely such formidable defenses would give him much to consider.

Grove Hill, Alabama was to be a shoe and money drop. I'd phoned Gus a few days earlier when I was in Laurel, Mississippi and asked him to send the leather and paper there. I had calculated that Grove Hill would arrive just as my money ran out. And, my faithful shoe friends, who had been my saviors way back in Alamagordo, New Mexico, and had served me wonderfully all the way to Alabama, were so run over they looked like a car going around a curve on two wheels.

Picture the toll the road can take on a pair of shoes if they are the only pair you have, and they are contacting hot asphalt, jagged gravel, and briars from daylight until dark, from New Mexico to Alabama.

If your chances of hitting a post office when it was open were five out of seven (Monday through Friday) or even five-and-a-half out of seven, (Some post offices are open on Saturday morning) you might think you had it made. Yet, it seemed often as not, I arrived at my post office on Sunday. While in Laurel, Mississippi I tried to calculate the day I would arrive in Grove Hill. But my arrival in Coffeyville, Alabama, 30 miles west of Grove Hill, told me I was going to hit it wrong. My pea brain told me I should hitch from Coffeyville into Grove Hill. It was early Saturday morning, and I was fairly certain I could make it before noon. I'd just have to take a chance that this was one of those post offices that was open until noon on Saturdays.

One of the many nice things that God gives His believers is an innocent faith in the inherent goodness of all men. That benefits the lowly hitchhiker. People who believe are generous with rides, especially preachers and born again Christians, those who've recently seen the light. Whether it's a call to spread the Word, simple innocence, or compassion for the less fortunate, it's still good news for the hitchhiker. Not that the hitcher comes out unscathed. The price of the ride is usually subjection to "Do you know the Lord, Son?" That question might make you squirm but that's okay, you're still getting a ride. The Lord sent me one of His true believers to take me from Coffeyville to Grove Hill.

There's a reason we believe in signs. Not "signs" such as the wooly caterpillar portending a severe winter, or a ring around the moon meaning rain the next day. I mean man-made signs. Something subconscious tells us if a person went to the trouble to make a sign, that sign must be telling the truth. But a person could make a big sign that's a lie.

"Warning: These Premises Protected by Security Dog" is a sign you take at face value when, in fact, there may be no dog at all.

"Yard Sale Today — 120 Monroe St." If the sign isn't curling at the edges, or the letters aren't running from the effects of rain we believe there's a yard sale on Monroe.

There's a big sign on the edge of Grove Hill, Alabama: "Welcome to the South's Friendliest Town."

The kind Christian man who gave me the ride took me out of his way and let me out at the post office. When I found that the post office was closed, I concluded that he thought it would be open, too.

This was depressing. I had wasted time and effort. Now I had to hitch back to Coffeyville, then walk back to Grove Hill. I'd arrive on a Sunday, and the post office would still be closed, and I'd have to keep walking past Grove Hill, and hitchhike back to Grove Hill from the other direction on Monday.

So much spinning of wheels (legs?) and all because I hadn't hit the post office during the week.

To sooth my bruised sensibilities I decided to give myself a rare treat and have a real breakfast in a real restaurant instead of my usual chocolate milk and tortilla chips.

No sooner had I stepped off the sidewalk in front of the post office when I was startled by a police car suddenly stopping beside me. With unnecessary haste, I thought, the officer jumped from the car. Did he think I was going to run with a 35-pound pack on my back?

"Grove Hill, The South's Friendliest Town." No sweat, I thought. The officer's greeting would go something like "Good morning, Sir. Welcome to Grove Hill. I saw your pack and was just curious to hear about your adventure."

That's not exactly the greeting I got.

"You got any ID?"

Maybe when we passed the sign at the edge of town we'd been going too fast to read the small print at the bottom saying: "For select individuals of our choosing. All others are subject to whim. Or any number of preconceived notions."

Are we humans still just basically animals? Is our suspicion nothing more than an instinct to protect and preserve our territory? Do strangers, all strangers, represent a threat.

After producing ID and my story the policeman acquiesced, but I suspected it was with some misgivings that he was returning me to his polite, genteel, Grove Hill society.

The chilly experience with the policeman hadn't dampened my desire for a hot breakfast. I found the town's only restaurant filled with the early morning regulars — mostly men having coffee with a donut and a chat before they started their work day, and men without jobs or hobbies who now fill their days with gossip.

I soon got the feeling I was the interest du jour.

Every eye seemed to pick me apart. Why was I there? A strange man in town. Veiled whispers sprang up, followed by slight shakes of the head, or small shrugs of the shoulders.

"Center of attention." Those words cover a lot of territory and emotions. They can create the best and worst of feelings. If you've been voted Mr Universe or Mother of the Year, that's good. The worst feeling is being the center of attention for all the wrong reasons. If you're the focus of suspicion it's definitely a bad "center of attention."

The waitress' obvious lack of enthusiasm made it seem as if lots had been cast to see who would wait on me, and she'd been the unfortunate loser.

My good breakfast had been spoiled by unreasonable, biased stupidity. Thank you, friendly Grove Hill.

I felt sorry for my hiking boots. They'd been as faithful as a dog. Way back in Alamogordo I'd had reservations about them. They were the only ones available, so I had no choice but to take a chance on them. They had rewarded me by taking me from New Mexico to Alabama. But now they looked like a 90-year-old man, so sad and run down.

I felt a tad uneasy because Gus had been out and I'd had to leave my message on his answering machine. Money and shoes arriving on schedule was vital to my mission. No money meant no food meaning no walk. And eventually the same could be said for shoes.

Grove Hill was a total wipeout for me. After hitchhiking 30 miles into town, I find the post office closed, and I'm made to feel like a leper. Then I hitch back to Coffeyville so as not to jeopardize my "walk every inch" vow. I walk back to, and through, Grove Hill because when I arrive the second time it's Sunday and the post office is still closed. On Monday I walk back into Grove Hill from the other direction. I present my picture ID at the post office and ask the postperson if he would kindly look to see if there's a general delivery for me.

"No, there isn't."

What! Gus has never failed me before. Waves of apprehension send me to the nearest phone. Gus is sorry (his words not mine). The only answer must be that, John, his teenage son has taken the answering machine message and forgotten to relay it. I explain that money is vital but boots aren't. We agree on another town farther down the road to make the drop.

I'd thought that my faithful boots were about to die, when in fact they carried me all the way into the next state, Georgia. Alamogordo, New Mexico to Blakely, Georgia. Surely these boots belong in the Guiness Book, or behind glass on a black-velvet-covered-pedestal in the Smithsonian. In fact, their dilapidated condition was to help get me out of a sticky situation in a central Alabama town called Perdue Hill.

Over my right shoulder a brewing storm was turning the sky into huge churning balls of gray-black cotton riding just above the ground.

The small grocery/post office combo I spotted was the sweetest sight just then. A public place I wouldn't be asked to leave, I hoped, while the storm raged. I'd ridden out storms like this in Mississippi standing head down in a pine woods wearing my 50-cent yard sale poncho. Weak armor when bristling lightning cracks its whip all about your head. It was nearly useless. And when I asked, at the first grocery I came to, if I could use the restroom to change into dry clothes my request was denied. Hospitality strikes again.

This Alabama grocery/post office had a price, too. It may have sheltered me from the lightning, but it couldn't protect me from something else that made me feel uncomfortable. After I'd bought my de rigueur chocolate milk, chips and M & Ms, and I'd inspected every item in the store, the storm had abated and I felt I couldn't, in good conscience, stay in the store any longer.

The store's long covered porch would be my halfway house until the number of drops lessened even more. The store's porch even had chairs and a bench — a friendly gathering place, I judged, under better conditions. I sat looking out at the fat drops on an Alabama July afternoon. My wool gathering was interrupted by a car pulling up in front. Out stepped a black man. Not a man of great bulk, but still large. My attention was riveted immediately by the gun and holster on his hip, handcuffs on his belt, and a badge, but no uniform.

He went into the store and in a few minutes came out and sat beside me, kinda chummy like, but not really. I was sure the first thing out of his mouth would be, "You got any ID?"

Instead it was, "Where you headed?" His tone was only slightly less chilly than "You got any ID?"

"Where you headed" can mean two things: One says, "Gosh, tell me about your adventure," or "You weren't planning to stay long, were you?"

Just as soon as I'd made it through my Los Angeles-to-New York story, he said, in a tone with some suppressed contempt, "I've seen people like you before; rich guys who've done it all and are now doing something else weird."

I especially didn't care for the rich guy part. I'd have shrugged it off as ignorant bias if we hadn't been joined by a teenage boy. I didn't want his discrimination planting seeds in the boys mind. And "rich guy" might be all this boy heard and I didn't want him running to some of his friends with a there's-a-rich-guy-walking-down-the-road-alone story. I didn't like that scenario at all.

With some contempt of my own, I lifted my shoe and showed him the silver-dollar-sized hole nearly all the way through the bottom.

"Sure I'm rich, look at this."

He shrugged, spit, looked away.

"That doesn't mean anything."

I thought under the circumstances I'd best let it drop. It was a lose/lose situation. Though I couldn't help but add, "It does to me."

When the rain slowed to a drizzle I was eager to leave this dreary person. The gun and badge had given him power but not wisdom. I mentioned wanting to make it to Mexia before dark and stepped off the porch.

Fading light in Mexia made me violate two of the primary considerations of site selection: 1. Proximity of people. 2. Noise.

I had climbed a bank and gone back into a thinly wooded area.

A bad thing about choosing the wrong spot is that soon after you've made your decision it gets really dark and you're stuck there because it's too dark to find any other place.

Some people, more than others, are prone to yelling at or between one another. Not that it's a bad thing, they just communicate more in that fashion than most people do.

I hadn't known until after dark that my chosen Mexia home for the night was smack in the middle of a Bell (as in bellowing) Communication hotline. I hadn't seen the houses, or heard the voices, until it was too late.

The yelling back and forth gives birth to another problem for the roadside sleeper. Human yelling invariably sets into motion dog yelling. You'd think the dogs would ignore it after a while but there must be something about the pitch or tone of it that causes them to go bananas.

If Mexia and I ever cross paths again I'll tip my hat and wish her well, but as far as sleeping over goes, count me out. Sorry Mexia, no five star rating.

Stand on an overpass and look down at any Interstate traffic. Seattle, San Diego, Miami, Milwaukee — unless you knew where you were, you'd never be able to tell simply by looking at the traffic.

All Interstates have trucks, zillions of trucks. And cars, cars, cars speeding to where? And there is always a goodly number of campers–people getting back to nature, or so they like to delude themselves. Maybe it is better than being a couch potato, but neither are they camping nor getting back to nature. Call it something, just don't sully the experience of meeting the great outdoors on its terms by calling the people in those mobile metal boxes "campers." Their idea of roughing it is crossing Texas without cruise control.

I felt a little envious as I stood on US Highway 84 looking down at the people in those trucks and cars and campers passing beneath me on Interstate 65 in South Alabama. Running from Mobile to Chicago, Interstate 65 runs through Louisville and within 25 miles of where I was born and spent 39 years of my life. Though I called Gatlinburg, Tennessee home, my parents still lived there in Kentucky.

I couldn't help but think how nice it would be to stick out my thumb and in just a matter of a few short days trade blisters, aching shoulders and neck muscles, hot burning skin, inadequate and ill-prepared food, a nearly constant thirst, and cold and indifferent people for all the good feelings I'd have if I was back home among people who cared about me. But that would mean giving in, giving up. Succumbing to the siren call of I-65 meant failure. It would mean wimping out. All the pain that had gone before would account for little and I knew I'd rather endure the months of pain it took me to get to New York than endure a lifetime as a quitter.

The next day something happened to boost my moral over the top. It was one of those events that renews your faith in the goodness and beauty of life.

Most of the time I was just plain weary. The heavy pack and the endless miles had worn me to a nub.

Such was the case one afternoon when I spotted a cool-looking grassy spot beside the road. Technically, it was someone's yard but I think it was a case of a man who simply loved to ride his lawnmower. The house was way down the road and I couldn't see how the owner would object to my sitting in the shade of one of his trees for 15 minutes.

As I sat with my knees drawn up and my arms resting on them, I heaved a big sigh. I just wanted to melt like chocolate sauce down the sides of a giant sundae. I was so tuckered out I didn't even check for fire ants before I plopped down.

A car pulled to a stop off the edge of the road in front of me. I braced myself. I was still smarting from the, "People get shot around here for going on other people's property!"

It was with considerable relief that I saw the driver's door open and a young lady about 25 get out and head toward me, Coke in hand. It was such a meaningful event, and yet hardly any words were spoken.

"I thought you'd like this," was all she said.

And, all I could say was, "Thank you."

She got back in the car with her two small children and drove away.

I couldn't believe so much of what goodness and kindness is all about could be condensed into 15 or 20 seconds. I wanted to say more, I should have said more. I could have told her that on this trip I'd learned that the really remarkable kindnesses were the ones people did out of the pure goodness of their hearts with no expectation of reward. They knew they'd never see me again. They were kind to me simply because they were kind people.

Evergreen, Alabama. If a pleasant sounding name was all it took, that would be a nice place to live, don't you think?

Would you think alligators would like it there, though? It never would have crossed my mind. Coyotes in Alabama? Gators in Alabama? Where has reason flown?

On Friday's pop-quiz back in Tennessee, if one of the questions had been: Coyotes are found in Alabama. True or false? I'd have considered that a "gimme." Everybody knows there ain't no damned coyotes in Ala-freakin-bama. And there ain't no gators, either.

Wrong! I heard coyotes and I seen gators!

I just knew Florida was the only state that had gators. Well, I might have been persuaded to believe a few had slipped over the line into the Okefenokee Swamp in Georgia but south central Alabama; get real!

I had just left Evergreen (No, the pretty name wasn't enough to keep me.), and was crossing one of those long, low concrete highway bridges so common in the South. Bridges were always interesting. You could sleep under them, bathe under them, take shelter from an afternoon storm under them, even take care of nature calls under them. And if you didn't want to do anything *under* them, while you walked across you could look down and see what there might be under the bridge. Sorta like flying over in a plane. Any interesting snakes? Big fish? Muskrats? Bodies? It could happen!

And invariably I'd find a penny or two on the bridge. I picture people using the bridge and water below as sort of a drive-thru wishing well. I guess they toss a coin out the window as they cross and make a wish. No telling how many are on the bank or in the water below. I found the pennies that never made it to the "well," the ones that hit the concrete railing and bounced back onto the road. I wondered how many shattered wishes I picked up with these pennies.

As I crossed this long concrete bridge east of Evergreen my eyes were kept busy checking the bridge for money and looking down over the side for other interesting stuff.

As I scanned the creek below I noticed a small grassy island with something black on it.

My first thought was "alligator."

Now, I know that sounds odd when not five minutes ago I said I would have found it hard to believe there were alligators in Alabama, but I thought this was a rubber alligator. Before you conclude that I've really lost it, let me explain.

In trucker C.B. lingo an alligator is one of those long, wide strips of rubber that has separated from a tire. The ones you have to dodge on the Interstate. I have to tip my hat to the guy who coined the phrase. The length, breadth, color and tread on its "back" do resemble a gator.

At first glance I didn't even formulate anything concrete in my mind about it. It was just like a thousand things we see every day and our minds make an instant evaluation about. I saw this long black thing lying on a small island under the bridge.

Only after I had studied the object for another half second did I realize this was no "highway gator." This one had a definite head, eyes, teeth and tail.

It blew me away!

Chapter 63
I Opt Not to Opp

Stop the average man on the street. Stop the average woman, boy, girl on the street, ask them to name the two most valuable things in the world. Wouldn't, often as not, the answer be gold and silver, love and peace, chocolate and coke, depending on the people you stopped? I believe you'd get a wide range of answers, when there can only be one answer — air and water. They are both things we take so much for granted that their real worth is something we never stop to consider. Without them there can be nothing else. Everything that man values must fall in place behind them.

My first introduction to the real value of water was while I was in the Navy. When my ship would go to sea we had fresh water for a few days, then that ran out and the only water we had was desalinated seawater. Trust me it ain't like the real thing. It may be okay for your body, but it tastes salty and flat.

Then several years after I got out of the Navy I bought a small farm that had no water. My wife and I moved there and had to carry water until we could dig a well. Carrying every drop you use home in plastic jugs can give you a whole new appreciation.

In all my earlier water appreciation experiences, there had been plenty of water it was just the awkward way it was obtained that made me appreciate it.

The person who said, "You never miss the water 'til the well runs dry" was one of our greatest sages. You can't sit in your home where all you have to do is turn a knob and have any real appreciation of what water means to you. You have to really want it and need it and not be able to get it before you can see its true worth.

I've read that it takes over 300 gallons of water a day to supply the needs, on average, of every American. And every last one of us will jump up and say in indignation, "That's crazy! No way do I use 300 gallons of water a day!" It's obvious we don't drink any amount close to 300 gallons, but we never stop to think about all the hidden water we use. There's toilet flushing, body washing, clothes washing, cooking, dish washing, water used to supply us with heating, cooling, car washing, and lawn sprinkling. How long would your list be even if you could think of every way we use water. I suspect about 300 gallons long. Try to envision, if you can, reducing your water consumption from a probably realistic 300 gallons down to an "in-your-face" gallon or even a half-gallon. You can picture it would create some heavy-duty changes on your part.

Car washing and lawn sprinkling would soon lose their importance. Your thirst would teach you all the priorities you needed to know.

The equation is simple, concrete and as absolute as any physical law in the universe. If you have three hundred gallons of water you'll wash your car. If you have a half-gallon you'll send it carefully down your throat. Each drop becomes more than liquid gold; it becomes liquid life.

Only when there was water over and above what my throat and body demanded, did I move up the water usage scale to the next level — teeth brushing, face washing and shaving.

Even though the Navy and farm life had taught me how I could get by on a lot less if I tried, I never knew how far that lesson could be stretched until I crossed the desert. I found it was possible to wash my face, shave, brush my teeth and wet my hair so it would lay in one direction all on slightly less than a quart of water. Just for fun, try it, then ask yourself if 300 gallons is such a farfetched figure, after all. 300 gallons of water a day is a "creature comfort." We're so lucky. All the water we need, plus Wal-Mart and McDonald's. Do other people in the world see us as living like kings?

Even the lowly coast-to-coast walker has his "creature comforts." After the necessities — food, water and moleskin there are things a hiker thinks he needs. Things that make life more bearable. After days of searching I found one of the hiker's creature comforts in Opp, Alabama. I could have found this item just about anywhere, but I needed it packaged in hiker form.

The item I was looking for was usually packaged with a snap-on lid. And that's something I didn't need. Snap-on lids are fine for bathroom or kitchen shelves. For backpackers, though, using them is flirting with disaster. Even if you've never had a pack on your back or hiked any farther than the corner convenience store, you can picture the mood of a hiker who looks in his pack and discovers the mess created by a jar of strawberry jam or pimiento cheese whose lid had come off. It only has to happen once for you to ban snap-on lids forever.

A person contemplating a long, long walk (the weird few) will logically contemplate for months beforehand all the things he possibly will need. And yet as surely as he'll make a few bad choices (See: "Ingenious Stool" Chapter 4), he'll also forget things like glass cleaner that are very important.

Sitting there on the couch in January, with the snow blowing outside, trying to picture everything you'll need while walking down the road in some far away environment in July is tough. Of course, you picture the obvious food, clothing, shelter, and even the less obvious sunglasses, toenail clipper, and writing pen. But would you also picture Windex and Vaseline?

The necessity I had been looking for and finally found in Opp, Alabama was Vaseline. I know you're wondering how I made it from Los Angeles to Alabama without something I'm now calling a "necessity." Oh, I knew about Vaseline. I learned of its goodness on other walks in North Carolina and Florida and I'd had some with me all along until I somehow lost my small jar with a screw-on lid back in Mississippi.

I was constantly pulling stuff out of my pack and laying it on the ground while I searched for other stuff buried deeper. And though I religiously searched the area before I left, somehow my Vaseline must have fallen through the cracks. As an added measure I had developed a habit I used without fail on this walk. After I had hoisted my pack to my back, and was ready to start walking again I took three or four steps away, then stopped, turned around and looked back at the spot where I'd just been as a final survey of the area. Still nothing is foolproof, bombproof or unsinkable and my Vaseline somehow was gone.

I can see the puzzlement on your face: Vaseline? A necessity?

Note: It's August in Alabama, all day is spent walking down the road. You sweat like a mule in plow harness. A tiny river of sweat, with its headwaters at your neck, courses its way down your backbone and follows the natural channel created by the crack of your behind. The salt content in the sweat soon grates raw any delicate tissue. Do the words "Vaseline" and "necessity" take on new meaning?

Why could I not find Vaseline before Opp? I could have. But it was in big heavy, snap-on-lid jars. I was looking for one of those dainty purse-size squeeze tubes that a lady might carry in her purse. Only Opp was big enough, cultured enough, refined enough to have exactly what I was looking for.

It wasn't just the fact that Opp had properly-packaged Vaseline that spoke of its culture and sophistication. I saw a sign that said, "Chamber of Commerce." It takes a town of some pride in its self-worth to maintain a functioning Chamber of Commerce. Not that it denotes an inflated ego, more just an indication of dignity and satisfaction with who you are. It reminds me of Dolly Parton's advice to women who complain that men don't pay enough attention to them. With her salty, Tennessee hills, no-nonsense brand of insight, she said, "Hell, fix yourself up a little!"

A Chamber of Commerce is an indication that a town is trying to fix itself up a little. When I saw the green sign with the arrow pointing to the right I did something out of character for me on this walk — I decided to deviate from my planned route and visit the Opp Chamber of Commerce.

That, in itself, holds scant meaning for a motorized, wheeled society. A flick of the finger, an ever so slight push on the foot pedal and in a few seconds you're parked in front of the Chamber. The walker spends a few extra moments weighing any deviations from the straight and narrow.

What's the harm done by a sidetrack of a few blocks when the overall picture is one of thousands of miles and millions of steps? I can only say you have to be there. Side trips are a needless addition to your pain. And I can't say why the Opp Chamber of Commerce sign caused a deviation in my steps.

It was a nice day. Things were going well, I'd found my Vaseline (in its proper container) and the Blister dogs weren't straining with foamed mouths at their chains.

But the name Opp intrigued me. I still can hardly write it without adding a period after the last "P". It looks like an abbreviation — maybe short for Oppenheimer or Opportunity. Wouldn't that make sense for this little "fix itself up a little" town with its Chamber of Commerce and the correct Vaseline? Surely Opp is an abbreviation for Opportunity. Curiosity and a feel good day, that's what made me sidetrack to the Chamber office. Where better to find out how a town was bestowed or stuck with such a name.

When you think about it, "Chamber" seems an odd label to put on a place that dispenses information and good will. "Chamber," too often, follows "horror" or "judges," neither of which conjure up pleasant thoughts. But invariably these "Chambers" are peopled by kind, little old ladies who are eager to be out of the house and to feel useful. Most likely they were born in the town, lived their whole lives there and took pride in extolling its virtues.

A wave of deliciously cold air greeted me as I swung the Chamber door. I parked my pack at my feet between me and the chest high counter. The lady was all smiles. Somehow, I could tell it wasn't one of those *required* smiles.

"Hi, just a question," I said. "I was passing through your fair town and couldn't help but be intrigued by its name. How did it get the name Opp?"

Before she responded there was a small chuckle that said, "Yeah, we get that a lot."

She took her glasses off and let them dangle from a chain around her neck.

For just a second I thought I would be sorry I asked. In my experience, the glasses maneuver usually signals something lengthy is on the way. I didn't really want a discourse by the town historian — just a simple explanation.

"Well," she began ("Well" scares me a little, too) "It's really very simple. In its early days the town was floundering. Businesses came and went quickly. For a while it looked as if the town might not continue to exist at all. Then a local lawyer, who cared about the town and its future, thought of a way to give it a shot in the arm. He convinced a railroad company that it would be of benefit to them if they'd come through their town. They did, and it was successful for all concerned. Out of gratitude, the town fathers decided to change the name of the town to the lawyer's which was "Opp.""

There was no hint of embarrassment, no regret in her voice that she was stuck in a town with a name like Opp. Maybe the town's folk are glad they aren't saddled with a bland and generic name like Cloverdale, Grove City or Washington Square.

I smiled and said, "On my way over here I was thinking about the name and thought it might be short for opportunity."

"That'd be nice, too, but I'm afraid the truth isn't as colorful as that," she said.

So that's the story of Opp. A town with a name only a mother or grateful town could love.

After the nice Chamber lady had told me the fable of the enchanted city of Opp I thanked her. As I turned to leave she added, with another hint of pride, "If you can prolong your visit for another week, Opp hosts one of the largest rattlesnake roundups in the world." My nervous laugh said why I opted not to Opp.

Chapter 64
Somewhere in My Broken Heart

Better than his storytelling, in my opinion, are Mark Twain's insightful, humorous, philosophical witticisms. His views on just about any human condition had a different slant, not only funny, but usually containing a message.

One of my favorites is, "Live your life so that when you die even the undertaker will be sorry." It's so true and yet how many people actually achieve it? Few who consciously try. It's the people who are naturally kind and loving who live and end their lives and everyone is sorry.

Who among us won't have at least one person who, upon hearing of our death, won't think, "Hell, I never liked the S.O.B. anyway!"

Either through dumb luck or God's good graces I was married to one of those rare people whom everyone liked.

And death hasn't softened nor glittered my view as death can sometimes do. Death sometimes brings a sympathy not accorded the living.

I say with confidence that everyone, upon hearing of my wife's death felt a twinge of sadness. She viewed, not only her fellow humans but all of God's creatures as equals and treated them with kindness, love and compassion. There's no doubt in my mind the undertaker was sorry, too.

You can picture that in 3800-plus miles of walking I had plenty of time to reflect on what might have beens, and wish that things had turned out differently. On one particularly lonely night in the Arizona desert as I lay looking up at the countless stars I asked her, if she could, to come and talk to me for just five minutes. I explained to her that it was the desert and there was no one for miles around. And even if she came, and I told people she came, no one would believe me anyway. It seemed the perfect time for her to come if she could come. I pleaded, but she didn't come. I once asked a person whose intelligence I respected if they thought it possible that my wife could be aware of what was happening down here. She had no definite answer either, but I liked the answer she gave. She said that it may be possible that she knew and saw what was happening, but that she now existed on a plane different from us, one in which communication was impossible.

On this walk not only did I miss my late wife, there often were times I missed having anyone to talk with and experience things with. At least a few times, I remarked to people along the way that I wished I had someone with me if only to argue with. Many prisoners have testified that solitary is the worst form of punishment.

One of my favorite stories concerns that very subject. In fact, I was so fascinated by it that it transformed me from a lackadaisical, disinterested, rebellious, gazing-out-the-window student to one who saw the joy and entertainment and education that could be obtained through books. It's a short story written by Anton Chekhov called *The Bet*. The story is fictional, but based on the debate as to whether it would be better to be imprisoned for your lifetime, or executed immediately if you had to choose.

The beginning of the story takes place at a party in what must have been England in the 1800s. Two men at the party became engaged in an argument as to whether solitary imprisonment or capital punishment should be the preferable choice for a wise man who found himself in a situation and had the power to choose.

One of the men was a rich old banker and chose the quick ending of pain through execution. The other man was a young lawyer and chose solitary confinement, reasoning some form of living was desirable to none.

The argument became heated and the rich man blurted out that the other man was wrong and furthermore he wouldn't have the fortitude and determination to live with such a decision.

The banker said to prove his point, he'd bet the lawyer he couldn't stay five years in solitary confinement if it was within his power to terminate his stay at his own time and choosing. In fact, if he stayed the entire five years he'd give him a million dollars. But if the poor man violated the agreement and asked to be released even one minute before the agreed five years, then the rich man owed him nothing.

In the heat of the argument and to prove his point the young lawyer foolishly bragged that not only would he stay the agreed five years, but an additional ten years.

The rich man felt smug in his belief that now there was no way he could lose the bet. The poor man could never stay five years, and fifteen years was sheer folly.

It was agreed the poor man would be confined in a cottage on the back of the rich man's property. There would be no locks so he could leave at anytime but with the full understanding that in so doing, he would lose the bet. Food would be left for him.

It was agreed that the prisoner would be allowed books.

During the first year he requested books of mostly a light nature, thrillers, fantasies and comedies.

In the second year he wanted only classics.

By the sixth year he had turned to the study of six languages and read only about philosophy and history.

In one year all he requested was the Bible.

And in the fourteenth and fifteenth years there was no theme to his requests and he might indiscriminately ask to be brought books on the sciences, chemistry, medicine or Byron or Shakespeare.

At the beginning of the bet the rich man hadn't been concerned because the loss of a million would not hurt him and he knew in his heart that the man couldn't possibly endure more than a few years of voluntary imprisonment.

Now it was nearly time for the bet to end and he was very worried. During the 15 years his business fortunes had reversed and now the loss of a million would ruin him.

He felt bitterness toward the prisoner. To himself he thought, "Now it is he who will be free and rich."

He devised a plan to kill the prisoner, casting the suspicions on the gardener, and thus freeing himself from the foolish and soon to be devastating bet.

On the night before the release date the man went to the cottage with a pillow, intending to smother the prisoner in his sleep. To his amazement the prisoner was gone. On the table was a note: "At twelve o'clock tomorrow I regain my freedom and the right to associate with others. But I think fit, before I leave this room for the sunlight to address a few words to you. I have spent fifteen years intently studying life on earth. True, I have not set eyes on the earth and its peoples, but in your books I have drunk fragrant wine, sung songs, hunted stags and wild boars in the forests, loved women. Created by the magic of your inspired poets, beautiful girls, ethereal as clouds have visited me at night and whispered in my ears magical tales that have made my head reel. In your books I have climbed the peaks of Elbrus and Mont Blanc, whence I have watched the sun rising in the morning and flooding the sky, the ocean and the mountain peaks with crimson gold in the evening. From there I have watched lightning flash and cleave the storm clouds. I have seen green forests, fields, rivers, lakes, cities. I have heard the singing of the sirens and the strains of shepherd's pipes. I have touched the wings of beautiful angels who flew to me to converse of God. In your books I have plunged into the bottomless pit, performed miracles, murdered, burnt towns, preached new religions, conquered whole kingdoms.

"Your books have given me wisdom. All that man's brain has created over the centuries has been compressed into a small nodule inside my head. And I hate what I have learned about man and this world. Everything is fleeting, ghostly, illusory as a mirage. Proud, wise and handsome as man might be, death will wipe him from the face of the earth along with the mice burrowing under the floor. Your posterity, your history, your geniuses all will freeze or burn along with the terrestrial globe."

"You have lost your senses and are on the wrong path. You take lies for truth and ugliness for beauty. You would be surprised if apple and orange trees somehow sprouted frogs and lizards instead of fruit, or if roses smelt like a sweating horse. No less surprised am I at you, who have exchanged heaven for earth. I do not want to understand you."

"To give you a practical demonstration of my contempt for what you live by, I hereby renounce the money that I once yearned for as one might for paradise, but which I now scorn. To disqualify myself from receiving it I shall leave here five hours before the time fixed, thus breaking the contract."

The stories' message had a profound effect on me.

There's a song from the 60s or 70s called *Games People Play* that contains the words: "Placing value on the worthless, disregarding priceless wealth." To me that's a summation of *The Bet*.

Have I strayed from my original intent? Is any of this connected to the loneliness of the cross-country hiker? People need people.

It was ironic that on one of my particularly bad Nancy days (I called it a Nancy day when the longing for her was particularly bad) I came upon a cemetery set right beside the road. And next to the road was a new grave. It was covered with dirt and flowers. There was a young woman kneeling beside the grave and she was crying. I felt sorry for her in part because her grief was so obvious. She was right next to the road and was making no attempt to hide her tears nor muffle her sobs.

I might have passed her by out of respect for her dignity if I hadn't been having a Nancy day myself. It was easy for me to feel what she was feeling.

I started toward her. I wanted to say a few words of consolation. I knew that while consolation is a noble endeavor, it doesn't always achieve the desired effect. I knew it would be hard to console her, being a stranger and a strange looking stranger at that.

Maybe God let her see into my heart as I walked toward her, she gave no indication that this strange looking thing coming toward her frightened her. The tremendous grief she was feeling at that moment was completely barring all other emotions.

I asked her to excuse me for intruding, but something had happened to me recently that made me feel I had to say something to her. I told her I could understand her grief (She said the person was her husband) because I had recently lost my wife of 25 years to cancer.

Anyway, I told her what I felt. I don't remember my exact words but the essence was that the pain of losing someone you love never goes away. In fact, there are times when the pain is as sharp and real as the first day, but God, in his infinite wisdom and mercy, allows those times to occur less and less frequently with the passage of time. I knew it to be fact.

After I left her my condition was pretty shabby, too. The girl's grief had brought my own grief back to me. And when you're walking down the road alone there's no diversion to help you shake it.

When I saw the Western Steer Buffet on the outskirts of Dothan, Alabama I thought surely the sight and smell of real food would help pull me out of my reverie.

It helped. My heartstrings weren't twanging nearly so loud, the lump in my throat had mostly subsided, and things were going better until, just as I'd sat down after my fifth trip to the hot bar, I heard over the restaurant's sound system Billy Dean's song, "*Somewhere in My Broken Heart.*"

It all tugged at my heart—the graveside girl, Billy Dean's song, the too-many-to-count trips to the buffet. For several more hours that Dothan afternoon they all weighed heavy on my old, sad heart.

Chapter 65
I, Too, Lay an Old Friend
or Two, to Rest

I sometimes wondered how much side-to-side head movement and tongue clicking occurred after I had passed through an area. I must have been the source of more than a little amusement in a community for several days after I'd been there.

Picture a sleepy, Mayberry-ish Georgia town named "Sylvester." How often would someone pass through who was walking coast to coast? Maybe, just maybe, someone walking from Savannah to the West coast might pass through Sylvester. But Los Angeles to New York? Through Sylvester? For starters, no one with half a brain is going to attempt to walk from Los Angeles to New York. Secondly, if a fool did try it, they'd have smarts enough to know you didn't pass through Sylvester, Georgia. Kansas City, Indianapolis, or Pittsburgh maybe. But Sylvester, Georgia? What a hoot. Even I had to smile. In Dothan, Alabama I'd been within 15 miles of the Florida state line. Nobody walking from Los Angeles to New York City should be way down here.

And I was hesitant about going two blocks out of my way to visit the Opp, Alabama Chamber of Commerce. How ludicrous that seems, when in the over-all picture, I added about 800 miles to the length of my trip by being down there within kissing distance of Florida.

When I told people why I'd made such an exaggerated loop, I think it was lost on them. Surely they thought no one with a 3000-mile walk staring them in the face would voluntarily take an 800-mile side trip. Wouldn't someone with half a brain go as the crow's flies? I wanted to walk through the Old South. Since my mother took me to see *Gone When the Wind* when I was about five or six years old, it has always fascinated me. The pioneering movie director, D.W. Griffith, was from my home county in Kentucky and our lone, small theater was aptly named The Griffith. When *Gone With the Wind* made it to our tiny town and theater it was cause for excitement. And right or wrong, it planted a seed in lots of people's minds about life in the Deep South.

I believe I'm fairly safe in saying that most Kentuckians consider themselves southern. That may be stretching it a bit, still I think that's the picture they like to paint of themselves. So, being sired and raised in the Bluegrass, and having traveled throughout the South, you'd think I wouldn't be so fascinated that I'd walk 800 miles out of my way just to pass through it.

The flip side is that I've also been in Kansas City, Indianapolis, and Pittsburgh. The defense rests.

Through a series of snafus, my buddy, Gus, and I had never gotten together on a place to send my much needed new boots. When I bought my last boots in Alamogordo, New Mexico not in my wildest dreams did I think I'd still be wearing them in Alabama. And in fact they were ready for retirement as I was leaving Mississippi. I tried then to coordinate a drop point with Gus but for one reason or another it never happened, and now I was in Georgia still wearing them. The silver-dollar-sized hole in the right sole was beginning to inflate to some larger denomination.

Finally, the small town of Blakely, Georgia was agreed upon.

It was with both anticipation and trepidation that I walked up to the window at the post office. The thought of new boots was exciting. On the other hand, "new" could also mean "blister."

I carried the box outside. Being seen changing boots under a shade tree would draw less attention than doing same in the post office.

In California you could do it anywhere and never raise an eyebrow, but this was Blakely, Georgia. Bizarre is almost the norm in Los Angeles. Here it can get the cops called. I didn't need that. Besides, I wanted to turn my new friends (or foes − I hadn't forgotten the "boots from Hell" and the White Sands Missile Range) over in my hands and cuddle them like my firstborn. I wanted to get off on the right foot (sorry) with these new comrades in arms. I knew it could go either way. The next couple of days would be crucial. We could easily become inseparable friends or bitter (but still inseparable) enemies.

It may sound a little silly to the person whose "distance walking" consists of the span between the couch and the refrigerator, or the ground between their car and the door of the 7-11. These people (Of course, we know *you* aren't in this group) are totally oblivious to what's on their feet. It's of so little concern that they'd have to look down to see.

Try 3813 miles and see if new boots aren't something that takes on major meaning.

You can see why the shade tree next to the post office in Blakely, Georgia is forever etched in my memory. In a way, new boots meant the adventure was starting all over. I took them out of the box and turned them over lovingly in my hands. I admired their beauty and their virginity, their youth and innocence. They'd never so much as touched the ground.

On the phone, I'd done my best to convey to Gus what I needed in a boot. He lives close to Louisville and his chances of finding what I required were far better than mine. My first glance told me he'd done well. They looked like more than just a pretty face.

Having the advantage of hindsight (which is always 20/20) I know now I should have bought at least three pairs of boots in the months of pre-walk planning. I should have broken then in before I ever took the first step of this odyssey. But at the time I was viewing this adventure from an entirely different perspective. I knew I had the will, but did I have the heart?

I had a questionable knee from an injury sustained during an ill-fated attempt to carry a water-laden kayak (don't ask, it's another long story) up a steep, muddy bank. Even if I had the heart, did I have the knee for such an undertaking?

At the time it seemed silly to buy three pairs of boots, not knowing if I'd make it a hundred miles. I did have enough cautious optimism to buy a second pair (See Chapter 27, "The Boots from Hell") but not the good sense to try them on. You can see how important this day in Blakely, Georgia was for me. All that had gone before made this much more than simply picking up the boots at the post office, slipping them on, and skipping merrily down the yellow brick road.

"Run down at the heels" can apply to boots or the human spirit. I doubt you've ever seen anything so "run down at the heels" as my Alamogordo to Blakely boots were. If you set them down, they'd just wonk over to the side as if they'd lost their will to live. They were tired, old warriors. In truth, they had saved this entire trip. If they hadn't rescued me in Alamogordo I doubt I could have summoned the courage to fight through the blister pain and the heat of the desert Southwest. They represented far more than just something without life or soul to me.

No dearly-departed friend was ever laid more tenderly or lovingly to rest than these boots were as I placed them in their box, sealed them, and handed them to the post person for their final journey back to Kentucky for safekeeping. They'd always have a place in my heart and on my mantle (at least figuratively). I suspect I'll always have them around in my attic or basement somewhere to run across every year or so.

Chapter 66
Sylvester's Courage and That Noodly Stuff

My new boot friends and I marched away from Blakely. Maybe they could never replace my Alamogordo boots in my heart but somehow, I could tell after just a few miles that our relationship was going to be cordial. Not that we weren't going to have to go through a period of adjustment. But isn't some give and take on both parts common in a lasting friendship?

Haven't we all heard that in Arizona it gets to be a 120 degrees but you don't notice it because it's a *dry* heat. I agree that dry heat beats wet heat but your armpits still flow like the Rio Grande.

South Georgia's heat is like having hot pancake syrup poured over you. It has a stifling, suffocating quality. Ordinary breathing suddenly takes a conscious effort. Going into air conditioning is like going from Hell to Heaven.

The Pizza Hut in Sylvester, Georgia was a cool haven on an August afternoon. The lunch buffet had all the pizza, salad and sweet iced tea you could hold. And in the cool! God must be in the back tossing pizzas 'cause this was heaven. Even the glum, what-are-you-smiling-at look the waitress gave me wasn't going to spoil this.

All of us have had things happen to us in our childhood that have a profound effect on us; things that may pass as insignificant to anyone else but form indelible memories that, even though we are children, stamp impressions on our brains that are never erased. One of mine crossed my mind as I sat enjoying the lunch buffet at the Pizza Hut in Sylvester, Georgia. Between giant bites and huge gulps I paused long enough to gaze out the window and noticed a black man passing by on the sidewalk across the street. Just at that instant he triggered one of my childhood memories — a black and white memory.

When I was eight years old my father, who had been an auto mechanic most of his adult life, managed to purchase a service station of his own. I grew up hanging around it. It was the late forties before television had ripped our social fabric to shreds. People still visited and had the time to just sit around and talk. My dad kept the station open six days a week from six in the morning until nine at night. After supper (it wasn't called "dinner" yet. At least not in the rural Kentucky circles my folks traveled in.) a collection of men came to the station to loaf. When my dad bought the station there was a "No Loafing" sign over the door. I suppose it must have been the gasoline company's policy but no one gave it any thought. I think it could just as readily have said, "Welcome Loafers."

Occasionally, a new cast member would appear to add spice and interest or a new perspective.

But my special memory that flashed across my mind as I gazed out the Pizza Hut window was of a black man who only came for about two weeks every summer.

This was Kentucky in the late forties and though I don't remember any overt racism we hadn't even approached "separate but equal." Blacks and whites seemed to get along okay but there was no mixing or interaction between the races.

Maybe he was welcome because he was "safe". It was safe to say he'd be gone in two weeks and wouldn't be back until next year. You could associate with him without being thought of as becoming too chummy with blacks. Actually, the words were more cutting and vicious than "chummy" but you see my point.

I think if this black man had been a "normal" black he wouldn't have been accepted into the circle of white loafers at all. This man was thought to be, to use a term from that period, a "simpleton." No one could fault you for being kind to, as Scarlett's father called them, "Inferiors."

Even though I was just a kid, I never bought into the accepted belief that this black man wasn't bright. I think he wasn't bright in the sense that Helen Keller, in her youth, was thought of as "not bright." At that time if you couldn't express yourself then you must be dumb. And this black man was "dumb" for much the same reasons Helen Keller was. He was, in fact, deaf and dumb. It typecasts that person.

Although it's nearly 40 years since I've seen that black man, two things stay clear in my mind. And those two things remind me of something I once read that said that almost certainly neither Presidents Garfield nor McKinley would have died of their wounds if modern medical techniques had been available. I believe if it hadn't been the forties or he hadn't been black he could have been helped to hear and speak.

Occasionally, a man would come to the station and bring his accordion. On a few occasions the black man happened to be there when the white man played. If the tune was lively enough, the black man would point to his ear and then point to the accordion and smile.

And even though it was always summer when the black man came he always wore a cap with sheepskin lining. I was never sure if the black man started this to show people he had the ability to say something, or if it was a result of a white person's training, but if you took his hat off and pointed to the sheepskin lining he would go "Baa" like a sheep. I wondered how he could imitate a sheep yet he couldn't say any other words.

I can't say with any certainty but I believe the reason we only saw the man two weeks out of the year was because he was institutionalized the rest of the year. It would have been the common thing at that time.

After several years his visits stopped. There was nothing else for me to assume but that he died.

But why did all these things about this poor black man come back to me while I was scarfing down pizza nearly 40 years later in a small, south Georgia town? It's really very simple. The name of the town was Sylvester, and so was his.

There are people in this world whose actions aren't guided by what others would do. They aren't afraid to strike out in a direction that others would be afraid to take.

Maybe these people pay dearly for their boldness. But on the other hand, maybe they live with more excitement, substance and backbone than the less adventurous.

I have a David saying, "Either you happen to life or life happens to you." By that I mean either you grab your destiny by the scruff of the neck and take control and purposefully move in the direction your heart and mind tell you, or you sit back and passively let life dish out the menu she likes.

The latter course may be the easier to take, but it is simply existing, it isn't really living. Courageous risk taking is the only rewarding life when it comes time to look back and see what it was all about.

One such risk-taker slowed to a stop beside me one oppressive south Georgia afternoon.

"I saw you walking when I was on my way to work this morning. Where are you going?"

It was a young woman, who was alone on a stretch of highway well away from the protection of houses, businesses, and other people.

By rote, I went through the well-worn litany. I had repeated it so often that I had to remind myself to keep it fresh. It may be old hat to me but it was new to them. And it really wasn't all that hard to get up for the performance. Vanity breeds enthusiasm.

"Where do you sleep?"

"At this point, God only knows, but if form holds it will be in a hay field or woods."

"My mother would kill me if she knew I was saying this, but you can sleep on my couch tonight if you'd like."

And I know that right now 99 percent of you would agree with her mother. Where in the world was this girl's head? But ye of too much television have become jaded.

Ed McMahan and Dick Clark *might* knock on your door, but the odds are about 250,000,000 to one against it. I *might* slit her throat. But I like to think there's a better chance that Ed and Dick will knock on her door.

Anyone should use their best judgment but not be so afraid that they never take a chance. You miss too much of life that way.

The girl looked at me, sized me up, used her best judgment, determined I could add something to her life's experience and decided to take the risk.

Was she smart or dumb? Did I offer enough to make it worth the risk? I'd like to think so. On the other hand, you might think she was just plain dumb.

Soon after our arrival at her place she started dinner. In the movie *The Apartment,* Jack Lemmon plays a bachelor caught up in the whole New York City rat race. It won best picture around 1960. I remember in one scene he was cooking dinner and he drained his spaghetti on a tennis racket. Such is bachelorhood. I never saw any wet tennis rackets at my benefactor's apartment, but the ambiance pointed to rackets as a possible kitchen utensil.

She opened a box and a can or two.

"You're welcome to take a shower while I fix us something to eat." (What is this thing about my being offered the use of a shower by everyone who comes in contact with me?) "Hope you like Hamburger Helper."

After I'd scraped away several layers of topmost Georgia in the shower I sat down to a giant plate of noodly stuff. It looked like Jack Lemmon's dinner, but I was starving, and it tasted like haute cuisine to me.

"I'm sorry it isn't much but it's all I've got in the house until payday."

"Hey, no apology needed on this end. If you knew what my diet consisted of you'd understand how good this tastes to me. Even the Greyhound Bus Station would be an upgrade from candy bars and chips. But please don't misunderstand, I'm not comparing this to the bus station."

"Well, my mother visits some and I think she sees some similarities," she laughed.

"What kind of job do you have?" I asked.

"I'm a social worker. I deal mostly with unwanted, underprivileged, abused minority children."

Her accent told me she was a Yankee.

"Does your accent cause you many problems here?" I knew the old South.

"Oh yeah, I get some looks that no one would want to get. But the people who really matter are the kids who are my clients. Most are poor, unloved, and unwanted, so they don't care about the difference in my voice."

"Yeah, I guess it's nice to be around someone prejudice hasn't tainted yet," I said.

"Yeah."

A full stomach and a couch to spend the night on. I slept the sleep of the innocent and pure of heart.

She had to go to work the next morning so, after a bowl of Cheerios, she took me back to the spot where she'd picked me up outside town.

I wonder if she ever told her mother?

Chapter 67
Lions and Tigers and Bears

I enthusiastically endorse a long walk for everyone. I can't think of anyone who wouldn't benefit by a severing the stranglehold television and the automobile have on us. All too often, we experience Mother Nature from our living room windows, or as she zooms by at 65 mph on the Interstate.

A long, solitary walk not only seems to cleanse the mind and body, I can't think of a better way to commune with Mother Earth and Father Sky. You are able to see your world much as an Indian must have seen it. Of course, the opportunities to see the world he saw are dwindling daily. McDonald's, Wal-Mart, billboards and urban sprawl are quickly shrinking what the Indians saw.

Still there are places that haven't been sullied by man. To be at those places when the temperature and the lighting and the mood are all correct can be one of the most emotionally enhancing experiences you can have.

I once took a hitchhiking trip from Kentucky to Glacier National Park in Montana, down to New Orleans and back to Kentucky. As I was passing through Montana, I saw on the map that I was going to be close to Custer Battlefield. I told myself it was foolish to be that close and not see something so significant.

I can't remember why but I arrived just after dawn. I walked out on the battlefield and was the only person around. It gave me such an eerie feeling to be standing where so much history had taken place. If someone dressed like an Indian had walked up behind me and said "Boo," I'm sure my heart would have stopped.

Standing there, I could see the soldiers and the Indians. It was an exciting, spooky feeling. One I could never have experienced through a book or a movie or on television. If other people had been there it wouldn't have been the same. Conditions were right just at that moment and probably never would have been again.

One night in south Georgia conditions were again right for a very unique experience; an experience I hope I never have again.

Darkness was approaching, necessitating that dreaded daily search for a place to spend the night.

There were railroad tracks running beside the road. That would mean little to most people but to the person who has to find his bed where he can find it, a railroad is of special interest.

Railroads create a corridor of sorts. Given a choice, people usually don't "crowd" the railroad. There's the noise to put up with. And trains can block your way if you want to get to the other side of the track. Trains often carry hazardous stuff. Man has wisely let trains have their own space whenever possible. So there's less man intrusion along a railway.

It may take quite a bit of walking to find a suitable spot to put down along a highway. Houses and businesses are located along them. Trains have sort of a highway of their own, though. And in most cases the houses are missing and have been replaced by woods and brush.

Though railroads are often good places to find campsites, they aren't good places to walk along. You have to keep checking with your eyes to the front, and your ears to the back, so you are always on edge wondering if your ears are doing their job. Rocks are used under, around and between the ties, and the rocks are too big to walk on comfortably. And the spacing of the crossties is wrong for the average person's stride — stepping on every tie is too short, every other tie is too far.

I seriously doubt railroads were purposely designed to discourage walking along but maybe it's a good by-product that they are. Scraping and shoveling the remaining pieces of train track walkers into a bucket after their ears failed to do their jobs would be an unpleasant job for most.

So I was pleased to find a railroad and a highway traveling arm in arm.

At a crossing I pulled <u>my</u> train-switching switch and shifted <u>my</u> wheels over to the railroad. It didn't take long before I was out of sight and sound of the highway. It was then a simple matter of picking my spot along the railroad "right of way" to spend the night.

I know you're wondering if it's scary, sleeping that close to something so big, noisy and deadly. After all, trains do turn over, they do jump the tracks. But trains are just so wide and are confined to a narrow track. So you can plan accordingly. For good measure add an extra margin of space between you and the track and, notwithstanding the periodic noise that shakes you loose from your skin, railroads offer a secure place to spend the night.

There was a depression running beside the track where I found myself at dark. I call it a depression rather than a ditch because you could walk across. It was just a matter of descending down from the track, then up a short bank. At a level spot on the bank I pitched my tent among some bushes.

This was an ideal spot. I was out of sight of the butcher, the baker, and the candlestick maker. Not even the engineer, the brakeman or the caboose man could see me.

I could enjoy my dinner Doritos, Payday candy bar and Kool-Aid, and settle down to a peaceful night's sleep, secure in my own little world. And I did just that. South Georgia in August seldom serves up a cool enough night for good sleeping, but I was blessed with one that night.

I wonder how many people would walk from Los Angeles to New York City and wear a watch? I'm sure a lot would. It seems ludicrous to me, though. What would you need a watch for? Isn't your day governed pretty much by the sun and moon?

So, when I say I was awakened during the night by that Kool-Aid call of nature at around three, I'm only guessing. It just *seemed* like three. I had no way of knowing. I slept in the same pajamas as the Indians so if there'd been eyes to see I would have cut a cute figure, standing a few yards from my tent answering the call in the "altogether." The only item breaking the continuity of my white skin against the dark trees was my hiking boots. I was willing to get out of my tent naked, but not without my boots. I'd heard enough rattler stories and seen enough fire ants to make me gun-shy about parading around barefoot.

As you know, my tent was little more than a glorified body bag. It was a long, screened tube with a nylon floor. If I turned over during the night it had to be a revolution in one spot. To enter it I had to get down on my hands and knees and back in. If I went in headfirst there was no way to turn around. The tent was slightly wedge-shaped to allow for the fact that shoulders are wider than feet, and I only made the mistake once of going in head first. I had to back out. Thankfully, it was in the Southwest desert with only "desert critter" eyes there to smile at my ignominy.

You've heard that it's possible to be scared so badly that you cannot make a sound, not even a scream. Hard to believe, isn't it? You'd think if you're scared badly enough, you're going to scream — case closed. There really is a step beyond scared. It's called terrified. I suppose like everyone I'd been scared before. Who hasn't? It wasn't until this south Georgia night by the tracks that I experienced terror.

I'd finished the business that had forced me out of the tent in the first place. (After this night I made it a point to find a bottle, can or cup to take inside with me.) I had unzipped the small door to my tent to re-enter (You only leave it unzipped once. Because that was the time you came back and found about a hundred of those sweet Georgia brown mosquitoes had invaded your home during your brief absence. On numbers two through gazillion trips you zip the tent as you leave), and had begun to back my skinny, little white butt into the tent. I was at the point where only my shoulders and head were still sticking out. It was a twixt-and-between situation where grace never resides and the one in which you feel most awkward and vulnerable. It's like a turtle must feel when he sees the bobcat's paw coming but he hasn't got that complete lock and set on his shell yet. Or possibly when a woman has one leg in her girdle and the doorbell rings.

Anyway, just as I was almost in, but not quite, I suddenly heard some creature, beast, being, whatever, running bat-out-of-hell straight for my tent. The only thing I knew for sure was that it had four legs–two couldn't churn that fast!

In about one one-hundredth of a second I made my analysis: It was an animal, it had four legs, it was coming straight for me — fast! I couldn't determine its size nor intent. Was I a target or did I just happen to be in the path of a frightened, escaping animal.

I had only one defense — scream. Not very manly but desperate situations call for desperate measures. And vanity seemed frivolous at this point.

Knowing my little, thin nylon tent was; at best, psychological protection, you can imagine the real terror this charging beast presented.

In that nanosecond all my computer could flash on the screen was — SCREAM! SCREAM! SCREAM!

Obeying instantly, and without question, I screamed. Would it stop the charging beast? None but the beast knew. I knew, though, that buck nekkid, on hands and knees, bass-ackwards, half in/half out of that tent my defense options had narrowed to one simple game plan — SCREAM!

"Scream" is synonymous with "noise," isn't it? Aren't "loud," "terrifying" and "noise" the operative words in "Scream?"

Picture my amazement when my best attempt produced nothing. Although I'd never consciously tried to scream, I felt that nature would take her course under these circumstances, (and I'd come up with a classic) but no sound came out. None!

Oh, Lord! My last and only defense and it has deserted me. What now? It's the belly of the beast for sure! I would never have guessed it would all come down to this — nuked by some unseen varmint from hell on a dark, south Georgia railroad right-of-way. Not a very noble ending for a life that held such promise.

Nothing to do but clinch my eyes and butt, hold my breath, and prepare for impact.

It was weeks later and hundreds of miles further down the road that it dawned on me why I didn't get eaten that night.

I thought I only had one defense — a scream. Turns out I had two; one I didn't even think about until I was well into South Carolina. It hit me one day like a bolt out of the blue. Without knowing, I had one of the best defenses known to man; a silent defense probably much more effective than my scream would have been. I had something that could turn a charging rhino, stop a lion in its tracks, make a wolf wimper. What was it? Are you ready? I'll give you a hint. You might have to hold your nose. That's right — good ol' American walking-down-the-road, sweatin-like-a-monkey, stinkin'-like-a-goat B.O.! I ask you, what critter, no matter how bad wouldn't be turned by that?

Just when I was sure that whatever was charging toward me was about to hit me, it swerved and ran in another direction. I really believe it was because it smelled the awfulness that was me.

Seriously though, more likely it was an animal running for its own life, pursued by its own devil and just happened to find itself bearing down on me.

Chapter 68
The Most Disheartening Episode

I guess it's only human nature that we like to be with our own kind. Maybe it's true with all animals. Sheep may get along with goats but wouldn't they just as soon associate strictly with other sheep?

I think feeling comfortable with your own kind is something deeper or different than race relations. It's a coveting of your comfort zone. You recognize and identify with other people who share your characteristics and background. It's only natural to gravitate toward the familiar.

But the thinking man doesn't stop there. He realizes that it's a big, exciting world out there, made so mostly, by people different from him. The wise man is willing to step out of his comfort zone and grasp the new and different, be they places or people.

Then you have the non-thinking man who refuses to recognize and greet anything or anyone who doesn't fit his mold. "Different" scares him. And being scared causes a lashing out.

I had the misfortune to be trudging slowly through the South while being quite different. I looked different, I talked different. And just those are enough to make people look that certain "we'd-rather-you-weren't-here" look. In the vast majority of cases it never goes beyond that "look."

However, an incident happened one afternoon that still confuses me by its lack of logic. I've never seen nor heard of a better picture of blind prejudice than what happened to me that afternoon. I couldn't see the logic in it then and I still am confused by such a random act of bigotry.

It was about five one-weekday afternoon. I was "out in the country" walking east on a divided four lane highway. The lanes going each way were divided by about 30 yards of median grass. There wasn't a lot of traffic; and since this was out in the country the cars going by were reason for more interest than if there had been more volume. After you've seen ten million pine trees and about a zillion acres of red and grey dirt a Toyota pickup going by that's sitting about six inches off the ground and has a bumper sticker that says: "Praise the Lowered" is cause for a second glance and a moment of smiling contemplation.

Pickups are the chariot of choice in the South and are so numerous that after a while sky-high, jacked-up bodies, big, mud slingin' tires, gun racks (gun or carpenter's level optional), with a coon hound in the back and a bumper sticker that says: "I didn't vote for President Clinton or her husband either!" hardly merit a sideways glance.

One pickup passed me that did, however. It was going the same direction I was with only the grass median separating us. It still confuses, perplexes, bewilders and saddens me when I think of what the man in the pickup did as he passed me. His act is even more puzzling due to the fact that he was alone. He couldn't have been showing off for someone else in the truck or someone coming down the road because there wasn't anyone else. It seemed his act was just a reflex of blind hatred born of years of non-thinking prejudice.

What made his act even more senseless was the fact that the man had never seen me or heard me, had no idea what I stood for or against, whether I was a nice or a mean person. The stupid, ironic part was I might have even thought like him, for all he knew. He was judging me solely on my looks. And, even that was stupid because without my pack and safari hat we probably looked similar. Asked to pick the red neck from the line-up I might just as easily have been picked as him.

No, it was an inbred distrust of anything different. It's the stuff hatred and wars have been made of since one man looked, acted, sounded, smelled different from another.

Maybe Rodney King, even though he didn't possess a lot of sterling qualities, was a philosopher of sorts when he said: "Why can't we all just get along?"

I think what disturbed me more than anything else after the man in the pickup passed was the thoughtlessness of his act.

Man is supposed to be the only animal that reasons. In this man I saw only an animal, a reactionary, who acts without reason and that's a scary, dangerous man or animal.

One man, any man is walking down the road, facing traffic. On the far side of a four-lane, divided highway a man is passing by going in the same direction. They don't know each other, have never seen each other. As the man in the pickup pulls even with the walking man he sticks his left arm out the truck window and gives the walker the "finger."

Just for a moment visualize this picture and see if you agree with me that this man's simple act said volumes about what has been one of man's biggest problem since he's been on this Earth.

Think, not of just the simple vulgar gesture but of the picture it paints of a much larger picture.

Frightening and sad, isn't it?

Chapter 69
Shootout at Ludowici

Why are seafood restaurants so often called "Captain Bill's or Captain Don's? How come none are ever called, "Deckhand Bob's?" How does the moniker "Captain" bestow any sterling qualities regarding the procurement, preparation and presentation of fine seafood?

And it's hard to picture the owner of a seafood restaurant in land-locked Jessup, Georgia being the captain of anything larger than a dinghy.

But the sight of any Seafood Buffet no matter who's in charge can straighten the spine of a slumping coast-to-coast walker. The once thought near dead suddenly develop spring in their step and luster to their eyes.

When I saw the sign that said Captain Joe's Seafood Buffet just east of Jessup, Georgia I was sure I had died and without possessing the qualities, requirements or credentials had suddenly found myself at Heaven's gate. This was walker's and hog's heaven.

And praise the Lord it was heavenly. From soup to nuts and on beyond to desserts it lay for the taking in quantities befitting the wants and needs of the tired, starving, hot, thirsty Los Angeles to New York walker.

Only a concentration camp survivor could have seen it with the same eyes, smelled it with the same nose, tasted it with the same lips as this Doritos and Kool-Aid survivor did.

I owe Captain Joe's such a debt. They allowed someone who looked like me to eat and eat and eat and didn't even charge me "pro rata." And all the sweet iced tea I could possibly hold!

Treat yourself to one of life's true joys — go Jessup, Georgia in mid-August, have someone drop you off about 15 miles out of town and point you in the direction of Captain Joe's. When you get there you'll be ready for, and have an appreciation of, what a really good appeasing of hunger and a quenching of thirst is all about.

Even though my stomach looked liked I'd swallowed a bowling ball and picking up my pack with its accompanying swing to my back nearly rushed a tidal wave of Captain Joe's Buffet toward my throat I managed to sway with blissful contentment toward South Carolina.

I was set. I wouldn't have to eat or drink until I was well over into South Carolina and it must have been 75 miles away.

Why is it that it never works that way? At twelve miles east of Jessup I came to Ludowici and the raging thirst had returned. I believe that is one of the indications of dehydration. If you drink all you can hold and in an hour you're really thirsty again, then your body needs much more than you can drink at one sitting, no matter how much that might be. What your body needs is a good drenching, a continual inner soaking spread over several days. One blast, no matter how big, isn't really adequate. It takes large quantities spread over several days for your body to recover from dehydration.

The problem was that I'd felt fine and not thirsty at all as I passed through the town of Ludowici. It was only as I passed the outskirts, and going back wasn't a desirable option, that thirst struck again. Then the eyes no longer notice the land, or the sky or any beauty they might contain. The eye becomes blind to anything other than what might bring relief to the throat. The throat becomes the master. You're driven by some inner need, a need that's stronger than any other need except the need to breathe. Then the eye becomes the slave of the throat, the throat's sentinel. King Throat commands Subject Eye to search relentlessly for any signs of wet relief for the king.

Such a fear had gripped my eyes when they spotted the Ludowici Truck Weigh Station. If King Throat had been cool and moist and appeased, then Slave Eye would never have registered to itself that this was a place for meeting any requirements that the King had.

Being a truck weigh station, why would there be anything wet or cool or satisfying there?

The eye fears the throat, though. And fear makes for desperate grasping of straws.

My eyes said it was *something* and anything was a straw to grab for. The King was in a bad mood. Something must be done!

The weigh station was a gray, unimposing, small rectangular box of metal that only Americans would view as something suitable as a work area. To most other people in the world, people who view long metal boxes as shelter, this would have been the home of probably ten or fifteen people. But we are rich. We made it into a truck weigh station.

The two "weighers" inside were nice and talkative, more I believe from boredom than any real inclination toward cross-country walkers. At least they weren't overtly suspicious as usually is the case in the South.

As I popped through the door I noticed a slight look of surprise on their faces. When I saw one lift a blind and check the scales outside, it dawned on me that it wasn't my looks that surprised them (check out a few truckers) rather they had been expecting a truck , if anything. I suspected that way out here anyone coming through the door had been preceded by some truck noises.

"Hey fellas, I was wondering if you could spare me a drink of water?" I wasn't sure why an answer required that he bring his tilted chair back down to all four legs on the floor but that's what he did before he answered.

And his partner gave another check out the window for that truck I was surely in and he'd surely missed the first time. This time his eyes broadened their sweep.

"Sure," the tilted chair guy said and flicked a finger in the direction of the fountain. "You walkin'?"

He said this just when I'd really begun to nurse that water fountain. I didn't want to give him an answer just then, even if it was a simple "Yeah."

I decided he could wait for two more big swallows but that it would be impolite to not acknowledge him after that. This was a fantastic water fountain and who knew how far it was to another like it. I didn't want to chance being run off for rudeness, though.

"Yes Sir," I said. "I'm attempting to walk from Los Angeles to New York City." This may have been eastern Georgia but I was still using "attempting."

"Holy Sweet Jesus! You mean you've walked all the way from Los Angeles to here? Naw! You mean you've gotten rides, too.

I could tell he was agitated. He even reached up and took the cigar stub out of his mouth. And it looked like the only time that happened was at bedtime, if then.

"No, not really. I've walked it all."

Then he turned to his partner, "Russell, what the hell you think of that? If you or I had to walk to Ludowici they wouldn't even bother to call the emergency squad, they'd just call the undertaker and tell 'em to bring a push broom and scoop."

Russell just gave a slight shake of his head and a smile.

I got the feeling he'd like to look outside just once more. I <u>had</u> to be pullin' their leg. There must be a truck out there somewhere.

"Hey, drink all the water you want? That's all we got to offer but you deserve something after doing that. When did you start?"

"April eighth."

"Good Lord! How many days have you rested?"

"One."

"Good Lord!"

"Well, I wouldn't call it a rest day. A violent Texas storm kept me in one day."

"Where do you sleep?"

"You name it. Practically anywhere but mostly fields and woods. Since you mention it, do you know of any place nearby I could put my tent up for the night?" I asked.

He thought for a second, then looked at Russell for what seemed a visual confirmation of what he was about to say. That seemed an exercise in futility since Russell hadn't contributed anything, plus or minus, to the entire discourse. Then he said, with nothing more than a slight jaw gape from Russell, "Across the road about a half mile away there's a river running parallel to the highway. It's kinda sandy down there, and people go there to fish. There's a road back to it about a quarter mile down the road. I'd say it'd be a pretty good place. I don't know if I'd do it on weekends, but now during the week should be okay. Most people right around here have jobs so they're usually in on weeknights."

Then the question I had for everyone — "How far would you guesstimate it is to the next grocery store?"

"Hmm, let's see. I guess it'd be that Quick Stop at Allenhurst 'bout nine mile."

I had begun to think Russell wasn't going to say anything the entire time I was at the weigh station, so I had to smile inside when he volunteered an observation at this point without any prompting from his partner, whose name I never knew because there were no introductions.

"Well, you know Ilene's brother-in-law Shelby opened a little bait store in Walthourville about a month ago. I think they carry bread and milk and cans of pork and beans and stuff like that. And it's only about seven miles up the road."

I silently blessed Russell for his contribution. Thinking about seven miles to the next food is better than thinking about nine miles to the next food.

I felt I'd about sucked the fountain dry and we'd covered about all the walking bases so I figured it was time for me to go. There were just two questions that remained.

How do you pronounce Ludowici?"

"It's "Loo-Dough-Wicki.

For an instant it crossed my mind to ask the weigh station guys where the name came from. Then I thought better of it. They didn't seem like history buffs. I still had one more question, though.

"Why is that bullet hole in your front window?"

"It's not just the front window. The back wall has a corresponding hole as well."

"Damn," I exclaim.

"Well, it could have been worse. Luckily no one was here at the time."

I just shook my head and stepped up for round two at the water fountain. Those tons of seafood back at Captain Joe's were like gasoline thrown on my already roaring bonfire of thirst.

Have you ever been so thirsty that you drank and drank at a cold water fountain until all the cold water was used up? As the water gets less and less cold, your pleasure begins to wane in direct proportion to the rising temperature of the water. I can tell you I've left regiments of fallen fountains, drained of their cold life's blood strewn across this walker's battlefields from sea to shining sea.

I'm sure the Ludowici weigh station water fountain is still on R. & R.

Chapter 70
The Most Bewildering Incident

One of the nice things about a long walk is that it's pretty clear cut. Your objective is point A to point B. You move your right foot in front of your left, then your left in front of the right. Do that enough and you reach point B.

Not too hard to figure out. Adventures will happen, of course, but they are above and beyond any mechanics of walking.

You can ponder life as you walk if it moves you, but it isn't required.

You're one of a minority of maybe one percent. Ninety-nine percent of the people are busy keeping the wolf from the door — getting up, going to work, coming home, eating dinner, watching a little television, then off to bed to repeat the cycle the next day. No matter where you go it's pretty much that way. People are born, people work, laugh, cry and grow old, then they die.

Cross continental walking is not going to change that. The walker observes life as it manifests itself all around him. He is only a casual observer passing through.

So, when something happens that doesn't fit the mold of human behavior it's news, it's puzzling, it's man-bites-dog stuff.

Late afternoon thunderstorms in August in South Georgia are more the rule than the exception (In Florida there are almost never any exceptions).

During a storm on the outskirts of Hinesville, I was fortunate to be able to reach the overhang on the front door of a church. It wasn't much, but it was better than the woods or field. It's funny how you feel safe from lightning under the flimsiest of shelters sometimes.

This storm lingered longer than most and it began to get dark.

When you have no reason for Thursday to be any different from Monday, or Tuesday to be different from Friday, it's easy to lose track of what day it really is.

And it wouldn't have mattered on the front porch of the Hinesville Church of God except with regard to when you can sleep in the backyards of churches and when you can't. As it became more evident that the storm wasn't going anywhere, I began trying to figure if this was a safe day of the week. After a few, long seconds of mental gymnastics with my hands pressed to the sides of my lowered head, I calculated it must be a Tuesday. Thank goodness — a safe day.

The last bits of daylight and the storm's passing were going to coincide, it seemed. I'd have just enough light left to pop up my tent in the backyard without fumbling in the dark.

You'd think a day of walking from daylight to dark would make for instant sleep as soon as the opportunity presented itself. But seldom did I fall asleep as soon as my head hit the pillow. There was always that period of transition, a sort of winding down. Maybe the wait under the church overhang had rested me. I could tell I wasn't going to be able to go to sleep quickly. Usually, when it happened I'd throw back the front flap of my tent and lay gazing at the stars through my screen door. My tent was unique in that I could roll back the front door flap, then roll up the flap that covered my feet and body, tie those two together, and have what, in effect, was a screen "house."

It was nice when the weather was warm and clear because you could lie on your back and star gaze to your heart's content. It didn't make for a very secure feeling, though. It was like lying outside. If you weren't presentable, there you were for the whole world to see. It was small, but if you saw it erected you'd definitely not confuse it with any other structure. It was small but there wouldn't be any doubt it was a tent.

And that's where the puzzlement comes in concerning that late evening behind the Hinesville church. As I lay on my back looking at the sky I was lost in my own reverie. It was Tuesday, I was behind the church out in the country, there was no church service, no one was around. Or, so I thought. Out of the blue and the corner of my eye, I detected movement. I jerked my head around just in time to see a teenage boy walking rather quickly past my tent. He was no more than ten feet away. He was moving like he was in a hurry, but not being chased; more as if he were late for supper and knew his mother would fuss at him.

But the surprising, confusing thing was, he gave no indication that he saw me. He passed so close to the head of my tent that it was impossible for him not to have seen me.

In the days following I replayed the event over and over in my mind as I walked down the road. I could only come to this conclusion: The boy was aware that something was there, but his mind rejected the idea of it being a tent. I compare it to passing by an elephant in your neighbor's back yard. You dismiss it because you *know* it isn't possible for an elephant to be in your neighbor's back yard. It was something big and gray but it couldn't have been an elephant.

I surmised all this in the days following the incident but at the time that wasn't my supposition at all.

When you are vulnerable, you think the worst about everything happening around you. Fear feeds bad thoughts about your situation.

At the time I thought the boy was just pretending to not see me and was going to tell a bunch of friends and they were going to come back after dark and do unspeakable things to me. What was I to do, though? I was in unfamiliar territory. Stumbling around in the dark terrified of what might be chasing me didn't seem a very viable alternative. I decided to just lay and listen. Every small sound became footsteps. Finally, after what must have been hours, my frazzled nerves suffered meltdown and I dropped off to sleep.

No one ever came that night. I suppose the boy just thought he saw an elephant.

Chapter 71
El Dorado — The Streets of Gold

During all the years of wishing and planning for my right foot in the Pacific and my left foot in the Atlantic, two things about the walk were always carved in stone. One was that the right foot would be dipped at one of the storied beaches off Los Angeles, and the other was that left foot at that old stalwart of the South — Savannah.

I had always just assumed Savannah was a city with beaches on the Atlantic. It isn't. It's close but only car close. It's not walking close.

After inspecting my map closely on the approach to Savannah I saw how flawed my assumption had been. And I wasn't so keen on "left foot" occurring in Savannah that I was willing to walk out of my way to achieve it.

I knew all along that I was going to walk up the east coast so contact with the Atlantic could occur at any number of places, and there need be no urgency about it being Savannah.

The route I'd chosen was to take me through the industrial backyard of the city. I saw sugar refineries and other businesses, but as for the historic Old South Savannah, I saw nothing.

While I was gawking at the Dixie Crystal Sugar Refinery and saying to myself, "Huh, so that's where Dixie Crystals come from," I nearly stepped on the biggest, fattest rattlesnake I'd seen outside Wild Kingdom. I'm sure the Dixie Crystal Refinery would have been leveled by the sonic boom coming from my throat if not for the fact that at the same instant I saw the snake, I realized it was dead.

Since the beginning of this walk, and especially in the desert Southwest, I had been warned repeatedly, "This is rattlesnake country, be careful."

Yet it was here in Savannah that I was to see my first rattlesnake. All the way from Los Angeles to Savannah I hadn't seen one alive or dead or any degree twixt the two. This one looked like it had just eaten a litter of pups for lunch and was crossing the highway when a Goodyear all-weather radial landed smack between pups number three and four.

Maybe it was because the course I took was one seldom covered on foot, and had the advantage of never being picked over but I couldn't believe the amount of money I started finding. I'd found money on a regular basis since leaving Los Angeles. Of course, the bulk being pennies, but nickels, dimes and quarters were common, too. When the accumulated change began to get bulky and heavy I'd stop and mail it back to my daughter, Erin, in

Kentucky. I didn't have any intention of spending the money I found. I wanted to save it all, so that after I'd reached New York I could count it, and indeed know how much money a person would find if they walked from Los Angeles to New York. I think that had always been a boyhood fascination of mine — maybe even preceding the fantasy of the walk itself. Here I was finding pennies way out of proportion to the penny rate that had occurred all across the United States.

It reminded me of when I was a small boy without much money of any kind and sometimes dreamed at night of finding large amounts of nickels, dimes and quarters in the gutters of streets. In my young mind, I didn't see paper money as lots of money. To me, then, coins represented the real money as long as there was piles of it. Savannah brought back memories of those dreams. It seemed every few steps I found a penny.

Finding the pennies so frequently was a two-edged sword. Picking any object off the ground isn't fun carrying a pack on your back, but bending over to pick them up was a balancing act each time it happened.

I was glad to find them, and of course, happier when the value of the coin was greater because I could see my grand total growing , and I still had several "rich" states to walk through.

It was after only about the third penny way back on the Pacific Coast Highway in Los Angeles that I discovered I'd have to develop a new technique if I was to continue to pick things up. You'd be surprised how often you do want to pick things up. Things were always coming along that needed a closer look. Oh, you could turn them over with your walking stick and give them a quick "Yea" or "Nay" as to whether they were worth the effort of bending over. And ninety percent of the objects encountered could be evaluated and rejected from the standing position. But the other ten percent required closer inspection. Naturally, that could only be achieved by bending and picking it up. Of course, money never had to go through the weeding out process. I picked up any and all money.

If I did what a person normally would do to pick up a penny, i.e. bend at the waist, the pack would want to shoot off over my head like a sled off the top of a snow-covered hill. At the beginning of this walk I cursed several pennies for making me grab desperately for that pack to keep it from shooting over my head. I soon learned I had to substitute a squat for a bend if I wanted to pick anything up. My back had to remain straight. Either way, I'm sure I looked fairly comical. It's odd that I became adept at spotting pennies that had lain there for so many years, and been run over so many times, the faces were ground off. No matter how defaced, I could spot money. Nothing else that occurred along the highway was quite that symmetrical.

Chapter 72
The Afrikan Nation

The backroads and streets of Savannah had been good to me, peaceful, with plenty of fun money added to the picture. It isn't the easiest thing to leave such a scene and venture into the unknown. But, Manhattan called and there was only one way to get there — keep placing my right in front of my left.

Speaking of the unknown, during this walk I had become so out of touch with what was happening in the world.

You'd think that since I passed through a place so slowly I'd be very familiar with a narrow strip of America from sea to shining sea. In a way, I was a stranger in a strange land, a man without a country. People only tolerated me. They allowed me to pass through, but I was never drawn into their world. Questions and answers were given and taken in only the most superficial manner. I would have had to stay in one spot for much longer, probably months and possibly years, before I'd have been trusted with local news and gossip.

And any newspapers, books or magazines were definitely extras I wouldn't carry. I was out of the loop with the locals, and didn't want to waste precious time visiting the local library to catch up on the news. I was pretty much an island in the sea of world happenings.

After my walk I was floored at how out of touch I'd been for the last five and a half months.

So, when I was on the road between Savannah and Charleston and saw a large, slightly askew, billboard with an arrow pointing down a side road that said, "The Afrikan Nation" — as seen on "Sixty Minutes" — I was definitely puzzled.

Television was as lacking in my realm as were magazines and newspapers and the sign proclaimed something so foreign to me.

I thought the Afrikan Nation was probably a small community ahead indicated by the arrow on the sign and I'd pass right by it.

When I came to a small grocery a few miles up the road, thoughts about the Afrikan Nation had been replaced by chocolate milk thoughts. So I was surprised when the owner addressed me as "Mon."

As in, "Would you like another Rum and Coca-Cola, Mon?"

As I drank my chocolate milk I roamed over to the sweets aisle. It was a busy grocery and several people came and went. I noticed they all had accents like the store owner.

Their accents weren't deep South or even American. And the women were dressed like actresses from *Porgy and Bess.*

It was confusing to me. This little ethnic section may have been here for years, still I blamed my ignorance on how out-of-touch I'd been during my walk.

Here was a nation within a nation and I knew nothing about it.

If, before my walk someone had said, "I want to pose a riddle to you — on this walk you will cross more than one nation. Can you explain that?"

I would have walked from Los Angeles all the way to South Carolina in complete perplexity, if indeed, I'd have given any credence in the first place to the riddler and his riddles.

Chapter 73
My First Real Bed Since Lamesa, Texas and the Emperor Gets New Clothes

If your knowledge of the South is obtained by traveling to Disney World on Interstate 75 from anywhere up North, you aren't aware of what the South's all about. One of the things it is about is the pine tree.

The pine tree is the grease that lubricates everything in the South. If it weren't for the money the pine tree generates I'd bet things would be vastly different. Remove the pine, and there'd have to be some quick re-tooling of mind and machine or lifestyles in the South would come to a grinding halt. As long as there are trees in the South there will be shoes on a lot of feet, and biscuits and gravy on lots of tables.

Naturally, those trees don't make money unless they are cut and hauled to the sawmill or pulp mill. They might be pretty and majestic, standing tall, but lying is where the dollars are. In the South you're seldom out of sight of the log truck or sound of the chainsaw.

As you might imagine on a 3813 mile/five-and-a-half month walk, you travel slowly and become lost in your own reverie. If nothing exciting or even interesting vies for your senses, it's easy to slip into a world other than the present. Thoughts of the past or future float through your mind as you plod mindlessly ahead. You see but don't, you hear but don't, until something so dramatic occurs it forces your senses back to the here and now.

An incident way back in Alabama comes to mind that's a good example of what I mean.

I was no longer surprised when a police car pulled alongside me. I was an oddity and it's a policeman's job to insure peace and normalcy. And since I knew my heart was pure, and our country was, at least on paper, still free, the sight of a policeman approaching didn't quicken my heart much.

But I was taken aback, and in the next breath amused, by what the officer said. As so often was the case I didn't seem to pose enough of a threat to merit getting out of the cruiser, so the officer just eased up beside me. I turned to look and that action alone seemed to answer his question. I was puzzled as to what there was about me that cleared the policeman's mind.

"We got a call a little while ago about a blind man walking down the road." I saw the faintest hint of a smile cross his face.

Assured that I had *most* of my faculties and that I was harmless the officer left me to my trudge.

The only explanation that I could come up with was that when the reporting person had seen the "blind man" it was because I had dropped off into one of my dreamworlds and was still moving forward but not really part of my surrounding world. Since I always used my walking stick the person calling in had assumed I was blind.

It's so easy to slip into that other world. Something always happens to bring you back. It can be fairly simple or quite dramatic.

An auto crash will do it every time. There's no other sound like it.

I was about 20 miles south of Charleston. I was approaching a crossroads with a store and a few other buildings. Not an important enough intersection to warrant a stop light, but one that had earned itself a caution light. As I was soon to learn "caution" was, is, and forever more should be, the operative word at this intersection.

I can only guess that I was in one of my dream worlds when a loud noise relayed the message to somewhere deep inside me that something dramatic was happening in the real, outside world.

It was a screeching, crashing, glass shattering, grab-every-scrap-of-your-attention-senses sound.

I was too deep within myself to say I actually observed what happened. As so often happens with accidents you hear the sound, snap to attention, look in the direction of the sound and realize that you *almost* just witnessed something.

An eerie thing about horrific accidents is that, although the sound is so gut wrenching, loud and horrible, it only lasts for a split second and then it's followed by the equally horrible few seconds of utter and complete silence.

By the time my eyes and senses had focused in the direction of the sound, the accident scene was already in its eerie noiseless state of aftershock.

People were then pouring out of places I had no earlier indication contained anyone. They were racing to the scene. My pack wouldn't allow me to be even one of the first several to reach the scene so I was just frozen to the spot, more or less.

A log truck with many logs sticking way out past the rear of the trailer had slowed to make a left turn. Evidently the driver of the car following didn't see or was, perhaps, like me, in his own never-never land of dreams. Consequently, he ran into the rear of the log truck resulting in one of the logs piercing the driver's vent window and exiting through the passenger side rear window. How the driver was not decapitated by the log I'll never know. Word filtering back through the crowd was that a girl in the back seat was injured but those injuries didn't appear to be "life threatening."

Once the ambulance had come and the excitement had given way to the inevitable clean up, it was time for me to continue my march to the sea.

Much to my chagrin, marshlands began to appear on each side of the road. That in itself would have been enjoyable enough, if I'd been traveling by car and a warm, dry bed waited at the end of the day.

Marshlands have a beauty of their own, but where I would spend the night began to concern me as I walked toward Charleston and saw watery marshes on each side of the road for as far as I could see. I grew increasingly uneasy.

There were no farmer's fields, no church back yards, no woods.

There was the option of walking all night. And I thought I might have to.

I was on a narrow, two-lane road, and I didn't relish walking it in the dark but twilight was upon me and I had no choice but to keep going.

My spirits soared when just ahead I saw the sign for a state park. I told myself that a state park had to have some solid ground.

It was completely dark when I arrived and lightning and thunder were approaching from the west. Behind some shrubbery at the entrance to the park was as good as I was likely to get.

Normally, approaching rainstorms caused my neck muscles to draw up ever-so-slightly in anticipation but the solid spot I'd found behind the shrubbery made even the coming storm seem bearable.

The Marshland storm that night at the park was what I call a "bully" storm. It was totally bluff and bluster. More fluff and feathers than any real threat. It sounded big but produced little.

I was so thankful for my patch of high ground that the storm was no more of a bother than a flea tickling a dog's ear.

The next day, Charleston; that delightful place where Rhett retreated to after Scarlett and the war to see if anything of honor and dignity (his words) still existed.

It does. And as Rhett felt Charleston was unique in his day, I found it unique, too.

When you approach most cities or towns you are greeted first by the occasional house, then more houses, then a convenience store, then a Wal-Mart, a McDonald's, houses closer and closer to each other and finally Main Street.

Much to my bewilderment Charleston has reversed the entire order of the typical town's structure. Suddenly you're on Main Street. There's none of the customary build-up. I suppose it has something to do with the wetlands crowding the city on the side from which I was approaching. I looked up and ahead was Main Street USA and to my back was knee-deep mud.

I hadn't slept in a real bed since Lamesa, Texas and though I wasn't trying to set any records, my tent and sleeping bag had become my way of life.

As soon as I saw what lay in front of me I knew that would change.

I knew I must look worse than any street person in Charleston. I ducked into a vacant drive-through car wash, took off my pack and began rummaging for my cleanest dirty shirt and pants. A quick search told me I couldn't improve my appearance much. I changed anyway, took off my silly looking safari hat, spit on my hands and slicked my hair down the best I could. I ran my boots over the car wash brushes to remove what mud I could, then stepped out in the light of day to try and fake my way into my first motel since Texas.

Luckily, I didn't have to present myself to too much of Charleston before a suitable motel appeared on my left. As it turned out the desk was being operated by the kind mother of the motel's owner. I gushed about the beauty of the area, apologized profusely about my appearance and related my story to further my cause.

I soon found myself watching TV on my first bed in months.

After a while there was a knock on the door. It was the motel owner.

"Hi, excuse me for bothering you. My mother told me about your walk. I recently cleaned out some closets and was going to give the clothes to the Goodwill. You're welcome to see if there's anything you can use."

So I really did look that bad, did I? I knew the car wash transformation hadn't accomplished much. Still, I was slightly embarrassed that I looked pitiful enough to elicit this kind attention. I jumped at the offer for two reasons. First, and mainly, I needed new clothes. I realized after only the first few days of my walk how hard I was on clothes. You'd think the simple act of walking down the road wouldn't create much stress on them. But when you sit down on hot asphalt, or lay on park benches, or in the grass, and walk in a cloud of dust, they don't last long. And the summer sun can be brutal when anything is exposed to it day after day. The shoulders of my shirts were so thin you could almost read a newspaper through them and my shoulders were as tanned as if I'd been walking without a shirt, which I never did. My shoulders looked funny. My thin shirts couldn't keep out the sun, but the thick straps of my backpack could. So I had two white stripes running over and down the tops of my brown shoulders.

The second reason I jumped at the offer of new clothes was, more than anything else on this walk, I hated to go to the laundromat. I found that about a week was the longest I could go without doing my laundry. But it was such a chore. It was time spent wastefully when all I really cared about was moving on down the road.

As we walked to the little shed in the back the owner said, "I hope you can get some good from some of this stuff. I called my nephew a couple of weeks ago and offered it to him but you know kids these days. If it isn't baggy, or faded, or you can't tattoo or pierce it, they don't want anything to do with it."

I just gave my best sympathetic "Kids — Whatcha-gonna-do" smile.

When I saw the clothes I knew why the nephew hadn't bothered. I wasn't a kid, and I wasn't really particular, but these clothes were dated. It was one of those curve balls life throws at you occasionally.

I didn't see how I could refuse his clothes without sounding ungrateful. I had to muddle through somehow and repay his kindness by sounding really glad to get new clothes. I was happy to get different clothes but these were *too* different.

I carried an armload of shirts and pants back across the parking lot.

I saw him looking at my boots.

"How many pairs of shoes have you worn out?"

"I'm on my third pair."

"Where do you live?"

"I'm a Kentucky native but I've lived about the last twelve years in Gatlinburg, Tennessee."

"Oh, my wife and I love Gatlinburg. The mountains are so pretty," he added.

I thought I may as well add my two cents.

"Isn't it funny that the people in the mountains go to the beach for vacations and the people at the ocean go to the mountains? I suppose everyone wants a change of scenery, though."

"When do you plan to get to New York?" he asked.

"Well, no real date in mind but, hopefully, before bad weather."

Then he added, "You have kinfolks there?"

"No, it's just a goal."

He held the door to my room open for me.

"Well, I hope you make it okay. Good luck."

During my pre-walk planning when I thought about clothes I figured taking three shirts and three pairs of pants would be about right.

I'd be wearing one all the time, and would have two backup sets. It seemed adequate and logical to me when I studied the limitations of space and weight. Now, too, I selected three shirts and three pants from my new choices. A light flickered in my head. Weren't these clothes too wintry for Charleston in August? But the excitement made me put a bushel over the light.

I thought it crude and thankless to leave my old clothes anywhere around the motel property, so though six sets of clothes were a strain and burden as I traipsed away the next morning I knew I'd jettison the old stuff at the first unwatched dumpster.

Chapter 74
I Still Look Pitiful
and the Shirt Off His Back

There's an old English saying (or maybe it's Welsh or Irish or Norse or any of a number of seafaring nations) that mentions something about "men going down to the sea in ships."

I was never too clear about its true wording or meaning and for the first few times I heard it as a boy, was confused as to how a man could go down to the sea in a ship.

Since time began men have been lured by the sea. And even though walking is my first love, I too, have a place in my heart for the call of the sea.

When I reached Charleston I couldn't see or touch the sea, so I couldn't achieve my major goal of "left foot in the Atlantic" here, but it was close enough to smell. And there's nothing like the smell of a sea breeze.

Route 17 follows the ocean's shore through much of South Carolina so I knew it was the logical choice for me. Just north of Charleston there's a large forest called Francis Marion National Forest. I haven't the foggiest notion who Francis Marion is, or was, or the horse's name he rode in on. And I could see on the map that my chosen Route17 ran straight as an arrow through Francis, starting from his toenails, through his gizzard and right on through his bald spot.

What concerned me was that Francis looked big, really big, a jolly green giant on the South Carolina landscape. National Forests have been a burr under my saddle in the past. Remember "National" precludes anything commercial that might mean food or drink. "National" scares me in any context other than when it precedes "Anthem." When Americans label anything "National" it means it's ours, but not necessarily *yours.*

To me "National" meant "desert" as far as my needs were concerned. There may be a house or two but, as for an oasis of convenience stores or gas stations, I'd be out of luck. It was the Arizona desert revisited, only in green versus brown.

When I looked at the map, Frances Marion looked to be roughly 40-plus miles across and I couldn't count on any sustenance until I got to the other side. I'd have to do what worked for me in the desert. Just before entering the National Forest I'd have to drink all I could possibly hold, fill my water jugs, drink sparingly the first day, drink all I was carrying that night, then hope I found water before I had to bed down the second night.

It was risky but still better than any other plan I could come up with. And it had never failed me.

Luck, of sorts, was with me on Route 17 through the Francis Marion National Forest. There's a house or two and an antique store and collectively they call themselves "Awendaw." (Don't ask.) "Wide spot in the road" is an appropriate translation. "Town or "village" would be much too strong.

As luck would have it, the antique store sold soft drinks and chips. Not having food and drink is the downside to a National Forest, but the upside is there are few cars and few people and it gives you the opportunity to commune with nature.

Francis had led with his chin in his fight with Hugo. Evidence was everywhere that Hurricane Hugo had ravaged the Francis Marion National Forest just a couple of years before I came through.

Charleston had been hit too, but National Forests don't have the advantage of government-guaranteed, low-interest loans with which to rebuild. Getting back to normal takes a little longer for Mother Nature. Rebuild she does, though, and probably better than man, given the time.

One thing was odd about the damage Hugo did to Marion. About 20 percent of the mature pine trees had been broken off. Not strange in itself, but it was the manner in which they were broken. There was a systematic uniformity that I thought would be inconsistent with a hurricane. The trees were all broken off at about the same height — approximately fifteen feet in the air.

I was puzzled as to why all the trees were decapitated at what seemed to be the precise same distance from the ground. I had plenty of time for mulling so I tried to reason it out. As usual my theorems came back shot full of holes.

My best idea was that if you took any number of standing wooden items whose bases were fixed and immobile and applied pressure to the tops, they'd all break at approximately the same height. Then, more reasoning brought out the old shotgun to shoot holes in my theory.

That reasoning might be sound if the hurricane was only applying pressure to the tops of the trees. I felt sure that the force of the hurricane was felt equally from the base to the top of the tree. That being the case, wouldn't the trees snap at the base?

Why, during Physics class, had I spent most of my time gazing out the window and thinking about that blond cheerleader?

Georgetown, South Carolina was my first sight of real, human habitation after Francis Marion, and the neon "Open" sign on Quincy's All You Can Eat Buffet was enough to curl my six remaining toenails.

It was Sunday and the after-church crowd had beaten me by just a few minutes. I felt slightly ashamed at my appearance. Francis Marion hadn't noticed, but I felt sure Georgetown's scrubbed and starched parishioners couldn't miss my chin stubble, my emaciated body, sweat-streaked shirt, crumpled, dusty, crease-free pants and not-quite-Irish-Spring smell.

One of the wonderful things about religion is that at least some of its followers actually practice what it preaches.

What am I trying to say? Well, there are a few people who attend church for reasons other than to show off their new bonnet. And on Thursday they are still filled with, and try to live, the same spirit they had when they left church on Sunday.

Little did I know that one of God's disciples was about to appear to me in Georgetown's Quincy's.

Just inside the door was an area for hanging coats. I was glad to see it because it gave me an opportunity to slip partially out of sight and make some adjustments, and hopefully, improvements to my appearance.

As I stuffed my shirttail into my pants, swished my hands across my wrinkled pants, and smacked at my dusty shoes I was unaware that someone had come up behind me.

When I straightened up I realized a man in a suit was standing looking at me.

My first thought was, "Oh no, there won't be any all you can eat buffet for bums or coast-to-coast walkers this Sunday afternoon."

Instead the man said, "Would you be offended if I bought your meal?"

Outside my body I heard, "No Sir, not at all." Inside I sang, "Glory, Glory, Hallelujah!"

A full 90 percent of the thrill created by the suited man was due to the restoring of my faith in man's humanity to man. The other ten percent was the prospect of a free meal. Vastly more important was the gesture of kindness on the man's part.

In retrospect I wondered why he thought I had no money when I was already inside. Maybe he just wanted me to save what little money I had.

Between mouthsful and platesful I went over to his table, where he sat with his wife and another couple and asked for his address so I could write him an official thank you note. That's what I told him, but what I really wanted to do was write later and tell him what I was doing, and that his was an act of true kindness and selflessness, the kind that made my walk really enjoyable and restored my faith in the overall goodness out there.

After too many desserts and sweetened iced teas to count, I was again north bound on Route 17 on a very hot, deep south Sunday afternoon.

About five o'clock that afternoon, I had passed the last house on the outskirts of Georgetown and was again alone with the pines, egrets, and palmetto of rural coastal South Carolina.

A car passed and slowed to a stop about 50 yards down the road. As I came alongside, a man and woman, both in their mid-40s, got out and beckoned me over. The man stuck out his hand. "We won't keep you but a minute. My wife and I have a dollar bet you can settle. We saw you on the other side of Georgetown earlier today. My wife said the Georgetown Lion's Club was sponsoring a walk to raise money for the Diabetes Foundation. It was a relay from Charleston to Wilmington. She said you were a part of that and I said not. Are you?"

I eased the pack to the ground. I sensed this would require more than a simple yes-or-no answer, and standing with that silly pack pulling downward was worse than when moving.

"No, I'm not part of that walk," I said.

A beer was offered and I declined as I recited the Los Angeles-New York tale.

There were the usual assorted oohs and aahs from the couple that, as always, salved my ego. By this time I *had* done something worthy of an ooh and aah. I had reason to be proud, and I was.

Then it was my turn.

"Everyone has a story. What's yours?"

"Well, I'm afraid it isn't as exciting as yours, but it's not exactly ho-hum either. We live aboard a sailboat and I write poetry for a living."

"Sounds good to me," I said.

"It's a little scary sometimes. We discussed it pretty thoroughly before we finally decided to give up two good, steady paychecks and run with this new lifestyle. We love it now, and we'd have to be desperate to go back to the dog-eat-dog..

After a few minutes more the man's eyes came to rest on my wintry looking, long sleeved shirt I'd gotten from the motel owner back on the far side of Charleston.

"Isn't that shirt hot?" Poetry Writing Sailor asked.

"Yes," said Walker Me with a what-else-can-a-poor-man-do shrug of my shoulders.

"Well," said Writer, "I'd be proud if my shirt was a part of the remainder of your walk to New York," as he pulls the pale blue Banana Republic, short -sleeved shirt over his head and hands it to me.

Of course, I was taken aback and gratified. Twice in the same day an unusual act of humanity and kindness. And I'd never come close to owning a shirt the quality of a Banana Republic shirt.

I figured if he could pull his shirt off right there on the side of the road I could do the same. It felt so good to exchange his cool short-sleeved cotton shirt for my hot long-sleeved polyester one.

He left bare-backed and bare-chested.

It became my main shirt from then until Manhattan. It was a quality shirt; strong, well-made, good looking, and most importantly, cool.

I continued to use the shirt long after my walk. Once it was lost in my utility room, and when found was covered with mildew spots. I decided they could be disguised with an old friend — purple Rit dye. Though the finished color was closer to lavender, and a strange, dotted pattern shown through, I wore that fine shirt for work around the house. Then for work under the car. Then, with shoulders that had become strings through wear and sun, my friend was sent to rag-bag heaven.

Chapter 75
Left Foot in the Atlantic

I had lived in Gatlinburg, Tennessee since 1979, and my wife and I had learned from locals and Rand McNally that if we had a yearning to walk along the beach, Myrtle Beach was the nearest spot to us; not necessarily the most idyllic or romantic, just nearest. And somewhere sprinkled in one of our conversations with friends we learned that Myrtle Beach, or more correctly a community ten miles south called Murrell's Inlet, was one of the best places in the world to obtain fresh seafood. Our bags were as good as packed.

In our early married days we'd even planned an entire vacation to New Orleans, strictly to experience as many four and five-star restaurants as we could in two weeks. I know gluttony is a sin, but it sure can be fun in New Orleans.

Nancy and I made several trips to Myrtle Beach for the sea and its food.

It was with some familiarity, more familiarity than anything up to this point, that I approached the outskirts of town.

I knew it was a lot of glitter and splashes of color. Anything to catch the eye of a child and make him tug on the pant leg of his father or mother, begging to go to the miniature golf course, the water slide, or the tilt-a-whirl.

Like any place where they tore down paradise and put up a parking lot, Mrytle Beach uses any hook it can to extract your money from your wallet. The business district is a five-mile strip of gaudiness, kept in check only by the ocean on one side and palmetto scrub on the other.

I was glad to see Myrtle Beach. It represented a happy past and a happy present. It was to be my designated spot for "left foot in the Atlantic."

I'd come all this way from Los Angeles and that "right foot in the Pacific," and I'd covered every inch by foot. I felt really proud. I had every right to be. I realized most anyone could do what I'd done if they really wanted to (anyone, that is, who can put one foot in front of the other and string a few million together.) It was more mental than physical. If you could stand the hassles, anyone could do it. It wasn't Everest nor paddling across the Pacific.

I was on a natural high as I walked up the street in Myrtle Beach. Just a few hundred feet to my right was a big goal. I could crawl on my stomach and attain it from here. If so inclined, I could quit now and not be ashamed. I'd still be in a very elite society. Since the Pilgrims jumped off the boat at Plymouth Rock how many people had walked from shore to shore? A few hundred? A few thousand? Not many, when you think about 260,000,000-plus living today and all the millions who have gone before.

Yes, through sweat and some blood and near tears, I had enrolled myself in a national honor society. Though I was proud, I couldn't be too smug. I'd done something worthy of pride, but I had to pull in my horns in homage to the people who had gone across on crutches, wheelchairs, roller skates and who knows what else. I'd even heard of a preacher who did it on his hands and knees. I'm not sure if he went coast to coast but I remember the distance was amazing.

I flashed back to a Mom and Pop grocery in Alabama where I'd stopped for Gatorade, chocolate milk, and M & Ms. The lady owner, after seeing my pack and asking my story, had asked if I'd seen the man with the cross. I don't think she expected me to know what she was talking about, but I did.

For years I'd known there was a guy who had walked through almost every country in the world, carrying a full-size replica of the cross Jesus carried. He'd even written a book which I'd read before my walk.

A few years earlier he had stopped with his cross at her store. She didn't say, but I detected a note of irony in her voice. First a man with a cross and now one with a silly safari hat.

It was with light feet and heart that I traversed Myrtle Beach this August morning. Webster says "August" means, "Inspiring awe or admiration; majestic." Yes, this *was* an August morning. I hadn't been so proud since I crossed into Louisiana from Texas and knew I'd won the West.

Just about every seaside town has signs with arrows along Main Street that say "To the Beach." I could have gone over to the ocean long before I did but I wanted it to be at the right place. Huntington Beach on the Pacific had been a populated play area. The roller-bladers, volleyballers, and strolling lovers created a neat atmosphere in which to launch my colossal endeavor.

I wanted something similar on the Atlantic side. I didn't want to walk down to put my left foot in the Atlantic and have such a momentous event witnessed only by sea gulls and sand crabs.

So, I wanted to wait until I was in the heart of Myrtle Beach and I saw one of those "To the Beach" signs. I felt a rush as I saw one up ahead and said to myself, "This is the one; this is the right place to do it."

I turned right and, after a few hundred feet, the street ended and sandy beach began. I looked up and there she was in her morning curls and waves — my goal, the beautiful Miss Atlantic. Not only was "left foot in the Atlantic" going to be a triumphant celebration, it was going to be a cooling treat for at least 50 percent of my lower extremities.

Maybe it was the early morning hour, or school had taken up, or it was simply the difference between the coasts, but the roller-bladers, volley-ballers, and lovers had been replaced by one lone lady, reading a book in a low-slung, legless beach chair.

You would think that the Hunchback of Notre Dame gait I had to use having one shoe on, one shoe off would have caused the book lady to, at least, glance up to see what kind of lumbering beast was returning to its briny beginnings. But no, she kept her nose glued to those pages.

"Left foot in the Atlantic" was nearly a mirror image of "right foot in the Pacific." This was merely a symbolic gesture. As I swished my left foot around and squished the sand between my toes, I looked out at the endless horizon, broken only by a distant shrimp boat.

Strange, in a way, why the ocean holds such allure when and all there is to see is water meeting sky. Maybe it's the mystery of what lies beyond that mystical, unattainable line. I stood there savoring the moment awash in the sense of accomplishment.

There had been a lot of doubt in the preceding years and months as to whether I had it in me to actually connect and complete right foot in the Pacific-left foot in the Atlantic. It was a nice feeling, standing there letting the cool waves wash over and around my left foot.

I knew, though, that this was only a way station on the path to my intended destination, that being the Empire State Building.

I backed up a few feet, sat down on dry sand. I did my best to keep sand out of my sock as I dried my foot with a bandanna and put my shoe and sock back on. Three thousand miles of blisters had made me very aware of the fact that you can't be too careful when you're dealing with sand, shoes, and feet. Carelessness can be very painful.

A shod biped once more, I did my slinging-the-pack-to-the-back-dance and headed back for the concrete sidewalk of Myrtle Beach.

As far as I knew the book lady had never looked up. So as I walked back toward her, I just couldn't let her slip past this momentous occasion with her nose glued to some pulp fiction. I stopped in front of her and announced, "You just witnessed history!"

Nose still maintains contact. I stood there frozen — she sat frozen.

It only took a few seconds to realize she had no intention of acknowledging my presence. And in a flash of brilliant cognizance I realized that if I didn't move away from her quickly, she was going to start to scream. I could have some heavy-duty explaining to do to the police. Though my pack may add some credence to my feeble story, my appearance would probably negate any credibility my story might have.

I quickly made a discretionary, circling retreat, as if she had turned into a rattlesnake.

Continuing north through the streets of Myrtle Beach, I pondered the woman's actions, or rather her body language. There really were no actions.

It caused me to think back to a small grocery in Alabama where my concepts of how things should have been were completely convoluted. It had me feeling pretty much as the lady on the beach had made me feel.

It was a day like any other in the South on a hot summer afternoon. I stopped at a tiny, old grocery, owned and run by a young black girl.

After I purchased my usual drinks and sweets I noticed an overturned nail keg toward the rear of the store and decided to sit on it and savor. I could see her behind the counter but I'm not sure she realized it.

A few minutes later a black man came in whom I gathered she knew. After he'd made his purchase and he was about to leave, she gave a signal with her eyes and a slight turn of her head, indicating she wanted him to stay until I left. I was floored. I couldn't comprehend that anyone would be frightened by *me*. Me, who grasps small critters and escorts them out of the house in a Kleenex to keep from killing them. Me, who had only admiration for what the young girl was accomplishing with her business.

We're puzzled when others don't see us as we see ourselves.

Chapter 76
The King Size Waterbed

If you write to the Myrtle Beach Chamber of Commerce asking about vacation opportunities you're sure to receive tons of pamphlets extolling the sea, sun and fun. And I'm sure one of those pamphlets is going to point out that Myrtle Beach has more golf courses per square whatever than any place on earth. True or not, one of them was my refuge the only night I spent in Myrtle Beach.

Myrtle Beach is so long it's almost impossible to walk from one end to the other in one day. Well, the business part of the town can be covered in one day but you're still really in town and we've already discussed "town" and the nemesis it is for someone sleeping out.

Golf courses are seldom ringed completely by houses and I was counting on that. Trees and bushes usually fill the spaces between houses, and I thought I could find a spot among the bushes to conceal myself for the night.

I finally spotted a golf course just off the main street. Good thing too, because it was getting very late.

One thing I hadn't counted on was the fanaticism of golfers. I should have known. Barring snow, sleet, atomic blast or anything below eight-point-five on the Richter Scale, there'll be golfers out on the course until they can't possibly see what they're doing.

I had counted on the gloom of night to make the golfers pack it in so I could make camp, but that was naive. If the US Postal Service wasn't deterred by the gloom of night why did I think golfers would be. I was just a few feet from one of the greens and woefully, inadequately hidden in a clump of bushes. Golfers came and went, chattering about strokes and clubs, slices and hooks.

I praised the twilight because I could have easily been detected if any of them had looked in my direction and squinted.

When any golfer came onto the green next to me I'd freeze like a lawn jockey.

Finally, after the sky was the color of pitch, the last crazy golfer gave up and I was left to the solitude of my bush hideout.

Most all my energies, both mental and physical, for the past couple of months had been directed toward swishing my left foot in the Atlantic. Now that I'd accomplished that and I was out in the country again, I had time to sit down and think about my route through North Carolina, Virginia, and on to Manhattan. I didn't care for what I saw. One area on the map had several dotted parallel lines piled one on top the other, and scattered among the lines were things that looked like tufts of grass. I knew that meant one thing–swamp! I could have trouble finding a high and dry place for my tent that was free from armies of mosquitoes. But it seemed the price I'd have to pay for choosing a route along the coast.

Green Swamp, Holly Shelter Swamp, Wolf Swamp all crowded next to the road on my northern route.

It felt strange to be thinking "North" now, when since April 8th all my thinking had been West to East. I had no choice but to take it one day at a time and trust in providence.

Near Holly Ridge, North Carolina I heard a local in a country grocery store say, "I can't remember when we've ever had this much rain."

It did seem like days since I'd seen the sun. It was my first experience on the walk with anything more than afternoon thunderstorms. My 50-cent yard sale army poncho was totally inadequate. An April shower was a strain on its defenses so given any sustained rain and it was ready to retreat or surrender.

On one particularly waterlogged day the approach of darkness found me near Holly Shelter Swamp. If I'd been in a better mood about the whole experience I'd have asked how it got the name Holly Shelter, but all I was really interested in was getting through and out of Pogo's turf.

I knew it would be no easy task finding a high and dry spot. Finally, I saw a spot that I thought would do. It caught my eye because it had a quality rarely found when you're looking for a place to put down.

I remembered from my boy scout days that the manual had said a more comfortable night's sleep could be obtained if, before lying down, you scooped out two shallow depressions — one for your hips, one for your shoulders. It made sense. But never had I seen one occurring naturally. Seems Mother Nature isn't too interested in whether man sleeps comfortably on the ground or not.

There it was, though, a spot of ground with two slight depressions that looked as if they'd match up with my hips and shoulders.

The last time I'd used the technique was way back in the sands of the desert Southwest. Scoops, or shallow depressions, require tools in most places, which I didn't have, but in sandy soil your hand works fine. And if it's strictly sand you can just lie down and squiggle your shoulders and hips and you'll naturally just settle down into the contour of your body.

Visions of a good night's rest danced before me as I positioned my tent just so over the two depressions.

Everything was great until another of the nearly constant rain showers started.

I wouldn't go so far as to say those first pings of raindrops on tent-top strike terror in the heart of the camper, but I'll bet any camper would admit they strike dread in their hearts.

I learned early in my walk that lightning didn't necessarily mean rain but if I heard thunder I could count on rain. Let's not try to interject logic at this point about one being impossible without the other. I *think* the reason I found this to be true was that it was possible for lightning to be far away and still be visible, if I heard thunder the storm must be close enough for it to affect me. Rarely was I wrong.

There's that first ping on the roof, then a few seconds, then three or four pings in a row, then another interval. And invariably during this interval you gain hope that the pings are over because this interval is usually longer than the time between the first ping and the second session of three or four drops.

But almost always your hopes get dashed if all you have between you and the awesome power of Mother Nature is one thin sheet of nylon.

In a tent, no matter if its the Cadillac of tents, if that ping, ping, ping, evolves into something like an AK-47, you're in deep do-do.

That was to be my experience this night in North Carolina. The rain seemed to go on forever. I didn't think nights could be this long. For the first few hours I was awake every few minutes. I'd feel around the outside of my sleeping bag, first at my shoulders then at my feet, to see if my brave little "I think I can, I think I can" tent still had its finger in the dike.

Things seemed to be going okay and because I had been lulled into a false sense of security by several dry tests of my immediate surroundings and worn down by a day of walking in the rain, I fell into a deep sleep. At what must surely have been near daylight I was in that state of half-in, half-out of consciousness. I felt like I was floating on air, or was it water? Whatever, it felt so good.

I had never owned a waterbed but in my state of stupor I thought, "This really feels good. So this is what it's like to have a waterbed. But then something else deeper in my brain clicked, another cog took hold. I sprang upright as much as my tent would permit. "Oh, my Lord, I'm floating in water!"

My little tent had lost a valiant fight — sleeping bag, clothes, everything was floating in water. What depression.

Luckily, it wasn't cold. I had no choice but to lie there and wait for daylight.

Picture the soggy mess I presented as I slogged back into town in search of a laundromat. I remembered a crossroads a mile or two back and figured that would be the best place to start my search for a laundromat.

Throughout this walk I'd had trials, even life-threatening situations, but somehow something always came along to rescue me.

I've always thought life held one of two destinies for me. Either I was being saved for a grand purpose, or saved for a very juicy end, as payment for my sins.

Hypothermia wasn't to be my juicy end. The clerk at a convenience store directed me to a laundromat. I could warm up and dry out.

Chapter 77
Through Persistence
My Life Is Saved

Blisters seemed to haunt me throughout my walk. For no rhyme nor reason they would come and go at will. Periods when they decided to be gone were the really joyous parts of the trip. But then they always came back with a vengeance.

I had started out in nylon socks because they were what I always wore and I never had any problems with blisters at home. Very quickly something told me it wasn't the same as walking daylight to dark.

Heat and friction are the spark and tinder necessary to build a big blister fire. Create a situation where both are present and you're in a whole heap of trouble. And if heat and friction become teammates, the game is over. You'll hobble to the sidelines. After my first blister attack in California I could think of nothing else but ways to find relief. I ran the entire gamut of blister remedies — powder, moleskin, adhesive foam, Band-Aids, lambs wool, prayer. I grasped at them as desperately as any drowning man grabbing a straw. If someone had said sour cream or the juice from a can of pork and beans would give relief from blisters, I'd have headed for the grocery.

Hobbling down the road in California I tried to think of anything at all that would give me relief. I thought maybe cotton socks were the answer. Cotton was natural, shouldn't it be more user friendly to my feet than something synthetic? I stopped at the next K-Mart and bought three pairs of cheap, grey cotton socks.

It was impossible to tell right away if they were the answer to my problem because my feet were already hamburger.

The condition of my feet continued to ebb and flow as I headed east. I suppose they were more often bearable than not as I couldn't have continued otherwise.

On more than one occasion I'd mentioned my pain to my buddy, Gus, when I called asking him to post me some sorely needed money.

Gus had done his share of outdoorsy stuff so I always gave some credence to any advice he gave concerning coping with Mother Nature on her terms. His advice was brief in the extreme. Wool!

I didn't want to hurt his feelings so I kept my initial reaction to myself. But my logical side was screaming, "Wool?" "Wool?" "Have you lost your mind? I'm walking through the desert, Gus, not snowshoeing in the Yukon. I want wool next to me like I want a mustard plaster on my backside."

All my life I'd hated wool, I mean *hated* wool! Thirty years earlier when I was in the Navy I was almost cornered by wool. We were issued white cotton summer uniforms and blue winter wool uniforms. I joined in June in San Diego so I didn't think much about wool and what was coming. Anyway, we'd never be wearing Blues, this was southern California, it doesn't rain or get cold. I was 22 and thought I could whip my weight in wildcats, what did I care if the uniform was a little scratchy.

I still remember the October day in 1962 when the order came down for the fleet to switch to winter Blues.

The next day when I got up and put those Blues on, it was all I could do to keep them on. They nearly drove me right up the bulkhead until I had my first day of liberty and was able to go ashore and find a seamstress who would line the inside of all of them with satin.

And Gus said, WOOL!!! I was out all day in the sun in hundred degree temperatures, sweat running down my backbone and into the crack of my behind, and Gus suggests hot, scratchy, drive-me-completely-nuts wool!

I don't know if it was the days of dampness or the complete soaking of everything that night in the tent but soon after that a crippling bout with blisters returned. Mid-North Carolina and they seemed to be the worst ever. At this juncture, this close to Manhattan, I didn't seriously think about quitting, but I questioned what I'd do if I didn't get relief. I'd tried every trick and remedy to no avail.

The obvious solution, the sane solution, could never enter my mind. It was too foreign to my makeup. Dumb as it sounds, I'd almost as quickly have given up and gone home as to try it. What was it? Take a few days off. That good reasoning was so lost on me. It was just too logical. I had only taken one day off the entire trip and that was way back in Lamesa, Texas and only because lightning cracked its hellish whip across every inch of Texas sky.

I couldn't stop now. This was North Carolina and I was so close. Something besides stopping or even taking a few days off had to present itself.

Enter Providence again. And in what a guise this time. It wore the cloak of money, or more correctly, the lack of it.

I was running out so I called Gus and asked if he could send me some to the post office in Greenville, which I guesstimated was about four days away. In the course of our talk I again mentioned the blister problem. And again, in his infinite wisdom, he spoke that single powerhouse of a word — WOOL! My defenses were in such shreds I didn't even groan when he said he'd send a pair of wool socks with the money.

In the days it took me to get to Greenville there was no joy in Mudville. I felt like this old Casey was about to strike out.

Gus' promise of wool held no more excitement for me than wool had ever held. I couldn't see how the socks were going to make any difference. Wool was damnable wool. In fact a shiver went up my back each time I thought about wool touching my hot, raw feet. It was comparable to rubbing salt in an open wound in my opinion.

I had forgotten about the wool socks by the time I reached Greenville. I was almost out of money and that was serious stuff. Wool socks wouldn't buy Gatorade, chocolate milk or Doritos so money was very much on my mind as I stepped up to the postal clerk in Greenville.

The promised wool socks only dawned on me when I saw my normally skinny money envelope had fat sides.

There were only two reasons I decided to give in to Gus and put on the socks. First, Gus had been a lifelong friend. I thought I owed him, at least, a trial run with the socks if he believed so strongly in their healing powers. Secondly, I was desperate as to how I was going to continue my walk with this hellish blister monkey on my back. I was resolute in my hatred of wool, yet almost at the point of tears as I sat on a town bench in Greenville. I cringed as I pulled on the socks over my tortured feet.

I put on my shoes and started North, saying to myself, "Gus I respect you but you only get six blocks or six traffic lights whichever comes first. And if these socks do what wool has always done to me, they're coming off as fast as I can find a place to do it.

As God is my witness, the transformation was as quick as the promise of a faith healer at a tent revival. I hadn't taken six steps before I saw the miracle of wool. Instantly the pain was relieved, not gone, of course, but definitely better.

I nearly shouted the praises of Gus and wool.

Chapter 78
The Blessed End of the Stinging, Biting Devils From Hell

Walking along one day in Coastal, Central North Carolina it dawned on me, "Hey, I haven't seen any damned fire ants lately."

Chapter 79
Thorns and Needles

Some of the best sleeping outdoors you can have is in the desert. Though it may be hell on wheels during the day, all the elements for a great night's sleep fall into place at night. That is, if you have adequate cover. The intense heat during the day can lull you into believing that you couldn't possibly need much over you in the desert at night. It isn't true. It can get downright cold at night. An adequate sleeping bag is a delightful plus. Your body has been broiled (or is it baked) all day and the coolness of the desert at night can feel delicious.

The coolness is only one of the factors that make sleeping in the desert so nice. In addition to coolness, there's zero humidity so you don't wake in the morning with clothes, shoes, and sleeping gear all damp. If you lie down in the sand and do a little squiggling, your body seeks its own level and you have a bed that's contoured to it.

There are no mosquitoes either, or any other flying, biting critters that I know of.

One of the best things about sleeping in the desert is experiencing the beauty of all the trillions of stars in the heavens. I've never understood why the lights of the cities block your view of the stars but I've read that is the case.

I'll bet if you took someone who'd spent their entire life in the inner city and let them spend a night in the desert they'd be flabbergasted at what they'd been missing. The stars are so much brighter, so much closer, and have about quadrupled in numbers. It's really something spectacular to see.

In addition to desert sleeping there's another delightful sleeping adventure. But instead of sand this one requires trees, namely pine trees. You've led a sheltered, guarded, dare I say deprived life, if you haven't slept on a bed of pine needles. I know, sleeping and needles? But take my word, it's the Beautyrest of Mother Nature's bedroom.

A few miles north of Greenville, I inadvertently stumbled upon a bed of pine needles one night. Just as surely as night fell, I had to go through that dreaded search for my daily bed and as luck would have it I spotted a Wal-Mart. And I'm probably one of two or three people in North and South America who would think of Wal-Mart as a place to sleep.

Here's the inside info on Wal-Mart if you need a place to sleep. I don't have to tell you Wal-Mart is big–big corporate-wise, big in their thinking, big in their doing, big in their building. And, as benefits those of us who search nightly for sleeping space, they buy big.

When they buy land for a store they don't just buy enough land for the building and parking lot, they buy acreage around the store. Maybe they do it so they can expand. Or maybe they want breathing space. Who knows. Who, including Wal-Mart, wouldn't buy elbowroom if money wasn't an object?

But all that surrounding land, especially the part behind the store, isn't being used. It's just lying fallow waiting to be cultivated by we sleeping spot farmers.

The Wal-Mart people in charge might have a local farmer come with his tractor and mower to keep their property looking respectable, but other than that the land is just there.

The store's security guard might in the beginning look out at the store's backyard, but it wouldn't be long before he realized the land wasn't doing anything, nor was anybody doing anything to it.

Enter the Knight of the Open Road.

Greenville's Wal-Mart is blessed and doesn't know it. Way back on the back of their property is a sparse pine woods. The ground is covered with a three-inch cushion of fallen pine needles.

If an apple is nature's toothbrush then surely a layer of pine needles is nature's comfy bed. Cover them with something to keep the prickly part of the needles from reaching you, have an adequate cover for warmth, and you will sleep like a babe snuggled next to Mother Nature's bosom. Add a breeze that wafts over you like cool velvet, and bliss awaits you.

But wait. It gets better. If that same breeze is strong enough to make the treetops sway you are in for another treat. The swaying branches make the stars in the background appear to twinkle.

People have long pondered why the beautiful and delicate rose lies so close to the ugly and prickly thorn. My late wife, who was a more astute scholar of the Bible than I, explained that God once gave us a choice and we blew it. Everything could have been beautiful on Earth.

It isn't too much of a stretch to see why the rose has thorns on its stems, though. The rose is delicate and needs protection. But why does the blackberry bush need thorns? Blackberries can take care of themselves — ever get a seed stuck in your teeth?

Personally, there's never been much love lost between me and blackberries. And I'll bet if you polled people whose experience extends beyond a manicured golf course or a Wal-Mart or McDonald's parking lot, you'd find an almost universal dislike for blackberry thickets. They grab at you, entangle your legs, scratch you, tear your pants and are a haven for snakes. That one I haven't figured out yet. Snakes don't eat blackberries, do they?

One late, late afternoon in northern North Carolina I spotted an oasis of green. It was an inviting island but it was surrounded and protected by a sea of tangled piranha — blackberry bushes.

I was so tired. It looked so inviting. A great green, soft bed of grass upon which to lay my tired body for the night.

How to reach the island, though? It was guarded by alert and well-armed sentries.

I stood at the roadside and assessed my arsenal. I wanted badly to reach the island but did I have the strength, courage and weapons to tackle the giant? I looked down at my walking stick.

Courage was the key. I thought of the old Chinese proverb, "A brave man dies but once, a coward a thousand times."

I stepped off the road toward the promised land. Almost immediately the ensnarling blackberry vines sprang, armed with a thousand knives. I flailed out with my walking stick as confident as David meeting the giant. I was making headway against what must have given birth to that old maxim, "The proverbial clinging vine," when I came to a water filled ditch. I was stopped dead. Across the ditch stood a solid wall of more blackberry vines, formidable but I hoped not too deep. I stood there in my narrow vine canyon. Was it forward or back? "Back" meant a renewed search for a place to spend the night, and the perfect spot was just on the other side of the briar wall.

But "forward" meant a quick stumbling, charging, swinging, balancing act. I saw what had to be done. My choice, if "forward", was to try and jump the water-filled ditch and land swinging, clearing enough vines with a few quick swings to remain standing on the far bank.

It sounds so dumb and improbable, sitting here in my Lay-Z-Boy, but at that time it looked do-able. In fact, it may have been, if not for a 35-pound pack on my back. Why not throw the pack across first? There was no place for the pack to land. And I didn't want to take a chance on the pack falling back into the watery ditch.

I backed up and screwed up my courage, then I launched. I felt both feet land on the other side and was prepared to start swinging my walking stick like a madman.

Only when my feet landed on the far bank did I realize I was tethered to the bank I had just jumped from. A long tendril of blackberry vine had latched onto the back of my pack. In effect, the vine created a bungee cord that pulled me back toward the launching pad. It didn't spring me back, though, only arrested my motion in mid-leap. There was no doubt what was coming next−a wet dunk in the ditch. What a mess!

I clawed my way up the bank I had intended to jump to, and proceeded to beat the vines back out of my way. The soaking from the ditch and the burning of my face and arms from the clutching thorns made me lose all patience with the blackberry vines. I attacked, with a vengeance, the remaining ones standing between me and my original green goal.

It was Utopia lost. I couldn't enjoy the spot even after I reached it. It was a night spent in semi-damp clothes with a smarting face and arms.

Chapter 80
The Yard Sale Breakfast

Even though Virginia joined the South during the Civil War and the Capitol of the Confederacy was Richmond, I've never thought of Virginia as a southern state — mid-Atlantic coastal was my mental picture.

As I neared the North Carolina/Virginia state line I did so with a little sadness. My heart had always been in Dixie and to my thinking leaving North Carolina meant leaving the last of the Old South. The pace would quicken (not mine, everyone else's), and I expected sympathy and appreciation for the cross-country walker to take a decided nosedive. I figured dodging speeding, chronically-pressed-for-time commuters would be my main concern.

One Saturday when I approached two men having a yard sale near the North Carolina/Virginia state line it wasn't bargains I was after. A local could tell me exactly how far it was to the Virginia line.

I've heard it said that in Japan it's in poor taste to come directly to the point if you want to ask a question. Japan is a country steeped in centuries of custom and strict adherence to the proper way to conduct oneself. Out of courtesy I looked over the fella's wares before I sprang my question on them.

"How ya doin', fellas? I know the question you hear most is 'Will you take less?' But I've got a different one for you. How far to the Virginia line?"

They looked at each other, then the one closest to me said, "You aren't planning to walk there, are you? It's twelve miles!"

"I think I can make it."

"Where have you walked from?"

"Los Angeles," I said

"Good gracious! I guess you can make it then. Yeah, it's about twelve miles on up the road."

"Los Angeles! When in the world did you leave?"

"April the eighth."

"Hey, you done pretty good."

They seemed to be mulling all this.

Since this was early morning, there wasn't any reason my head couldn't be resting on Virginia soil that night. I strolled among their wares. I knew it was unlikely I'd buy anything but I welcomed the break.

Although I swear I didn't prod or steer the conversation in that direction, for some reason, it gravitated toward food and whether I'd eaten.

One of the kind men said, "Me either. If you'd like I'll fix us some breakfast."

If I liked?

I noticed a decided limp from the yard sale man as we took the short walk back to his house.

I, being from the old school, thought it strange that he lit in on the skillet when his wife didn't seem to be doing much else.

He must have had some short-order experience, because in no time we had a spread of which anyone could be proud.

"You seem to know your way around the kitchen," I said as a compliment.

"Yeah, I was a cook in Nam, 'til one day we were overrun and I took a hit in my left leg. It was my ticket home. It was several years before people were brave enough to tease me about being a cook and still getting shot. One of the best ones was a guy I've known all my life. Said it was probably "friendly fire."

Breakfast was a rare treat for me. I mean a conventional breakfast. My usual breakfast was leftover Doritos, washed down with a few gulps of anything that I hadn't polished off during the night.

Eggs, sausage, toast, juice and hot chocolate were a banquet. All given freely and prepared by this kind man just twelve miles short of Virginia.

Chapter 81
I Almost Cry

I knew I was going to be walking through country steeped in history throughout the rest of my walk. And judging by the names on the map it was going to have a decidedly English flavor — Suffolk, Gloucester, Essex, Yorktown. I felt strangely like I was walking through a countryside in England; the town names, the looks of the houses and stores, and the narrow streets. The Old South seemed a million miles away.

Virginia, Maryland, Delaware, and New Jersey might be some of the flattest, greenest, most scenic walking I'd encounter the whole trip.

Another nice thing about traveling through countryside with such a long and checkered past is that roadside historical markers abound.

I noticed something about the markers that seemed very shortsighted. I figure they're really put alongside the road for the motoring public. So, why do so many have no pull-off next to them? If the purpose is to get people to read them, they're defeating their purpose if they don't provide pull-offs. Time is too precious for today's American to find a parking space and walk back to read the sign.

On the outskirts of Suffolk I noticed an historical marker ahead. Since I enjoyed reading them and no parking area was required for me, I stopped to see what it said.

The oldest church in the U.S. was just behind the sign. It was built in 1632.

My main function on this walk was to be getting on with the business of getting on. I wasn't happy unless I was pressing on toward Manhattan. But how could I justify, at some future date years from now, passing by something so historically significant? How could anyone not think it was worth a look? It's one of those things you must take time for even if you think you don't have time.

It seems silly to say the church looked well built. It hadn't been standing over 300 years because of any shoddy workmanship. The walls looked about two feet thick. I got the impression that the church had been kept up. It didn't look 300.

Looking at my map, I saw I was about to cross my first substantial body of water. With the exception of the Mississippi River, nothing more than step- across creeks, small lakes, and small rivers had crossed my path. For the first time the pale blue that represents water on Rand McNally appeared as more than a thin ribbon. If the pale blue on the map could barely be covered by the width of my little finger I was facing some substantial water.

Portsmouth and Newport News, Virginia are separated by what is technically the James River but more literally is a deep backwash of Chesapeake Bay. Even though the map bridge was only a fraction of an inch long, I knew this was going to be a substantial bridge, too.

I looked forward to walking across the bridge. No matter how long it was it would be refreshing to look out at the blue water. I could look at any boats that might be in view. And seagulls and pelicans. Not to mention, I could spit off the bridge several times (It's a guy thing). Boys have to spit off bridges for the same reason boys have to shove each other when a cute girl comes around.

It never crossed my mind that there might be a hassle about my walking across the bridge. Just about every bridge had a place for walkers except bridges that were part of an Interstate Highway.

As I approached I noticed what looked like a small guard's shack. It crossed my mind that it was odd because this wasn't a toll bridge. I thought that maybe since this was such a long bridge the guard shack was there to assist motorists who might have trouble while crossing the bridge. As I came in front of the shack a young man in uniform came outside, sized me up and said "You can't walk across the bridge." There was no malice, no spite, no animosity, nor even a hint of I-can-Lord-it-over-you, dirtbag, tone in the man's voice. He was simply stating an irrefutable fact.

It fell on my ears with the same force as if I'd been sitting in the doctor's office and he said, "I'm sorry, our tests reveal you have...(Fill in something very scary)."

Let me tell you why the guard's simple statement had such a devastating effect on me:

I had told myself long ago when this walk idea was nothing more than a gleam in my eye that if I ever did tackle this crazy thing I wouldn't accept rides, I wouldn't take shortcuts, I wouldn't cheat, I'd walk every inch. And I know you're saying to yourself, "Hey, Stooge, just forget this bridge. Go on up-river and cross somewhere else!"

It wasn't that easy. I didn't see a bridge for hundreds of miles on the map. I dreaded going out of my way for even a city block, and there was no telling how far I'd have to walk to find the next bridge. Even if I did, how did I know it allowed pedestrians? And you'd have to be in fair proximity to a bridge before anyone would know if it was crossable on foot. Besides, if I went too far, Richmond and even Washington, D.C. and all the mess they entailed were looming.

I wanted to take my pack off, sit on the ground, hold my head between my hands and make the world go away.

Begging crossed my mind. My feelings at this time were so strong I wasn't above it. I saw a way out. The young man had no animosity in his voice. He had his nameless, faceless orders. He didn't have to believe in them, just follow them. I sensed a door slightly ajar. The crack wasn't big enough for my foot but maybe big enough to let reason slip through. I decided to spill my guts. I splashed my story all over him about what I was doing and how traumatic it would be after all these months and miles to have to give up my walk-every-inch vow. My syrup and slobber covered the front of his shirt. I stopped just short of groveling.

They say a wild beast attacks those prey who show the slightest sign of weakness. The guard seemed to waiver almost imperceptibly. The hair on my neck raised in anticipation and my claws extended in readiness.

I spoke (or was it sprang) "It means so much to me. Can't you say you didn't see me? That would be believable and if I'm stopped by the police I'll say I never saw you either."

Reluctantly he relented and I shot for the bridge at a speed which wild beasts would have respected. Even if grass could have grown on this bridge it couldn't have grown under my feet. I was elated and my feet proved it!

About a third of the way across the most dreaded and feared thing happened. The beast with his blue light overtook this hapless prey. The policeman stopped on the bridge; got out at his own peril among the speeding cars and his arm beckoned.

I tried my best to give a brief, animated synopsis of the feature-length script I'd given the guard shack guard not ten minutes ago.

Even at the best of times, tales can leave an officer unmoved. Add having made him dodge racing commuters and your cause is the proverbial snowball in hell.

He told me to get into the back seat. The wire screen between us was intimidating but as we crossed the bridge I related more of my story in the nicest, most docile tone that could possibly emit from the human male.

I got nowhere. I knew my walk-every-inch vow was ruined. I could only hope, through sincerity and sweetness to save myself from incarceration or a ticket.

He muttered a few words about understanding but still being unable to allow me to walk across the bridge. I guess somewhere deep inside he felt a kinship because he stopped on the far edge and let me out without so much as a lecture.

I was still devastated. I was in a blind rage. I walked north but saw nothing. All I could think about was now I couldn't say I walked every inch. It probably wouldn't mean much to anyone but me, still I was crushed.

I thought to myself, "Just think of all the millions and millions of inches between Suffolk, Virginia and Los Angeles, California. I personally, with my own feet and legs covered every single one of them." But the reason I was so distressed was I didn't want my resume to say "Los Angeles to Suffolk", I wanted it to say "Los Angeles to Manhattan." I hated the thought of something so grand and something I'd worked so hard for, to from this day forward, for as long as I live, have an asterisk at the end of it. I didn't want any "buts" or "excepts" to follow this accomplishment.

"There's David Stoess, he once walked all the way from Los Angeles to New York, except..."

I knew it would be a long time before I got over this. Maybe never.

It was done now. I had a choice. I could quit and go home or I could take a deep breath, cinch up my intestinal fortitude and continue toward New York. I headed north. I had too much invested.

I could only hope that in the overall picture, my having to ride across a bridge wouldn't be a big deal to people. Surely it was a sin easily forgiven. My intentions had been the best. Heaven knows I paid enough penance.

To this day it occasionally flits across my mind to go to Suffolk and skirt that bridge and any other bridge that stands in my way, even if it means going by way of Canada to reach New York, City.

Chapter 82
Eclair, Not Salad, at Waldorf

Walking through northern Virginia wasn't nearly so much fun as the deserts of Arizona and New Mexico. Knowing how I'd suffered way back there I couldn't believe I was thinking that way. Here there always was an abundance of food and drink. The land was flat and green and the weather was tolerable. What was the cause of my malaise? Why was I dissatisfied now, when I'd been satisfied with less before?

It seemed to come down to one thing — people. It was the quantity. There were just too many. And too many in one spot breaks down most of the good characteristics that make people enjoyable and interesting. There is simply not enough time and there's too much scurrying. Interest in what others are doing, and time for smelling those roses has to take a back seat.

In Psych I in college I read about an interesting rat experiment some behavioral psychologist had conducted. As I got further and further north and the cars and people began to multiply by quantum leaps. The answers to my queries grew shorter and snappier, and the experiment came floating back to me.

Seems the doctor wanted to see what relationship, if any, population numbers had on the behavior of rats, and by extension what conclusions could be drawn regarding humans.

He took a large cage and put in a few rats. Things were fine. The rats seldom fought over food and had few other problems with relationships; their interactions were what one would expect from a few rats living together.

But then over a period of time the doctor continually added more rats and he noticed that there came a point where the peaceful co-existence among the rats began to break down. Fighting became commonplace. There didn't seem to be much peaceful interaction. Discord was rampant.

I began to see the Northeast as one big cage.

Probably, in the rat cage there were rats that were an exception — didn't bicker, they weren't petty, and they didn't fight.

And so it was with the Virginia, Maryland, Delaware, New Jersey and New York cage — exceptions existed.

One example was a nice lady I queried about the road ahead while at one of my eternal chocolate milk oases.

"If you walk through Waldorf on 301," the lady said, "there's a bakery on the left hand side. I can't remember it's name but it's been there probably a hundred years. They're famous for their chocolate eclairs. They will give you one if you say you're a first time visitor."

I was slightly abashed at my cynicism about the North after her statement. She had shown me a kindness and directed me to someone else who was kind.

On my way to the bakery I couldn't entirely suppress my cynicism, though. I thought the eclairs were probably reserved for visitors in Eddie Bauer shirts and Air Jordan shoes. Not for me in my run-down-at-the-heels, $39.95 walking boots and my not-quite-fresh-from-the-laundromat pants.

And there was another big obstacle yet to be surmounted before I could suck the filling out of that eclair. It was a word synonymous with depression−bridge.

I had to cross the Potomac River before I could reach Waldorf, Maryland. Like the James River back at Newport News, the Potomac, at the point I had to cross, was more bay than river. The bridge was several miles long.

I saw it was listed as a toll bridge. I was sunk. I knew the chances of my being able to walk across this bridge were slim and none.

Closer to the bridge I asked about the likelihood of my being allowed to walk across. No one could really shed any light on that, but one man did start a cog turning. He said, "If you'll go to the guard they will sometimes call the police to take pedestrians across."

Sounded logical to me but when I queried the guard lady she looked at me as if she didn't care if I swam, flew or tightroped across. Her only concern was to see that I didn't walk across.

Overcrowded rats strike again.

I backed off a few hundred yards from the bridge entrance to contemplate my dilemma. It finally occurred to me that someone might pick me up if they were assured they wouldn't have to put up with me but for just a few minutes.

I searched the roadside for a piece of cardboard, took out my for-postcards-to-home-ball-point, blocked out the words "Just across the bridge," then filled in the letters. Three hours later I was beginning to think nothing would work, when a very brave, foolish, or better yet, what we all should be, adventurous young man stopped.

I shoulda known! If I'd had the time before I took off running to where he had stopped I'd have given my forehead a dope slap. A pickup truck!

I sometimes come down hard on people in pickup trucks and yet more often than not my savior has been riding in one. Is it the company car for angels?

As I threw my pack in the back and hopped in the front I heaped praise upon the guy.

"Hey, man, thanks so much for stopping. I've been in that spot about three hours. About 10,000 cars have passed me and you're the first who didn't treat me like I was part of the scenery."

"No problem. Part of the reason I stopped was your unique sign. I didn't know exactly what "Just across the bridge" meant. There isn't anything just across the bridge."

By now, you know the script. I got the feeling the pickup angel already knew the script, too. My Los Angeles to New York story didn't elicit any "Sweet Jesus! You've *walked* all the way from Los Angeles" outburst.

All he did was give a soft "hmm." No outbursts, no questions.

You've seen the movie *It's a Wonderful Life*. I thought maybe I could catch him before he had time to regroup and see if he stuttered at my next question. If he stuttered I knew his name was Clarence and there'd be a ship's bell ring somewhere before we crossed the bridge.

"What line of work are you in?" I asked quickly.

"Well, as they say in Hollywood, I'm between engagements, but when I'm working I pilot yachts for the rich and famous. In the fall, I bring their boats down to Florida from up north and in the spring I do the reverse.

It's a service few people are aware of. It's for people who like to putter around in their boats close to home, but for reasons of time or other hassles, don't want to take them on long trips. Obviously, these are wealthy people who have winter and summer homes."

"Sounds like an envious and interesting occupation," I said.

"Yeah, but there's more and more big shipping every year. So much of what the United States uses is brought in on those big container ships and they're huge, scary really. They can make even the biggest boat I pilot look like a cracker box. It keeps you constantly on your toes staying out of their way."

When we stopped at the first pull-off I thanked him.

It had been a ride of only a few minutes and I wanted it to last longer. A comfortable seat, conversation with someone who cared. It was hard to tear myself away.

The old bridge pain returned. Maybe a bridge here, a bridge there seems of little consequence in the big picture of five and a half months, and 3000-plus miles, but it caused me no end of grief.

My pain was soothed somewhat by my free chocolate eclair in Waldorf. And the sweet girl at the bakery seemed not to notice my Jordanless and Bauerless wardrobe.

Chapter 83
I Am Pleasantly Surprised and Apologize to Maryland and Delaware

You've seen the signs, "Next mile adopted by the Wives and Daughters of our Gallant Men who Fight for the Glorification, Sanctity and Honor of our Beloved Confederacy." Thank goodness, they aren't quite that wordy. But they might say, "The next highway mile adopted by the Tappahannock Lions Club" or "Troop 14 Montross Boy Scouts." No matter the wording, you see the signs all over the U.S. And take it from someone who's been there, none of it means diddly.

If these are supposedly miles along the highway that have been taken under someone's wing for clean-up and beautification above and beyond what they receive from normal highway department care, (or lack of it) then there's something I'm missing. Many, many miles of experience told me one mile of highway is pretty much like the next.

I don't know where the fault lies but no matter what the sign says the quantity of soft drink bottles, beer cans, empty cigarette packs, lost work gloves and previously owned Pampers was as abundant in a mile of Mississippi roadside as in a mile of Maryland roadside.

Many people in many places are being deceived if they think their mile is getting special attention. I once saw a picture of an old muffler lying on a highway that had a bright new yellow paint stripe running across it. And one day I heard Paul Harvey say that, if you were on a certain highway in Minnesota it wasn't a speed bump you just ran over, the highway department paved over a dead deer.

I don't mean to sound like I'm slamming the highway department of any state. I'm not informed enough for that. All I can say is our priorities have broken down somewhere. We as a nation should be ashamed for the conditions for our roadsides.

But you can't judge by whizzing down the Interstate at 65 miles per. Get out of your car on any road and take a walk. A hundred yards will do it. Report back to me.

When I first saw the "This Highway Adopted By" signs I thought that it meant a bunch of the people whose names appeared on the sign met every Saturday morning or once a month and marched down their mile with black garbage bags in hand. When I walked mile after mile, state after state and never saw that happening, I refigured.

Somewhere I'd heard that a person or organization could sponsor their mile with donations, so that their mile got special attention and care, but they didn't physically have to do the work. I never saw any indication of that, either.

There are states that do better jobs of taking care of roadside trash than others. And they rank in almost inverse order from what you'd think. From all you've heard of California with its way-ahead-of-the-rest-of-the-nation enlightened population you'd think they'd rank number one on the cleaning-along-the-highway index. That wasn't my finding. I have no idea if anyone has ever compiled a ranking after inspecting all 50 states, but I'll bet California is not in the top 25.

Before I started my walk, if asked to compile my best guess list, based strictly on my hunches, I'd have rated California cleanest and New York least clean. And with my preconceived prejudices factored in, every state in the Northeast would be huddled down there cheek and jowl with New York.

Maryland and Delaware weren't the demons I thought they'd be. I owe them apologies. Pretty farmland far exceeds smokestacks. They each can hold their heads high.

They'd be right up there with the cleanest half.

Chapter 84
The Pigeon on the Bridge

In all the months, even years, spent contemplating my walk, one troubling thing kept popping up. How would I discourage dogs from following me? I'm sure most would think how am I going to keep dogs from *biting* me?

I'd done enough pre-walking to know that I could use my walking stick much as a lion tamer uses a chair. If the dog was really determined to sample some hiker ham, I could take off my pack and use it as a barrier between ham and incisor as ham slowly backed away. Being bitten wasn't a worry. What concerned me wasn't mean dogs, but overly friendly dogs.

I see that puzzled look on your face.

Seeing an animal in pain has always had a profound effect on me. Well, later it did. At first I was a boy. For the good of all animals there should never be boys.

My father and mother should never have let me have those BB guns and rifles. They make killing an easy and impersonal act. I'm ashamed when I think back to all the rabbits, squirrels, birds, fish, frogs, snakes, fishing worms, ants, (good ants, not fire ants – if someone had every fire ant in the world in a giant bottle I'd supply the gasoline and strike the match to send them all to hell). And how many other assorted creatures of which I can't recall went to heaven because of me?

I can't pinpoint the moment when I switched from killer to compassionate protector. The pendulum swinging of the killing axe was halted far off to one side at some point, for some reason, and it never returned to center again. A lot of the pain animals have to endure is human related.

Have you ever seen that puzzled "what happened" look in the eyes of a dog that's been hit by a car? That look of innocent bewilderment is enough to break your heart. They don't understand where all the pain is coming from. They didn't do anything to cause it.

I didn't want to have to experience that look from any animal ever again. I knew that if any dog started following me along the highway his chances of getting hit by a car were going to soar. I love dogs and having one along would be great fun and company but I didn't want the responsibility. A dog would either have to be on a leash or running loose. Neither would work for me.

From the first I tried to ignore any dog who wanted to get friendly. If that didn't work I gave my gruffest "Go home." Plan C was to reach down as if to pick up a rock. (You'd be surprised at the percentage of dogs who know what that means). Plan D, as a last resort, I actually threw the rock. I figured hurt feelings or hurt flank from a rock were better than a crushed body under the wheel of a car.

If the dog or cat was hit by a car and not killed what could I do? Listen to its cries of pain as I walked away from it? A rock in the flank didn't seem so cruel after all.

Plastered to the roads are bodies of creeping, crawling, waddling, trotting animals that either weren't "run back" or found themselves on the road, simply because roads are unavoidable.

In Delaware I was crossing a long, high bridge—one on which pedestrians were allowed.

In the middle of the bridge, at its highest point, I noticed a pigeon sitting at the edge of the road. Of course, that wasn't normal and I knew something was definitely wrong when I bent down for a closer look and the pigeon made no attempt to fly away.

I knew the pigeon had no chance if I left him there. Eventually a car would flatten him, either by accident or purpose and if he tried to move around on the edge of the bridge and couldn't fly he'd likely fall to the water below and drown. I'd been drawn into a dilemma. I picked the bird up and started carrying it with me off the bridge. I had no real plan, I just knew anything would be better than leaving it to its chances on the bridge.

Take it to a vet? Realistically, what could he do, or be willing to do, if I didn't have the money to pay for services? Where was a Vet? How far? Was it copping out? I wanted to help the pigeon but what direction to take and how much inconvenience to accept?

At the end of the bridge there was a tiny park. I took the bird over and sat it down on the grass. I knew I was copping out. Had I done the right thing? Not really. I knew I should have found that vet.

I wasn't very proud of myself. I'd only given lip service to my beliefs. The beginning of the Hippocratic oath is, "First, do no harm." I thought I'd, at least, done something for the bird. I'd gotten him out of an almost certain death situation. But was the grassy park any less of one if he couldn't fly?

I couldn't stand to ponder it. I had to walk away and try my best to think only good things would come to the pigeon.

Chapter 85
Scalpeled at the Rodeo

Discouraging critters who needed love from following me turned out to be more manageable than I'd thought. Maybe I didn't look very promising. Love is fine but a fella's gotta eat and I'm sure I didn't look like much of a star to latch on to.

It hurts to act mean when really there's only love and compassion in your heart. The recipient seldom understands tough love. There were times when I had to run critters off when I'm sure they saw me as their last hope.

I had to employ evasive action every time I encountered one of the unfortunates that had been hit on the highway. In a car you see a flash of red, some disarrayed flesh and you can divert your eyes and the whole gruesome scene is behind you in a heartbeat.

I don't have to tell you the walker is at a disadvantage when the carnage is encountered. I could see it coming for almost as far as I could see. Of course I could begin to plan then how I was best going to avoid the disheartening mess. Simply looking down worked until I actually came to the scene. Then I had one of three choices:

1. I could turn my head far to the left or right, looking out of the extreme corner of the leading eye until I was past.

2. When I came to the scene I could look up, focusing hard on the horizon until I inched myself past.

3. At the very last minute I could do a quick orientating survey as to the lay of the land concerning what I might stumble over. After imprinting that in my mind I'd close my eyes and do the best I could to not open them until I was past the scene.

Risky business all, but more pleasurable than the alternatives.

I was in waterland. The map said it, the bridges said it. Not marshland or swamp, like South and North Carolina, but land with bays and rivers. They abound in the Northeast.

I came to my third unwalkable bridge. This one had a Chamber of Commerce visitors center snuggled next to the entrance.

I decided to try the a-policeman-will-take-you-across theory once more. I told the old fable of the simpleton who decided to attempt a walk of Herculean proportions to the nice ladies at the Chamber.

I'm not sure if it was the fable or the kindness of the ladies but in no time flat a blue and white was parked out in front.

In my innocence of heart and intent I was surprised when the officer, out of some law enforcement policy, told me I'd have to put my pack in the trunk. I could have been any kind of loony though, for all he knew. The police stopped taking chances long ago.

As he opened the trunk for me to put my pack in he added, "Do you have any weapons?"

I thought that strange. If I did and had any intention of using them, would I tell him?

What was my response when asked if I had any weapons? You thought since I sent my slingshot and marbles back home when I was way back in California the only answer could be, "No." At the time the policeman asked the question I started to give a quick reply of, "No." Then I thought, "This sounds like a serious question. I know I don't have any weapons but what if I'm carrying something that might be construed as a weapon?" I gave a quick, mental picture, rundown of everything in my pack. I'd been in every nook and cranny hundreds of times. Of course, I wasn't carrying any weapons, but something did occur to me. It seemed silly to call it a weapon but I thought I'd better play it safe.

"The only thing I can think of that might be called a weapon is some scalpel blades I found back in the desert in New Mexico. I kept them because they were super sharp and since I wasn't carrying a knife I thought they might come in handy."

The officer asked if he could see one.

While I was digging them out he said, "Scalpel blades that you found beside the road? Aren't you afraid of A.I.D.S.?"

I assured him I was, but that these seemed okay because they'd never been taken out of their sealed aluminum-foil wrappers.

The officer seemed satisfied that the scalpel blades posed no threat, especially since they were going to be in the pack in the trunk.

He was a nice man with none of the usual officer/criminal, king/serf demeanor about him. If I had to ride across the bridge with him I was glad he didn't treat me as though I was a bother.

The far side of the bridge introduced me to the Garden State. All my life I thought surely that was a misnomer for New Jersey. Like Maryland and Delaware, though, I learned I had wrongly judged New Jersey.

Once off the bridge I had to head straight for the small village of Woodstown. Several days earlier back in Delaware I had called Gus to arrange for him to drop ship my last pair of boots to me.

It seemed that the pair I was wearing should have gotten me all the way to Manhattan since I had *just* started wearing them in Blakely, Georgia. The previous New Mexico to Georgia had spoiled me, though.

Upon learning of my Los Angeles-New York quest, a fellow in a grocery store in rural New Jersey said, "You're almost there." That simple statement boosted my spirits wonderfully.

I knew, though, that the shoes I was wearing weren't going to make it to Manhattan.

And again I had difficulty getting to the post office during business hours. Invariably when Gus sent money or shoes it required either a speed up or slow-down to coordinate mail, business hours, and my body so that they all arrived at the right spot at the right time. You can understand how tricky that is if you're on foot and the post office is in the next state.

Nowhere is the old saw about beauty being skin deep more true than in hiking boots. The new boots Gus sent me in Woodstown were pretty but was comeliness important at this advanced stage of the journey? Way back in Huntington Beach it may have been important to me that the boots I was starting such a momentous task with be aesthetically as well as functionally pleasing, but standing here in Woodstown, New Jersey, only a few hundred miles from Manhattan function preceded style.

In Shakespeare's *Macbeth,* there are witches stirring a cauldron and chanting, "Double, Double, toil and trouble."

They could have been cooking up my new hiking boots in that pot because these little jewels were "double toil and trouble."

Even Gus' miracle wool socks had to cling by their fingernails to keep that old blister wolf from the door.

By now I was determined nothing was going to stop my forward march. I gave the boots a choice: Straighten up and fly right or I'll stop at K-Mart, get me some $9.99 specials, send your butts back to Kentucky and you can forget about carving your place in history.

They got the message. They wanted to take me to Manhattan so they shaped up and did it.

Even at this late stage in New Jersey I still had to sometimes ask directions. I guess that isn't too hard to believe. If you go anywhere new, you might have to ask directions even if you're within two blocks of your destination.

I stopped at a small grocery to inquire how far it was until I turned left on Highway 54 on my way to Hammonton.

"Well," the fella says, "keep going down this road 'til you pass the rodeo on your right and 54 is the next road to the left."

Surely my face showed my dubiety. My nonplussed smile, then my voice quickly followed in doubt.

"A rodeo? A rodeo in New Jersey?"

The man reacted as if "New Jersey Rodeo" had no more of a funny ring to it than say, "Wyoming Rodeo."

I realized I was a long way from home, and my best option was to thank the man, hit the door and pay homage to the New Jersey Rodeo as I passed by.

Drawing closer to the Rodeo I thought about man having dominion over the fish of the sea, over the fowl of the air, over the cattle and every creeping thing that creepeth the earth.

I wondered, though, if that meant man had free rein to do as he pleased with all the other animals? An arguable point, I'm sure.

While I think that God intended animals for our welfare, surely He never intended man to demean animals.

In one sense I feel God means for animals to be our equals, sorta like a boss-employee relationship. One isn't necessarily better, in true worth, than the other, one is just boss.

I thought about the rodeo. Hasn't man overstepped his bounds? For his pleasure, does man have a right to train or artificially stimulate a horse or bull to buck on command? When a calf is running away at full speed, is lassoed, then jerked so violently off his feet that often he is facing the opposite direction, does that feel good to the calf? Does the calf get up and say, "Boy, I'm glad someone popped my neck. It was so stiff today."

I don't think we should use animals for sport. And I'm sure there are people who'd say, "Oh, they enjoy it." Not necessarily meaning the rodeo, but any number of other sports we involve animals in. How do we know for sure, though? They may be "enjoying" it for a reward.

We make it hard enough on animals. We squeeze them out of their habitats with shopping centers and subdivisions. They have to adapt to our cars and pollution. The places they have to live are smaller and less suited to their needs. Coyotes are forced to come down out of the hills and catch the cats of Bel-Air. Deer are forced to graze on subdivision lawns.

In Maryland I saw a small herd of deer standing just off the highway in a sparse grove of thin, short trees. We looked at each other as I passed, and they seemed embarrassed to have to be calling what they were doing "hiding." Deer like to hide during the day. It was degrading to both them and man that they were reduced to concealment in a sparse grove of trees.

I witnessed something else in New Jersey I thought was sad. I'm sure man's destruction of habitat was a contributing factor.

One morning just before noon (I'm guessing by the sun. There's no ethical, moral or legal reason for a hiker to wear a watch.) I noticed running toward me on the highway what, from a distance, looked like a large dog. But remember dogs didn't concern me because I had my walking stick and pack for protection.

As it got closer, though, I saw it was a fawn. It looked no more than a few days old. I thought something must be seriously wrong in its life, because normally, it would never leave its mother's side and be running as fast as it could down a New Jersey highway.

It seemed to be so afraid that it didn't even notice me until the last possible moment when it veered and ran off the highway. At first I blamed the fawn's erratic behavior on dogs but neither did I see nor hear any.

I still don't know why the deer was doing something so atypical of normal deer behavior. I do believe that had it been a hundred years earlier, the fawn could have found a hiding place and wouldn't have been reduced to running about wild-eyed in search of one.

Chapter 86
McDonald's Takes Its Last Prisoner and I Get Respectable in Perth Amboy

There's no love lost between me and McDonald's. I have no real animosity toward them, but to my way of thinking they've gone beyond where their talent should have taken them.

It was somewhere in Louisiana when it occurred to me that I'd like to be the first person in modern times to walk coast-to-coast and not eat at McDonald's once. Then I had to stop and think about their pervasiveness and their hype. In all my stops had I not been lured into a McDonald's before now?

I had. I remembered I'd slept behind a church in Cleburne, Texas and as I started for the edge of town the next morning I passed a McDonald's. I'd been in Texas long enough to know that you had better git while the gittin was good. In Texas you might not git for another 50 miles.

I went in and had breakfast. I remember it was more like a play breakfast. Everything, the eggs, the hash browns, the juice all seemed to be in miniature.

But breakfast it was, I guess. At least it had that label and it was enough to ruin my pledge to be McDonald's-free coast-to-coast.

My map told me the city of Perth Amboy was the last city before I crossed the Newark Bay Bridge and onto Staten Island.

Staten Island is one of the five boroughs of New York City. And Manhattan, my goal, was one of the other boroughs. I was getting excited.

I'd never been to Staten Island, but figured since it was a borough of New York City it must be crawling with people. The prospect intimidated me some and I figured it was time to make myself as presentable, and by extension as inconspicuous, as possible.

It must have been off-off season for the motel in Perth Amboy–they let me stay! This wasn't like the 13-dollar one I stayed at in Lamesa, Texas. This one even had an elevator.

I stood in the shower until I was "pruny" and removed as many layers of grit and smell as I could with those tiny bars of soap.

When I was buffed and shiny I laid all my clothes out on the bed and the surrounding floor to see what would best allow me to slip through Staten Island and Brooklyn, drawing the least attention to myself as possible.

I know what you're thinking, "Yeah, and that backpack's not going to stand out at all, is it, Dummy?"

Yes, but you'd have to get a lot weirder than that to turn an eye in New York. But I wasn't taking any chances. I couldn't see any way around carrying the backpack through Staten Island but I had a plan for Brooklyn. Visualize what shirts and pants would look like after they'd been worn days in the summer on a sweaty, stinky body, then wadded up and stuffed in a mailbox-sized compartment and left there for days.

After I'd chosen my cleanest dirty outfit I was forced out the door by my stomach's gnawing at my backbone.

I stepped out of the front door of the motel and looked to the right — no food in sight. I looked to the left — no food in sight. Nothing either way except a McDonald's.

It was dark and I had little inclination to venture in Perth Amboy. McDonald's it would be.

Walking toward McDonald's I knew full well what I was doing. But if I was folding under, at least, I could say I folded to one of the basest, strongest needs — hunger.

I had a choice — eat at McDonald's, or go to bed on crackers and cokes from the motel vending machine. I think I would have done that if my McDonald's track record had been intact. But that silly, little breakfast way back in Cleburne, Texas had spoiled all that. The all-powerful "Mickey D" had won again.

But I was glad McDonald's was there in Perth Amboy. I've gone to bed on crackers and coke.

The next morning I went to look at the bridge. At this late stage of the game I had viewed so many bridges and so many cars that I could look at the map and judge quite accurately what bridges would or wouldn't allow pedestrians. But my motel was close to the bridge across Newark Bay, so I thought it might be worth the short walk just to eyeball the bridge for possibilities to walk across. I figured the chances were slim and none, but I had nothing to lose.

Even my "BB-in-a-boxcar" sized brain evaluated the situation instantly. You'd have to be suicidal to set foot on that bridge.

I went back to the motel and did something totally out of character for me. I called a taxi.

On the way across the bridge I told the driver to stop at the first possible spot. I was surprised at how graciously he accepted my apology for not having a tip to give him.

Staten Island is a 13-mile-long strip of businesses and residences. I was surprised that there were more open spaces than I'd imagined. I'd always pictured it being all row houses and projects.

A 13-mile walk was a piece of cake by this time so by mid-afternoon I found myself facing the bridge connecting Staten Island and Brooklyn.

Chapter 87
The Hourly Rate Motel,
I Try To Win Over the Indians,
and the Natives Seem Friendly

A couple more giant steps and all the months, days, miles and inches come to a pointed end. The small flicker of light at the end of this 3000-plus-mile tunnel will soon look more like a Second World War searchlight.

I have to force my mind to force my body to carry me through the last few miles. I'd guess no more than ten miles remain, yet they are the most dreaded miles of the trip.

You'd think the first few miles would be the hardest, but for me it's just the opposite. Everything about New York City is foreign and intimidating to this boy from rural Kentucky and Tennessee.

There is too much bombarding the senses. Stimuli requiring immediate attention fly at you from every angle. There's no chance to evaluate with any leisure. Everything and everybody seems to be hurling somewhere and it feels like you're being sucked into the vortex. There are simply too many people rushing to too many places. The rat experiment has spilled out onto the streets.

I am apprehensive about Staten Island. It's a nervous thirteen miles. I cross it unscathed but I don't like it. I reach the end in mid-afternoon. Thirteen miles is hardly enough to bring beads of perspiration to my forehead at this late stage of the game. With any effort at all I could reach the Empire State Building today.

I dread the minefields of Brooklyn. I don't belong here. It isn't my land. I feel like a foreigner.

I decide to lay back and give a full, fresh day to the final assault. Except for my anxiety to put a cap on all this, I have no reason to hurry.

I rent another room at the last motel on the Brooklyn-end of Staten Island. In a way I hate to do it because by this time my practiced eye can spot places to camp even on Staten Island.

But I ask myself why should I push my luck at this late date when I'm, at least figuratively, within a good Tiger Woods golf drive from reaching my goal. A motel seemed a valorous discretion at this battle site. I had no doubt there was no shortage of Staten Island "bilin' pots" ready and willing to render me into little piggy sausages if I wasn't careful.

It would only be my fifth night that I stayed in a motel. Not bad in five- and-a-half months.

I once read a book written by a man who rode a bicycle coast-to-coast and never slept out once. He spent every night in a motel. In my mind his accomplishment wasn't much greater than if he'd counted the miles on a stationary bike in his home. I know that's stretching it a bit but he didn't experience enough or pay enough dues in my opinion.

So it is with mixed feelings that I approached the desk of the last motel on Staten Island. Staying in a motel always smacked of cheating to me. Each time I did it I could see the little smirks on the faces of Daniel Boone, Davy Crockett and Kit Carson.

I can paint you a picture of this motel with one word−curry. Someone said the East Indians have taken over the motel business much as the Chinese took over the laundry business at the turn of the century. I've concluded, through my travels, be it foot, bicycle, boat, truck or car that the vast majority of motels not part of a national chain are owned and run by East Indians. It isn't so much a statement of prejudice as one of fact.

At the desk, talking to the owner is a young woman, a girl really, negotiating for an hourly rate.

Some of you are saying to yourself, "No damn way I would stay in an hourly rate motel!" And you'd also say, "No damn way I would drink out of a toilet, newly flushed or not!" And "No damn way I would finish a half-eaten sandwich I found in a dumpster."

I'm here to say, "Yes, there is a damn way."

There's an old saying, "There's only three hours between fat and lean." Never say never. All of us, without exception, would sleep anywhere, drink anything and eat anything we could swallow, given enough time. I need a bed badly.

After the girl had gotten her key, the desk clerk turned toward me.

His curry fragrance reminds me of a garden. Mine probably reminds him of a garden, too — compost. He doesn't flinch as I request a room.

This night I lay out the best plan I can muster for the minefields of Brooklyn and Manhattan.

How to slip through the enemy lines?

I want to become as much of a spirit, a non-person, as I can manage. I want no attention drawn to me. First, I conclude the pack is a decided liability. It's hard not to notice a 35-pound glob on someone's back.

But how to complete the walk and still retrieve my pack afterward? Where to leave it? Who do you trust when you're on an island of cannibals?

I run down my list of friends on this island. My short list is also my long list. I have no friends here. Only two people know I exist at all — the hourly rate girl and the motel desk clerk. Not much of a support group.

The motel manager is my lone hope.

The next morning Bambi himself couldn't have fawned better. Honey drips from my lips as I relate my cross-country odyssey to the motel owner and how I'd be eternally grateful if he'd take protective custody of my pack until I walk to the Empire State Building and back.

As hard as I try to make the story unclouded and believable and to speak slowly and enunciate clearly, I could tell by the way his eyes and feet synchronize in their shifting back and forth that the whole concept is lost on him.

Walk from Los Angeles to New York? To what purpose, for God's sake? I can see in his face that walking anywhere is reserved for a good purpose; to get to work, secure milk for a child, or take a goat to market. You don't *just* walk anywhere.

I try another tactic. Game Plan B — the old end-around.

If not by direct words, I imply that since I'd given him business by staying in his motel he should do me this favor and watch and protect my pack for a few (actually several) hours.

As the chink in his armor reluctantly appears, I plead with my eyes. My back is to the wall.

Divine intervention again! Finally, just when I was beginning to believe everything I'd heard, or imagined, about New Yorkers was true, the motel manager gives an almost imperceptible shrug of his shoulders. It isn't one of those New York my-hands-are-tied-it's-all-controlled-by-the-mob shrugs, it's one of those Tennessee I-kinda-like-ya-kid-so-I-let-you-wear-me-down shrugs.

My best and biggest heartfelt smile covers my face.

He indicates a broom closet off to one side of the motel office.

I emphasize more than once that I'll make the trip to the Empire State Building as quickly as my unworthy feet can fly.

Although I more or less beg the man to let me leave the pack, it is with great trepidation. I am endowing all my worldly goods, at least the ones in New York, to a complete stranger. Upon my return, if his Okay-I'll-help-you shrug of his shoulders is replaced by the same shrug, only this one indicating I'm-sorry, I-don't-know-what-happened-to-your-pack I will be completely defenseless.

The fate of my pack rests entirely in this man's hands. His yet unknown honesty and kindness are my only hopes.

After having that pack on my back every day for five-and-a-half months, I feel naked and vulnerable as I walk down the street away from the motel.

Here I am in shark-infested waters with no cage, no armor, not even so much as my walking stick for protection.

The night before, a short walk, and some well-placed questions, told me I could catch a city bus from the edge of Staten Island over to the edge of Brooklyn. So, I head for the bus stop closest to the Verrazano Narrows Bridge.

This must be the craziest (I think that's what "Verrazano" means in Italian) bridge in the world. Even at normal speed the goings-on look like a Keystone Kops movie. As strong and ingrained as my walk-every-inch policy is, I wouldn't have attempted to walk across this bridge for a million dollars.

When I get off the bus at the first stop in Brooklyn I am pleasantly surprised. Everything isn't decaying, the people don't have horns or fangs. I see no street-corner gangs nor burned-out cars. There are trees and houses and shops and schools. People are doing pretty much in Brooklyn as they do in San Francisco, in Dallas, in Pocatello, Grinder's Switch or Bug Tussle. They are getting on with getting on. They don't seem inclined to bother or even notice me.

It is a pretty, warm September day. Kinda hard to grasp that all this started on another pretty, warm day way back in April at a California beach. I guess if a long journey starts and ends on a pretty day then any ugly days in between sorta lose some of their sting in your memory.

And here I am walking down a sidewalk in Brooklyn. It seems a little surreal—a little like it isn't really me doing it. Was it me that had the determination and fortitude to walk all that way? Could I really have persevered through the heat and thirst and loneliness of the desert? Was it me, that little boy from Tennessee, who'd survived the sudden, terrible Texas storms and the seemingly endless zillions of biting, stinging fire ants from Texas to North Carolina? That wasn't me was it?

When I realize that all that has gone before–the feet, the yards, the miles, every inch from sea to shining sea–I have met and conquered; or more correctly, Mother Nature has let me slip through, my heart feels lighter and my step has new spring.

Here I am in Brooklyn only one bridge away from the piece of land I'd been aiming for all this time.

My heart is lighter, not just because I'm walking toward the Brooklyn

Bridge, but because Brooklyn isn't the hellhole I had envisioned it to be. It is simply a case of too many people trying to do too much in too small a space.

I once worked in a shop that catered to tourists. It was in a mountain resort town so people came from all over the eastern US to visit. It didn't often happen, but occasionally I'd learn that someone was from New York City. And there was only one question I wanted to ask: Was it possible to walk across the Brooklyn Bridge? Of course, there can only be four answers — yes, no, maybe, and I don't know.

In retrospect it's odd that the Brooklyn Bridge was my only concern at that time. My walk was still in the future but I was planning, always planning. Yet at that time I innocently thought that I could walk across any bridge with the possible exception of the Brooklyn Bridge.

Strange how life can leave us twisting in the wind sometimes. The reality is that the Brooklyn Bridge is about the only bridge I *can* walk across. At least some of the New Yorkers I'd asked back in Tennessee had given me a "yes" to my question about the bridge. But I'd also gotten an equal number of each of the other three possible answers.

I am encouraged and hopeful as I approach the bridge, but still don't know for sure if this is going to be my final obstacle or not.

There is such joy in my heart as I see a walking/biking lane going across the bridge that is nearly as wide as an automobile lane.

Chapter 88
The Empire State Building Bares Her Chest and I Suckle at the Breast of Victory

I am glad it is a Tuesday. I think of Tuesdays and Thursdays as the generic days of the week. If the days of the week could be broken down into functional classifications Tuesdays and Thursdays would be our utility days. Sunday would be our somber, reverent, no-nonsense day and Monday our official, dreaded workday. And, of course, Wednesday has always been hump day. If you can make it through Wednesday the workweek is more than half over. Friday would be just what we have always labeled it — T. G. I. F. day. And of course Saturdays will always be classified as our Mardi Gras day.

Tuesdays and Thursdays. "Mac-Days," if you will. But they're my favorite days. You are more likely to have the world to yourself on Tuesdays and Thursdays. Everyone else is preoccupied with just getting through the workweek–their heads down, plodding ahead. They aren't in your way. They have no real interest in what you're doing. They are the best days for seeing a movie unhindered, and your favorite restaurant will be less crowded.

I think another reason Tuesdays and Thursdays have always been my favorite days is because I've always had this weird desire to be doing something different from what everyone else is doing at that particular moment. (See book title.) I've always enjoyed working when everyone else is sleeping or playing. I'd much rather work Saturdays and Sundays and be off Tuesdays and Thursdays.

It was just dumb luck that the last day of my walk fell on a Tuesday. No way, back on April 8th at Huntington Beach in Los Angeles when I took the first of what was to become millions of steps, could I have planned to bring this all to a conclusion on one of my favorite days. Oh, I could have sandbagged and made it happen, but it wasn't my nature.

But here I am on the Brooklyn Bridge and all systems are "Go."

September 24th, Tuesday, it's warm, the sky is blue and the air clear. Yes, it is New York City and it is clear.

As I cross the bridge, the combined power of the Budweiser Clydesdales couldn't prevent me from turning my head and craning my neck to see if I can spot what has been pulling at me like a magnet for five-and-a-half months. Yes, there she is! Standing tall above all the other mothers. The third tallest mother in the whole U.S. I can see her now. What joy! No more hunger, thirst, blisters, pain or sorrow. I have done it!

There, 30-odd blocks away stands heaven. I can walk on my hands and make it from here. I can sneeze and blow myself backward there. Thirty blocks, now, is no more than a puddle jump for me.

I suspect if you asked the average American to walk 30 blocks they'd have a fainting spell. They'd have to have a cold rag put to their head just at the thought of it. For me, it was a skip around the mulberry bush, a short burst between the monkey bars and the sliding board. Only a nuclear disaster could stop me now.

I step from the Brooklyn Bridge and into the caverns and canyons of Wall Street and the business district of Manhattan.

Brooklyn had been small businesses and homes. This is all three piece, button down, briefcases.

If I had been apprehensive in Brooklyn, that's all gone in Manhattan. People are scurrying like rats. They each have their own agenda, their own walks to finish, their own empires to reach. They have no interest in me. I am just another nameless face in the crowd. I like that. I can relax and enjoy 30-odd (Yes, odd) blocks of the Big Apple.

New York City is like New Orleans, San Francisco, Miami, in fact, like all really large cities — you might see anything — nothing surprises you.

Pushcart owners are hawking Italian sausages on a bun smothered with onions and green peppers or flavored ice in a cone. Card tables are hastily set up on the sidewalks diverting your attention to wristwatches, sunglasses, T-shirts and just about anything else you can think of. Assorted street musicians strum, pluck, beat and blow instruments for a few coins in their hat, or a chance to sell you a tape of their latest strummings or pluckings.

Everyday the circus comes to town in New York City. The sights and sounds and smells are all there, from the elephant droppings to the peanut shells. It's a crazy, but exhilarating world.

I soak it all in as my light feet fairly float toward 33rd Street and that tall, tall monument to concrete, steel, and being the biggest.

I eat their sausages, drop coins in their hats, try on and reject their sunglasses, accept and promptly drop into the next trash container their pamphlets.

It's a world pulling me in all directions, vying for my interests, and my money. You either love it, are immune to it, or it drives you crazy.

As the block numbers add one upon the other upward toward 33 and where the Empire State Building stands, I assume they'll gather momentum like a snowball downhill and soon my feet will have trouble keeping up with my body It doesn't work that way, though. As I get into the streets numbered in the 20s, I begin to wonder if someone is scooting the Empire State Building backward away from me, like she is a queen on a chess board trying to escape capture by this knight.

I had miscalculated how fast 30 city blocks would fly by. My enthusiasm has suppressed good reason. The 33rd block is becoming as illusive as safety is in a bad dream. Everything else seems to be speeding up while my legs are moving at a snail's pace.

When I was a small boy I loved horses in the daylight but at night, in my dreams, they must have taken on a different meaning. Several times a month one would be chasing me down the street and just when I'd get almost home, my legs would turn to jelly. I'd be on all fours crawling with nearly useless legs. The dream would always end with me just at my doorstep and my last sight being the fire breathing horse bearing down on me. He never caught me but the fear couldn't have been worse if he had.

Actually, my Empire State Building quest isn't as bad as all that. If I practice patience the street numbers will add up in good time. I am just too anxious. I tell myself to back off a notch or two; slow down and appreciate New York City. I don't have to like it, but I shouldn't let the experience pass me by without savoring it.

So, I force my body to slow until it is once again positioned directly over my legs. I force my eyes to do more than focus on the street and sidewalk. I tell them they won't have this opportunity often, so they'd better make the best of it. We all know more than we need to know about asphalt and concrete. It's what's walking and sitting on them that should merit our attention. It's better to stumble occasionally than to look down constantly.

It makes more sense to savor these last few hundred yards. I have made it. There is no reason to think I won't. It will be over in just a matter of a few feet and a few minutes.

I'll have a lifetime to look back on this and the memories will be better and remain sharper if these last few blocks and minutes are savored.

Since I entered Manhattan I've been walking north on Broadway but I know from my Rand McNally that the further north Broadway goes the more it angles away from the Empire State Building at 33rd and Fifth Avenue. So, when I reached 30th street I decide it is time for me to take a right and go over to Fifth, then north on Fifth to 33rd.

As I turn north on Fifth, there she is in all her magnificent granite splendor. She looks danged beautiful to me.

I walk up beside her, but I'm careful not to touch her. I want to admire and appreciate her for a moment at a distance, even if that distance is only ten or 15 feet. I look up to see the top but it isn't possible, standing so close. I can't look up for long because it feels like I'm going to topple over backward. It feels as if I'm looking back *beyond* perpendicular.

So, here I am–the finish line. Three or four steps added to how many millions and it will all be over.

The years of planning, wishing, dreaming really, since I was a young boy, have all come down to just three or four steps. The indisputable fact that it is real doesn't seem real.

The price, the huge price, I had had to pay to be able to stand in this spot.

I had sat on hot asphalt in the direct sun because there was no shade. I had sought the pitiful bit of shade provided by a mailbox or a telephone pole, grasping at any scrap of protection from the broiling sun.

I had saved the last swallow of my more-precious-than-gold Gatorade so that when ravaging thirst drove me out of my sleep during the night it would be there.

I had drunk from stock tanks, windmills, even tanks holding water for toilet flushing purposes. I had gone without water when water was the only thought that occupied my mind.

Then I had endured water when there was too much water, nearly drowning under roads from fast-rising water. Terrible electric storms from which I had no protection, I had endured.

The multitude of blisters and the thousands of miles that turned my feet to hamburger, cost me six of ten toenails and made my feet hardly recognizable, even to me.

The smothering onslaught of the stinging, biting hordes of fire ants I had somehow lived through.

And the times in Louisiana when the suffocating clouds of mosquitoes were so thick, so armed with their tormenting hypodermics, that getting in and out of my tent at night required a constant swinging of my towel about my head and body with one hand while I did whatever needed to be done with the other.

There had been the loneliness, the awful feeling in the desert that I was the only person left on earth. I think of the times I wished I'd had someone with me, and when I had to make my bed among strangers whose intentions I knew not.

In the deep South I had endured feeling like I was a stranger in a strange land – my own land! I had some inkling of the terrible Amish practice of shunning. All because my appearance wasn't exactly like theirs.

Was it worth all that and more to able to stand here at last beside her grey eminence?

I answer with a resounding, Yes!!! The thrill of victory vastly outweighs those agonies of defeat. Cheap was the price I paid. I will be rewarded each time, throughout the rest of my life when I look back at what I have accomplished. I have bought myself membership in a very exclusive country club — a Walk-Across-the-Country-Club. I am finished. I have met all the requirements, paid all the dues.

My reverie is interrupted when I notice a man selling post cards on the sidewalk. I step over to investigate and am not surprised to see they are of the Empire State Building. He has cards depicting every angle and pose of the building – a virtual Swimsuit Edition of the Empire State Building. I have to have some.

It occurred to me in the last few months that not everyone would believe I'd walked all the way across the country. And that didn't really bother me as long as I knew the truth. But I want some postcards as sorta bragging rights; a kind of proof that I'd been here. After all, postcards of the Empire State Building aren't available in Wikieup, Arizona; Blanket, Texas; Hot Coffee, Mississippi; or Bacon, Georgia, so I buy several postcards with different "poses" from the seemingly disinterested man.

The bored look on the face of the man selling the postcards makes me wonder if he ever even looks at the building anymore. Is he like the person who makes the doughnuts for 30 years but the thought of actually eating one repulses him.

Is the postcard man just weary of all the hype?

Of course, you've read *The Grapes of Wrath*. What? Put this trash down and go read it right now! I'll wait.

For today's times its ending would be blase and mild, but viewed from the perspective of the late 1930s it was shocking. In fact, when John Steinbeck submitted it, the publishers said if he wasn't willing to change the ending they couldn't publish the book. But Steinbeck stood his ground. He wrote back, saying he felt the ending was an integral part of the message he was trying to convey and that he had no intentions of changing the ending. But if it came to that, he'd just as soon see the book remain unpublished.

I suspect the editors and publishers realized the magnitude of what they held in their hands and decided discretion was the better part of valor. To our great joy and enrichment we can now enjoy a classic of writing, thanks to Steinbeck's insistence.

I spot a shiny, foot-square brass plaque on the side of the building. It says, "The Empire State Building."

And here as I stand next to the Empire State Building, it suddenly dawns on me that life (mine) is going to imitate art (Steinbeck's). I walk over and press my lips to it.

Epilogue
Dry Technical Stuff

It was never my intention to write a book about this walk. The walk was something I did simply because it had been a dream of mine since I was a small boy. I did it for the adventure and to see if I had it in me.

After I kissed the plaque on the Empire State Building I returned to Tennessee and did what I'd done most of my life — worked at a job and started the dream planning of my next adventure. My wife of 25 years had passed away before my walk, and after I got back home I began tossing around the idea of looking up an old grade school love whom I hadn't seen or heard from in 30 odd years.

Every few years I'd run into an aunt of hers who lived in the same town as my parents back in Kentucky. So, I had some limited knowledge of how her life had progressed through the years.

As luck would have it, one day when I was visiting my parents, I ran into the aunt again and saw it as a good chance to catch up on my grade school love, Alyce.

The aunt said Alyce was doing well and wasn't married and was living in a small town about 15 miles away. And she felt Alyce would love to hear from me.

When I got back to Tennessee I wrote, then she wrote. Then the writing became almost daily.

Naturally, in the course of our getting re-acquainted we each had to give a thumbnail sketch of what had transpired in the 30 years since we'd seen each other. Of course, the walk was one of the things I mentioned.

On one slow news day, I decided I'd insert the Ocotillo Wells short shower story, just to have something to say. At the time I gave it no more thought than it may be something Alyce would enjoy hearing.

In a return letter she said she had thought the story interesting and funny and that I should consider writing a book about my walk, since in addition to the Ocotillo Wells story, there must be scores of other stories.

I pooh-poohed the idea at first. I knew the walk contained lots of happenings, but was it in me to compile them in any manner that would appeal to anyone.

One slow day at work I thought, just for the fun of it, I'd jot down as many weird, unusual or noteworthy things that had happened to me between Los Angeles and New York

City as I could remember. I was amazed that after only a short time that day, and in a couple of nights at home, with hardly any effort, I had 279 items jotted down.

Before, during and after my walk I never had the slightest intention of writing about it so I never took notes. And we know that a camera would have been much too extravagant weight-wise for me to carry so I had no pictures except the ones I retained in my head.

Yet, the 279 (and still growing) memories fairly floated out of my head.

You don't sit on your first cactus thorn in the desert and forget it easily.

Nor do you walk from Seminole, Texas to Charleston, South Carolina and never wear a jacket nor sleep in a real bed without it staying in your memory.

The inescapable summer sun in the desert will never let you forget it. It seemed relentless in the ways it could torture. As you know by now, having read this far, the sun tortures not only the body's exterior but its innards as well. The sun was well represented in the memory countdown.

I said at the beginning of this book I never intended (nor could I) make this book a travelogue. I simply wanted to relate what a walk from Los Angeles to New York City might be like. I didn't want to paint an eight by ten color glossy of this old USA. I just wanted to relate, as best I could, what I experienced and the thoughts that arose from those experiences.

If you walked it, you'd experience, in one form or another, to one degree or another, your own sights, smells, feelings.

I think if you bothered to read this book, then somewhere deep in there you've at least wondered, if only for a split second, what it would be like to walk from coast to coast. Having done it, I whole-heartedly and enthusiastically encourage you to give it a try. Not only will you get an up close and personal, intimate, slow and easily digestible view of what this country is all about; just as importantly you'll learn what *you* are all about.

It might be easier for you, it might be harder for you. You might see more beauty than I, you may see more ugly.

Go! Do it! See what our country's made of. See what you're made of.

They say never give advice because a wise man doesn't need it and a fool won't heed it. So, I won't advise. But I will tell you things I would change if I ever did something like it again.

First, take a kindred spirit with you. A love mate would be heavenly, but kindred spirit may be more important.

Prisons were built because mankind learned that the worst form of punishment is loneliness.

Toward the end of my walk I concluded that a coast-to-coast walk would be the ultimate form of marriage counseling. If you're still speaking when you reach the far coast then I guarantee Paul Harvey will one day say, "And today in Tuscaloosa John and Mary Smith still have that small sign in the rear window of their car that says, Just Married — 65 years."

The second thing I would change is that I wouldn't carry anything on my back. I know, everything you've seen, heard or read tells you a backpack is the way to go. You've seen pictures of climbers scaling Everest or hikers enjoying one of our national parks, and they are all wearing packs.

I contend they are because they have no choice. If you hike country rough enough then a pack is about the only answer. But the roads, rather than backcountry, have always been my cup of tea and where there are roads wheels are possible.

A word about backcountry vs. road walking: Backcountry is fine if you want to escape the rat race and commune with nature. But we are people-people. Whether we realize it or not, we thrive on human contact. And it's a rare person who can go long periods alone and really enjoy himself.

That's why I prefer road walking. You get to see the countryside but you also get to experience what I think makes the trip fun and memorable — the people you meet along the way.

There's a song from the movie *Pocahontas* that can teach us a lot about respect for nature but it also teaches us respect and understanding about everyone else occupying planet Earth.

Pocahontas is singing to John Smith who, along with his fellow Englishmen, had always ridden roughshod over America, the land as well as Pocahontas' people. In one part of the song she says something I think is good to remember when you travel anywhere outside your little world. Heck, it's even good advice *within* your little world. She says to John Smith, "You think the only people who are people, are people who look and think like you. But, if you walk the footprints of a stranger you'll learn things you never knew you never knew."

But I've strayed way away from the road and wheels and not carrying things on my back.

There's a man from England who holds the record for the longest continuous walk. He walked from the extreme tip of South America at Tierra del Fuego to Point Barrow, Alaska. He didn't carry a backpack. He took all his belongings in one of those two-wheeled carts like little old ladies in England pull their groceries in. No doubt he had his beefed up to industrial strength.

If I went again I'd capitalize on his idea. Let something with wheels be my back, whether grocery cart, bicycle or pull-along golf cart. I realize something that bulky would create its own set of problems but the trade-off is of small consequence.

I feel sure if you were to slip the pack and all I carried from coast to coast onto your back you'd say, "Heck, this isn't heavy." And I do believe I went across as light as is possible. I carried no food, no cooking gear, next to no rain gear and the minimum of clothing. So, I agree my pack wouldn't feel heavy *at first*. But you haven't multiplied those first few seconds by millions. I liken it to carrying a piece of luggage through the airport. When you first pick it up with your right hand, it doesn't seem too heavy but when the terminal turns out to be further away than you thought, soon you tell yourself I "think" I'll switch to my left hand. For a while that seems easy. But soon you find yourself switching hands more frequently. And it's great that you have two hands. But remember you only have one back–no switching allowed.

You put on a pack in Los Angeles and take it off 8,388,600 steps later in New York. Not quite true, literally, but you see my point.

While I'm giving advice, which I said I wouldn't give, I want to add two cents more.

If you decide to go on any adventure, let's say a long walk, a bike trip, boat trip, etc. where Mother Nature, not you, is in charge, buy the best clothing and equipment there is.

I know you're thinking, "Oh, he means buy good stuff to take with you." No, I mean buy the best there is.

About halfway through my walk I formulated this original saying about clothing and equipment, "Don't buy the best you can afford, buy the best there is."

There's an old saying in horse racing circles, "Breed the best to the best and hope for the best." It applies when you pit yourself against Mother Nature. Of course, you won't win unless she lets you. But I think she looks more favorably on those with enough gumption to prepare well.

When you think about what to take on a trip I guarantee the only picture your enthusiastic gosh-this-is-going-to-be-fun-I'm-rearing-to-go mind will be able to come up with is of one of those warm, sunny, spring days when bees are buzzing and flowers are in bloom and a Hanes T-shirt and cut off Levis are the uniform of the day.

Forget that crap! Do not let your mind lead you down that flower-strewn path. Believe me, it only leads to the gas chamber.

Instead, (I know it will be hard) picture yourself standing in a grove of trees, during a driving rain, dejected with head bent, a cold trickle coursing down your backbone. Or sitting under a bridge on a rock waiting out a storm that seems like it will never end and all the while your body heat is draining rapidly away and you feel the first sign that your teeth are going to start chattering.

I still have vivid memories of the indignity visited upon me one April day in the North Carolina mountains. It was several years before my Los Angeles to New York walk. I was on a spur of the moment, ill-prepared, 100-mile mountain walk when I started seeing snowflakes. Snowflakes in April in North Carolina? Who are they trying to kid? Ha Ha. The harsh reality was that April snow had me scouring in the first roadside dumpster for something, anything to put on my shivering body. The only thing I could come up with was a giant, plastic garbage bag *after* I'd dumped the garbage out of it. I tore a head hole and two arm holes. And, believe me, I was thrilled beyond words to have it.

Think of those days, for as surely as you set your foot outside your snug, little domicile, they will visit you.

The warm, sunny days require no thought. They'll take care of themselves, but force yourself to think of the vilest, nastiest, coldest, wettest days and nights and plan for them.

In the final analysis what is your butt worth to you? When you stand there shivering uncontrollably on the verge of hypothermia, if you have an ounce of reasoning power left, you're going to wonder what you spent the money on that you saved by going to K-Mart.

When, literally, your life depends on your equipment I think it's a no- brainer — you buy the best.

It's what I'll do next time. I've learned my lesson. I found out Mother Nature giggles with delight and rubs her hands with glee when someone like me thinks they can tackle her with a 50-cent yard sale poncho as I did.

I like to call it naive when really, the only label you can put on it is stupid.

Mother Nature may not be the Wicked Witch of the West; she may not be out to get you, but she simply does her thing and sometimes it can be violent and unforgiving. There's no way you'll think the money ill spent if you use it to prepare well.

And finally, (I think and you hope) my last piece of unsolicited advice.

If you feel moved to venture out, to go forth and experience the myriad of possibilities out there, don't be deterred by the doomsdayers and naysayers. If you let them they'll keep you at home on your couch. Their fear of the unknown keeps them there, but what have they gained?

I love Chinese proverbs. There's one I like that applies to being brave enough to venture out: "A brave man dies but once, a coward a thousand times."

I blame television for a lot of our national hysteria. I read somewhere that if murders occurred at the same rate in real life as they do on TV, in 50 days there'd only be one person left on earth.

Television's goal is to keep us watching. It has to be exciting and interesting to get and keep our attention. "Axe murderer dismembers eleven" is attention-getting. Everyday stuff like working, eating, sleeping, line dancing on Saturday night isn't exciting enough to make us watch. Television has to find stuff to hold our attention so a high percentage has to come from the weird, gruesome and bizarre. We begin to see Charles Manson and Lizzie Borden in everyone.

If all of a person's exposure to the outside world came through TV, they would think 90 percent of the people are bad and 10 percent good, when in fact, those figures are reversed. As a whole, the US is filled with kind, or at worst, disinterested people. They have their own agenda. Harassing you isn't part of it. And the best part is you often find that people take time from their busy day to be kind to you. In my five-and-a-half-month Los Angeles-New York adventure I was as vulnerable as a person could be. I presented the golden opportunity if someone wanted to do harm to me. I carried no weapon and unbelievable as it sounds, I crossed the entire state of New Mexico and never saw a policeman. Yet, not once in my entire walk was anyone mean to me.

I admit I sometimes got looks but I'd be the first to admit I was strange looking and that was to be expected.

I read something that sums it up nicely: The everyday kindnesses of the back roads more than make up for the acts of greed in the headlines.

Of course, only a fool would deny danger is out there. Sure danger exists. But not to the degree that we are led to believe.

Ninety-nine percent of the people out there are the ones working, eating, sleeping, and line dancing on Saturday night. That doesn't mean they're uninteresting or dull, quite the contrary. They're only trying to keep the wolf from the door.

Of course, you wouldn't walk with reckless abandon just anywhere at night in Detroit, Chicago, New York, or Los Angeles. Common sense should dictate your actions. Avoid what you feel might be trouble spots. But you don't let those spots completely discourage you from going out and meeting this great world head on.

Remember the young man who told me he wouldn't be afraid to walk anywhere in the toughest parts of New York wearing a tuxedo? He said this after I voiced my concerns about walking through Brooklyn. He said, "It's all a matter of attitude."

I agree to a great extent. Your attitude and by extension your viewable actions can and do often determine how another person is going to react to you.

The Queen of England is stiff, prim and proper, so I doubt anyone is going to go up, slap her on the back and shout, "Hey, Queenie, old girl, waz happenin'?"

It's a perfect example of how your actions can affect other's reactions. Of course, put yourself in harm's way and your attitude won't mean diddly to someone who needs your cash for his overdue fix.

But walking down Highway 83 in Nebraska enjoying a beautiful sunrise on a June morning you'd be relatively safe.

As Chicken Little contends, the sky *could* fall on you. Anything and everything *is* possible. But if you let that control your life, you're really little better than one of those poor people who have that phobia about ever leaving their house. Be overly cautious and you might live to be 90 and die in your sleep but what did you miss on the way to 90?

So, go and enjoy.

When it finally hit me that there might be a book in all this I knew, or thought I knew, that books begin with titles. I suspect that's really not the case but with me it seemed a prerequisite, a cornerstone upon which to build my thoughts.

With very little thought the title presented itself to me. The act of right foot in the Pacific, left foot in the Atlantic had been part of my plan all along, if indeed the walk ever got off the ground.

But as more and more recollections about the walk occured to me, I had to smile to myself when I thought that tongue-in-cheek I should sub-title the book: *A Chocolate Milk Lover's Guide to North America.*

When I got into the meat and potatoes of actually writing the book, I wished I had taken notes concerning all the different brands of chocolate milk I was exposed to and drank relishly (I know it isn't a word but it describes it best).

I'd liked to have given my critique and star-rating to each brand I tried. Time and the return to home have mercifully faded most of the brand names from memory, so that only the very good or the very bad remain. Time, too, has erased a lot of the bitterness I felt at the time toward the dairies who cared only for my money and put alkaline, brown syrupy water in the carton.

At the time I would have exposed them to the world in a heartbeat but now I've mellowed some and don't see their sinful deception worth my time and effort.

The bad won't get into my "Chocolate Milk Lover's Hall of Fame" and that punishment alone fits the crime.

As a kindness to you for buying this book (You didn't *borrow* it, did you?!) I'll give you the benefit of my vast and extensive, and I can assure you, comprehensive field testing.

From someone who's tried them all, here are my top three choices. They are all so close in excellent taste and quality that I won't further break them down into good, better, best. In no particular order here are my top three:

1. Dean's Chocolate Milk, Home Office — Franklin Park, Illinois. If Jack Daniels is the sippin' whiskey of the whiskey world, then Dean's is the sipper of Chocoholics. You miss so much if you simply drink it. This nectar of the cow vine wants/needs/cries to be savored.

2. Darn, I can't remember the name but I'm sure it's the only dairy in Kosciusko, Mississippi. Can "brown" and "gold" both describe milk? This jewel can in no way be portrayed if you are confined by the totally inadequate words "chocolate" and "milk".

3. Green Springs Dairy, Home Office–Baltimore, Maryland. This one was like a phantom — The Flying Dutchman emerging from a fogbank, a ghost out of the mist. At a small Mom and Pop grocery in tiny Church Hill, Maryland was the one and only time I was able to get it. So you know it must have been special to imprint itself on my memory with so little exposure.

There isn't a sliver of doubt in my mind that there were times in Arizona, New Mexico, and Texas that I could have downed a gallon of chocolate milk at one sitting.

On a few occasions I've been asked what part of the country I liked best, which state was my favorite, where the people were the nicest. I've had lots of time to reflect and here are some of my best and worst picks:

Though I spent half the book complaining about it, the Southwest still holds the most fascination for me. It's just so different and mysterious to a boy from Kentucky. It can be cruelly harsh, yet it still grips me somehow. Its mystique holds you in awe. It's stark, seemingly unlivable, ungodly hot and completely foreign to anyone east of the Mississippi, yet it can have a strange mysterious hold on you once you've spent time within it. At the time I thought I hated it, but it's a place that grabs your heart.

The surrealness of the Southwest, the stark, lonely landscape makes you feel like you're alone on another planet. It's scary, yet exhilarating. Maybe it's fascinating because we subconsciously want to be alone, away from the madding crowd for at least a while, and the Southwest can grant that wish in spades.

It reminds me of Thoreau's *Tonic of Wildness,* although I never knew Thoreau saw the desert Southwest. Maybe he meant any place untouched by man.

And I have almost the opposite feelings about the East. I don't like it, but can't really say why. After the North Carolina/Virginia state line I never felt completely safe.

My walk did nothing to change my lifelong fascination with California. It was and remains my favorite state. I speak of natural beauty, man and his trappings aren't included. It has such diversity, surely anyone could find enough beauty to satisfy them.

The state that appealed to me least? Sad to say it was Louisiana. I expected more from her and all I got was denuded logging moonscapes, an endless caravan of speeding log trucks, choking clouds of mosquitoes, and zillions of smothering, stinging, biting fire ants from hell. New Orleans I'll take. Perish the thought of every other parish.

Best and worst towns? This list is strictly from my point of view. Any place listed here can rightfully claim it was mentioned due only to the demented ramblings of a person of diminished capacity.

To keep from seeming to play favorites I decided to list the towns from West to East rather than alphabetically or numerically.

Favorite Towns:

1. Salome, Arizona. A tiny, truly western town without any pretension about its uniqueness.

2. Fort Thomas, Arizona. Just a smattering of houses but kind of a tight-knit little world of its own; dry, but as clean as if it were hand washed each morning before sunrise.

3. Superior, Arizona. Deep in the heart of mining country and for that reason I'm surprised it made the list. I think its uniqueness was what drew me. It sits snuggled up against the side of a mountain like a bunch of buildings that gathered there to get in out of the rain in 1820, and they just stayed. The twentieth century came and didn't notice them, and they escaped change.

4. Albany, Texas. The picture of Norman Rockwell's small town America — clean streets, white picket fences, people who wave when they meet. And I'll bet lots of the old guys drive with their first finger continuously held in the air over the steering wheel as a permanent "wave" to whomever they meet. I didn't look but I'll bet there's a Cleaver listed in the phone book and the sheriff's name is probably Taylor.

5. Collins, Mississippi. If they shot a scaled-down version of *Gone With the Wind* they'd choose Collins. I picture everyone except maybe Scarlett, Rhett and that whiny Suellen being happy here. Rhett and Scarlett would be just too Charleston-ish and Savannah-ish for Collins and Suellen would whine no matter where she was. But Collins is the epitome of the slow, southern town. If you like "laid back," go see Collins.

Does it say something that three of my favorite towns were in Arizona and there are no favorites east of Mississippi?

Places I disliked:

1. Corsicana, Texas. Other than having a great hundred-year-old bakery that ships fruit cakes to the stars, I found little to commend Corsicana. One disclaimer may be that I walked through on Sunday, a dead day in most cities. It reminded me of a once booming oil town that had nothing to offer anymore — kinda depressing, really.

2. Clarence, Louisiana. Though dirt poor, Clarence may have been interesting if I hadn't felt so out of place and unwanted. I'm sure it's a feeling visited upon people of color quite often, but I'd never been the only white person in town, and I couldn't escape that uneasy feeling of racial inadequacy.

3. Grove Hill, Alabama. I still can't believe the billboard at the edge of town proclaims Grove Hill "The South's Friendliest Town." I found it a closed society whose only interest seemed to be why I'd dragged my suspicious-looking carcass through their town.

4. Sylvester, Georgia. As I sat in the Pizza Hut in Sylvester looking out the window I thought if I had to live in a place with no more imagination than to continue to call itself Sylvester, I'd throw myself under the first John Deere coming down main street.

5. Blackshear, Georgia. Bigotry and racism just seem to ooze out of Blackshear.

6. Kinston, North Carolina. An old, dirty-looking mill town, whether it has a mill or not. The South has many towns that appeared to once have had money yet are still hanging around when there is no longer any sustenance.

7. Pick a town in New Jersey. It's odd that I liked most of the "Best" places for some physical quality and disliked the "Worst" places for some intangible that I simply "felt."

Where did I like the people the best? Strange as it seems, Eastern New Mexico. Why? It might be because there are so few and they are so spread out, that they haven't become tainted by civilization. They still welcome human contact. They aren't jaded nor suspicious.

Where did I like the people the least? Well, in general the East, and in particular New York City.

I don't think New Yorkers are inherently different from anyone else, it's just that their living conditions have robbed them of any time to be nice. They scurry around so fast that civility can't keep up. And surely the cramping of so many bodies one on top of another like cordwood would shorten any fuse.

New York City does hold some allure, though, at least in the very short term. There's a sort of bustling fascination about it. After my walk I concluded that being in New York City was like being thrown into a barrel of rats — but *interesting rats.*

Finale

I love freedom stories. I think I like them because at heart I've always been a hobo. And "hobo" has always gotten a bad rap, in my opinion. People lump the phrases, and by extension the people, labeled "hoboes," "tramps," and bums all together, when really they are separate and unequal entities.

By definition and practice the three can be separated this way:

1. Bum — A person who sits in one place and will not work.
2. Tramp — A bum who travels.
3. Hobo — A person who travels and takes odd jobs when and where he can find them.

I guess if you judged me from this book and my walk across the US, you'd label me a Tramp. But the reasons I didn't work were that I had saved enough money to see me through the walk, and I was concerned about the time factor involved if I stopped to work. I didn't know how long it would take to reach New York City and I was concerned that cold weather and possibly icy rain and snow would catch me before I was able to finish. The idea of walking and stopping along the way to take odd jobs did appeal to me, though.

But getting back to freedom stories, I've always admired, and been fascinated by, people who wanted to be free and had the courage of their convictions and actually took action that resulted in the freedom they desired.

Two stories come to mind and I relate them for two reasons. One, I like them for their gutsy neatness and, two, because they say that anything is possible if you just do it.

If you want to attempt something like my L.A. — N.Y. walk you can if you have a mixture of courage and reckless abandon.

The first story was told to me long ago by a farmer. It concerned a fella who was a mutual acquaintance of ours. The farmer telling me the story once had this man working for him. And one day the man was plowing some ground with a tractor. It was getting late in the afternoon and the farmer knew that the plowing should be finished and that the man should have come back to the house by this time.

In the back of any farmer's mind is the possibility of an accident, so the farmer thought he'd better walk out and check on him.

As the farmer approached the field he noticed the tractor sitting in the middle of the partially-plowed field. No one was in sight so the farmer quickened his pace toward the tractor. When he got close enough he could hear the tractor just sitting there idling.

The man working for him was nowhere in sight. It was months later that he heard that the man was working in the Oklahoma oil fields.

The farmer's only conclusion was that the mood had hit the man to move on and it had come in the middle of a plowed field.

The second story I read somewhere. It concerned a man who had always wanted to fly. But not necessarily *airplane* fly. *He* wanted to fly.

Realizing that was improbable, nay, impossible, he decided on the next best thing.

Being a man with limited resources he rigged what he could. He filled about 50 balloons with helium and tied them to a lawn chaise lounge. He rigged his airship with food, drink and a B.B. gun for descending when the time came.

He succeeded his expectations and rose higher and higher until he was in the air approach to his city's airport. Several planes reported him and when he did decide to return to Mother Earth several of the gendarmes were there to greet him.

Far from being sorry that he'd done it, he was elated that, at least, he'd flown like the birds. When asked if he'd ever do something like that again he replied, "No." When asked if he was glad he did it he said, "Hell, yes."

I had to smile to myself when I read the "freedom balloonist" had said that, because it reminded me of my own trip.

On the few occasions when I've been asked if I'd ever do something like my walk again, I have replied with a definite but understated, "Yes!" And I have a simple, straightforward (well, maybe a little more imposing and elevated) answer to those who've asked if I ever wanted to quit during my walk. "Hell, yes!"

My next sentence was going to be something about your thinking those two stories were better examples of childish irresponsibility than ones of freedom. But then it occurred to me that, that probably wouldn't happen because the person who'd feel that way is probably too stodgy to be reading this book anyway.

I believe if you've come this far with me, there's some degree of hobo, in you, and like me, you can appreciate the love of freedom that resides in each.

I'm reminded of a quote from Walt Whitman's *Song of the Open Road.*

For all of us, you and I, who love freedom and can see ourselves walking across America, no better inspirational words have been spoken or written. I don't see how anyone could read Whitman's words and not feel his own feet inching toward the door.

"From this hour I ordain myself loos'd of limits and imaginery lines, going where I list, my own master total and absolute, listening to others, considering well what they say, pausing, searching, receiving, contemplating, gently, but with undeniable will, divesting myself of the holds that would hold me."

Finis

Now it's come to this: I promised at the beginning of this book that I would reveal the amount of money I found on this walk. But before I could count it I spent it. SIT DOWN!! I'm just teasing. You know I wouldn't spend that money.

But truth is I haven't counted it. It's been in a rather fat, zip-up pouch in the top of my bedroom closet. It represents an accumulation of all the times I sent the coins I found back to my daughter. When I got home I was surprised at the volume and weight of the coins.

Out of curiosity, I scooted some coins around and came across a man's ring with a "diamond" filled horseshoe on top. I had forgotten about it. It looks cheap and I've never considered it to be of any value.

I uncovered something else that I thought rather odd. I found many coins on my walk but only one dollar bill. I'd thought I'd find more. Within ten miles of my home I once found a ten-dollar bill while on a walk. On another occasion while running, I found an envelope with $32 in it.

One day Alyce, my goad, naysayer, co-typist, spellchecker, proofreader and fellow bon vivant asked me if I was going to spend the money after I counted it.

I did jump to my feet!

"Are you crazy, woman?"

Those pieces of copper and nickel mean much more to me than anything I might buy with them. Only at the point of keeping body and soul together would I ever consider using that money.

Not only that, a great percentage of it is hardly recognizable and probably non-spendable anyway. It's been run over hundreds, maybe thousands of times, and been lying exposed to sun, sand and asphalt for months or years.

The very first sentence of this book states that we all see pennies on the ground occasionally and even nickels, dimes and quarters. But invariably those coins are found singly. It would be rare to find more than one coin at any one spot.

Knowing that to be true, I was made starkly aware of how many times I stopped to reach/squat for coins all across America. After dumping the fat, zippered pouch on the kitchen table, then counting not the value but just the number of coins, I calculated I squatted, reached, and bent 868 times. That sounds like a lot to me. My *knees* think it sounds like a lot!

I saw a few coins that I decided shouldn't be included in an appraisal of the money you'd find on an *American* coast-to-coast walk. These were Mexican, Canadian and what looks like Vietnamese coins. I didn't include any of that in the total.

Okay, now I'm going to end this for all time by telling you the total amount of money you're likely to find on a typical Los Angeles to New York walk.

But first I'm going to give the screw one final turn.

I could just tell you the amount and that would be fair for those of you who bought and read this book. But it would be rewarding those spiders who picked up the book, read the first few paragraphs, and said to themselves, "This looks lame. I'll just flip to the last page and see how much money you'd find."

But I can't see how to reward the faithful without giving the spider the same reward.

Poor reader, *you* poor reader, the faithful who've struggled and strove to this point and who must unfortunately suffer, too, for the spider's attempt to suck the life's blood from this book and leave it a hollow shell dangling on its web. It's a shame that all must pay for the transgressions of a few. (The whole class had to stay in at recess because I wouldn't confess it was me who "baa-ed" like a sheep when the teacher stepped out to speak to someone in the hall.)

So, my apologies for making you, along with the bad guys, get out your pencil.

Here is the total:

Pennies: 742 Quarters: 30

Nickels: 43 Dimes: 53

Dollar Bills: 1